kick the clutter

clutter

CLEAR OUT EXCESS STUFF
WITHOUT LOSING WHAT YOU LOVE

ellen phillips

RODALE

To everyone who struggles to fit too much stuff into too little space
(no matter how much space that is).
And to my mother, who taught me the secret of gracious living.

Mention of specific companies, organizations, or authorities in this book does not imply
endorsement by the author or publisher, nor does mention of specific companies, organizations,
or authorities imply that they endorse this book, its author, or the publisher.

Internet addresses and telephone numbers given in this book were accurate
at the time it went to press.

Direct edition first published in 2007. Trade edition published in 2008.

Printed in the United States of America
Rodale Inc. makes every effort to use acid-free ∞, recycled paper ♲.

Illustrations by Michael Gellatly
Cover design by Susan Eugster
Interior design by Patricia Field

Library of Congress Cataloging-in-Publication Data

Phillips, Ellen.
    Kick the clutter : clear out excess stuff without losing what
you love / Ellen Phillips.
        p.   cm.
    Includes index.
    ISBN-13 978–1–59486–717–0   hardcover
    ISBN-10 1–59486–717–8   hardcover
    1. Storage in the home.   2. Orderliness.   I. Title.
TX309.P56   2007
648'.8—dc22   2007018711

2   4   6   8   10   9   7   5   3   1   hardcover

We inspire and enable people to improve their lives and the world around them

For more of our products visit **rodalestore.com** or call 800-848-4735

CONTENTS

Part One: Clutter-Kicking Basics

Part Two: Clutter-Kicking Room by Room

Part Three: Clutter-Kicking Outside the House

Part Four: Trash (Yours) to Treasure (Theirs)

Part Five: Controlling Clutter Creep

ACKNOWLEDGMENTS

If you enjoy this book and find it helpful, it's because of the many friends and family members who have so generously shared their tips, their clutter woes and triumphs, and their expertise with me—and now, with you. Special thanks to my wonderful editors, Anne Halpin White and Karen Bolesta; project editor Hope Clarke; copy editors Erana Bumbardatore and Amy Kovalski; designers Susan Eugster and Patricia Field; and illustrator Michael Gellatly, all of whose enthusiastic participation in this project has been invaluable; and to the professionals who generously gave of their time and expertise to make this a better book, especially Diane Albright, Janet Brito, Patrick McWilliams, Karen Moyer, Pat Robertson, Jaap van Liere, Brendan Strasser, and Jackie Tepper. Many thanks to the many friends who contributed their first-person experience to help augment mine, especially Jennifer Bright Reich and Christine Bucks. And my most sincere thanks to the members of the Kutztown Curves, who got almost as excited about the book as I was; to my boyfriend, Rob Hays, who kept his sense of humor throughout the project and helped me keep my sense of perspective, and to his father, George Hays, who is eagerly awaiting his copy; to my own father, who graciously put up with my taking over his office and working 'til all hours to get the book finished when I was supposed to be visiting him; and to Pat Brown, who invented the word "dustables." Finally, special thanks to Janine, Katrina, and Karen for believing.

INTRODUCTION

Are you ready to stop stumbling over your clutter and start kicking it out of your house and your life? If you are, this book is for you. You may be a first-time clutter fighter: Clutter may have crept into your home gradually, and you've just recently realized that you have a problem. Or you may be a seasoned veteran: You've been trying to shovel out for years and have either given up after a struggle or have finally cleared out all the clutter, only to watch with dismay as it piled back in. Whether you fall at either end of this spectrum or somewhere in the middle, these pages contain tips and tools to help you. And I think you'll have fun as you go!

That's because *Kick the Clutter* goes where other clutter books fear to tread—to the heart of controlling clutter once and for all. The chapters in Part One: Clutter-Kicking Basics (beginning on page 1) give you the basic tools you need, from the real secret of lasting clutter control to a five-step clutter-kicking program, an overview of organizing and storage aids, and lots of 5-minute fixes that let you jump-start the clutter-kicking process.

In Part Two: Clutter-Kicking Room by Room (beginning on page 69) and Part Three: Clutter-Kicking Outside the House (beginning on page 289), you'll find hundreds of tips to help you conquer your particular clutter issues, whether you're trying to make more room in an apartment or RV, combine two households in marriage or partnership, or deal with an avalanche of inherited clutter (from parents or kids or both). Each chapter will show you how to prioritize your clutter-kicking strategy for that room or space and give you a unique tool to inspire you to clear out the clutter *and* help you keep it from coming back.

What happens when you've amassed a pile of stuff to get rid of? That depends on the stuff—and on you. You can have a lot of fun with this part of clutter-kicking, as you'll see in Part Four: Trash (Yours) to Treasure (Theirs), beginning on page 349. You can help people in need, swap stuff you don't need for things you do, or even make some money from your clutter. The choice is yours!

The High Cost of Clutter

Clutter costs us. Clutter is not just an inconvenience or an eyesore—it's an industry. Several, actually. Consider some of the hidden costs of clutter:

❉ The sadly ironic name "self-storage facility" is only too accurate. We'd rather pay a hefty monthly charge to store our stuff than just get rid of it. Since the first self-storage facility appeared in 1966, their numbers have increased to a whopping 55,000 US facilities today. That's 6.68 square feet of storage space for every US resident—for a total of 72 square miles of American land not just storing clutter but also covered up by the clutter of these metal structures.

❉ One in 11 US households rents a self-storage unit, for a total cost of almost $20 billion a year.

❉ Despite the fact that household size continues to dwindle (2.57 people per household in 2004), the houses themselves just keep getting bigger. The average home size has been supersized, French-fry fashion, from 1,500 square feet in 1970 to 2,400 square feet today. With the fastest-growing housing segment being singles and couples, what's occupying all that space? You guessed it: stuff.

❉ Top 10 self-storage states (accounting for almost half of all self-storage facilities): California, Florida, Georgia, Illinois, Michigan, New York, North Carolina, Ohio, Pennsylvania, and Texas.

❉ Another outgrowth of our increasing clutter and its related chaos is the professional organizer, who charges an hourly fee to help get your clutter (and life) back under control. The National Association of Professional Organizers has more than 3,900 members.

❉ Believe it or not, there are 12-step programs (like Alcoholics Anonymous) for clutterers, including Clutterers Anonymous and Messies Anonymous.

❉ Randy Frost, PhD, professor of psychology at Smith College and an expert in obsessive-compulsive disorder, studied compulsive hoarders, the most extreme form of clutterer, in the 1990s. He estimates that there are as many as four million hoarders in the United States alone.

❉ A Google search for "Clutter" brings up 37,600,000 results. If you search on Amazon, you'll get 45,793 results for "clutter"; add "organizing," and you'll get 158,983 more, for a grand total of 204,776. Yikes!

What's the Deal with Dustables?

You'll find a lot about dustables in *Kick the Clutter*. What are they? Those knick-knacks, collectibles, art objects, or what have you that just sit around collecting dust. My friend Pat Brown coined this delightful word, and now it's become so much a part of my thought process that the "dustables light" will often go on when I'm out shopping and see a particularly intriguing kitchen gadget, antique, or craft item. Hard as they are to resist, unless I know I have the perfect place for them, I leave them on the shelf. After all, who likes dusting?

Finally, there's that little issue of keeping your clutter from creeping back into the house, like those unwanted pounds that always seem to make their way to your midsection minutes before swimsuit season begins. You'll learn the tricks to keeping clutter at bay in Part Five: Controlling Clutter Creep, beginning on page 439.

Throughout *Kick the Clutter,* I've only included tips that I know will work. And I've also been up front about what *won't* work and what happens when real life intrudes on your clutter-kicking plans. I'll be speaking directly to you on every page because I want you to not just succeed at kicking your clutter, but to have a good time while you're doing it. (And yes, of course you can!)

There's one more thing about *Kick the Clutter* that I want you to know: It's not just about me talking to you. This is an interactive experience, and I want you to be a very big part of it because unless you are, you won't get the most out of it. Throughout the book I've included formats for various worksheets and exercises for you to do because I want it to be *your* book, and only you can make it your book. If you do, you'll do more than kick your clutter. You'll finally know exactly what you need to make the home you have into the home you love. And that's a promise.

Ellen Phillips

PART ONE

Clutter-Kicking Basics

Chapter 1

Get a Clutter-Clearing Mind-Set

It's safe to say that, if you actually live in your home, you live with clutter. And that's true whether you live in an eight-bedroom mansion or a one-room apartment with a sofa bed. Those photos in design magazines of immaculate rooms with empty shelves and one perfectly placed *objet d'art* on the coffee table are essentially sets, unlived in and unloved. You may have a little clutter, you may have a lot of clutter, but you *do* have clutter.

Why is that? It's because—and we should face this up front—clutter is simply part of the human condition. But that doesn't mean we're stuck with the messy, stacked-up status quo. You *can* kick the clutter, as you'll see throughout this book. And the best—really, the only effective—way to start is by figuring out how bad your "clutter condition" is and how it happened. So let's begin at the beginning: How bad *is* it?

THE CLUTTER SCALE

There's clutter, and then there's clutter. Before you get rid of it, you have to understand what your clutter is, so take a deep breath, take a good look around your

The Clutter-Hoarding Scale

You may think you have it bad—or just wonder how bad you have it. Find out by seeing where you—or someone you live with or care about—fall on the National Study Group on Chronic Disorganization's Clutter-Hoarding Scale (at www.nsgcd.org).

Yikes! This is very serious stuff. The organization categorizes clutter levels in four different areas—structure and zoning issues, pets and rodents, household functions, and sanitation and cleanliness—and then rates you on a scale depending on how you score in each area. The scale rates you from Level I (all doors and stairways accessible, clutter not excessive, no odors, and so on) to Level V (rodents—and they don't mean pets!—evident and in sight, kitchen and bathroom unusable due to clutter, client sleeping elsewhere as house is not livable, and so on). If you or someone you know scores above Level I, you can find referrals and assistance on the organization's Web site.

house, and then ask yourself what you mean when you say that it's cluttered or messy. Do you mean that there's a pile of magazines, catalogs, papers, and assorted bric-a-brac all over the coffee table and you have to shove it all out of the way (often accidentally spilling it in a heap on the floor) in order to set a cup down? Or do you mean that there are so many boxes, piles, and heaps of stuff in the room that you've given up on spending time there and instead navigate from the front door to the kitchen through a narrow path you've left between piles?

How did you—or more accurately, your home—get into this mess?

YOUR CLUTTER, YOURSELF

There are lots of ways to end up with a cluttered home, and the best way to start dealing with your own clutter is to see why you have it to begin with. The categories below describe several clutter-attracting "types," and as you read through them you may find one that seems to have been written just for you. Of course, you may also find that several of these categories apply to you—you might be a Collector and a Compulsive Shopper, for example—but that just means that you'll need to fight clutter on two (or more) fronts instead of just one. And the same holds true if you're a

Compulsive Shopper and your spouse or partner is a Collector. But don't panic! Knowledge is power here, so let's take a look at the causes of clutter—*your* clutter.

The Collector

I'm starting with this category because I'm in it. You name it—kaleidoscopes, fossils, shells, books, guitars, Pueblo pottery, beads, vintage Christmas ornaments, Audubon prints, yarn—I collect it. Hopefully, if you fall into this category, you collect only one or two things. But even so, it's all too easy for a collection to take over every available shelf and display area, then start taking over actual living

Clutter and Capitalism

You may be thinking that your clutter really isn't your fault—and of course you're at least partially right. We live in a capitalist society; the production and consumption of goods are the foundation of our economy. So the goal of our economy is to persuade us all to keep buying . . . and buying. And buying. Clutter is one of capitalism's unwanted side effects. After all, when you buy more than you need without tossing what you already have, things start to pile up!

I once read that if no more shirts were ever made, there would still be enough shirts in existence to clothe all of humanity for all time. Talk about a sobering thought! So if there are already enough shirts out there for the duration, why do we keep making—and buying—more? Because our society tells us that it's not fashionable to wear the same style or color season after season or year after year. Because it's socially unacceptable to wear the same shirt to work more than once a week, even if it's washed between wearings. Because, because. I'm sure you can think of plenty of other reasons—and so can the advertisers who spend billions of dollars to persuade us that we need this exclusive designer top or that fantastic bargain blouse.

What does this mean for you? Should you stop buying new shirts? Not much chance of that, right? (And of course I don't mean to pick on shirts here—I'm really talking about all nonperishable items.) But it does help to be aware that you're being bombarded with messages to buy, so that next time you head off to the store, pick up a catalog, or shop online, you can at least make it a two-step process. Before you buy the next new thing, ask yourself: What old thing will I get rid of to make space for this?

The Accidental Collector

Sometimes, becoming a collector is an accident. As people's gift lists become longer and time to buy presents seems to always grow shorter, everyone's tempted to take the easy way out. So if they think a friend, family member, or co-worker collects something affordable, they'll keep an eye out for the collectible objects and add them to their gift stash. A sure hit, and one more thing off the list, right? Not necessarily, as these stories show.

Miss Piggy

I'll never forget the first time I went to see the office manager of sales at the company I worked for at the time. Patsy's cubicle was literally crammed with pigs. Pig statuettes of every conceivable material and style leered down at me from every surface. There were hundreds of them. I was so appalled I almost forgot why I'd come up to see Patsy.

Someone else in sales explained that Patsy adored pigs. The whole sales department made a point of bringing Patsy, a delightful person, pig collectibles of every conceivable kind back from their (frequent) travels. Patsy's pig collection grew exponentially as the years went by.

Eventually, Patsy retired. As I passed her abandoned cubicle, I noticed that every single pig was still there! Astounded, I asked another co-worker about this. Can you guess her answer? Patsy never really liked pigs at all. That poor woman. Surrounded all those years by a horde of unwanted "dustables," all because she was too sweet, too polite, to say no.

How had this false notion of Patsy's love for pigs gotten started in the first place? I can only guess. Maybe a grandchild had gotten her a little china pig for some occasion, and Patsy, the proud grandma, had brought it into the office to display. Whatever the case, I'm sure she never foresaw the result of her modest display. I still think of her working among all those pigs for decades, loathing them all the while.

spaces by cluttering up tables and counters. Take it from one who knows: It doesn't have to be that way. There are two ways to escape from the Collector trap—without giving up your beloved collections.

Review. Tastes change—even yours. Trust me. As you learn more and your collection evolves, you'll find that some of your early treasures begin to lose their appeal. In fact, you may be humiliated to recall that you once thought that garish

If you can relate to Patsy's story, let me just say that it doesn't have to be that way. Here's how another friend escaped from a similar situation.

Just Say No

My friend Sandy loves Majolica ware, including colorful statues of hens and roosters. She also loves ceramic representations of fruits and vegetables, and she both gardens and raises chickens. What could be easier than getting her ceramic chickens and ceramic fruits and veggies for every occasion? They sound like the perfect gifts, right?

Wrong. After a few years of being barraged with hens, roosters, and a cornucopia of ceramic produce, Sandy stared at her shrinking counter and storage space and took action. She began telling all her friends and relatives about how Majolica was a very special kind of ceramic and that, in general, she really despised crockery, stoneware, and country ceramics of all kinds. Because she was so particular, she explained, she felt that it would be best if people let her choose her own ornaments rather than trying to guess her taste. Then, Sandy packed up all the gift chickens and veggies and traded them at a favorite antique store for something she really wanted.

This may sound harsh, but it saved Sandy from Patsy's fate. You can bet that, after one of these "talks," no one ever gave Sandy a chicken—or any other decorative "dustable"—again! But at least a few of the well-intentioned gift-givers may have been taken aback by her directness. In my view, it would have been even better for Sandy to have told people what she'd appreciate instead—a fruit basket, locally made jams and jellies, a gift certificate to her favorite book or clothing store. If you find yourself in this position—the recipient of collectibles you don't want—I suggest that you let the gift-givers off the hook by giving them an easy gift option that you'd really appreciate.

mass-produced vase was a priceless Native American collectible. Rather than mindlessly amassing more and more, make a point of reviewing your holdings monthly, twice yearly, or whenever you add a new piece to your collection. See if there isn't something you could dispose of now without feeling deprived. Remember that there are probably collectors out there for your former treasures—*you* bought it at one point, after all—and selling it now will free up more money for your current collection. Don't be ashamed of your early purchases—collecting is educational, if nothing else. Pack up the pieces you've decided you can live without, say good-bye, and turn your attention to streamlining your collection.

Rotate. Here in America, we like to display *all* our treasures. One of my (as yet unrealized) dreams is to have all of my books out on shelves where I can see them at a glance. We like to have all our Hummel figurines or Hallmark ornaments or first editions or Colonial textiles on display. And what do we get? Dustables. Unless you're lucky enough to have glass-fronted display cases or shelves, every object you choose to display will have to be dusted, again and again and again. Instead, let me suggest a brilliant alternative from the Far East.

One of the things I collect is shells, and of course I have books about shells, as well. In one of them, one of the great American shell collectors recounted his surprise when he went to visit a Japanese counterpart. The Japanese collector was reputed to hold one of the greatest collections of shells in the world. The American shell collector was practically drooling when he arrived at his host's residence for a rare viewing. But to the American's dismay, instead of being shown room after room and case after case of beautiful shells, he was taken to the living room and decorously seated. Then, a servant brought out . . . *one* shell. After a half hour, the servant removed the shell and returned with . . . another shell. In the course of the visit, the astounded American was shown perhaps five shells. To the Japanese collector, appreciating the rarity and beauty of a single shell was more important than displaying the entire collection.

The lesson here is that you really don't have to set out every last bear carving or Roman coin you own at the same time. Instead, rotate your collection, choosing a few choice specimens to display at any given time. This will keep your collection fresh to viewers as well as to you. And if you happen to collect paintings or first-edition prints or photographs, this tactic is especially useful. You can enjoy open wall space and still display your collection of original Julia Longacre barn paintings. Just make sure you have proper storage for the pieces that are not on display.

The Inheritor

A variant of the Collector is the Inheritor, the person who's inherited his or her parents' stuff, in-laws' stuff, great-aunt's stuff, or even grown kids' stuff. This is worse than being a Collector—unless you're an Accidental Collector—because you never asked for or would have chosen this stuff, but now there it is in your house, jostling with all your own stuff and filling up every available nook and cranny. People who haven't experienced this (yet) may wonder what the big deal is—why don't you just get rid of it? But if you're in this place, you *know*.

Sentiment can play a big role in turning you into an Inheritor. That was Great-Aunt Ethel's giant armoire! Those were Grandma Jones's second-best breakfast dishes! But there can be more to it than that.

For example, my sister's small, super-cluttered house includes a Victorian sofa, coffee table, and two chairs that she inherited from our grandmother. She doesn't like them and has no space for them—and to top it all off, she could use the money she'd get from selling them to a local antique store. But she doesn't dare sell them because she knows our father would be horrified if she tried to unload his mother's precious stuff, even though he himself has no room for it. And my sister is quite right—I've heard him rave about it myself. In fact, I have another Victorian sofa set from the same grandmother. It's taking up an entire room in my tiny cottage, and I don't sell it for the same reason: What if my father came to visit and saw that it was gone?

Being the recipient of unwanted or unneeded wedding presents may inadvertently turn you into an Inheritor, as well. You may have an atticful of bulky boxes you haven't opened in 25 years. And what if you're in an apartment? I recently saw a home show on HGTV where the cabinets of the newlyweds' apartment kitchen were all filled to bursting, not with dishes and pantry staples, but with boxes of wedding presents. Yikes! But, of course, Aunt Peggy would never forgive you if she came over and saw that her gilded epergne had vanished from your dining room table, right?

If you're thinking of marrying (or remarrying), it's not too late to preempt the gift debacle. (See "Beat the Wedding Blues" on page 10.) But if you're thinking about all the drawers and closets and attic space you've filled with wedding presents as you read this, all is not lost.

The trick is to be bold but tactful. If you never liked the crystal Aunt Martha gave you but your cousin chose it as her own pattern, give it to your cousin. Explain that it doesn't really go with your china and it would make you very happy to think of her using it—plus it's great insurance against breakage!—and

Beat the Wedding Blues

Engagement presents. Shower presents. Wedding presents. I'll bet if you had it to do over again—or ever found yourself actually doing it over again—you'd ask for cash, checks, and gift certificates, right? In the past, people thought it was crass to ask for or give money or gift certificates instead of actual gifts, so a pileup of wedding presents was virtually inevitable (unless you eloped). But these days, when many marriages involve combining two households (or apartments), even Miss Manners couldn't object to a couple's asking for what they actually want rather than just sitting back and waiting for the gift avalanche.

So don't be shy! If you're getting married, ask for what you want, and simply explain that you already have all the possessions you could possibly use and would rather remember the gift-givers by treating yourself to Italian or horseback riding lessons, going on a romantic getaway, indulging in a spa day, or enjoying a delightful dinner at the best new restaurant in town. And if you really, really don't need or want a thing, either say so nicely and insist on "no gifts" early on and again in the invitations, or ask that donations be made in your names to your favorite charity or charities, instead. No fuss, no muss, no clutter!

steel yourself to tell Aunt Martha the same thing if it ever comes up. (Believe it or not, chances are it won't.) Or donate the crystal to a charity auction or consignment shop whose proceeds are given to Aunt Martha's favorite charity or cause. Or sell the crystal on eBay, to an antiques store, or at auction.

The Parent

Your kids are grown and gone. But somehow, they've left all their stuff behind. "Don't throw it out—we might need it!" "We'll be back for it . . . someday." "We don't have room for it right now . . . we can't afford a mover . . . we're too busy . . . we live too far away . . . ." The excuses are endless, but they all boil down to the same thing: We love our childhood stuff, but we don't want to deal with it, so *you* keep it. And don't you dare throw it out!

I've met lots of moms who have fallen for this and who have told me over and over that they don't have room for the kids' stuff anymore—especially if they've become Inheritors and are also trying to find space for their parents' or in-laws' stuff. But of course they feel trapped, since they're afraid the kids will think they don't love them anymore if they get rid of their things. Luckily, I also met one mom who had come up with a no-fail solution.

Diane, one of the members at my local Curves fitness center and also one of the most practical people I've ever met, told me this story: "One year, I went upstairs to the attic to get the Christmas ornaments, and I realized I couldn't even get *into* the attic, much less find the ornaments, because of all the stuff my kids had left behind. So I brought down every single thing that belonged to my kids and put it all in the guest room. Then I told them that they had 2 weeks to come and pick up their stuff, and whatever was left after 2 weeks was going. Sure enough, every kid appeared like magic. And now I can find everything in my attic!"

Not only did Diane get rid of the next generation's junk, she did it without the sky falling. Each and every child still calls and visits as much as ever. So don't despair. Use Diane's technique, explain firmly but gently that it all must go, and then sit back and bask in your own happy ending!

The Compulsive Shopper

Okay, no one likes to think of herself as a Compulsive Shopper, so if you'd rather call yourself a Bargain Hunter, Smart Shopper, or anything else that lets you see yourself here, go right ahead. But whether you can't resist a great deal—whether you need the stuff or not—or you find yourself shopping for entertainment and then buying (and buying), you have come to the right category.

Sometimes, the Compulsive Shopper merges with the Scout (see page 13), justifying extreme purchasing on the grounds that now he or she is prepared for an emergency or breakdown. Here's one chilling example.

When my friend Carolyn heard that I was writing this book, she asked if I had seen her down-the-street neighbor's yard. Apparently this guy had bought so many lawn mowers, snow blowers, lawn tractors, and every other kind of equipment at auctions and yard sales that the stuff now spilled out of his overflowing garage and covered the entire lawn. (Hey, they were great deals! And what if he needed a replacement part?) Carolyn even suggested that a photo of his "private junkyard" would make a great cover for this book. Yuck! The scariest part to me is that the guy has a wife and a daughter, who of course are forbidden to touch his precious junk. I hate to think of them living up there, creeping like rats among all those piles of future scrap.

Thank goodness, most Shoppers are compulsive about smaller and nicer things. But they can still add up. And when your great buys start spilling out of drawers and off surfaces, they no longer look so nice. In fact, they look just like junk.

Fortunately, there are two ways you can still enjoy your shopping habit without letting it take over the house (or your credit cards). The first way works best if you have lots of so-so stuff you really ought to get rid of, be it dishware, clothes, jewelry, or CDs. The other works well to keep you from refilling the house with more.

Trade up. The first way is to trade in all that okay stuff for a few pieces of really good stuff. Sell your masses of so-so jewelry on eBay or through a consignment shop, yard sale, or flea market stand. (You don't have to have one of your own—see if a seasoned yard-saler or flea-marketer will buy the stuff from you.) Then take the proceeds (and yes, you'll end up with a lot less than you thought; this isn't *Antiques Roadshow,* but it will still be good money) and buy something really nice for yourself, a piece or two you'll love and be proud of. See Part Four: Trash (Yours) to Treasure (Theirs), beginning on page 349, for a wide range of ways to sell your stuff.

Specialize. The second way is to narrow your hunt. Rather than heading down to the antiques mall with your checkbook blazing, prepared to get whatever strikes you (and it's amazing how striking all that stuff always is), set a goal and stick to it. Here's how this works: You adore Christmas ornaments. But when you head to the store, you are *not* looking for Christmas ornaments. Instead, you are looking for a heavy green German-made kugel Christmas ornament from the 1920s. Or maybe you love cookware. But when you head to the store, you are *not* looking for cookware. You are looking for a 4-quart Le Creuset Dutch oven in Lemongrass. This way, you still get to go shop and enjoy yourself, but your money usually stays in your billfold and your house stays clutter-free. You can still enjoy the thrill of the chase—now more than ever, since you're chasing something specific. And just think how delighted you'll be if you happen to stumble on that kugel ornament or Dutch oven!

The Scout

I really wanted to call this one the Survivalist, but I didn't, since I want you all to read it. Instead, I settled on the Scout because it's all about that famous Boy and Girl Scout motto, "Be Prepared." If you still have boxes of canned food under the bed from the Y2K scare, or you can't throw out an empty mayonnaise jar because you might need it for canning someday, or your fridge is full of bottles and jars with a half-spoonful of whatever was in it because "it's still good" or "it's a sin to waste it," you are definitely a Scout. (So am I, by the way. Not because of mostly empty bottles and bags, but because I find things like wind-up radios and battery-operated lanterns absolutely irresistible. After all, what if there was a power outage?)

The Great Depression in the 1930s created an entire generation of Scouts, people who were so poor as children—and for whom so many goods were so unavailable—that they had to use foil gum wrappers to make Christmas ornaments. Saving rubber bands, string, bits of soap, clean foil, and jars was serious business— it could be the difference between comfort and want. (I still remember seeing a book about this sort of "Yankee frugality" called *String Too Short to Be Saved*.)

Fortunately, most of us in America aren't faced with these shortages today. But we *are* faced with such hazards as power outages, climbing gas prices, technological breakdowns, downsizing and layoffs, and terrorist threats. Some of you may have stocked up on duct tape and plastic sheeting a few years ago at the government's urging, in case the country faced a terrorist attack.

Being prepared can seem like plain old common sense, and it is . . . to a point.

But if it means turning your home into a garrison, with emergency supplies and "extras" taking up so much space in the basement, attic, garage, closets, and under the beds—everywhere!—that you have no space for "normal" stuff, it's out of control. It's clutter. You don't really need an entire bathroom full of 24-packs of toilet paper, unless you're running a summer camp out of your home.

Use common sense—and use your available space in the ways that make the most sense. (And that includes *open* space for people to move and breathe and relax in.) A kitchen drawer full of rubber bands, bottle caps, and twist-ties could hold a lot of utensils or silverware or teas or spices, instead. And know what? You can buy a whole pack of rubber bands if you really need them. So don't be penny-wise and pound-foolish. Buy what you need, buy what you can use, buy what you have room for. And buy no more!

The Host(ess)

Another friend, Margaret, loves to entertain. She has two kitchens inside and one outside, all loaded with appliances, dishes, cookware, and cooking staples. Oh, and did I mention the bar? But because she and her partner, Frank, who loves cooking and entertaining as much as she does, planned the house around this, there's plenty of room for all their paraphernalia.

If you love to entertain but are trying to do it from the family kitchen, where space is almost always at a premium, repeat after me: You are not, you don't have to be, Martha Stewart (or even Margaret). You can enjoy having people over just as much as Martha and Margaret do, as long as you keep the entertainments in scale with your home's physical limitations—not to mention your own.

My mother was the perfect hostess. Every formal dinner, every party, was just *perfect*. Mama would spend days, sometimes weeks, cooking. We'd all spend days polishing silver, hand-washing fragile china and crystal, laundering linens, cleaning, and decorating. By the time of the big event, everything looked stunning. The food was phenomenal. And my mother, a frail person, was completely wiped out.

After years of watching this cycle repeat itself, I've developed my own rule of entertaining: If the food is good, the hosts are happy, and the company is congenial, everybody's going to have a great time. I really enjoy decorating and cooking, but I make sure I keep my goals realistic and don't attempt more than I can fit into my schedule—and kitchen. As a result, my guests are happy; my boyfriend, Rob, and I are happy; and everybody has a good time.

Scaling back the scope of your entertaining may simply mean keeping less entertainment-specific stuff around taking up space. Sure, the Christmas plates and Santa mugs are cheerful, the snowman placemats are adorable, the snowman salt and pepper shakers are cute, the Christmas tree dishtowels are . . . well, you can see what I'm getting at. One of the smartest tips I've ever heard is this: Resist buying holiday-specific tableware because you use it once a year but have to store it *all* year. It makes a lot more sense to buy seasonal accessories—placemats and napkins in fall colors, for example—that you can use for many months each year and for all the holidays that fall in that season. The same goes for party napkins and the like. Trust me, your guests will *not* miss them!

From Weakness to Strength

Once you know your susceptibilities, you can fight them. And you can win! You just have to make sure they don't creep back in and bite you from behind. If you're a Parent or Scout, for example, buying ingenious clutter-control tools might really help you keep stuff contained and free up space. But I'm a Collector. If I start buying clutter-control containers, racks, and the like, before I know it, I'll have a new collection—of them.

For many of these categories, avoiding temptation is the best policy. If you're trying to lose 5 pounds and you absolutely adore the cannoli at Louie's Italian Bakery, it's not rocket science to keep out of Louie's until the weight is off. If you're a Compulsive Shopper and you know there are certain stores you can't resist, consider them off-limits until you've kicked your clutter. Then see if you can handle limited exposure—but watch the number of times you find yourself there and the number of bags you bring home! If you're starting to see a pattern re-forming, kick the habit so you don't have to start kicking clutter all over again.

Laissez-faire is also a good way to handle some kinds of temptation. For example, I love catalogs. I read catalogs to relax when I'm too wiped out for a maga-zine, much less a book. And of course, when I get my favorite catalogs, I want lots of the goodies shown and described so alluringly inside. But instead of rushing to the phone—unless I actually need something, like a replacement for a worn-out skirt—I tell myself, "I'll get that tomorrow." You won't be surprised to hear that tomorrow pretty much never comes.

So keep your weak spots in mind as you read through the rest of this book, because not all of the ideas in here will work for you. (What a relief that there are so many to choose from!) Pick the ones that you *can* work with, and you, too, will be a clutter-kicking success story.

CLUTTER-KICKING STRATEGIES

Right about now, you're probably itching to embark on your new clutter-free life. Try these tactics to get started. There's a clutter-control program in Chapter 4— Five Simple Steps to Kick Your Clutter, beginning on page 54. In addition, the room-by-room chapters in Part Two contain some "5-Minute Fixes" that will let you start to make a difference in your clutter in a hurry. But whatever else you do to control clutter, keep the simple strategies below in mind and you'll have some great can't-fail backup plans.

Clutter Mythbusters: One In, One (or Two) Out

I was talking about clutter control with a group of women at my local Curves in Kutztown, Pennsylvania. One of them, Sylvia—not surprisingly, an interior decorator—said that she kept clutter out by a strict policy: If something came in, something had to go out. That makes sense, I thought. And in fact it's a classic approach to keeping clutter-free. But the one in, one out rule just helps you maintain the status quo, so as far as getting *rid* of clutter, it's a myth. Here's a way to beat it. Another Curves member, Diane, says that *her* policy is that when one thing comes in, *two* have to go out. Yes! If you can do that, your clutter will melt away. Try it—aim for at least one thing, a one-for-one exchange. If you can think of—and bear to sacrifice—two things (or three, or four . . .), do it. Your clutter will head out the door even faster.

When in Doubt . . .

My dear friend Cole is an inveterate Collector like me, though his partner, Bruce, is anything but. Bruce's idea of clutter is an extra napkin in the drawer. When I asked him about his philosophy of clutter control, he replied, "When in doubt, throw it out!" (Can't you just picture me and Cole wincing?) If you can achieve Bruce's take-no-prisoners mind-set, clutter won't stand a chance. But don't try it on your family's precious stuff without their permission, or you may find yourself on *Family Feud!* Stick to your own stuff and generic stuff that other family members won't miss, like the seven extra Pyrex pie plates you have in the cupboard "just in case," or that stack of plastic bags under the sink.

Throw the Guilt Out First

In both of these cases (the "one, two, or more" switch and the "when in doubt" approach), I'm saying, "throw it out." But that's not necessarily what I mean. Bruce, a committed environmentalist, would never really throw anything out. But he *would* recycle, compost, donate, or give it away. If trashing stuff makes you feel guilty, or if you can't bear the thought of losing money on something you paid for, turn to Part Four: Trash (Yours) to Treasure (Theirs), for a wealth of guilt-free suggestions for disposing of your clutter without throwing it out.

Set Priorities

When clutter confronts you everywhere you look, it's easy to be so overwhelmed that you become paralyzed. Your good intentions give way to procrastination— you'll deal with it tomorrow. And of course, that particular tomorrow never comes. Instead, try this: Go into all your downstairs (or public, if you live in a one-story house) rooms and decide on the worst clutter problem you have in each room. Don't dither—just look around and see what hits you in the face first. Then deal with that one thing in each room.

After that, set the next level of priorities: Do you want to do the same for the upstairs (or private) rooms? Or should you choose the second-worst clutter problem in each downstairs room and tackle each of those? Or maybe you'll focus on one room (see Part Two: Clutter-Kicking Room by Room, beginning on page 69) and keep tackling the clutter issues there in order from worst to least bad until the job is completely done?

It's a lot easier when you have a plan of action—and follow it!

Take Small Bites

Related to setting priorities is keeping your clutter-kicking goals manageable. There's nothing as horrible as pulling everything out of a closet (or cabinet, dresser, pantry—you know what I mean), then realizing you don't have time to deal with it right now and shoving it all back in. Ouch! Instead, tackle just your shoes. Or just *some* shoes. Purses. Sweaters. Underwear. Whatever.

Budget your time realistically. Every morning, after I finish my household chores and before I start working, I try to accomplish one clutter-kicking task, whether it's tossing outdated coupons, packing up plastic bags to drop off at the grocery or magazines to take to the library "free" boxes, or cleaning out a drawer and bagging the discards for Goodwill, the Salvation Army, or the Society of St. Vincent de Paul. I always feel great starting my day with a small accomplishment,

the Pros Know

Throughout this book you'll find great clutter-kicking ideas from a variety of professionals in de-cluttering and related fields. But in this case, the pros I'm referring to are the professional diet experts and organizations. Reputable diet pros know that you can't crash-diet and hope to keep the weight off long-term because no one can sustain the severity of a crash diet and remain healthy or sane for long periods of time.

Sure, you can lose 20 pounds in 6 weeks if you eat nothing but grapefruit, but the minute you stop eating grapefruit and start eating normal food, the weight will all come rushing back. The only way to lose weight and keep it off for good is to change your basic eating and exercise patterns and to take the weight off slowly but surely. It's not glamorous and it's not a magic bullet, but it works.

The same thing holds true for clutter. Yes, you can hire an organizer to go through your house and toss everything that's not absolutely essential. But not only will the rest of your family hate you, you'll also be horrified to see the clutter piling back in the minute your back is turned. That's because you and your family won't have learned how to manage your clutter in a way that fits your lifestyle and personal styles.

With clutter as with weight loss, slowly but surely wins the race.

but I make sure I don't launch into a big, distracting project that I can't finish—or that will eat up the whole morning at the expense of work.

Jobs, families, friends, a household to manage, pets to play with, errands to run . . . unless huge piles of clutter are threatening to topple over and kill somebody, clearing out just isn't going to be your top priority. But that's no excuse for embracing the status quo. I say, break it up and get it done. Book by book, bra by bra, paper clip by paper clip. If you keep at it, one day you're going to look around and realize that the clutter that comes into the house today (and don't kid yourself, it *will* come—in the mail, with the kids, in a shopping bag, and so forth) is the only clutter you have to deal with. Aaaah, what a feeling!

To get started, I recommend trying the "5-Minute Fixes" in the chapters in Part Two. You'll find fast ideas for accomplishing some clutter-kicking. And when you see how much difference even 5 minutes can make—both in a room's appearance and in how good you feel—I think you'll be hooked.

Be Entertaining

There's a story I've always appreciated about a slovenly woman whose house was dirty and cluttered—which is to say, a real mess. One day, someone gave the woman some beautiful roses. Thrilled, she dug out a vase, washed it off, and put the roses in it. Then she set the gleaming vase with its beautiful flowers on her cluttered, dusty table. Immediately, she saw that it looked terrible, so she cleared off the table and dusted it, then set the vase back in its place. But as she looked at her now-shining table with its beautiful vase of flowers, the woman realized that the area around it looked terrible with all the chaos, mess, and dirt. So she began cleaning it up so her flowers would look nice. Of course, you can see where this is going. Before she knew it, our heroine had cleaned the entire room—and all because of a vase of flowers!

For most of us, it's not a vase of flowers but the impending arrival of guests that triggers our long-dormant desire to de-clutter and clean our houses—or at least our "public rooms." I say, make the most of this: Have people over as often as you can manage, and see what a transformation it makes in your home! You don't need to engage in grand-scale entertaining to make this work for you. An informal dinner with friends; an afternoon get-together to cook, knit, or chat; a monthly book club meeting—whatever you'd actually enjoy works fine, as long as it's on a regular and fairly frequent schedule. My friend Carolyn and her husband, Gary, host a weekly "Friday Night Supper Club" for a group of friends at their house. You can bet it's always spotless when we arrive!

Get Help

I'm not referring to professional help here, though a team of in-shape guys to haul off heavy stuff or move things around can sure come in handy. Instead, I'm talking about asking your family to pitch in and help you kick your collective clutter.

To use another example from the world of dieting, professionals always tell you to get your family, friends, and co-workers on board before you try to lose weight. If you explain to them that you're counting on them to help you stay motivated, praise your progress, and keep you away from temptation (for example, by going with you on a walk or to a show as a social outing rather than to the ice-cream

The Unwilling Accomplice

What if your spouse or partner *won't* help? What if he or she is the root cause of your clutter problem? If you or the kids are the main culprits, though your spouse or partner may not lift a finger to help you, he or she will probably be relieved to get rid of the mess. It's not ideal, but you'll still end up with a clean, de-cluttered house.

If you're in it together, you can start small and make it a contest—sort of like *The Biggest Loser*. Then, rather than a threat, he or she may see it as a fun competition and get into the spirit. You'll get help—*and* a de-cluttered house.

If he or she is the real clutterer in your home, though, it's super-important to be reassuring: Tell your spouse that you'll work with them to take it in easy stages, and promise not to ever get rid of anything they love. Assure them that they'll be consulted at every stage. (This is important no matter what your situation is—even if you have the world's most enthusiastic clutter-kicker for a spouse or partner. And remind them that they need to consult *you*, too.) If you think they might go for it, share some of the "5-Minute Fixes" in Part Two to see if you can get them interested.

But what if you've tried everything and you can't get your significant other to budge at all? He or she announces, in effect, and despite all your efforts, "It's my stuff and it's staying. Got that?" I'm no psychiatrist, but I'd say that's a control issue. If you're in this situation—and I hope nobody reading this is!—you're not really dealing with clutter; you're dealing with a basic couples problem. I'd say it's time to call in the professionals for a consultation—and I don't mean professional organizers!

stand or coffee shop), you're much more likely to succeed. This is even more true when we're talking about clutter. After all, your family can't literally put food in your mouth, but they can put stuff in your house!

So shamelessly steal this tip from successful dieters and put it to work for you. Get your spouse on board first, then hold a family meeting. Tell the kids what you're doing, why you're doing it, and how everyone can help. (See page 216 for more on getting everyone from toddlers to teens in on the act.) Suit the tasks you want your kids to do to their ages, and for goodness' sake, don't make them overwhelming! After all, *you* haven't been able to cope with the clutter, so you can't expect your kids (or spouse, partner, roommate, or live-in parents) to do any better.

Keep it fun, upbeat, and manageable, but most of all, keep at it. And don't forget to praise everyone for his or her progress.

What about nonfamily members? Tell friends, co-workers, and anyone else who might give you things that your house is bursting at the seams and you can't accept another *anything*. Ask them for clutter tips and favorite clutter-control and organizing tools. (They might have great ideas!) And let it be known that you want gifts like food, flowers, donations made in your name, memberships, or gift certificates rather than things, however lovely, that will pile up.

ONWARD!

I hope that, after reading this chapter, you've found the reasons why you have clutter that needs kicking, you've evaluated how bad your clutter problems really are, and you've already started to think of ways you can get to work to get rid of unwanted and unneeded stuff.

But please, before you begin kicking your clutter, bear in mind that "unwanted" and "unneeded" aren't the same thing. Before you toss the first rubber band, make sure you know the difference between simple clutter and something—however useless—that you really love. Chapter 2—Sorting It All Out, or How Much Do You Love It?, is all about thinking through your stuff and pinpointing where it falls in your affections (or dislikes). Making sure you keep all of your most-loved things—be they cracked, moth-eaten, ugly, or even unrecognizable to anyone else—is the key to successfully kicking your clutter once and for all.

Now, let's get started!

Sorting It All Out,

OR HOW MUCH DO YOU LOVE IT?

This chapter is going to be short but sweet because its focus is narrow but totally essential. It's about recognizing and keeping what you love, no matter what anybody else says. If you don't do that, you'll never be able to kick your clutter. Why? Because if you toss or give away what actually matters to you—from a chipped mug your first love gave you to the stuffed animal you carried around obsessively when you were 2 years old—you will not only regret it for the rest of your life, you will also become angry with clutter control and you'll retaliate by trying to compensate for the loss with more stuff.

Now, what does all that mean? Let's look again at dieting; it's closely related to de-cluttering, because when you diet, you're trying to change your eating and exercise habits to de-clutter your body of excess pounds. Okay, if you love low-fat, low-carb eating and strenuous daily exercise, you probably don't need to diet, now do you? But if you hate exercise and love carbs and fat—and have packed on the pounds as a result—to get and keep them off, you have to make a deal with yourself. Draconian diets that make you eat salads with no dressing, skinless chicken, and steamed veggies with no butter will *not* work—at least not for long—unless you're in prison and have no other choice. If you have to give up every single thing you love, you will fail, because really—who can do that for the rest of his life?

The diets that work are the ones that let you indulge in your favorite foods, but only occasionally and only in moderation. That way, you don't feel deprived. You feel like you can keep going if you know that you can have a Krispy Kreme doughnut once a week—but only one Krispy Kreme, and only once a week. If you felt that you could *never* eat another Krispy Kreme, guess what? One day, you'd find yourself eating a whole box of Krispy Kremes and hating yourself. Or a whole bag of M&Ms. Or a big plate of French fries. Or whatever.

Just as people throughout human history have prized fat, salt, and sugar because they make us feel good, at least for a little while, people prize objects that trigger positive associations for them—happy childhood memories, things that create a sense of connection (such as a family heirloom), things that mark important occasions, things that commemorate personal milestones and achievements, and things that remind us of people, pets, or places we love. These objects become symbols of who we are, and their loss is devastating.

I still remember an adult friend's inconsolable grief when her favorite stuffed animal was stolen, along with a gym bag, from her car. The surprised thieves probably tossed the stuffed toy in the nearest dumpster, but my bereft friend put up "missing person" posters—complete with a photo of her stolen hedgehog—all over town. And in case you're wondering, my friend never found her beloved toy, but her story *does* have a happy ending: Years later, she saw another one in the window of a secondhand store in the town where she was living. Though the original was lost, she now has Hedgehog II to fill its place.

THE FIRST ESSENTIAL CLUTTER RULE

This is *so* important that I'm going to put it in big letters so you can find it easily whenever you feel pressure from friends or family members to throw out something you cherish. I call it the First Essential Clutter Rule, and you should remind yourself of it often. Here it is:

$$\left[\begin{array}{c} \text{If you love it or you use it,} \\ \text{it's not clutter.} \end{array} \right]$$

Dear Claire,

When I married, my great-aunt Violet gave me her mother's antique cherub bowl. This heirloom is made of pink bisque with gold dots all over it and has a cluster of cherubs hovering around the rim. It's huge and fragile, and my whole family hates it. I could use the attic space taken up by the big box I have to keep it in. My husband thinks I should take it to an antiques dealer or an eBay store, but it's been in my family for more than 100 years and I feel like a traitor when I think about getting rid of it. What should I do?

—Cherubic

Dear Cherubic,

Is dear Great-Aunt Violet still extant? If not, you might present it to one of her offspring—or their offspring—as a touching memento of their mother or grandmother. If she had no offspring, take your husband's advice—it's excellent. Unless, of course, one of your other relatives is always commenting on the bowl when she visits you. In that case, you should give it to her at the next opportunity (even if the relative is your mother). And if she suddenly has some reason why she couldn't possibly take it, tell her you understand, but you wanted to make sure she had the opportunity before you sold it. If Great-Aunt Violet is still alive, you could always return the bowl to her, telling her how much you've appreciated her gift over the years but that you couldn't possibly keep it with rambunctious children in the house—you'd never forgive yourself if it got broken. When she eventually leaves it to you in her will—and steel yourself, she will—take your husband's great advice and sell it. Perhaps you'll be pleasantly surprised at its value!

Good luck,
Claire

The key to successful clutter control is really that simple. I don't care what it is, and I don't care what shape it's in, if you love it, or if you use it, it's not clutter—no matter what anybody says. As I write this, I have in my attic the stuffed lion that, though it was bigger than I was, I carried with me everywhere when I was 2 years old. (Thank goodness the pacifier and baby blanket I also carried everywhere are long lost.) My boyfriend, Rob, has the antique model of a Chinese junk (a kind of

Love It–Lose It Spectrum

Lose it	Don't like it	Don't especially like it	Don't like it much but have a sentimental attachment	It's okay	Like it	Like it a lot	Love it!
			grandma's rocking chair				
silver plate							
				floor lamp			
	coffee maker						
		plaid bathrobe					
							Pendleton blanket
							paper shredder
				fireplace screen			
		blue martini glasses					
						hot pink raincoat & umbrella	
					ceramic toothbrush holder		

Your first step is to evaluate each of your possessions on this Love It–Lose It Spectrum. Here's my version and how I rated some of my things. Create your own spectrum and rate your personal items, then move on to the Useful–Useless Spectrum on page 28. Make it easy on yourself and use a separate spectrum for each room!

boat) that his father bought him when Rob was a child living in Hong Kong. Its sails are too tattered to actually attach to the model, but they're lovingly stored away, and someday Rob hopes to have new ones made that he can attach to his model junk, based on the antique prototypes.

The same rule holds true if you use something. If you till your garden with an old wheel-hoe every spring, it's not clutter. If you knit gift scarves and mittens every year with some of your massive yarn collection, it's not clutter. If you make homemade sauerkraut with your antique mandoline, it's not clutter.

True, in both cases—love and use—other people might call any and all of these objects clutter, or even junk (so to speak). But they're *not*. You know it, and by God, you owe it to yourself to defend your well-loved and well-used possessions against the forces that want them out.

However.

If you find yourself clinging to *everything* on the basis that you love or use it, you're probably deceiving yourself. Rather than being defensive to the point of coming to a clutter-kicking standstill, look at your possessions as falling on a scale—the Love It–Lose It Spectrum. You can create your own scale based on your feelings about things, or you can rate your stuff on mine. I'm reproducing it on the opposite page so you can use it.

When you're thinking about getting rid of any given object, do a quick mental check to see where it falls on the Love It–Lose It Spectrum. Even if it's as battered as the sails on my boyfriend's boat, if you love it, keep it. (But keep it out of sight—see "The Second Essential Clutter Rule" on page 32.) You should probably keep anything that winds up in the "Like it a lot" range, too, and should consider the merits of keeping versus tossing anything in the "Like it" range. Don't like Aunt Adele's Victorian china but have a sentimental attachment? Keep a piece or a photo and sell the rest. Anything scoring below "Like it" that's not an heirloom should go in the get-it-out pile, unless it belongs to someone else in the family. Ask everyone to rate their stuff on the Love It–Lose It Spectrum as well, so you don't inadvertently toss something another family member treasures. (Check out Chapter 11—Clutter-Free Kids' Rooms, beginning on page 207, for advice on how to kick your kids' clutter.)

I Don't Like It, but I Use It

What if you couldn't care less about it as an object, but you think it's useful? This can apply to everything from a leaf-eater to a deicer, from Great-Grandma's potato masher to the only vacuum cleaner that actually sucks up pet hair. Here's another case where you may not love it, but if you really use it, it's not clutter. Before you throw out a tool or kitchen utensil, ask yourself (and your family, if it's someone

Useful–Useless Spectrum

Don't know what it is	Don't use it, don't like it	Don't use it	Don't use it, but keep it because it might come in handy	Use it seasonally	Use it once a month	Use it at least once a week	Use it at least once a day
	grandma's rocking chair						
	silver plate						
							floor lamp
							coffee maker
			plaid bathrobe				
				Pendleton blanket			
						paper shredder	
				fireplace screen			
	blue martini glasses				hot pink raincoat & umbrella		
							ceramic toothbrush holder

Once you've placed your items on the Love It–Lose It Spectrum, it's time to rate each of your possessions in terms of its usefulness. This chart shows how I evaluated some of my possessions. Once you create your own charts, move on to the Item Action Plan on page 30.

else's) to rate it on the Useful–Useless Spectrum. As with the Love It–Lose It Spectrum, I'm reproducing mine for ready reference, but feel free to create something that works better for you and your family.

You may not "like" your slow cooker or air popper, but if you use them regularly, they're not clutter. The same is true of your silver-polishing cloths, even if you use them only before Christmas. But if you have duplicates of useful things—several electric razors, in case something happens to the one you use, or, God forbid,

How Much Do I Need?

If you found that you fall into the Scout category in Chapter 1 (see page 13), you've probably stocked up on staples of all kinds, from toilet paper to batteries, first-aid kits to bottled water, reflective blankets to flashlights. After all, you might need them someday!

And yes, if there's an emergency, you really might need extras of basic necessities. If your area is prone to ice storms in winter, it's smart to keep extra staples on hand *in winter*—toilet paper, milk, butter, eggs, tissues, bread, and anything else you and your family might use up in less than a week. The same holds true if your area is prone to power outages. In my case, if the power goes off, so does my septic system, so I keep jugs of water on hand for manual flushing, just in case. But how much is enough?

Certain faiths believe in "preparedness," the stocking up of staples so that families could survive a disaster of considerable magnitude, one serious enough to interrupt supply lines for anywhere from 6 months to 2 years. Survivalists and some Libertarians also believe that this is smart practice. And once again, if you're concerned about the stability of our supply system *and* you have the space for storage, go for it.

The keys here are to stock only what your family will actually consume—it won't help you to stock up on split peas if your family won't eat them—and then to rotate your stored goods. You want to use the oldest stores first. If you don't cook from your home storage, there's no point in keeping it. Fortunately, there are books, magazines, and online guides to help you. Three that leap to mind are *Backwoods Home* magazine, their book *Backwoods Home Cooking*, and *Cookin' with Home Storage*.

If your "preparedness" is more a matter of compulsion than a religious tenet or a carefully planned life strategy, you can probably put your shelf space to better use. After all, those unused batteries get old, and who needs a fossilized box (or 10) of laundry detergent? Instead, for frequently used items, use the one-plus rule: What you're using currently and a spare. Then make sure you use the spare next and replace it with the new spare, and you'll be sure to keep things current and fresh. As always, use your good sense: If your kids drink three bottles of fruit juice a day, you'll need more than three extras unless you go to the grocery every day. (Or you could switch to space-saving concentrate!) Balance your needs with your storage space, though—more frequent shopping trips make more sense, clutter-wise, than pantry items stacked all over the house and spilling out of closets and entryways.

Item Action Plan

Item	How I listed it on the Love It-Lose It Spectrum	How I listed it on the Useful-Useless Spectrum	Action(s) I will take
grandma's rocking chair	Don't like it too much but have a sentimental attachment	Don't use it	See if any relative wants it; if not, take it to local antiques store or consignment shop
silver plate	Hate it	Don't use it/ Don't like it	Take it to antiques auction
floor lamp	It's okay	Use it at least once a day	Keep an eye out for one I like better & replace when I find one
coffee maker	Don't like it	Use it at least once a day	Replace now. Donate old coffee maker & get receipt for taxes
plaid bathrobe	Don't especially like it	Don't use it but keep it because it might come in handy	Never worn designer robe; sell through upscale consignment shop or eBay drop-off store
Pendleton blanket	Love it!	Use it seasonally	Keep it
paper shredder	Love it!	Use it at least once a week	Keep it
fireplace screen	It's okay	Use it seasonally	Replace when I have the money & see one I really like
blue martini glasses	Don't especially like them	Don't use it/ Don't like it	Sell through an eBay drop-off store or an antiques store or secondhand shop
hot pink raincoat & umbrella	Like them a lot	Use it once a month	Keep them
ceramic toothbrush holder	Like it	Use it at least once a day	Keep it

After listing your possessions and evaluating them on the Love It-Lose It and Useful-Useless Spectrums (pages 26 and 28), it's time to decide what you'll do with each item. Keep it, give it away, toss it, donate it, sell it, or replace it—the choice is up to you. Here's how I'll be handling some of the clutter in my life. Create an Item Action Plan for your possessions, then get started on de-cluttering!

multiple lawn mowers and large appliances (because you just might need that black-and-white television set one day)—it's time to reevaluate. Think of the space saved (and potential money earned) by clearing out those "extras."

If you inherited Grandpa's antique hand tools and you don't know what they are, much less how to use them, you can either sell them or keep them and display them. (We'll get to both options later.) In either case, there's no reason to feel guilty. Just be honest with yourself and your family as to what you really want to do with them, and then do it. Maybe your favorite nephew has decided to become a house carpenter. Voilà! You've given him the gift of a lifetime and cleared out your garage at the same time.

In my opinion, anything that falls within the "Use it at least once a day" through "Use it seasonally" categories is worth keeping, though if you're really short on space, I could make a strong argument for renting the seasonal stuff rather than owning it. Unless you live in a mansion and have space for a museum's worth of stuff—in which case, why are you reading this?—everything else falls into the sell it/donate it/give it away/trash or recycle it category. To borrow a phrase from Dr. Phil, let's get real. If you're not using it, you *don't* need it. It's just taking up space. So get it out!

PUTTING IT ALL TOGETHER

To get the truest picture of where your possessions fall in the scale of trash or treasure, you need to put together your Love It–Lose It Spectrum and your Useful–Useless Spectrum for any given item. Let's combine them into an Item Action Plan.

Use your Item Action Plan as a guide to show you what to do with your stuff. As you list each item and see how it lines up on the Love It–Lose It Spectrum and the Useful–Useless Spectrum that you created earlier, you'll be able to see clearly what you should do with it. If you love it and use it daily, it's a clear keeper. If you hate it but use it daily or weekly, it's a good candidate for replacement. (After all, if you hate your coffeepot but use it constantly, wouldn't it be a good idea to replace it with one you love? And the same is true of your everyday dishware and the clothes you wear to work.) If you hate it and never use it, for goodness' sake, toss, sell, donate, or give it away. Ask yourself why you're letting it take up space to begin with!

Obviously, it makes no sense (unless you've just won the lottery) to replace every single object you're not wild about but use, so prioritize: Try to replace the ones you use or look at most often (the ones, for example, that live on your kitchen counter) when the opportunity presents itself. If you really hate your blow-dryer and you use it every day, it makes more sense to replace it than to replace the clunky leaf shredder you use for 2 weeks every fall. It may take a while, but if you make it a priority, a year or so from now, you'll be delighted to find that you really like the equipment or utensils you actually use. And isn't that worth it?

THE SECOND
ESSENTIAL CLUTTER RULE

Before we leave this chapter and dig into kicking our clutter, I want to share with you my Second Essential Clutter Rule. Here it is:

$$\left[\text{ If you can't see it, it's not clutter. } \right]$$

If my boyfriend's, Rob's, beloved model trains (tracks, buildings, accessories . . .) are piled in and out of boxes that are spilling out all over the floor and stacked all over the tables and chairs, they're clutter. If they're neatly boxed and shelved or displayed attractively on their own table, they're not. If my cats' toys are thrown all over the floor, they're clutter—potentially hazardous clutter, at that!—but if they're kept in a toy box on a closet shelf and brought out for playtime only, they're not. If your houseplants, watering can, extra pots, fertilizers, and the like are mixed in with everything else on the kitchen counter, they're clutter; if the plants are displayed on an attractive stand with a storage cabinet for their accessories, they're not.

The same holds true for big and infrequently used objects. If your pressure canner is out on the counter all year, it's about the only thing that will fit on there because it's so huge. And unless you can all year, you'll want it out for only a few weeks in late summer. But if you can fit it under the sink, it's there when you want it—convenient but out of sight. It may be big and ugly, but it's not clutter. (Unless you never use it!) The same is true of power tools, the chipper-shredder, and the

The Artful Dodger

One very clever, very creative way to deal with potential clutter is to turn it into a decorative display. Remember my Collector friend Cole and his minimalist partner, Bruce, from Chapter 1? Cole has accumulated and inherited a wonderful collection of handmade and antique baskets, wooden bowls, and other rustic kitchen-related implements. But instead of trying to set them around the house or put them out on the kitchen counters, both of which would have aggravated Bruce and caused his clutter-kicking to really go into overdrive, Cole did something brilliant: He created a decorative tableau.

Cole and Bruce live in a wonderful and largely handmade house, and the kitchen has a fine set of rustic handmade wooden cabinets. Because the roof slants upward, there's quite a bit of room above one wall of cabinets. Cole created a montage of his rustic kitchen baskets and bowls, even including an old rocking chair at the high end of the ceiling. The result is a beautiful display that's totally in keeping with the look of the kitchen—and also out of everybody's way. It was the perfect solution for both Bruce and Cole. And, of course, their guests enjoy it, too.

So don't overlook seemingly "dead" space when you're thinking about what to do with beloved possessions, and don't forget the power of an effective combination. (For tons of ideas on creative ways to combine things, pick up a stack of back issues of *Martha Stewart Living* and *Mary Engelbreit's Home Companion* at your library. Then return them so *they* don't become clutter!) Just remember, setting out everything you own in a cheek-by-jowl fashion is *not* creating a display, attractive or otherwise; instead, you're just making more dustables. Using some restraint, mixing and matching different things, and varying the scale and texture will give you the most pleasing results. (For example, Cole's baskets and wooden bowls look better together than either group would have looked alone.)

chainsaw. If they're out rusting on the lawn or waiting to break someone's neck on the garage or mudroom floor, they're clutter. But if they're put neatly in the tool shed or on a shelf or wall peg in the garage, they're useful tools.

Mind you, there are limits. If your massive collection of LPs or antique pitchers is out of sight because they're stored in pieces of furniture bought expressly to hold them and then crammed all over the living room, you still have clutter. But now it's a clutter of furniture! I'm convinced that there are appropriate, attractive ways to store just about anything, as long as you're not trying to store too many of too many different things. (See Chapter 3—Tooling Up for some great storage options.) Choose either the LPs or the pitchers. Or some LPs and some pitchers. Unless, of course, you have the room but just don't know how to do it. In either case, read on! And make sure you didn't skip "The Artful Dodger," on page 33.

ONWARD!

Now that you feel confident that the things you really love will be safe from your clutter-kicking work and you've confessed that, yes, you *do* own things that you don't really love, it's time to get to work. And as with all work, the right tools can make a huge difference in the ease of and pleasure you'll take in the job. So let's head to Chapter 3—Tooling Up, and take a look at what's out there to help you turn the things you choose to keep into objects that are orderly, easy to find, and attractively displayed—rather than just a bunch of clutter.

Tooling Up

Sometimes kicking your clutter is as simple as finding the right place to put it. In this chapter, you'll discover where to get the best organizational tools, from ingenious storage systems and professional shelving systems to simple containers and functional furniture. The right tools can make the job of clutter control so much simpler, and that will save time—and your sanity, too!

But tooling up isn't just about actual tools like buckets and files. It's also about finding the right help for your clutter-kicking needs, whether it's a great book, magazine, or Web site; a professional organization; or a support group. You'll find those here, too.

Most books bury their resources lists in the back, as if they were afterthoughts. But as you'll see, not just in this chapter but throughout this book, I think being able to find and use the right tools and resources can make all the difference in whether your clutter-kicking efforts succeed or fail.

In fact, if you've tried to get your clutter under control in the past and it hasn't worked, this list may be the missing link. So not only am I putting this chapter right up front, but I've also included appropriate tools and resources in every chapter in Parts Two, Three, and Four. That way, you'll have the resources you need where you need them, and you'll be able to act on a great tip immediately, while you're feeling inspired! Tools and other resources are recommended throughout the tips, but look for the specially marked sidebars "Tools of the Trade" and "Love

It or Lose It?" to find some of my favorites—plus tools that are often recommended but are, in my opinion, overrated.

MY TOP 11 CLUTTER-KICKING TOOLS

Let me start by recommending the clutter-kicking tools I can't live without. These certainly aren't the only ones that work. (See "The Pros Know" on page 40 for some excellent suggestions from Diane Albright, a professional organizer.) But these tools are the ones I use every single day to keep my own home (and life) in order. Some are old favorites, dating back to my first dorm room and even before, while others are essentials I've discovered over the past 5 years. Some are free, most are inexpensive, and a couple cost a bit more (though you can often find them for much less if you buy them used).

Because your house is different from mine and your needs are probably different, too, please don't consider this the end-all and be-all list. I don't: My list is always growing as I add new finds! And the list doesn't even include two things that are absolutely essential for me—adequate bookshelf space to have all my books easily accessible and enough CD display and storage space to house my collection—since they're about me, but maybe not you. What I *have* included here are things I think everyone could use. See if you agree!

1. **Plastic storage boxes.** These inexpensive storage containers can be found everywhere, from supermarkets and pharmacies to home improvement stores. They come in all sizes, from tiny (great for pins, staples, and other office and crafts accessories) to huge (such as under-bed storage containers for clothes and bins for basement and garage storage). I like the ones with handles and side clamps best, since they're easiest to move. One definite advantage of these containers is that they're clear or translucent, so you can see what's inside!

2. **ClickClacks.** These rectangular and square plastic storage containers have lock-down lids to keep all sorts of food safe and fresh. I love them because they stack very nicely, saving you valuable storage space; you can see what's inside, so you can tell at a glance if you need more rice, cereal, dried fruit, or what have you; and they keep food pest-free. For more on ClickClacks, see "Tools of the Trade" on page 92.

3. **Copy-paper boxes.** I couldn't manage without copy-paper boxes, those sturdy, heavy-duty lidded cardboard boxes that are the perfect size for lifting—not too heavy!—and will hold a lot. I keep tax records, yarn, collectibles not currently on display, Christmas ornaments, and many, many other things stored in these boxes. I keep my "wrapping station" in two boxes, with wrapping paper, tissue paper, and gift bags in one box and ribbon, bows, and other adornments in the other. And I find that these boxes are perfect for storing framed (and unframed) artworks upright and safe, with paper or bubble wrap between them, when it's not their turn for wall display. I always label the top and all sides of the boxes so I can tell what's inside no matter what part of the box I can see. And of course, I wouldn't store cardboard boxes anywhere damp, such as in a basement or garage. (See "Plastic storage boxes," above—they're great for damp storage.) I used to get empty copy-paper boxes at the corporation where I worked. Now that I work from home, I ask my boyfriend, Rob, to collect them for me at the college where he teaches, and I also beg them from my local office-supply store.

4. **Shower and bath storage.** I absolutely love the wire baskets that you hang over the showerhead or suction to the walls of the bath or shower stall. They hold all your bath and shower essentials high and dry, so they're not sitting at the corners of the tub, collecting grunge and falling into the tub or shower. (See "Stash the shampoo" on page 132 for more on these bathroom lifesavers.)

5. **Under-sink shelves.** Unlike many organizing devices that end up taking up so much space that you actually lose storage space when you install them, the plastic shelving systems that snap together under the kitchen or bathroom sink are fantastic. (See "Tools of the Trade" on page 112.) They instantly double your storage space, are supereasy to install (even for a klutz like me), and let you actually see what you have stored in there. I have one in the bathroom and one in the kitchen, and I'm grateful for them every single day!

6. **Rolling carts.** I suppose you could call me a cart junkie. I have four of them in my house and use them constantly. In my opinion, they're clutter-kicking lifesavers. I have one in the kitchen with a butcher-block top that serves as a mobile island and storage unit; one in the living room with the TV,

DVD/VCR combo, remotes, and other accessories, so we can roll it out when someone's watching TV but keep it out of the middle of the floor the rest of the time; one in my office, holding projects I'm currently working on conveniently next to the computer; and one in my plant room, with houseplants and supplies conveniently corralled in one attractive display. (That one has glass surfaces to contain spills.) I bought mine new at various times, but I often see them selling for almost nothing at thrift shops and secondhand furniture stores.

7. **Metal storage tins.** These convenient cylindrical tins come in any number of attractive colors and designs (some of mine have beautiful songbirds on them, while others have whimsical pet art and still others have Colonial toile fabric designs), so you can display them wherever you need pest- (or possibly pet-) proof storage. They're capacious and easy to stack and access. I keep seed for my outdoor birdfeeders; dry dog and cat food; parrot toys; and kitchen staples like chocolate and butterscotch chips, dried fruit, beans, and pasta in mine. (Not together, please!)

8. **Plastic buckets.** Like metal bins, plastic buckets make great clutter-containers. I use heavy plastic buckets with lock-on lids to hold my bunny and chicken feed, potting soil, and other gardening supplies like orchid bark. Smaller buckets keep my cleaning supplies and small gardening tools like trowels, pruners, and weeders contained in one easy-to-find place. I also keep a small covered bucket to hold kitchen scraps for the compost heap. Handles make plastic buckets and bins easy to pick up and carry to where they're needed, and they stack easily, too, for the most efficient use of space. Unlike decorative metal tins, plastic buckets aren't attractive enough to display in plain sight. I keep mine in the mudroom, laundry room, greenhouse, and under the kitchen sink.

9. **File cabinets.** I love my two-drawer file cabinets! I bought them used at a secondhand office supply store in an assortment of cheerful colors, getting them over time as I needed them. I keep hanging folders in them with work-related files, topical files that are relevant to me (such as a home-repair file) or simply of interest (a backyard chicken file), a bills file, and even files of garden catalogs. (For more on my bill-filing system, see "Bite the bill bullet"

on page 242.) They keep information organized and easy to find. I keep my work files in a separate cabinet from my personal files, and I keep all file folders labeled and alphabetized by topic. A file cabinet can be an organizational lifesaver—no more time wasted looking for a paper or article that "you know you have somewhere." Everything's right there when you need it. But any filing system is useful only if it's maintained. If you have drawers of outdated stuff or papers packed in so tightly that you're afraid to pull out a file lest a volcano of papers erupts from the drawer, or if nothing's in a recognizable order, so you might as well have shoved it all in a box in the attic, then file cabinets won't help you. The trick is to buy them, keep them clean, keep them organized, keep them current—and they'll keep *you* happy!

10. **Desk planner.** My yearly desk planner is my lifesaver. Every December, I pick up one of these compact books (the size of a small notebook) at a local bookstore, and I'm set for the year. I like the ones that show a week on each two-page spread, since they have plenty of room to write but aren't too bulky. I write in appointments, upcoming events, work-related things like meetings and deadlines, vacations, birthdays, payment-due dates—anything that's time-sensitive. If a time is involved, I'll include that ("supper Carolyn's 7 p.m."); if it's an appointment, I'll include the phone number so it's right there if I need to call for any reason. I check the planner every evening to make sure I'm on top of upcoming obligations, and I check it again the next day as I progress through the day's events. (As you can probably guess, I keep my planner on the rolling cart next to my computer desk!) This does away with the clutter of sticky notes all over the fridge, computer, bathroom mirror, desktop, and other places I've seen people post notes in usually futile attempts to remind themselves of upcoming events. (After all, once the surface is bristling with notes, who even reads them anymore?) And it keeps track of all your engagements and obligations in one place, so you don't waste time looking through computer and print calendars trying to remember if some appointment has slipped your mind.

11. **Your eyes.** They're your best clutter-kicking tool, so keep them open. Familiarity breeds oblivion. When you see the same clutter all the time, you just stop seeing it. Make sure you look at your rooms, yard, car, closets,

(continued on page 43)

the Pros Know

In the realm of clutter-kicking tools, I know what works for me (see "My Top 11 Clutter-Kicking Tools" on page 36). But I wanted to know what a professional organizer—someone who's helped at least hundreds of people choose the best tools to de-clutter their homes and get their stuff organized and contained—would recommend. Fortunately, Diane Albright, organizing expert and owner of All Bright Ideas (see page 48) in nearby Emmaus, Pennsylvania, agreed to share her expertise with all of us. Diane not only sells wonderful tools and organizing systems through her store and Web site (www.allbrightideas.com), she also consults with residential and business clients and teaches seminars on organizing and clutter control. I have been consistently impressed with Diane's tool selection over the years and originally discovered some of my own favorites, including ClickClacks and the showerhead organizer, in the All Bright Ideas store, so she was the first person I thought of when I started writing this chapter. I think you'll find her advice as useful and down-to-earth as I did!

Q: If someone's working their way into de-cluttering or getting organized and can't afford to do it all at once, how (or where) would you suggest that they start?

A: Getting organized does not necessarily mean that you'll need to spend money hiring a professional to work on the project—that is, if you are capable of doing it on your own. Nor does it mean buying containers or totes. As a matter of fact, getting organized should save you money because you will see what you already have and won't be buying duplicates or replacements when you can't find what you need.

The first step to getting organized is de-cluttering, so you can see what you have left to organize and store. After you have thoroughly de-cluttered, you may be surprised at how much you have pared down your belongings. If you find yourself in need of containers or totes to organize your belongings more efficiently, try reusing something you already have.

I recommend keeping a stash of containers or baskets that you no longer need. Keep this stash on a shelf in your basement or attic. Every time you need a storage container, browse your stash.

However, there are times that it is better to buy an organizing product than to try to use a makeshift one. If you aren't finding a container that suits your needs in your own stash, consider purchasing an item that is specifically made for that purpose.

Q: What do you consider the one essential big-ticket organizing tool, and why?

A: The most worthwhile item to invest in is a closet system. A closet typically has an enormous amount of wasted space. If designed correctly, a closet can easily double your storage space and save you significant time when you're searching for a particular item. Your redesigned closet does not need to be elaborate. If you shop around for a good-quality closet system that is designed for homeowner installation, you should be able to find one for under $300. You *do* need to make sure you are purchasing a quality system.

A standard closet in most homes is a 6-foot reach-in closet with one single rod and one shelf above it, providing 6 feet of long hanging space and 6 feet of shelf storage. Unfortunately, this type of closet does not maximize your storage space. With a good closet system, you can easily increase your storage space to 8 feet of hanging space for short items like shirts and skirts, 2 feet of hanging space for long items like dresses and bathrobes, and 14 feet of shelf storage space. To do it, remove the old system and install two 4-foot rods, one at 84 inches from the floor and the other at 42 inches from the floor. Also include a 2-foot rod for hanging long clothes, with two 2-foot shelves above it; an upper 6-foot shelf spanning the width of the closet at the top, and a 4-foot shelf above the bottom double hanging rod.

Q: What would you consider the most essential small organizing tools, and why?

A: I'd recommend these six small organizing tools for every home.

1. Every house should have a junk-drawer organizer (even though most houses have five junk drawers in the kitchen alone). By using a junk-drawer organizer, you have a place to toss paper clips, rubber bands, scissors, pens, pencils, erasers, and other small items. The ultimate junk-drawer organizer has a sliding top tray, giving you two tiers of compartments.

2. Always have a place to put your keys. It can be a wall plaque with hooks or a box you keep in a drawer or set out on a piece of furniture. You need somewhere to habitually put your keys so they're always in the same place.

3. If you have a family, a sales receipt storage box is a must. The ideal size is 4 by 6 by 6 inches deep. The box can be plastic or, if storage space is at a premium, you can use a decorative box that can be left out as part of your decor. Put index cards labeled from A to Z in the box so you can sort your receipts alphabetically. Just toss your receipt behind the alphabetical letter of the store name.

(continued)

the **Pros Know**

(cont.)

4. Use two coupon organizers—one for grocery store coupons and a separate one for restaurant and retail store coupons. The organizer for the restaurants and retail stores will need to accommodate a larger coupon. I recommend keeping both coupon organizers in your car—this way you won't forget them. If you walk into a store or restaurant without your coupon organizer, it is very easy to go out to the parking lot to retrieve the coupon rather than driving all the way home.

5. No tools required for this one: Put your spices in alphabetical order. The order doesn't have to be exact; instead, it can be a grouping of spices under each letter or group of letters ("A,B,C," and so on).

6. Buy a desktop file box, typically 12 inches wide by 10 inches high by 7 inches deep, to hold file folders for the papers you most frequently refer to throughout the week. You may have files such as "bills," "to do," and "to read," or special projects such as "house hunting" or "college search."

Q: Do you have any tips you'd like to share with our readers on how to kick clutter or get more organized?

A: The key to being organized is having a designated place for everything. So first designate "homes" for all your belongings, even socks with missing mates and mystery keys that unlock who-knows-what.

Next, institute "Clutter Patrol" in your household. "Clutter Patrol" is a daily designated time when your entire family puts away their belongings. Now you may laugh and say that the first patrol would take a few days. That may be true, but instead, start out with 20 minutes a night until it is down to 10 minutes or less. If you have five family members and each of you goes on "Clutter Patrol" for 10 minutes a day, that adds up to 50 minutes a day putting away clutter. You may need to motivate your family to go on "Clutter Patrol." Do what works best in your household: Postpone a privilege or add a privilege to inspire your family to get it done.

Q: Finally, do you have any advice on how people can keep clutter from coming back?

A: Once you have your home organized, you shouldn't need to have a big de-cluttering project ever again. Instead, keep a give-away box or bag in a convenient location like your garage or coat closet. Every time you discover something that doesn't fit or that you don't want, put it in the bag or box. Donate the contents to charity.

and other spaces with "fresh eyes"—a realtor's eyes, a guest's eyes, your boss's eyes, Martha Stewart's eyes, whatever works for you—and see what they'd see. It will help keep you sensitized, not just to the clutter that's there now, but to that insidious phenomenon, clutter creep.

[Familiarity breeds oblivion.
Just because the clutter's been there
so long you don't even see it anymore
doesn't mean it's not still clutter.]

CLUTTER-KICKING RESOURCES

Beyond individual tools, consider this section your clutter-kicking toolkit. You'll find links to clutter-fighting organizations; professional organizers; Web sites, stores, and catalogs full of great clutter-beating products; plus organizations and links that can help you offload clutter once you've isolated it from the rest of your stuff. If you have a computer with an Internet connection, you can go online and check out any of these resources that interest you right away. (Ah, the joys of instant gratification!) In case you don't, I've tried to provide a phone number and address (where possible) so you can still contact the ones you want to know more about. Bear in mind that most libraries provide Internet access, and the librarians would be happy to help you get online and explore Web sites if you feel uncomfortable venturing into computerland by yourself. Read on and see what's out there!

Organizations and Programs

If you do better when you have a support group or you're in a structured program, one of these organizations may be for you. Check them all out and see which one is most appealing—and most affordable. (Many are online groups, so it helps to have computer access.) Then try the one you like best and see if it works for you. If not, keep in mind that as with diets, you may have to try several before you hit on the right one. In any case, good luck!

The Clutter Diet
LivingOrder, Inc.
PO Box 40460
Austin, TX 78704
866-915-3438
www.clutterdiet.com
program works like a diet

Clutterers Anonymous
PO Box 91413
Los Angeles, CA 90009-1413
310-281-6064
www.clutterersanonymous.net
12-step support group

Clutterless Recovery Groups,
   Inc.
5413 N. 32nd Street
McAllen, TX 78504-1560
512-351-4058
www.clutterless.org

FlyLady and Company, Inc.
www.flylady.net
*FlyLady Marla Cilley's
Web site; see also* Sink
Reflections, *page 52,
and "Tools of the Trade,"
page 237*

Messies Anonymous
5025 SW 114th Avenue
Miami, FL 33165
800-637-7292
www.messies.com
12-step support group

The National Study Group
   on Chronic Disorganization
   (NSGCD)
4728 Hedgemont Drive
St. Louis, MO 63128
314-416-2236
www.nsgcd.org
Clutter-Hoarding Scale

Organize Yourself Online
www.organizeyourself
   online.com

Professional Organizers

These aren't individual organizers; they're organizations and groups of organizers who can refer you to an organizer in your area. Their sites often provide organizing tips, as well.

National Association of
   Professional Organizers
   (NAPO)
4700 West Lake Avenue
Glenview, IL 60025
847-375-4746
www.napo.net

The National Study Group
   on Chronic Disorganization
   (NSGCD)
4728 Hedgemont Drive
St. Louis, MO 63128
314-416-2236
www.nsgcd.org
*gives referrals to local
professional organizers*

www.OnlineOrganizing.com
PO Box 1942
Clinton, MD 20735
301-659-2203
www.onlineorganizing.com

Professional Organizers Web
   Ring (POWR)
PO Box 298
Mt. Ephraim, NJ 08059
www.organizerswebring.com

Catalogs and Web Sites

You'll notice that I recommend many catalogs in this book. I'll confess that I'm a catalog junkie. I enjoy the adventure of browsing through catalogs, never knowing what I'll find on the next page. And the same is true of product-oriented Web sites, with their virtual catalogs. But the catalogs and Web sites I'm recommending here really do have wonderful furniture, tools, products, and organizing systems of all kinds that make it easier on you when you're trying to kick your clutter. If you have Internet access, you can go to the Web sites and browse, and then either buy if you find something you like (or want to get something I've recommended) or ask them to send you a catalog. Most of these companies also have stores in various locations. If you're lucky enough to live near one, you can go check out their wares in person. Store locations are listed in their catalogs and on their Web sites. If no street address is given here, it's a Web site– or catalog-only company.

As with everything else in this chapter, I'm sure there are many fantastic stores, catalogs, and Web sites I don't know about. If you don't see some of your favorites here, write them in the margins under the appropriate category so you'll have them right where you need them.

Closets

If you're trying to get your closets under control, look no further—these companies specialize in closet organization. Many offer free consultations, and many also have franchises or sell through other retailers across the country, so call or check the Web sites rather than going by the parent office's address. They may be closer than you think!

California Closets
1000 4th Street, Suite 800
San Rafael, CA 94901
800-274-6754
www.calclosets.com

Closet Factory
12800 S. Broadway
Los Angeles, CA 90061
800-634-9000
www.closetfactory.com

ClosetMaid
650 SW 27th Avenue
PO Box 4400
Ocala, FL 34474
800-227-8319
www.closetmaid.com

Closet Masters, Inc.
9515 Deerico Road, Suite 1012
Timonium, MD 21093
800-548-1868
www.closet-masters.com

Closets By Design
13151 South Western Avenue
Gardena, CA 90249
800-293-3744
www.closets-by-design.com

Contemporary Closets
19 Chapin Road, Building D
Pine Brook, NJ 07058
877-647-7331
www.contemporaryclosets.com

Easy Closets
19 Chapin Road, Building D
Pine Brook, NJ 07058
800-910-0129
www.easyclosets.com

Containers

We can all use some good containers, right? Check out these companies and see what they have to offer. You'll be amazed at the variety of containers that are available! Choose the ones that work for you.

Clares Closet
58 Noble Street
Kutztown, PA 19530
610-683-8112
www.shopatclares.com
eBay store: clares_closet

The Container Store
500 Freeport Parkway
Coppell, TX 75019
888-266-8246
www.containerstore.com

Organize.com
PO Box 2348
Riverside, CA 92516
800-600-9817
www.organize.com

Stacks & Stacks
1045 Hensley Street
Richmond, CA 94801
800-761-5222
www.stacksandstacks.com

Furnishings and Accessories

These companies also have containers but don't specialize in them like the companies listed in the "Containers" section. Look here for furniture designed specially for storage and all sorts of other intriguing and effective innovations. Don't forget to check their Web sites or catalogs for store locations near you.

Ballard Designs
5568 West Chester Road
West Chester, OH 45069
800-536-7551
www.ballarddesigns.com

Bed Bath & Beyond
650 Liberty Avenue
Union, NJ 07083
800-462-3966
www.bedbathandbeyond.com

Crate & Barrel
PO Box 3210
Naperville, IL 60566-7210
800-967-6696
www.crateandbarrel.com

Exposures
1 Memory Lane
PO Box 3615
Oshkosh, WI 54903-3615
800-222-4947
www.exposuresonline.com
albums and archival materials

Frontgate
5666 West Chester Road
West Chester, OH 45069
888-263-9850
www.frontgate.com

Gaiam Living/Harmony
Gaiam, Inc.
360 Interlocken Boulevard,
  Suite 300
Broomfield, CO 80021
877-989-6321
www.gaiamliving.com

Home Decorators Collection
8920 Pershall Road
Hazelwood, MO 63042
877-537-8539
www.homedecorators.com

The Home Depot
8920 Paces Ferry Road NW
Atlanta, GA 30339
800-533-3199
www.homedepot.com

IKEA
498 W. Germantown Pike
Plymouth Meeting, PA 19462
www.ikea.com

Kitchen Accessories Unlimited
1136-1146 Stratford Avenue
Stratford, CT 06615
800-667-8721
www.kitchensource.com

L.L. Bean Home
Casco Street
Freeport, ME 04033
800-411-5713
www.llbean.com

The Lane Co., Inc.
Altavista, VA 24517
800-750-5263
cedar chests

Lillian Vernon
100 Lillian Vernon Drive
Virginia Beach, VA 23479-0002
800-901-9291
www.lillianvernon.com

Linens 'n Things
6 Brighton Road
Clifton, NJ 07012
866-568-7578
www.lnt.com

Lowe's
1000 Lowe's Boulevard
Mooresville, NC 28117
www.lowes.com

Michaels, The Arts and Crafts
  Store
8000 Bent Branch Drive
Irving, TX 75063
800-642-4235
www.michaels.com

Moss
150 Greene Street
New York, NY 10012
866-888-6677
www.mossonline.com
individual pieces of china, flatware, and crystal

NapaStyle
574 Gateway Drive
Napa, CA 94558
866-776-6272
www.napastyle.com

OXO International
C/O Helen of Troy
1 Helen of Troy Plaza
El Paso, TX 79912
800-545-4411
www.oxo.com
  kitchen organizers and tools

Pier 1 Imports
100 Pier 1 Place
Fort Worth, TX 76102
800-245-4595
www.pier1.com

Plow & Hearth
PO Box 6000
Madison, VA 22727-1600
800-494-7544
www.plowandhearth.com

Pottery Barn
3250 Van Ness Avenue
San Francisco, CA 94109
888-779-5176
www.potterybarn.com

Pottery Barn Kids
3250 Van Ness Avenue
San Francisco, CA 94109
800-993-4923
www.potterybarnkids.com

Shaker Workshops
PO Box 8001
Ashburnham, MA 01430-
  8001
800-840-9121
www.shakerworkshops.com

Sturbridge Yankee Workshop
90 Blueberry Road
Portland, ME 04102
800-343-1144
www.sturbridgeyankee.com

Target
1000 Nicollet Mall
Minneapolis, MN 55403
800-440-0680
www.target.com

Through the Country Door
1112 7th Avenue
Monroe, WI 53566-1364
800-341-9477
www.countrydoor.com

The Vermont Country Store
PO Box 6999
Rutland, VT 05702-6999
802-362-8460
www.vermontcountrystore.com

West Elm
3250 Van Ness Avenue
San Francisco, CA 94109
888-922-4119
www.westelm.com

Williams-Sonoma
Mail Order Department
PO Box 7456
San Francisco, CA 94120-7456
877-812-6235
www.williams-sonoma.com

Home Office

Try these companies first when you're looking for equipment and tools to organize your home office.

FileSolutions Filing Systems
PO Box 671295
Dallas, TX 75367
800-336-2046
www.filesolutions.com

FlyLady and Company, Inc.
Mail Order
703 N. Broad Street
Brevard, NC 28712
www.flylady.net
  *"Office in a Bag" and "The
  Office Pack"*

Kiplinger's Taming the Paper
  Tiger
The Monticello Corporation
4060 Peachtree Road, Suite
  D-339
Atlanta, GA 30319-3020
800-430-0794
www.thepapertiger.com
  software system

Office Depot
Corporate Support Center
2200 Old Germantown Road
Delray Beach, FL 33445
800-463-3768
www.officedepot.com

OfficeMax
3605 Warrensville Center
  Road
Shaker Heights, OH 44122
800-283-7674
www.officemax.com

OnlineOrganizing.com
PO Box 1942
Clinton, MD 20735
301-659-2203
www.onlineorganizing.com
  *"Office-on-the-Go" System,
  a traveling "office" that fits
  in your car's trunk*

Staples
500 Staples Drive
Framingham, MA 01702
800-378-2753
www.staples.com

Tax Tabs
PO Box 54513
Atlanta, GA 30308
www.onlineorganizing.com

Problem Solvers

These catalogs seem especially designed to solve homeowners' problems, including clutter, storage, and organizational issues. They're amazing!

Hammacher Schlemmer
147 E. 57th Street
New York, NY 10022
800-321-1484
www.hammacher.com

Herrington
3 Symmes Drive
Londonderry, NH 03053
800-903-2878
www.herringtoncatalog.com

Improvements
5566 West Chester Road
West Chester, OH 45069
800-634-9484
www.improvementscatalog.com

The Sharper Image
350 The Embarcadero, 6th
  Floor
San Francisco, CA 94105-1218
800-344-4444
www.sharperimage.com

Solutions
PO Box 6878
Portland, OR 97228
800-821-1282
www.solutions.com

Storage Systems

I discuss these storage systems, most of which are designed to cover entire walls and offer a range of customized storage options, in more detail in Chapter 15— Cleaning Out the Garage, beginning on page 311.

The Accessories Group (TAG)
1123 Delaware Street
Salem, VA 24153
866-404-8570
www.theaccessoriesgroup.com
  garage storage systems

All Bright Ideas
217 Main Street
Emmaus, PA 18049
866-632-8911
www.allbrightideas.com

Gladiator GarageWorks
Whirlpool Corporation
Benton Harbor, MI 49022
866-342-4089
www.gladiatorgw.com
  GearWall systems

Grid Iron
222 S. Promenade Avenue
Corona, CA 92879
800-486-4932
www.gridironusa.com

ONRAX
815 Houser Way N.,
  Suite C
Renton, WA 98055
866-637-8828
www.onrax.com
  overhead storage racks

ORG
Windquest Companies Inc.
3311 Windquest Drive
Holland, MI 49424
800-562-4257
www.home-org.com

Organize.com
PO Box 2348
Riverside, CA 92516
800-600-9817
www.organize.com

Racor Home Storage Products
102 S. 1st Avenue
Sandpoint, ID 83864
800-783-7725
www.racorinc.com

Rubbermaid Inc.
Attn: Consumer Service
3320 W. Market Street
Fairlawn, OH 44333-3306
888-895-2110
www.rubbermaid.com
  FastTrack system

SCHULTE Corporation
12115 Ellington Court
Cincinnati, OH 45249
800-669-3225
www.schultestorage.com

storeWALL
4119 W. Green Tree Road
Milwaukee, WI 53209
866-889-2502
www.storewall.com

I'm a *real* sucker when it comes to gardening catalogs! Here are some of my favorites for yard and garden clutter control and useful gadgets. (Just be glad I'm not listing all my favorite nursery and seed catalogs! That would be a book in itself.)

Cabela's
One Cabela Drive
Sidney, NE 69160
800-243-6626
www.cabelas.com

Charley's Greenhouse &
  Garden
17979 State Route 536
Mt. Vernon, WA 98273
800-322-4707
www.charleysgreenhouse.com

Gardener's Supply Company
128 Intervale Road
Burlington, VT 05401
800-876-5520
www.gardeners.com

Gardens Alive!
5100 Schenley Place
Lawrenceburg, IN 47025
513-354-1482
www.gardensalive.com

Growers Supply
1440 Field of Dreams Way
Dyersville, IA 52040
800-476-9715
www.growerssupply.com

Kinsman Company
PO Box 428
Pipersville, PA 18947
800-733-4146
www.kinsmangarden.com

Orvis
178 Conservation Way
Sunderland, VT 05250
888-235-9763
www.orvis.com

Smith & Hawken
PO Box 8690
Pueblo, CO 81008-9998
800-940-1170
www.smithandhawken.com

Worm's Way
7850 N. State Road 37
Bloomington, IN 47404
800-274-9676
www.wormsway.com

Donations, Barter, Junk Removal, Free Stuff, and Yard Sales

Do you have something to give away, sell, or trade? Or some stuff that's in such bad shape you'd just like someone to come haul it off? Not sure where to donate something? Start with these organizations. Some of them, like Earth 911, JustGive, and Excess Access, specialize in matching donors with nonprofit organizations. Others accept specific types of donations. A few, including Craigslist, Freecycle, and Trashbank, encourage various sorts of barter, giveaways, and (in the case of Craigslist and Trashbank) sales. Got Junk and TrashBusters have hauling franchises across the country. And Winning Edge has resources for yard sales. Please don't assume that just because the organizations' headquarters are in particular places, the programs and services they offer aren't national in scope—they are! Check out their Web sites to see the extent of their outreach.

America's Second Harvest
35 E. Wacker Drive, #2000
Chicago, IL 60601
800-771-2303
www.secondharvest.org
  *the national food bank and
  food-rescue network*

BookEnds
6520 Platt Avenue #331
West Hills, CA 91307
818-716-1198
www.bookends.org
  children's books

Books for America
1417 22nd Street NW
Washington, DC 20037
202-835-2665
www.booksforamerica.org
  books

Career Gear
120 Broadway, 36th Floor
New York, NY 10271
212-577-6190
www.careergear.org
men's work clothes

Computers & Education
   Computer Recycling Center
1275 4th Street
Lockbox 200 PMB
Santa Rosa, CA 95404
888-887-3372
www.crc.org

Computers for Schools
   Program
3350 N. Kedzie Avenue
Chicago, IL 60618
800-939-6000
www.pcsforschools.org

Craigslist
60 Spear Street, 9th Floor
San Francisco, CA 94105
415-566-6394
www.craigslist.org
   classified ads, barter, and
   free stuff

Dress for Success
32 E. 31st Street, 7th Floor
New York, NY 10016
212-532-1922
www.dressforsuccess.org
   women's work clothes

Earth 911
14646 N. Kierland Boulevard,
   Suite 100
Scottsdale, AZ 85254
480-889-2650
www.earth911.org

Excess Access
5813 Geary Boulevard, Box 111
San Francisco, CA 94121
415-242-6041
www.excessaccess.org

The Freecycle Network
PO Box 294
Tucson, AZ 85702
www.freecycle.org

Goodwill Industries
15810 Indianola Drive
Rockville, MD 20855
800-741-0186
www.goodwill.org

Got Junk
8th Floor, 1055 W. Hastings
   Street
Vancouver, BC V6E 2E9
Canada
800-468-5865
www.1800gotjunk.com
   hauling service, franchises
   across the United States

Habitat for Humanity
121 Habitat Street
Americus, GA 31709
229-924-6935, ext. 2551
www.habitat.org

Hear Now
The Starkey Hearing
   Foundation
6700 Washington Avenue S
Eden Prairie, MN 55344
800-648-2327
www.sotheworldmayhear.org/
   hearnow/
   hearing aids

JustGive
312 Sutter Street, Suite 410
San Francisco, CA 94108
866-587-8448
www.justgive.org

Lion's Clubs International
   Headquarters
300 W. 22nd Street
Oak Brook, IL 60523-8842
630-571-5466
www.lionsclubs.org
   eyeglasses

Pets 911
14646 N. Kierland Boulevard,
   Suite 100
Scottsdale, AZ 85254
480-889-2640
www.pets911.com
   pet-related donations

Play It Again Sports
Winmark Corporation
4200 Dahlberg Drive, Suite 100
Minneapolis, MN 55422
800-567-6600
www.playitagainsports.com
   used and new sporting
   equipment

The Salvation Army National
   Headquarters
615 Slaters Lane
PO Box 269
Alexandria, VA 22313
800-958-7825
www.salvationarmyusa.org

Share the Technology
www.sharetechnology.org
   online computer donation
   service

TechSoup
435 Brannan Street, Suite 100
San Francisco, CA 94107
415-633-9300
www.techsoup.org/recycle
   computers

Trashbank
www.trashbank.com
   barter, sell, trade, or swap
   online

TrashBusters Garbage and
   Trash Removal Service
PO Box 2530
Blaine, WA 98231-2530
800-743-6348
www.trashbusters.com
   hauling service

Winning Edge
2440 Willow Glen Drive
Colorado Springs, CO 80920-
   1200
800-841-4248
www.win-edge.com/
   GarageSale.shtml
   online garage sales expertise

The Women's Alliance
3745 NE 171st Street, Suite 62
Miami, FL 33160
305-762-6400
www.thewomensalliance.org
   women's work clothes

eBay

Start with eBay's official site, then explore the other Web sites listed here to check out eBay drop-off stores, insider eBay selling tools, and eBay's official payment service, PayPal. (See Chapter 19—eBay and Other Online Auction Sites, beginning on page 372, for more links to online auction venues and drop-off stores.)

AuctionDrop
1355-B Adams Court
Menlo Park, CA 94055
650-470-6920
www.auctiondrop.com
  eBay drop-off stores

Cool eBay Tools
www.coolebaytools.com
  *Web site of Marsha Collier,
  author of* eBay for Dummies
  and many other eBay books

eBay Inc.
2145 Hamilton Avenue
San Jose, CA 95125
866-696-3229
www.ebay.com

iSold It
155 S. Highway 101 #7
Solana Beach, CA 92075
858-436-2800
www.i-soldit.com
  eBay drop-off stores

PayPal
2211 N. 1st Street
San Jose, CA 95131
402-935-2050
www.paypal.com

QuikDrop International
3151 Airway Avenue, Suite M-3
Costa Mesa, CA 92626
714-429-1040
www.quikdrop.com
  eBay drop-off stores

Antiques

If you have antiques and think they may be worth more than you could get from a consignment shop, an eBay auction, or even a local antiques store, check out these resources. Appraisers evaluate your antiques and estimate their worth. Christie's, Skinner, and Sotheby's are three of the premiere auction houses worldwide.

American Society of
  Appraisers
555 Herndon Parkway,
  Suite 125
Herndon, VA 20170
703-478-2228
www.appraisers.org

Antiques Roadshow Online
www.pbs.org/roadshow
  *antiques and show infor-
  mation; links to appraisers*

Appraisers Association of
  America
386 Park Avenue S, Suite 2000
New York, NY 10016
212-889-5404, ext. 11
www.appraisersassoc.org

Auction Guide
www.auctionguide.com
  online live auction locator

AuctionZip
www.auctionzip.com
  online live auction locator

Christie's
20 Rockefeller Plaza
New York, NY 10020
212-636-2000
www.christies.com
  antiques auctions

Guide to Auctions
www.guidetoauctions.com
  *links to auctions and auction
  sites*

Internet Auction List
www.internetauctionlist.com
  list of online auction sites

New England Appraisers
  Association
5 Gill Terrace
Ludlow, VT 05149
802-228-7444
www.newenglandappraisers.
  net

Skinner, Inc.
63 Park Plaza
Boston, MA 02116
617-350-5400
www.skinnerinc.com
  antiques auctions

Sotheby's
1334 York Avenue
New York, NY 10021
541-312-5682
www.sothebys.com
  antiques auctions

GREAT CLUTTER-RELATED BOOKS

I love books. They're incredibly handy, useful references, and I turn to them first when I'm facing an especially challenging clutter problem. Here are some of my favorites. Once again, this list isn't meant to be comprehensive by any means—I'm sure there are plenty of great books out there that I'm not familiar with. And as you'll discover, I've recommended many topic-specific books, such as *eBay for Dummies,* in the chapters where they're relevant. The books listed here are the broad-based clutter-control books I own and use—my personal clutter library. Check them out and see if you want a few for your permanent collection!

Alexander, Skye. *10-Minute Clutter Control Room by Room.* Gloucester, MA: Fair
     Winds Press, 2005.

———. *10-Minute Clutter Control.* Gloucester, MA: Fair Winds Press, 2004.
     Skye is a feng shui master and brings her feng shui sensibility to clutter
     control—a great combination. Try Skye's quick tips, and see if they bring you feng
     shui benefits such as prosperity and good fortune as well as clutter control!

Aronson, Tara. *Mrs. Clean Jeans' Housekeeping with Kids.* Emmaus, PA: Rodale Books,
     2004.
     When Tara, aka Mrs. Clean Jeans, wrote this book, she had a toddler, a pre-
     teen, and a teenager in the house. Lucky for her, she knew how to get them all
     (even 2-year-old Payne) to pitch in with the household chores. And lucky for us,
     she's shared her tips, rules, and chore lists (divided by age) with us. If you have
     kids (or grandkids), you need this book!

Aslett, Don. *Clutter's Last Stand,* 2nd ed. Avon, MA: Adams Media, 2005.
     Don Aslett has written an armful of cleaning and clutter-control books over
     the years, and I own several of them, but I've chosen to list this one as a great
     starting place mostly because I love the title so much. Don is the Dr. Phil of clutter
     control—he steps right up and tells you to get real about your mess and its cost to
     you in terms of time, money, and quality of life.

Baird, Lori, ed. *Cut the Clutter and Stow the Stuff.* Emmaus, PA: Rodale Books, 2002.
     This clutter classic is packed with tips. Lori and her team interviewed dozens
     of "everyday experts"—folks who use their hard-won wisdom every day—to
     come up with a wealth of practical information.

Cilley, Marla. *Sink Reflections.* New York: Bantam Books, 2002.
     Marla, aka FlyLady, sets forth her principles for changing your life and con-
     quering clutter by learning her system for overcoming clutter and CHAOS (Can't
     Have Anyone Over Syndrome), starting with cleaning your sink (hence the book's
     title). For more on Marla, see "Organizations and Programs" on page 43 and
     "Tools of the Trade" on page 237.

Cobb, Linda. *The Queen of Clean Conquers Clutter.* New York: Pocket Books, 2002.
     Linda Cobb, the Queen of Clean, is one of my personal heroes. When it comes

to cleaning and laundry, she's been there, done that—*all* of that. So when Linda says something works—or doesn't work—I listen. In this book, the Queen turns her attention to clutter control, but you'll still find tons of great cleaning tips thrown into the mix. Enjoy!

Culbertson, Judi, and Marj Decker. *Scaling Down*. Emmaus, PA: Rodale Books, 2005.
 Though aimed at people who are moving to smaller homes or retirement homes or who are helping their parents do so, this book offers wise, compassionate advice to anyone who's trying to kick their clutter. If you're having trouble letting go of your stuff—or need some help persuading your parents that it's time to release the death grip on their clutter—Judi and Marj will come to your rescue.

Koopersmith, Linda. *The Beverly Hills Organizer's Home Organizing Bible*. Gloucester, MA: Fair Winds Press, 2005.
 Linda's approach to clutter control is unique, and it makes a ton of sense. Her book is organized like a cookbook, with step-by-step directions and photos, a list of essential tools, the degree of difficulty, and how long it takes for every organizing "recipe," so nothing is left to chance. The recipes break organizing down into manageable bites, so you won't be overwhelmed by the scope of the task. And after helping thousands of clients organize their homes, Linda knows all the best tools and shares them in her book.

Stewart, Martha. *Martha Stewart's Homekeeping Handbook*. New York: Clarkson Potter, 2006.
 Leave it to Martha to produce the *Joy of Cooking* for the home. In addition to providing great organizing tips, she covers cleaning and maintaining every room in the house, with weekly, monthly, and seasonal checklists, as well as how to perform household repairs. While I'm talking about Martha, please check out *Martha Stewart Living* magazine's Web site, www.marthastewart.com, for tons of ingenious organizing tips.

ONWARD!

I hope you feel as if, at this point, you have all the resources you could possibly need to corral your clutter and organize every part of your house and yard. You may not be ready to use them yet, but it never hurts to order some catalogs (I'd start with the "Problem Solvers" on page 48) and start seeing what's out there. As you read the room-by-room tips in Part Two and yard and garden tips in Part Three, you can return to this chapter to get things you've decided you need. And all the resources I mention in Part Four, on how to unload your clutter, are here in one convenient place. But first, let's take in the big picture—a five-step plan to kick your clutter. Turn the page and start bringing your clutter under control right now!

Chapter 4

Five Simple Steps to Kick Your Clutter

Now that you know what's causing the clutter, how to evaluate your clutter, and what clutter-clearing tools are available, it's time to dig in! Follow these five simple steps, and you're on the way to a clutter-free life.

WHY STEPS?

Multistep programs aren't for everyone, and if you don't think they're for you, you can skip this chapter and move on to Part Two: Clutter-Kicking Room by Room. I'd suggest that you at least read through the chapter first, though, because it might give you some useful ideas as you tackle your own clutter problems.

For those who are open to them, step programs offer some real advantages: First, they give you a clear, straightforward plan of attack, so you know what you'll be doing every step of the way. (As one of my fellow fitness-club members remarked, "I just want to know that I'm doing it right!") Second, they break the plan into distinct phases, so you're not overwhelmed. And third, they pace the steps so that you move through the plan in logical order, from a motivating beginning to a triumphant end. You can review the plan anytime you need an overview,

the Pros Know

Want to customize your own multistep clutter-control program? Turn to the pros. Look at step programs in other areas, including weight loss, business success, overcoming addictions, and spiritual progress. Maybe Dr. Phil McGraw's "7 Keys to Weight Loss Freedom" from his book *The Ultimate Weight Solution* will inspire you to apply his approach to your clutter problems. Perhaps Deepak Chopra's approach in *The Seven Spiritual Laws of Success*, Stephen R. Covey's in *The 7 Habits of Highly Effective People*, or Suze Orman's in *9 Steps to Financial Freedom* will strike a chord.

These are just a few possibilities to explore in a sea of multistep options, from getting fit to mastering guitar to attracting romance. Don't limit yourself—pick a favorite expert or topic and see what you can apply when you change the topic to clutter control. Then don't be afraid to mix and match! The program that works best for you may not yet have been created—but you can create it yourself by pulling the steps that seem most sensible and workable from various programs and combining them to make a master program. After all, you know yourself better than anyone else does, so you're the best judge of what's likely to help you succeed!

and if you faithfully stick to the program, you *will* get results. So look this one over, and if it makes sense to you, give it a try. You won't be sorry!

FIVE STEPS TO A CLUTTER-FREE LIFE

That's a big promise from just a few steps. But if you try them, you'll find that I'm not exaggerating. Let them help you break the bonds of clutter and start living clutter-free right now!

What are these miracle steps? We'll discuss each one in detail, but basically, they are:

1. **Get a contract**. Motivate yourself to kick the clutter out of your home and your life. Make a commitment to yourself to tackle your clutter problem once and for all—and stick to it!

2. **Get prioritized**. Decide which areas to tackle first, next, and so on, and make a priority list so you can check off each area as you move along, until you've finished the whole list.

5-Minute Fixes

In later chapters, you'll find "5-Minute Fixes" with quick fixes for different rooms. But this time, I'm talking about taking 5 minutes, or 10, or 15, instead of tackling an entire room at once. It's a lot easier to tackle your clutter if you break down each task into manageable chunks. After all, who has hours to spend sorting through stuff? And even if you did, who'd *want* to spend hours that way?

For example, think about taking down your Christmas ornaments. If you decorate the way I do, it seems to take as long to get those ornaments down and packed up as to perform all the other tasks of the Christmas season combined! Instead of working 'til you drop (and breaking a few heirloom ornaments in the process), you'll have a much easier time if you divide the chores over an entire week. One day, tidy away the things under the tree. Another day, take down the outside display. Then put away the ornaments on the tree. Then the lights. Then the other ornaments in the house. Then take out or put away the tree. And so on. Not only does this make the job more manageable, it also gives everyone a chance to say good-bye to the tree and ornaments for another year.

So pick a time limit based on your time constraints and the task at hand, and get going. Make sure you don't overshoot—if you can't keep up with the time commitments you make to yourself, you will get discouraged and won't stick with it. To keep track, you can set an alarm clock or kitchen timer. When you hear the ding, you know it's time to stop.

This is a good way to motivate your kids to pitch in, too. You can make it a game and see who gets the most done before the timer goes off. It's fun!

Remember how the exercise gurus say that working out in 10-minute increments spread throughout the day is just as effective as doing the entire workout at once? The same is true of a clutter-kicking "workout." And in both cases, if you stick to your workout because you're doing it bit by bit, it will be a lot more effective than if you try to do it all at once and then give up because it's too hard.

3. **Get started.** It's easy to get so caught up in planning the details that you never get around to actually de-cluttering. Instead, plunge in right away while your resolve is still strong. Once you start seeing how much better things look, how quickly you can make a difference, and how much better and more in control you feel, you'll keep on going!

4. **Get organized**. As you clear out each area, organize what's left so it looks great and it's easy to find everything. You'll get rid of the frustration and wasted time you experience every time you try to find stuff you know is in there (somewhere), only to give up and buy it again and again.

5. **Get rid of it**. Toss it, sell it, give it away—but get it out of there! Otherwise, it will just pile up somewhere else, and your sense of accomplishment will evaporate. Kick it out once and for all.

Let's look at the steps one by one and see how to go about them.

Get a Contract

By drawing up a clutter-kicking contract, you make a concrete commitment to getting out from under your clutter. A contract also helps you visualize the scope of your clutter-control needs. It also lets you set a time frame that will be there, staring you in the face in black and white (or blue and white) every day, reminding you that you need to get going—and keep going until the job's done.

What should your contract contain? A good contract should include these features:

❏ **The date.** You need to be able to see when you started kicking your clutter.

❏ **The agreement.** State clearly exactly what you intend to do and the date when you will finish.

❏ **The terms.** Break the process into manageable chunks, and set goal dates for those chunks. This gives you checkpoints to measure your progress and keeps you from waiting 'til the last minute to start.

❏ **The payoff.** Here's where you can assign yourself rewards to mark your progress. List the reward you'll give yourself for a job well done after each chunk is finished. And make sure you think of something really special to do for yourself when it's *all* done!

❏ **The sign-off.** Your signature and date make the contract official. You're making an important agreement with yourself here, so don't skip this step. It's a strong psychological reminder that you've literally signed on for the long haul.

—— SAMPLE CLUTTER-KICKING CONTRACT ——

Clutter-Kicking Contract

January 1, 2___

I, _____, do hereby agree to go through every room in my house and systematically get rid of the clutter in each room, permanently removing any object that is not useful or valued and organizing the rest in an attractive, easy-to-find, easy-to-use manner on or before July 1, 2___.

I will proceed in the following manner:

- By January 31, 2___, I will have reviewed each and every room in my house and made notes of the clutter in each room and what needs to be removed, as well as noting messiness that needs to be cleaned up and organized and potential furniture or equipment needed to control or contain the items I want to keep.
- By March 1, 2___, I will have de-cluttered and organized every room on the first floor of my house.
- By April 1, 2___, I will have de-cluttered and organized every room on the second floor of my house.
- By June 1, 2___, I will have de-cluttered and organized the attic and garage of my house.
- By July 1, 2___, I will have de-cluttered and organized the basement of my house.

In return for faithfully meeting these deadlines, I will reward myself as follows:

- On January 31, 2___, or within the following week, I will treat myself to a spa day.
- On March 1, 2___, or within the following week, my husband has agreed to take me to dinner at the restaurant of my choice, followed by the entertainment of my choice. This agreement is here signed and dated by him: _____
- On April 1, 2___, or within the following week, I will treat myself and two friends to a shopping day in New York.
- On June 1, 2___, or within the following week, my husband has agreed to treat the family to a week at the shore. This agreement is here signed and dated by him:

  _____
- On July 1, 2___, or within the following week, I will treat myself to the new appliance of my choice.

This agreement is hereby signed and witnessed by me:

_____ <Signature> _____ <Date>

─── MY CLUTTER-KICKING CONTRACT ───

Clutter-Kicking Contract

_____ <Date>

I, _____, do hereby agree to _____ on or before _____.

I will proceed in the following manner:

- By _____, I will have _____
  _____.

- By _____, I will have _____
  _____.

- By _____, I will have _____
  _____.

- By _____, I will have _____
  _____.

- By _____, I will have _____
  _____.

In return for faithfully meeting these deadlines, I will reward myself as follows:

- On _____, or within _____, I will _____
  _____.

- On _____, or within _____, I will _____
  _____.

- On _____, or within _____, I will _____
  _____.

- On _____, or within _____, I will _____
  _____.

- On _____, or within _____, I will _____
  _____.

This agreement is hereby signed and witnessed by me:

_____ <Signature> _____ <Date>

A Quick Note on Worksheets

This book has been designed as an interactive workbook, so that it can help you work through your clutter. In addition to the contract on page 59, I've included sample worksheets in all the room-by-room and outdoor chapters so you can target each area where clutter has a foothold. I encourage you to make a clutter-kicking notebook with your own worksheets, so you'll have one easy-to-find reference for your clutter record and clutter-kicking strategies. But if you'd rather not write in the book, you can make photocopies of the workbook pages in each chapter. If you do use photocopies of sheets of paper for these exercises, I'd recommend that you create a "Clutter-Kicking Notebook" or folder where you can keep them together so they're easy to find when you need to refer to them. Otherwise, they may get scattered everywhere and simply create more clutter!

Check out the sample contract on page 58. Then photocopy the contract form on page 59 and write your own contract—or, if you'd like, write it right in the book! If you want your family to pitch in, discuss the idea of a contract with them and get them on board. Then you can have each person create his or her own clutter-kicking contract. Just make sure you read it closely before signing off, especially in regard to the tasks, deadlines, and, of course, rewards!

Get Prioritized

In clutter-kicking as in life, your priorities should reflect what really matters to you. And you absolutely *must* set them. Otherwise, if you're dealing with clutter in more than one room, you'll bog down and give up—guaranteed. But if you set your priorities based on what matters most to you—or what bothers you the most—and then follow them, you'll end up getting the job done. And you'll have the satisfaction of eliminating the most aggravating annoyances first!

You'll find a form on page 63 to use in setting down your priorities (you can make photocopies or work right in the book, if you prefer). But first, let's take a look at some typical priorities to jump-start your thinking:

- ❏ Clear out and straighten up the main entrance to the house.
- ❏ De-clutter the rooms visitors see most.
- ❏ Clear off the kitchen counters.
- ❏ Empty out the bedroom closet.
- ❏ Empty out and organize the hall closet.
- ❏ Pick up anything on the floor that's not supposed to be on the floor.
- ❏ Clean the clutter out of the car.
- ❏ Clear out the fridge.
- ❏ Take any outgrown clothes to Goodwill/the consignment shop/your cousin.
- ❏ De-clutter the main/kids'/guest bathroom.
- ❏ Make the guest bedroom look like a guest room, not a storage room.
- ❏ De-clutter your bedroom and make it look nice and inviting.
- ❏ Clean out the garage so there's actually room for cars.
- ❏ Tackle the piles of newspapers, magazines, and catalogs.
- ❏ Haul the expired/"we're never gonna eat this" food out of the pantry.
- ❏ Finish the first floor before starting on the rest of the house.

I'm sure you can think of plenty more. Obviously, in this case, we're talking about big priorities, the large-scale projects that will get you to your contract goals. There are also plenty of helpful small priorities, such as "Every day, I'll put three more things in the Salvation Army bag" or "Every day, I'll go through and recycle or give away one magazine or catalog." These small priorities will encourage you to keep kicking your clutter because you really will see the little things add up, and faster than you think. Even something like "Every day, I'll make sure there's no clutter on the stairs" or "Every day, I'll make sure the waste baskets are emptied" will make a big difference in how the house looks and how you feel about it.

Big or small, your priorities should reflect both your feelings and your situation. If paper pileup has reached mountainous proportions, dealing with it should go on your priority list. If cans and boxes fall on you every time you open the kitchen cabinets, dealing with that should be a priority. If you cringe at the thought of inviting friends over because of the state of your living room, put de-cluttering that on your priority list. If you're sick to death of shoveling through toothbrushes,

Make It Rewarding

I'm a big believer in rewards as motivation. It goes without saying that seeing an attractive, clutter-free drawer, room, or home is a reward in itself. But when you are faced with a dusty, dirty mess or feel like you should start kicking some clutter but really aren't in the mood, sometimes you just need something more.

Now, I'm not advocating a massive expenditure every time you toss a plastic bag or clean the refrigerator. I think the best rewards are in scale with the task accomplished. I also am not suggesting that you buy more stuff to re-clutter your newly cleared space! Instead, think of all those pleasures you enjoy but don't usually make time for, and pick one each time you need a reward. Here are a few examples to get you started:

✳ Light the candles and have wine with dinner.

✳ Get out a pretty vase and buy some fresh flowers to put on that newly cleared-off table.

✳ Before bed, take the time to actually *use* that luxurious foot cream you bought months ago or got as a gift.

✳ Treat yourself to the latest issue of a magazine you love but don't often indulge in. (But make a vow to pass it on after you've read it.)

✳ Get some great DVDs and popcorn and invite some friends over for a "girls' (or guys') night in."

✳ Get your car washed, waxed, and vacuumed.

✳ Make the time to go to a concert or a game.

✳ Have your favorite jewelry cleaned.

You can bet I use this tactic on myself when I want to get going! As you might guess, I love to write. But to make sure I keep going, I choose a little reward for myself at the end of every chapter. When I've finished, I "collect" my reward for what I hope is a job well done!

toothpaste tubes, and other bathroom detritus to clear off enough counter space to set down a hairbrush, put the counter on your list. Make it work with your needs.

Thinking about what areas to tackle first also helps put your overall clutter situation in clear focus. You may be so inspired that you'll make lists of second- and third-tier priorities, and once you do, you'll have your clutter-kicking checklist set and ready to go!

My Clutter-Kicking Priority List

❏ _____

❏ _____

❏ _____

❏ _____

❏ _____

❏ _____

❏ _____

❏ _____

❏ _____

❏ _____

❏ _____

❏ _____

❏ _____

❏ _____

❏ _____

❏ _____

❏ _____

Get Started

You'll never finish kicking your clutter if you never get started. And as we all know, it's easy to procrastinate, fixating on something or other and telling ourselves that "we'll start de-cluttering as soon as . . ." Uh-huh.

Rather than waiting, start doing something, anything, to clear out some of your clutter *now*. (Well, when you finish reading this chapter, anyway.) The "5-Minute Fixes" you will find will help you jump-start the process. Look there to find suggestions for fast things you can do to start getting your clutter under control room by room. Just tossing a few almost-empty shampoo bottles into the recycling can give you the lift you need to keep going—because you'll see the difference even something that small can make.

Get Organized

Okay, I know it's not as easy to get organized as it is to get started, or even to write your Clutter-Kicking Contract or your Clutter-Kicking Priority List. But take heart: You don't have to organize until you've kicked the clutter.

That's the plus side. The minus side is that you *do* have to organize every single time you kick some clutter—or you'll just end up in a hopeless mess again.

The secret is to organize as you go along. That's what keeps the task manageable. Once you've cleared out a drawer in the bathroom, organize what you've kept so you know what's in there and can find it easily. Same for your underwear drawer, pantry shelf, and shoe rack.

Shoe rack, you say? Ha! You think you had one of those at one point, but you haven't seen it in years. In fact, you haven't seen the closet floor in years. Well, don't despair. Once you've gotten rid of old, damaged, and beat-up shoes, not to mention shoes you never actually wear, shoes that don't fit, and shoes you don't like, you'll find that there are a whole lot fewer to organize. And if, as it happens, you *don't* have a shoe rack—or a shampoo holder, or some other gadget that will make organizing your stuff a whole lot simpler—turn back to Chapter 3—Tooling Up (beginning on page 35) and remind yourself what's out there. Check the "Tools of the Trade" features in upcoming chapters, too. Remember, the right tools can be better—and cheaper!—than a good professional organizer.

5-Minute Fixes

Here are five things you can get rid of right now to put yourself on the fast track to a clutter-free life. They may not seem like much—which is the point—but they will make a difference. Every little bit helps!

1 Toss out every pair of snagged, run, or otherwise beat-up pantyhose you own.

2 Toss out every stubby pencil and dried-up pen you can get your hands on.

3 Toss that broken umbrella you've been keeping "just in case."

4 Empty and recycle those dusty, musty old spice bottles that have been hanging around for the past decade.

5 Recycle all the duplicate catalogs that have gotten buried in piles of mail, magazines, and other "someday" reading.

Think of how good it will feel to actually know what you have and where it is. Instead of spending precious time looking for things, you could spend it on something you enjoy—or actually need to do. You'll be able to see right away if you need to replace something. (If all your umbrellas are broken or none of your dress shoes fit comfortably, it's time to buy that one new umbrella or one new pair of heels that works for you.) Have you ever been in the position of buying something you think you already have—you're *sure* you already have, and you actually have a suspicion you have several of—but you can't find it anywhere? Well, once you get organized, you'll never have to go through that embarrassment, frustration, and waste of time and money again. So, make a vow to yourself right now:

> [The Organizing Vow: Every single time I clear out any clutter, I will not consider the job done until I've organized the things that are left so they're easy to find and use.]

Every time, every single time you clear out any clutter, be it just recycling those duplicate catalogs or tossing outdated coupons, you will not consider the task finished until you've put what's left in good and logical order. And remind yourself of your vow as you go through all the chapters in Part Two: Clutter-Kicking Room by Room (beginning on page 69). If it will help you stay focused, write your vow on a few sticky notes and put one on the refrigerator, one on the bathroom mirror, one on your closet door, one on the dashboard of your car, and anywhere else you see often.

Don't overlook the organizing step. It's every bit as important as getting rid of the clutter. Because, after all, anything that's messy and disorganized is, by its very nature, clutter!

Get Rid of It

You've dutifully cleared out the kids' closets and drawers and amassed three big garbage bags of beat-up, despised, and outgrown stuff for Goodwill. Good for you! But there's a problem: Those big bags are still sitting by the front door 3 weeks later.

> [Collected clutter is still clutter as long as it's still sitting around.]

It may seem obvious, but it bears repeating: Collected clutter is still clutter as long as it's still sitting around.

I'm a huge fan of reuse, and I've devoted an entire section of this book—Part Four: Trash (Yours) to Treasure (Theirs), beginning on page 349—to telling you all the ways you can donate, recycle, and sell your former clutter. But I will say this loud and clear: If you know for a fact that, with the best intentions or otherwise, you will not get that collected clutter out the door if it means taking it someplace farther than the trash can, *throw it out*.

It may seem like a shame, or even a crime, when the Salvation Army is 10 miles down the road or you think your cousin John could use that trench coat or clunky old grill. But if you've tried to take stuff away before and found that final step overwhelming, and if you can't think of a zealous friend or sibling who'd actually enjoy doing it for you, it's better to put it out for the trash than not to put it out at

Dear Claire,

What about regifting? Isn't that a good way to get rid of stuff you don't like (not to mention the money you'll save on gift purchases)?

—*Thrifty Giver*

Dear Thrifty,

Regifting is fine as long as you know that the person you're giving the item to would *really* like it. Be honest about this: If you're not absolutely sure they'd want it, "regift" it to Goodwill instead. And remember the two drawbacks of regifting: First, you'll need to keep track so you don't inadvertently regift something to its original giver or anyone he or she knows. And second, if the gift is not your taste and you pass it on to someone else, don't be surprised if you start getting things like it from that person in the future. After all, you must have loved it or you wouldn't have given it to them!

My own favorite form of regifting is to have a gag gift that circulates among family and friends year after year. In my case, a dear friend had come upon—in a junk shop, appropriately enough—a large, hideous bird ornament with gaudily dyed real feathers. That Christmas, the bird materialized in another friend's pile of packages; the following year, it returned to its original purchaser; the next year, his sister was the lucky recipient; and so it went. Of course, he made sure the joke was obvious and got real presents for the recipients, as well. It was fun to speculate about who'd be getting "the bird" for Christmas!

Good luck,
Claire

all. (And who knows? Maybe somebody will be passing by and decide to "collect" it for themselves!)

Of course, I'd feel a lot better—and I think you would, too—if you recycled, gave away, donated, or sold your excess stuff. Think how great it would be to get that check from the eBay store or the consignment shop, hand over your donations list to your accountant to reduce that tax bite, or see your sister's face light up when you give her the sweater she's always admired and you haven't (ahem) been able to squeeze into for years.

the Pros Know

Every now and then, you need a good talking to. Psychologists, motivational speakers, and life coaches all know that the way you think about and talk about a challenge influences the outcome. As they say, if you think you can't do it, you're probably right. You'll find yourself getting a lot more from your clutter-kicking efforts—maybe even enjoying them!—and you'll find it easier to keep going if you can catch negative-speak in the act and replace it with something positive.

For example, let's say you're confronting a chaotic, cluttered closet with the attitude of, "I'll never get this mess cleaned out!" After working in there 'til you're exhausted, you look at the stuff still to be dealt with and you think, "See? I *knew* I could never do it!" What will you be most likely to do next—keep at it or shut the door on the problem and eat a bag of potato chips?

Now suppose you confronted that same chaotic, cluttered closet and said to yourself, "Let's see what I can do here in 10 minutes." At the end of 10 minutes, you'd say to yourself, "I've found six pieces of clothing and a pair of shoes that I can bag for the Salvation Army. That's made some space in here. I'll do another 10 minutes this afternoon and see if I can add to the bag or find some better clothes for the consignment shop."

Who's more likely to end up kicking their clutter, the can't-do you or the will-do you?

ONWARD!

Now that you know the Five Steps to a Clutter-Free Life, it's time to really get your feet wet. In the next section, Clutter-Kicking Room by Room, you'll find hundreds of ways to conquer and contain clutter in every part of the house. So pick a room, any room . . . and let's go!

PART TWO

Clutter-Kicking Room by Room

Chapter 5

Incoming Clutter

HALLS, STAIRS, MUDROOMS, AND DOORWAYS

It's all too easy for stuff to stop coming into the house as soon as it starts. And when your entryways turn into drop-off sites, the result is a pileup of bags, backpacks, shoes, umbrellas, gear, coats, and other paraphernalia just inside every door and spilling down every hall (not to mention up the steps). Eventually you're picking (or tripping) your way among piles of clutter, trying to find enough bare space to set down your keys, never mind your purse or coat. What a way to say "Welcome home!" Use the tips in this chapter to get the clutter up and out (of sight, anyway).

PRIORITIES FOR ENTRYWAYS

Unless you have so little stuff cluttering your entryways that 10 minutes of straightening will tidy it all away, you should begin clearing the entries to your home by setting some clutter-kicking priorities. Set your priorities by first focusing on what matters most to you about how the entryway looks. Then keep moving along to what matters least. The best way to do this is to take a good, hard look at the "before" state of the room and then visualize the "after."

An Entryway Visualization

To get to the "after" of your entry, you need to start with the "before"—the way things look right now. So get out some paper or use the "My Entryway—Before" form (or make a photocopy of it and write on that). Write down every place around the entrances to your home where there's clutter, and note what that clutter is. It might help to remember the Love It–Lose It Spectrum (see page 26) as you consider what needs to go. Go on—you can do it!

Once you've jotted down an inventory of the clutter in your entryway, it's time to move on to the "after"—what you want to happen and in what order. To get there, describe how you want the room or area to look when you've kicked the clutter. As a reality check, make sure you look at the room every few minutes while you're doing this.

Your description can be short and to the point: I don't want to see coats piled on all the chairs; piles of keys, change, and other stuff spilling over the hall table and onto the floor; and kids' toys, dogs' toys, and shoes scattered all over the floor. I'd like an entry that looks clean and welcoming. I'd like a place to put my keys and I'd like to easily find the day's mail. I want a place to showcase my antique table (or bench, or a painting or vase). I need an easy-to-see place for boots and umbrellas.

If you want, you can make a detailed picture of exactly how you'd like your room to look if it were perfect (for you). You can picture the colors of the walls and what would be on them, the rugs, furniture, flooring—everything. Write it all down on a piece of paper or on the "My Entryway—After" form—or on as many photocopies of it as you need to do it justice. (If you use photocopies, keep them all together in a "clutter" file so you can refer back when you need them.)

Getting There

Now that you've captured your entryway's "before" condition (including all the specifics) and you've imagined its "after" appearance, you can finally set priorities that will let you get there from here. Again, bearing both "before" and "after" in mind, I'd recommend starting with what bothers you most about the "before" condition and working down from there to make a list of what needs to be done.

My Entryway—Before

My Entryway—After

My Entryway Priority List

_____

_____

_____

_____

_____

_____

_____

_____

_____

Maybe you're concerned that toys, bags, and other stuff on the stairway poses a tripping hazard and you want it cleared up first. Or you're sick of having your floors ruined by wet, dripping shoes. Or you want to scream every time you even think about cleaning up those muddy shoe and paw prints. Or you'd really like to be able to sit down on a chair—without having to shovel coats and backpacks off it first—to take off your boots on a rainy day.

Get your priorities straight by writing down whatever's driving you to distraction on the "My Entryway Priority List" (or photocopy it, if you'd prefer). Work in descending order from most to least maddening. Once you've finished, you can turn to the tips below to find ingenious ways of dealing with each problem.

THE ENTRYWAY TIPS

Now it's time to get your hands dirty. Dig into whichever tips appeal to you or suit your circumstances, and bid hallway and mudroom clutter good-bye.

Table it. When you come in the door, you pile all the loose stuff on the nearest surface: keys, cell phone, sunglasses, purse or billfold, cigarettes, chewing gum, mail, gloves, dog treats, change—whatever it is, down it goes. And it may keep going down, all over the floor or under furniture, never to be seen again, as each member of the family dumps their stuff on top of yours when _they_ come in. You'll have a better chance of keeping everything together if you put a table near the door where everybody has room to dump their stuff. If it's a butler's table with a raised edge around the outside, so much the better—nothing can slide or roll off.

Add a basket. Better yet, add several low, open, square or rectangular baskets to your hall table. Label or color-code one basket for each family member so they can put their own change, sunglasses, mail, and the like in it. The table will look a lot neater, and you'll cut down on fighting. ("That's *my* quarter!")

Don't forget Fideaux. If you have a canine companion, you know that there's little chance of getting in or out the door without an enthusiastic greeting. You'll probably have a package of mini-treats, maybe a clicker (a popular obedience tool), and a toy or two adding to the hallway clutter. If it's also the door he uses to go in and out, there'll be at least one leash and possibly an electric-fence collar and "zapper" as well. So why not give him his own labeled or color-coded basket? Then everyone will know where to find his stuff. Just make sure it's out of his reach!

Box it up. An assortment of attractive wooden, lacquer, or toile boxes can also contain the tabletop clutter. If they have tops, everybody's stuff will be both contained and out of sight.

Take a tip from the kitchen. Rather than a box or basket, use a decorative utensil organizer to hold tabletop clutter. I've seen some really attractive wicker and cane versions. The dividers are just the thing for containing wallets, cell phones, sunglasses, and mail.

👍 Love It *or* Lose It? 👎

What about hat racks, coat trees, hall trees—whatever you prefer to call those Victorian footed stands with branched arms at the top to hold outerwear? At first glance, they may seem like a space-saving solution for corralling coats, scarves, hats, raingear, umbrellas, and other outerwear. But I'd think twice before you rush out to buy one. Instead, picture what that rack will look like laden down with, most likely, several layers of everybody's stuff. It may look like an organizing solution to some, but it just looks like more clutter to me.

Verdict: Lose it!

5-Minute Fixes for Entries and Exits

Here are five fast ways to jump into controlling clutter in entryways. Once you see how much you can accomplish in 5 minutes, you'll be energized and confident enough to tackle some bigger projects.

Start with a stand. An umbrella stand, that is. These old-fashioned ceramic, metal, wooden, or bamboo cylinders once stood in every home's entryway, and they're still available for very reasonable prices at flea markets and antique stores across the country. I recommend a ceramic stand, since wet umbrellas won't rot or rust them. You'll be surprised by how many umbrellas they hold—all upright for easy grabbing. They also work to neatly contain other upright objects like baseball bats and brooms.

Take a tip from the Shakers. The ever-practical Shakers installed strips of wooden pegs in their halls for hanging their coats, capes, and hats. If you do the same, your family and guests can hang up coats, backpacks, purses, and the like when they come in the door, and everything will be easy to see and grab when it's time to go back out. Pegs make hanging almost two-dimensional, unlike a space-eating coat rack. (Not to mention that coat racks look hideous once you hang coats on them.) You can order peg racks by mail from Shaker Workshops (see page 47) or buy them from your local home store.

Box your boots. Nothing says clutter—or maybe that's "squalor"—like a pile of wet, muddy, or otherwise grungy footwear by the door. Not to mention all the mud, melting snow, grass stains, and other tracked-in stuff all over the floor. But

Hang your keys. I know—in "5-Minute Fixes for Entries and Exits" I said that hanging keys look unsightly, but there are ways to make it work and preserve the aesthetics of your entryway. Keep keys from becoming clutter by putting a small bulletin board, corkboard, pegboard, or square of wood on your wall and attaching hooks for the household and car keys. You can also buy key holders ready-made from accessories shops. Keep everybody's straight by using the color-coders or personalizers you can slip over the backs of keys (you can find them at any hardware store), by making sure everybody has distinctive key chains (mine is hot pink and has a compass and mini-flashlight attached), or by putting labels under each hook. Make sure the key board is out of reach of small hands. And needless fortunately, some ingenious companies have come up with wonderful rectangular shoe-and-boot organizers that will keep that footwear in line (literally). They are durable, come in several sizes, and even feature optional rubber inserts so water can drain right through and your boots and shoes can dry faster. You can find them in mail-order catalogs like Smith & Hawken, Plow & Hearth, and Gardener's Supply Company (see pages 47 and 49). Your entryway or mudroom will look much neater (and stay much cleaner) if you get a boot box and insist that your family use it.

Buy a hall bench. These are available with a seat that lifts up to reveal a storage compartment underneath, or with rectangular storage baskets that fit neatly in place under the seat. You can stash mittens, gloves, scarves, and other outdoor essentials within easy reach but out of sight—and create welcome seating in your hall or mudroom. And they're so much neater and more attractive than a mass of knitwear all over the place. I see these offered in mail-order catalogs all the time. These convenient benches serve double duty as seating and storage—a good idea!

Try a silver salver. Or something similar that suits your taste or matches your decor. Why? To hold keys and other car-related clutter that often gets spilled out all over the closest surface to the door. Yuck! Hanging keys up on a rack is just as unsightly, unless it's in the garage, so make sure you keep a covered container on the hall table that's big enough to hold keys, sunglasses, and the occasional wallet.

to say, don't put your keys where they can be seen from outside! Make sure your curtains or blinds hide the key board from view from the door and windows, or put it where a cabinet, clock, mirror, or picture blocks it from view. Better safe than sorry!

Get a key cabinet. A small wall cabinet is a decorative way to keep keys within easy reach and organized but out of sight. Attach hooks to the inside back for the keys.

Clock it. A grandfather clock can add elegance to an entrance, but working grandfather clocks—whether new or antique—are pricey. Instead, look for a "gutted" one at a flea market, junk shop, or secondhand store, and use it to control

SANITY SAVERS

The entryway your family uses most is the best place to locate essential things that everyone uses. The problem is, you want them to be easily accessible, but you *don't* want them to turn into yet more clutter. The solution is to give each item its own attractive, easy-access place. Then, as each family member passes through, they can check to see if there's anything for them. Here are some ideas:

✳ A "Lost and Found" bin, box, or basket. Whether it's a misplaced button or sock, a CD case, reading glasses, a homework assignment, or a toy, if everyone knows to put straying items in the Lost and Found and everyone knows to look for them there, you will cut down on a lot of wasted time and annoying whining.

✳ A "Post Office." This should have separate sections for incoming and outgoing mail and be placed where the family has easy access but addresses can't be seen from the door or windows. If you have a space for stamps and self-sticking address labels, it will be easy for everyone to make sure the outgoing mail is ready to go (or for you to do it if they forget). It'll be easy to see when it's time to buy stamps, too.

✳ A "Happy Returns" bin, basket, or shelf for library books, DVDs, borrowed toys, magazines, and anything else that needs to go back whence it came. Say good-bye to late fees!

Success with the Lost and Found bin, the Post Office, and Happy Returns depends on everyone knowing where they are and what they're for, and agreeing to use them. Make it happen!

hallway clutter. The clock will be as handsome as a functioning model, and you can put hooks in the empty case for scarves, purses, leashes, and the like. You can also use the tall, narrow space inside the case for baseball bats, hockey sticks, golf clubs, or fishing rods.

Get the skinny. Sometimes the only storage space available is beside the door—and since hallways are often narrow, there's not a lot of width to work with. In this case, a tall, narrow cabinet—known as a chimney cupboard because it's shaped like a chimney—can be a clutter-kicker's best friend. Tuck it beside the door (or place one on each side of the door), and you'll have shelf space for mittens, scarves, earmuffs, sweaters, purses, travel umbrellas, hats, a box of tissues, and the like. There will even be space for a basket or box for keys, cell phones, change, mints, hand sanitizers, hand lotion, and other items that always seem to escape as soon as they're put down. And the bottom's big enough for attaché and computer cases.

Borrow a bookcase. Another tall, skinny option is a narrow bookcase. On the plus side, you can see at a glance what's on the shelves. On the minus side, you can see at a glance what's on the shelves. It will be off the floor, but if it's not attractively organized, it can still look like clutter. Assigning shelves for like items—all hats on one shelf, a to-be-returned shelf for library books and DVDs—is one way to make your stuff look orderly.

Add a shelf. Instead of simply installing a plain strip of pegs—which is actually pretty decorative in its own right—you might consider a peg shelf, which is exactly what it sounds like: a strip of pegs with a shelf on top to display ornaments or hold boxes, baskets, and so on. Shaker Workshops (see page 47) makes these in a range of lengths, and they're as beautiful as they are functional. You can also get more contemporary-looking versions from L.L. Bean (see page 46) with a shelf, hooks, and cubbies, and from Sturbridge Yankee Workshop (see page 47), with pegs, two shelves, and rectangular baskets to hold bills, keys, and the like. I'm sure there are many more.

Walk up to a wine rack. Wooden wine racks can make great, attractive, off-the-floor shoe storage, with a shoe in each bottle opening. I've found used wine racks in perfect shape many a time at Goodwill, the Salvation Army, and the Society of St. Vincent de Paul—usually for less than $4!

KID-FRIENDLY CLUTTER CONTROL

It's not rocket science to realize that kids won't hang up their stuff if they can't reach the hangers. Just as you want to put adults-only stuff like keys up high out of little ones' reach, if you want your kids to be responsible for putting up and taking down their outerwear and gear, make sure it's easy for them to do. Get a second strip of Shaker pegboard and put it at chair-rail height, or attach a strip of wood with decorative but durable blunt-ended hooks (brass hooks work well).

Dress it up. If you have room, a dresser is a great place for out-of-sight hall storage. (I have one in my mudroom that I found beside the dumpster at a long-ago apartment. I dressed it up with paint, and now I use it to hold tools and supplies.) If you put a dresser in your hallway, make sure its style suits your decor. Dressers are, of course, ideal for sweaters, scarves, mittens, hats, and the like—as long as they're dry—but can also be used to hold briefcases and computer cases, paper, and backpacks, too.

Wash it up. My editor Anne recommends putting an old-fashioned washstand in the hall. They're great for smaller halls because they take up so little space, and they add a stylish touch, too. "I had one in my house in Allentown that I wish I still had!" Anne says.

Screen it. What could be more attractive than a decorative folding screen in a corner at the end of your hall? And no one needs to know that it's literally screening anything from storage shelves and sports equipment to your recycling. As before, use a decorator's eye when choosing the screen—try a light color like natural wicker or rattan if the hallway's dark, or perhaps a Japanese lacquer screen in an art nouveau house. You can often find screen frames that have lost some or all of their screening. If you are handy or know an upholsterer or someone who's good at alterations, look for these screenless screens at bargain prices at flea markets, yard sales, and junk shops. You can put curtains or upholstery fabric on them, and voilà! No one outside the family needs to know what's behind curtain number three.

Use some kitchen leftovers. If you're remodeling your kitchen, hang one or more of the old cabinets in your mudroom for storage. They're roomy and useful. Obviously, you wouldn't want to put kitchen cabinets in an entrance hall, but a mudroom or other informal entrance is the perfect place for this sturdy, roomy, *free* storage unit. No remodeling plans? See if any of your friends or co-workers are remodeling, and offer to pick up and haul the cabinets away. Or check flea markets and secondhand home shops, or place an ad on www.craigslist.com or another local service for bargains.

Try the medicine cabinet. If you happen to be redoing the bathroom instead of the kitchen, consider using your old medicine cabinet in an informal family entryway. Not only will it have a mirror so people can check themselves out on the way out the door, but the handy shelves inside will hold tissues, gum, cough drops, breath mints, bandages, hand lotion, hand sanitizers, and anything else that's likely to be in demand on the way in or out.

Hope for a hope chest. A blanket chest makes a wonderful storage bin for sweaters, coats, hats, scarves, and mittens. It's decorative, so it will look good in your entryway. If you don't have a door at the end of the hall, you can set it against the wall there as a focal point. You could even place decorative cushions on top so people can use it as a bench if they need to sit down to remove outerwear or shoes (but try it first—very carefully!—to make sure the chest will take the added weight). Or try a trunk for storage in your entryway.

👍 Love It *or* Lose It? 👎

A hall wastebasket seems so obvious, but I can't say I've ever seen one in anybody's entrance hall. But think about it. A hall wastebasket. People are coming into your house. They have wrappers, empty bottles, tissues, bags, receipts, who knows what. What could be more logical than putting a wastebasket in your entryway so family and guests can toss their trash as they come in? It's the perfect place to unload unwanted mail, too—as soon as you get it inside. Of course, you don't want the wastebasket to look like another piece of unsightly clutter, so get one that matches your decor, and empty it regularly. Tuck it under a hall table to make it more inconspicuous. If everyone enters your house on all but formal occasions through a mudroom, the garage, or the deck door, you can set up a three-bin system for trash, recycling, and shredding. But if you do, think about color-coding the bins as well as using readable labels.

Verdict: Love it!

Add an armoire. If you have a spacious entryway but no hall closet for your family's and guests' outerwear, take a tip from our ancestors and use an armoire. These large, spacious freestanding clothes closets were in vogue in the days before houses had built-in closets. They're roomy enough for outerwear and decorative enough for display.

Aim for the moon. A demilune ("half-moon") table, that is. These rectangular tables fit flat against the wall but are rounded in front, making them perfect for entry halls because no one will get hooked by a corner as they pass by.

Go back to school. They were ugly, all right, but those school lockers sure held a lot of gear. You can put up your own metal lockers in a mudroom or secondary entry if you want to, but fortunately, you also have more attractive alternatives. For example, L.L. Bean (see page 46) now offers a wooden "Mudroom Locker" in a variety of bright colors. It comes with adjustable shelves, jacket hooks, behind-closed-door storage cabinets, and containers to collect loose odds and ends.

Set out a secretary. Not a live one, of course. (You wish.) You can now find small secretaries, aka drop-front desks, in home stores and catalogs. They are small enough to tuck against the back wall of the hallway and will hide mail, rubber bands, keys, and all the other doodads of coming and going behind the raised front, which turns into a writing desktop or organizing station when it folds down. There's a drawer, too, for even more storage options. L.L. Bean (see page 46) even offers one with a book rack at the bottom. A great place for those borrowed library books and DVDs!

Watch those cords. Lamp cords are the worst kind of clutter in an entryway

👍 Love It *or* Lose It? 👎

What about plant stands? They're attractive, affordable, and they certainly don't take up much space. My feelings about them are split: If you want to display a vase or other decorative object or add some life to your entryway with live plants, I think they're great. (Just keep them out of the line of traffic.) But as clutter-controllers, their surfaces are too small to do much more than hold one purse—precariously, at that.

Verdict: Love it for plants; lose it for clutter control.

because they're tripping hazards and can cause lamp breakage as well as bone breakage. Floor lamps pose a double hazard, since, even without the cord issue, they're easy to knock over as people go in and out with parcels or pets and kids race heedlessly through the hall. So skip the floor lamps in your entryways—unless you have a live butler to preside over comings and goings. Instead, opt for ceiling or wall lighting. If you want to put a lamp on your table or on another piece of furniture, make sure the piece of furniture is securely against the wall and the cord runs down behind it, where it's out of tripping (and chewing) reach.

Keep steps clear. Cat toys, cups and saucers, dirty clothes, games, shoes, grocery bags, mail—all sorts of stuff can end up on the stairs. And that's not just unsightly, it's also dangerous. Make keeping all your stairways clutter-free a priority, and make sure it's a priority for everybody else in the household, too (except, of course, the cats). See "Tools of the Trade" for a handy gadget that can help you.

Go belowstairs. If your staircase has either open space below it or a door under it, you can use the space for storage. If it has a door, it's as good as a mini-attic—and a great place for storing holiday ornaments and other things that are used seasonally and then stored. If it's open space, you'll need to put attractive storage containers under it, since people will be able to see inside. Low shelves with decorative rectangular baskets are one option; wicker hampers are another; decorative

trunks and bandboxes stacked with the largest at the bottom are yet another. If you have a solid wood wall under your staircase, you might consider asking a carpenter to see if he or she could cut a door and create a storage space for you.

ONWARD!

You've gotten your feet wet—probably literally!—in your hall, mudroom, and other entrances. Now it's time to tackle a real challenge. Are you with me? In Chapter 6 we'll take a look at one of the most cluttered rooms in the house—the kitchen.

Kitchen Clutter Control

Food. Dishes. Homework. Bills. Art supplies. Knickknacks. Junk. Clutter accumulates in kitchens faster than anywhere else—sometimes it seems impossible to find enough counter or table space to set down a mug, much less make a meal. Some kitchen clutter can create safety issues. Papers piled too close to the stove could start a fire. Appliances can clog counters, and their cords can become a tangled mess. Drawers and cabinets overflow with years' worth of pie pans, canning jars, cookie sheets, dishes, and glassware—way more than you use or need. This chapter helps you sort through the stuff, kick the hoarding habit, "find" more storage space, and create displays that are as practical as they are attractive.

PRIORITIES FOR KITCHENS

Start your kitchen de-cluttering process by setting some clutter-kicking priorities. To do that, focus first on what matters most to you about the way your kitchen looks. That will be your first clutter-kicking priority. Then you'll work your way through the clutter problems until you get to what matters least. The best way to do this is to take a good, hard look at the "before" state of the room and then visualize the "after"—how you want the kitchen to look when all the clutter's gone.

A Kitchen Visualization

To get to your "after," you need to start with the "before"—the way things look right now. Maybe your countertops are buried under mounds of mail and coupons and grocery bags. Or you have the food processor, blender, mixer, toaster, toaster oven, microwave, popcorn popper, and milkshake maker all sitting there. Open some drawers and cabinet doors—what do you see? Open the refrigerator, too—how's *that* look? Get out some paper or use the "My Kitchen—Before" form (or make a photocopy of it and write on that). Write down every place there's clutter and note what that clutter is. Don't let yourself be overwhelmed or discouraged, even if every drawer and surface looks like complete chaos. Instead, keep the list simple and remember that you'll be breaking the actual work down into manageable bites.

Once you've jotted down a quick clutter inventory of your kitchen's "before" state, it's time to move on to the "after"—how you want the room to look when you've kicked the clutter. Write it all down on a piece of paper or on the "My Kitchen—After" form (or on as many photocopies of it as you need to do it justice). To make sure you're being realistic, look at the room every few minutes while you're doing this.

Your description can be short and to the point: "I want a clear counter space where I can actually work without having to shove things out of the way. I want to open the cabinet without a mug or glass falling out. I want to be able to see—and reach—everything in the refrigerator." Or it can be a detailed picture of exactly how you'd like your room to look if it were perfect (for you). You can picture the colors of the walls, cabinets, and appliances; what the cabinets and countertops would be made of; your dream appliances; whether there would be an island, a wine rack, or a gorgeous set of copper pots and pans hanging from the ceiling; what the lighting would look like; if there would be an eating area—everything.

Getting There

Now that you've captured your kitchen's "before" condition, listing all the specifics, and you've imagined its "after" appearance, you can finally prioritize the steps you need to take to get there from here. Again, bearing both "before" and "after"

My Kitchen—Before

_____
_____
_____
_____
_____
_____
_____
_____
_____
_____

My Kitchen—After

_____
_____
_____
_____
_____
_____
_____
_____
_____
_____
_____

My Kitchen Priority List

_____

_____

_____

_____

_____

_____

_____

_____

_____

in mind, I'd recommend starting with what bothers you most about the "before" condition and working down from there.

Maybe you're concerned that the drawers stick because they're jammed too full to open, and that when you do pry them open, you can't find what you need because of all the junk inside. Or you want to have all your spices in one place. Or you never get to the older cans and boxes of food because of the mass of new ones piled in front of them.

Write down whatever's driving you to distraction on the "My Kitchen Priority List" (or on a photocopy of it, if you'd prefer) in descending order from most to least maddening. Now you have your priorities straight! Once you've finished, you can turn to the tips below to find ingenious ways of dealing with each problem.

THE KITCHEN TIPS

Because so much goes on in the kitchen, I've divided the tips in this chapter into sections and grouped them by topic so it will be easier for you to find what you're looking for. Dig in!

Cabinets, Shelves, and Pantries

Say adieu to ancient spices. If your herbs and spices have become bleach-blondes because you've had them for so long, or if their labels have faded beyond recognition, or if they no longer taste or smell distinctive and fresh, dump them. If you're reluctant to just throw them out, you can add them to the compost pile or, if they still have *some* fragrance, add them to potpourris. This time, replace only the ones you really use—and keep them in a dark, *cool* place, not on a spice rack over the stove like, ahem, I used to do.

Clear out empty cartons. There's always someone who leaves a carton in the cabinet with just one cracker, half a cookie, or a disintegrated pile of cereal in the bottom. (You know who you are.) Make it your mission to find these and toss them. You may find that you don't even need to replace half of them, creating instant shelf space.

Bag the empty bags. Now it's time to tackle the bags—those same one-cracker culprits tend to leave bags on the shelf with a few broken pretzels or crumbling chips. Toss the almost-empties (give the dog the broken pretzels) and see if you need to replace all of them or if there were really four half-empty Doritos bags and you can replace them with just one.

Toss stale stuff. While we're talking about crackers and chips, throw out the

👍 Love It *or* Lose It? 👎

Lazy Susans are another organizer favorite. Go to any kitchen design store and you'll see them as practically standard equipment. The theory is that they help you get to all your stuff in deep cabinets, especially corner cabinets, since instead of having to root around in there you can just give Miss Susan a turn and see all your stuff circle within easy reach. This makes sense if you don't need a lot of space or have a lot of stuff—because sure enough, lazy Susans are huge space-wasters. My friend Rudy got them when he had his kitchen redone, and I was appalled at how little he could get into those beautiful new cherry cabinets. There are better ways to get to your stuff; you'll find many right here.

Verdict: Lose it!

5-Minute Fixes for the Kitchen

Here are eight fast fixes to get your clutter-kicking started in the kitchen.

Trash the trash bags. If you—yes, you—have an accumulation of paper or plastic grocery bags lying around, pull them out and throw them out. You say you use them to pick up after the dog or to line your trash cans? Okay. Do a quick calculation: How many do you use each week? How many do you usually bring into the house each week? Keep enough for one week and toss the rest, or take them to the supermarket's recycling bin—you'll replenish your stash fast enough.

Raid the fridge. Throw out five old, mostly empty bottles or jars right now. It's that easy! Make a note of anything you need to replace.

Try a fridge facelift. Take down five things from the front of the fridge—outdated notes, old menus, tattered artworks, faded photos.

Toss the take-out junk. If you save the stuff that comes with take-out food—little plastic bags of sauce, packets of plastic utensils and paper napkins, salt and pepper packets, and the like—round them up, put them in a bag, and throw them out. Come on, buy a bottle of soy sauce, for goodness' sake! You'll always be able to find it and use it—and you can get the brand you like. No more horrible little squishy bags littering your drawers!

stale stuff. Okay, so you set out only 10 of those crackers at your dinner party. That was 3 months ago. Who's going to eat them now? Check your boxes and bags and toss anything you wouldn't eat—with pleasure—right now.

Try the cookie-sheet solution. I read this wonderful reader tip in an issue of *Cook's Country* magazine. The reader wanted an inexpensive but effective way to reach the stuff at the back of her cabinets. Instead of buying expensive organizing supplies, she bought used cookie sheets (the kind with shallow edges) and put them on the cabinet shelves, then put her supplies on top. When she needed something from the shelf, she simply pulled the cookie sheet forward until she could reach what she wanted. Great idea! No more groping around. Two caveats if you try this, though: Make sure you don't pull the sheet too far forward, or you'll have an instant avalanche. And you have to play fair and store stuff one layer deep!

Round up the rubber bands. And the twist-ties, paper clips, and similar stuff that's found its way all over your kitchen drawers. (Start with one drawer, then move on to others as you find time.) If you want to save these little items, sort through them, toss any that are dried out, bent, shredded, or otherwise useless, and put the rest in a zipper-lock bag so they're all together and easy to find. They'll take up a lot less space, and the next time you bring some into the house you'll be able to toss them because you'll see how many you already have—or to add them to the bag if you feel you need more.

Cut the coupons. Throw out as many expired coupons as you can in 5 minutes. Bet you'll find you've done them all!

Sort your coupons. Go through your coupons regularly to get rid of any that have expired. Once you've thrown out the expired coupons, you can put the remaining coupons in order by expiration date. That way, you can just check the front of the pile to see what's coming up and make sure you use them before they expire. Now you won't have wasted time cutting them out for nothing!

Clean a cabinet. Not the *whole* cabinet—if you can do that in 5 minutes, either you don't cook or you don't need this book. Instead, find five cans that are outdated or that contain food that you and your family will never eat. Toss them! It's a start.

Put in pull-outs. Home improvement stores and organizing stores, catalogs, and Web sites have wire pull-out shelves on rollers that you can install in cabinets to create more efficient storage space. Because they're rectangular, they make the best use of the space, and their wire-mesh sides keep the contents from spilling out. When you need something from the middle or back, pull out the shelf until it's easy to reach the jar, box, or bottle in question.

Add more shelves. Kitchen cabinets tend to have a set number and arrangement of shelves, which can leave a lot of unused space above the items you store on them. Rather than stacking mugs or cans, you can make better use of the space by adding more shelves. But there's a trade-off: You get more (stable, as opposed to stacked-up) storage space, but the less space there is between shelves, the harder it is to reach the back of the shelf. If you do decide to add shelves, consider the cookie-sheet idea above—unless you seldom or never use the things you put at the backs of your shelves. (And if you don't use them, why are they there?)

Stack 'em up. Buy some wire stacking shelves to put in your cabinets. (Again, they're available from home and organizing stores, catalogs, and Web sites.) These cabinet stackers create a shelf-on-shelf effect to hold additional plates, bowls, and other things so you don't have a single giant stack piled to the top of the next shelf. If you put dinner plates on the bottom and lunch or salad plates on the stacking shelf, you won't have to lift off the salad plates every time you want to set the table for dinner. Ditto for bowls. Using stackers cuts down on the chances of a china avalanche and the resulting broken china.

Use your cabinet tops. There's usually a good bit of space between the tops of your cabinets and the kitchen ceiling. Don't let it go to waste! Store seldom-used items in attractive, lightweight covered baskets that are easy to take down when you need them. This is a great place to put linens, seasonal items (if you can't bring yourself to sell or donate them), decorative cookie tins, party goods, even your sterling silver service (neatly wrapped in tarnish-proof cloth, of course). Label the baskets if you don't think you'll remember what's in them.

Use the cabinet sides, too. Your cabinets probably have exposed sides that

$$\boxed{\text{Tools of the Trade}}$$

Honestly, I try to resist either buying or recommending a lot of organizing gizmos. (I have enough stuff already, and more than enough claims on my checkbook.) But I have to put in a good word for ClickClack food storage containers (available through cooking and organizing stores and Web sites). These square and rectangular clear plastic containers are rigid, well-made, and durable—we're not talking about flexible opaque plastic containers—and they have lock-down lids that easily snap on and off (thus, "ClickClack"). They are just the best for storing perishable stuff that comes in bags and boxes, from flour, sugar, and popcorn to pasta, cereal, and lentils. (You can, of course, store anything in them, including craft and office supplies, but they're pricey, so I'd at least start with the basics and add on as your budget allows.) They come in numerous sizes and stack to make the most of cabinet space. They will keep your food fresh and pest-proof, won't spill if they're knocked over, and let you see what and how much is in them at a glance. Bravo!

aren't doing too much besides holding them up. Add hooks and hang potholders or trivets, cutting boards, or anything else that's useful and flat (and not too ugly to have out in plain sight). Remember that anything you can see can quickly contribute to visual (and actual) clutter if it isn't attractively organized, so don't litter your cabinet sides with stuff.

Use the cabinet bottoms. You can buy and install wire under-cabinet glass racks from home stores like Pier 1. They're inexpensive and can be great space-savers for wine glasses, martini glasses, and any other stemmed glassware that hangs upside-down from the rack. But! Don't hang glasses you don't use at least weekly, or they'll just become dustables. And don't hang them where someone is likely to smash them while doing something on the counter below.

Hook your mugs. You can also attach hooks under a cabinet to hang your mugs. The same caveats apply here as for the under-cabinet glass racks: Hang the mugs you actually use, and hang them out of harm's way.

Hang your paper-towel holder. Why waste counter space with an upright paper-towel holder when you can hang one horizontally under a cabinet? The towels will be easier to pull off the roll, too.

Don't forget the cabinet doors. You can also hook things to the insides of your cabinet doors—as long as they're flat and lightweight but unlikely to come loose and go flying everywhere when you open the door. Pot holders are a good choice. Or you can tack a calendar flat (if it will stay flat) against the inside of the door, where you can consult it easily but it isn't adding visual clutter to the room.

Turn your doors into towel racks. Thanks to stainless steel hangers that fit right over the door (and install without tools!), you can turn a lower cabinet door into an instant towel bar for dish towels. Or add a convenient double-hook hanger for pot holders. Look for them in catalogs like Solutions (see page 48) and at housewares stores.

Magnetize your cabinet doors. Attach a magnetic board inside a cabinet door and put important (but unsightly) refrigerator magnets there—the ones with addresses and contact data for the doctor, dentist, vet, ambulance, fire company, furnace company, auto dealer, and take-out pizza place. Make sure everyone knows where they are, and if you have smaller kids who can't reach an upper cabinet, either put the board on a lower cabinet door or install a duplicate down where they can get to it if they have to.

Recognize your pantry. Think you don't have a pantry? If your concept of a pantry is like mine—my grandmother's fabulous, roomy, walk-in area with a window (she always had plants on the sill) and tons of storage space—you may think you don't have one. But think again: The tall cabinet that's at the end of the counter in most kitchens is the modern equivalent. Treat it like a pantry and use it to store your staples. True, you may not be able to hang brooms and mops on the back of the door, but your "pantry" can hold a surprising amount of stuff—once you kick out the clutter. Which brings me to . . .

Make a date with your pantry. Painful as it is, you really need to pull the stuff out of your pantry and put it back in reverse order. I know—how I know!—it's easier to just put the newly bought stuff in the front and let the older stuff age to greatness in the dark at the back of the shelves, but really, what's the point? Get a notepad and pen and a garbage bag and settle in. (Remember, you can do this a shelf at a time if you can't face tackling the whole pantry at once.) Pull everything off the shelf and put anything that's outdated in the trash bag. If you actually use whatever it is, make a note on the pad that you need more of it. But be realistic. If you've never used it, let it go, even if your mother insisted that every well-stocked pantry had to have it. If you use it once a year, buy it when you're ready to use it. (If some national crisis keeps you from buying the cranberry sauce, I think you'll have other things to think about!) If you don't use it but it hasn't expired, set it aside for the local food bank. Give the now-empty shelf a quick swipe with a dust cloth. Then put everything back with the oldest stuff in the front, where you'll use it first, and the newer replacements in the back. Make sure the stuff you use most often is on the shelves that are easiest to reach. Think of the satisfaction of knowing that from now on you won't be wasting food because you've forgotten it was in there or you just didn't feel like digging for it.

Light your pantry. If your pantry is a walk-in or closet rather than a cabinet, add lighting so it's easy to find what you need and see what's there. Have an electrician install ceiling lights or buy cordless, battery-powered lights and install a row of them. They are inexpensive; use long-lasting LED bulbs; are easy to install with adhesive, nails, or screws; and are readily available from home catalogs, home improvements stores, and hardware stores.

Add more shelves. If your pantry shelves are so deep that you're stacking things in dangerous towers or wasting space, add more shelves to suit your needs. Use metal strips and brackets or other attachments for wooden shelves, insert free-standing wire shelves that fit on top of existing shelves, or add under-shelf wire or plastic shelving that simply slides in.

Put the snacks up front. Save time for everyone by putting cookies, corn chips, granola bars, and other snacks within easy reach (and sight). Save the upper and lower shelves for less frequently eaten (or needed) items. For example, you can store canning supplies and seldom-used appliances or dishes on the top shelf.

Use the pantry floor. Use the pantry floor under the lower shelf (or use the lower shelf, if it's a long cabinet) to store cleaning supplies, buckets, dishpans, paper garbage bags, and other necessary cleaning supplies. If you have young children or pets with free access to the pantry, make sure you keep any potentially harmful cleaning supplies under the kitchen sink with a childproof lock on the cabinet doors.

Use your pantry door. Pantries, including those tall cabinets, have long doors that are great for stashing necessary stuff out of sight. If your pantry is a closet and there's room between the door and the shelves, you can use clasping hooks to securely hang up brooms, mops, dustpans, and other cleaning necessities. If it's a long cabinet, there's still space to tack or hang up memos, add a magnetic board (see page 93) or a chalkboard, and keep your take-out and local restaurant menus where they're easy to find (more on this in the next tip). You can even use special chalkboard paint (available from home improvement centers) to create a chalkboard inside the door for everybody's messages, doodles, and so on. Just make sure you attach a little wire or plastic storage rack for chalk, pens, and other supplies.

Hang your take-out menus. Ever notice those hanging files in your doctor's office? They're on the doors of all the examining rooms so the doctor can quickly check a patient's chart and history. Put these hanging files to good use holding take-out and local restaurant menus inside the pantry door. They're available from office-supply stores.

Put your wraps on the door. You can also get special racks just for aluminum foil, plastic wrap, parchment, and wax paper. Check out organizing stores, catalogs, and Web sites for lots of options. These racks attach to the inside of the door and are a very convenient way to store wraps within easy reach.

Put up a pegboard. The pantry door (or inside wall, if you have a walk-in pantry) is also a great place to put a pegboard. Use it to hang up cleaning tools or small utensils that you don't use often but can never find when you need them, and you'll free up space in your drawers and under the sink.

Hang up a bag holder. The pantry door is also a great place to hang up one of those cloth tubes for holding plastic grocery bags. My friend Edith gave me one of these "bag sausages" for Christmas years ago, and it's a great invention. Just shove the bags into it the way you'd stuff a sausage, and pull one out when you need it. (Yes, we all do use them, for storing onions, picking up after the dog, and other necessities.) My rule is that once the bag holder is full, you take the rest of the bags back to the supermarket and recycle them in the bin outside the door. No more plastic bags spilling out from under the sink!

Contain the kid stuff. If you have kids—or grandkids who visit frequently—and they make the kitchen table command central for projects and homework, stash their supplies on your pantry shelves where they're easy for the kids to reach. Use the lightweight and inexpensive (but sturdy) plastic storage containers with handles and lock-down lids—they're easy to lift and carry, even for small kids, and you can quickly see what's inside. They're available at every pharmacy, department store, grocery store, and housewares store, in a huge assortment of sizes. (Keep them on the small side for small hands.) Perfect for art supplies, school supplies, or toys!

Collect the pet treats and toys. Plastic storage containers (see the previous tip) are also perfect for storing pet toys and treats, not to mention things like fish food and aquarium supplies. Instead of a gadzillion toys and little bags and containers of treats all over the place, you'll have them all rounded up in your pantry in one easy-to-find location.

Corral craft supplies. If you enjoy working on scrapbooking, knitting, beading, or other crafts in your kitchen, you can use lightweight plastic storage containers with lock-down lids and handles to hold your own supplies, too. There's bound to be a size that works for your stuff. You can see what's in the container and fit it neatly on a pantry shelf, where it's ready when you are.

Don't forget first aid. People are more likely to get cut, burned, scraped, or stung in the kitchen or outside than anywhere else, so it makes sense to keep a first-aid kit in the pantry rather than letting it languish somewhere it's unlikely to be found (or used).

Pet Alert!

If you have pets, chances are they share the kitchen with you. There are a few tricks you can use to contain their clutter (and chaos) so you can all just enjoy being together. I use a (waterproof) doormat under my golden retriever's, Molly's, food and water bowls—no fuss, no muss. My friend Anne uses vinyl placemats under her dog's dishes and they work fine, too. I also have Molly's feeding area tucked against the wall on the side of one set of cabinets, so nobody's tripping over it.

If you have cats but no dogs, you can put their bowls on a mat like Molly's. But I have cats *and* the dog, so I had to convert my shorter countertop to a cat-feeding station or the poor cats would never get a mouthful. (They take the high road and Molly takes the low road.) I keep their food and treats in attractive but vermin-proof canisters on "their" counter, so I don't have bags of cat food lying around. Molly's food and treats go into large Molly-proof canisters by her feeding station. I keep the food scoops in the canisters so they're with the food and not adding visual clutter. If you have room, you can store your pet food under the sink (in vermin-proof containers, please).

Those Dreaded Drawers

Cut back to one junk drawer. One day when I was working out at my local Curves, I was told this classic anecdote by Sherry, another member. "A friend was in my kitchen when I opened a drawer to get something and a lot of stuff burst out. 'That's all right, Sherry,' she told me. 'Everyone has a junk drawer.' I couldn't bring myself to tell her that that wasn't my junk drawer!"

If your kitchen drawers are in this shape, get a big trash bag. Then open your drawers and pull out everything that isn't a kitchen implement. Put stuff that should really be in a different room in one pile, stuff that you need in the kitchen (like a flashlight) in a second pile, and stuff you don't really need at all in the trash bag. Your goal is to get the "stuff you need in the kitchen" pile so small that you can fit it all in a single drawer, so be ruthless. Imagine all the drawer space you're freeing up for your utensils and small-but-essential kitchen gadgets! Finish what you start, though: Put the stuff that stays in the kitchen in its drawer, take the stuff that should be elsewhere to wherever it belongs, and throw that trash bag out.

Divide and conquer. Use an old utensil or silverware organizer to corral the jumble in your junk drawer. Put like with like so it's easy to see what—and how much—you have. The organizer will help keep sharp objects like scissors and utility knives away from vulnerable fingers; keep the flashlight and batteries from rolling around; and keep tape, correction fluid, and other seeming necessities upright. If you don't have an ugly organizer you'd like to upgrade for your utensils, thrift stores are full of them.

Keep just one tool. Maybe you're using your junk drawer as a second tool chest—after all, you might need a hammer, pliers, two kinds of screwdrivers. . . . Yes, you *might* need them, but why take up all your junk-drawer space with them when you can buy a multitool that combines 12 or so common tools in one? Whether you get a classic Swiss Army Knife, a Leatherman multitool, or anything in between, you'll save oodles of space by stashing a multitool in the junk drawer and keeping your "real" tools in the tool chest. These tools are built to last and are available from home improvement centers, home catalogs, and camping suppliers like Cabela's and L.L. Bean. If the multitool doesn't handle whatever you need to do, you can always get the single-purpose tool for a given job. (But please put it back in the toolbox afterwards!)

Monitor the junk drawer. After all, it's not called the junk drawer for nothing. Junk has a way of creeping in there, seemingly from nowhere. Once a month, take 5 minutes and give the drawer a good going-over, tossing what you can, putting anything that's strayed in there by accident where it belongs, and neatening up what's left so it's easy to see and reach. Small plastic storage containers and glass spice jars both make good holders for little stuff like twist-ties, paper clips, tacks, magnets, and rubber bands. So do baby-food jars. They all fit nicely in the drawer. Just make sure you buy colorful sticky dots at a stationery or office-supply store and label the containers' lids so you can tell what's inside at a glance.

Store spices heads-up. Now that you've freed up all that drawer space, you can devote one to herb and spice storage. You know that herbs and spices should be stored in a dark, dry, cool place, so choose a drawer that isn't near the stove.

I saw the neatest drawer spice display in, where else, *Martha Stewart Living*. Martha had her spices neatly lined up in a kitchen drawer. She had dealt with the problem of how to know which spice is which when all you can see are the caps by making beautiful vanilla-and-robin's-egg-blue round labels for all the tops, with the name of each herb or spice elegantly printed on the label. Pull out the drawer and you could see every herb and spice at a glance! Being Martha, she had put all the spices into matching glass spice jars (available from housewares stores), a nice "extra" if you want to go to the trouble.

I don't know if they'll still be there by the time this book comes out, but you could find Martha's gorgeous labels online and download them yourself from her Web site. (Go to www.marthastewart.com and search for "spice jar labels.") If they're not still available, you could always e-mail the site and see if someone could locate them for you. Of course, you can also create homemade versions by writing the names of your herbs and spices on those colorful round sticky dots you can buy at office-supply stores.

They'll stay fresh and keep their color longer—and it's amazing how many spice jars you can fit in a drawer when you stand them upright!

Centralize your cookie cutters. If you love making and decorating cookies, designate another of those freed-up drawers for cookie-making supplies. Stash your cookie cutters and containers of colored sugars, jimmies, cinnamon dots, and all those other cookie-making essentials in the drawer. No more time wasted trying to find it all! And you can admire all those wonderful cookie-cutter shapes every time you open the drawer.

Appliances and Gadgets

Don't keep duplicate appliances. How many homes have you been in where multiple coffeemakers, microwaves, and other appliances and gadgets were taking up valuable storage space, "just in case" the one in use broke? Guess what: They're not planning to stop making them anytime soon. And meanwhile, you could use that space. So give the extras to friends and family who don't have one, sell them at a yard sale, or donate them to Goodwill, the Salvation Army, or the Society of St. Vincent de Paul.

[Don't hoard what's easily replaceable.]

If it's broken, toss it. Or fix it—unless you've already bought a replacement. If you're not ready to take it to the repair shop right now, get rid of it. And bear in mind that a replacement is probably cheaper than a repair.

If it malfunctions, toss it. Okay, it's not *really* broken—the lights just go on and off sporadically when you're using it, it sometimes shuts off halfway through, or it works only half the time. As Dr. Phil says, get real! Get it fixed (and see the previous tip on this), or get rid of it and buy a fully functioning model.

If it's missing parts, toss it. Again, why use up valuable space storing that lidless blender, that pot with the broken handle, the serving fork you used to use all the time before a tine broke? If you can repair it or replace what's broken (and haven't already bought a replacement), go for it. But frankly, if you were going to do that, wouldn't you have done it by now? Be honest with yourself and throw it out or donate it.

If you don't use it, don't keep it. If you've bought every gadget on late-night TV but find that you've never used any of them, or you decided to invest in the latest hot appliance only to realize that your family didn't really like fresh spinach-beet juice no matter how healthful it was, it's time for deaccessioning. Sell those unused gadgets on eBay. Donate them. Give them away or—if they've never been used and are still in their "As Seen on TV!" boxes—give them as gifts. Yes, that appliance or gizmo cost money—sometimes, lots of it. And maybe you can make some (or even all) of it back if you sell it. But one thing is sure: It's making you no money sitting on or under your counter, and it's taking up valuable space.

If it does the same thing, don't keep it. If you use your food processor as a blender, you probably don't need your blender. But if you find that you *only* use your food processor as a blender, maybe you should give *it* away and keep your blender. Don't keep multiple appliances that do the same thing—keep the one you like and find yourself using and get rid of the rest.

SANITY SAVERS

If you're crafty, there's no end to the creative ways you can reuse beloved kitchen objects. Except for Native American baskets, the most wonderful basket I ever saw was made of grapevines twined around and through red plastic heart-shaped cookie cutters. It was in a fine crafts shop in Virginia, and I fell in love with it at once. (But no, I didn't buy it. I'm trying to abide by the "if you can't picture a place for it, don't get it" rule.) What a fantastic idea! It transformed those cookie cutters into a work of art. Think of how you can incorporate objects you love but don't use into something you can display proudly.

If you haven't used it in a while, don't keep it. This one is harder. Give yourself a bearable deadline—have you used it in a year, 2 years, 5 years?—and look at your tools and appliances with that in mind. If you haven't used that aspic ring in 20 years, you're not likely to use it now. If you've long since abandoned your food mill for a food processor, it's time to send the mill packing. If your bread machine, yogurt maker, or sprouter have seen no use since the Stone Age (or ever), find better homes for them. Mind you, sometimes what goes around does come (back) around—you could have used that Crock-Pot from the seventies when slow cookers came back big-time in the nineties. But you could also just go out and buy another Crock-Pot if you want to give slow cooking another try. And there are plenty still out there at secondhand shops if you don't want to spring for a new one!

If you can't bear to lose it, reuse it. What if you simply love the look of that old butter mold or whisk or copper chocolate-melter, even though you know you'll never use it? Or you have such a strong sentimental attachment to Grandma's antique wooden spoon or potato masher that you can't bear to part with it? Give them a new life as kitchen wall art. My father's girlfriend has a huge brick wall in her kitchen, and she's hung dozens of antique cooking implements on it. If you enjoy cooking, as I do, it's a fascinating display—like a culinary museum. Most of us may not have that kind of display area, but there's probably some wall space where you could hang one or two implements. I once found a very old handmade wooden washboard at an antiques store. When I turned it on its side, it looked just like a fish. My unique "fish" has been hanging on the kitchen wall ever since. Bear in mind that unless you have a huge display space, it's better to showcase like items together for the most attractive, coherent presentation—a group of cookie cutters, some antique silver spoons. You can even frame them or put them in a shadowbox.

Ditch the hanging baskets. Not plant baskets—those three-tiered wire baskets for fruit, onions, and so on. It may look like Old World charm to you, but it looks like visual clutter to me. Any time you have a bunch of different stuff hanging down, it looks messy and cluttered. So store your produce in bowls or baskets on the counter (or under the counter or on a table or in the fridge) instead. Take the hanging baskets to Goodwill, give them away, or turn them into plant baskets—fill them with flowering vines, and hang them from a tree.

Where to Put the Pots and Pans

Make your stove a storage center. When you're not using your oven to cook, use it to store pots, pans, baking sheets, cookie tins, and the like. Yes, you'll have to take them out to use the oven, so be realistic about how much you're prepared to haul around. (I think of it as doing arm-toning exercises.) If you're not the only one who's likely to turn on the oven, make sure everything you store in there is ovenproof!

Make the most of your stovetop. Keep the teakettle and the pots and pans you use every day right on the stove. I keep mine on the burners I use them on, with a smaller pan in the center front that I switch off with my teakettle. Everything else is shelved or in drawers where it won't collect dust between uses. Admittedly, my used-every-day cookware is beautiful Le Creuset enameled cast iron (worth every penny, if you can lift it), so it gives me joy to see it out and waiting. But even if yours isn't quite so attractive, I'd think it would be cheering to see these faithful kitchen helpers waiting to greet you as you begin preparing each meal. And it certainly saves time and effort getting them out and putting them up every time!

Use stoveside storage. My beloved old Caloric (!) gas stove came with my house. It has a tall, narrow storage drawer on the left side that's as deep as the stove itself and another storage drawer below that's as wide as the stove. I store baking pans, racks, spatter screens, and cutting boards in the tall, narrow drawer, and I keep the broiler and assorted pan lids in the under-stove drawer.

Double up your pots. Use your big pots to store smaller ones. If you have Dutch ovens, deep steamer pans, or any capacious cookware, it makes sense to keep

Dustables

Home-decorating magazines are full of great-looking ceiling hangers for pots and pans. You probably know at least one person who has one. People who have beautiful pots and pans like to keep them in sight, and at first blush it may seem like a brilliant storage solution, freeing up cabinets and counters. But unless you own a restaurant and use all those pots every day, they're dustables. Do you really want to spend your free time risking a broken neck as you clamber up there and dust all those pots and pans? I didn't think so.

smaller pots and other cookware items like soufflé ramekins tucked inside. Again, make sure the doubled-up pots aren't too heavy for you to lift comfortably.

Make a wall hanging. If it will look good with your decor, you can hang a few pans on the wall beside the stove. But hang only the ones you use (and wash) regularly, or you're just creating dustables. And remember that anything hung near the stove is going to get gummy and spattered. Pans hung like this will be very eye-catching, so you (and everyone else) will be spending more time than usual staring at their undersides, which translates into more time scrubbing them. Why do I say it's all right to do this and all wrong to hang them from the ceiling? (See "Dustables.") Pans hung flat on a wall—as long as there are just a few and they're decoratively spaced—are flat, so they reduce visual clutter. Pans hanging in midair create a "flying clutter" effect.

Put up a pegboard. My editor, Anne, says the best thing she did in her small kitchen was to put up a pegboard in an alcove near (but not too near) the stove. She hangs pots, lids, strainers and colanders, potholders, oven mitts, and dish towels—all things she uses regularly, so dust and grime aren't problems.

Rack it up. Do you have wire cooling racks for cookies, cakes, bread, and other baked goods? If so—and if they have no plastic parts—you can store them in the bottom of the oven, below the lowest oven rack. They fit neatly and don't have to be removed when you use the oven, unless you're cooking something really messy.

Utensils and Dishware

Group the utensils you use most often. At the back of my stove, I keep the gorgeous handmade ceramic crock that holds the utensils I really use—wooden and bamboo spoons, pasta tongs, spatulas, potato masher, soup ladle. (The less-often-used utensils are in the drawers on either side of the stove so they're easy to reach as needed.) You can use a jar, a sturdy vase, a *big* coffee mug—anything that will hold all your most-used utensils. Keep them on the stove or nearby on the counter. They'll be tidy, upright, and in easy reach. Note: Make sure the mouth of the container is as wide as its body. I started out using a lovely handmade bowl with a narrow mouth but switched to my current crock after having too many utensil avalanches.

Minimize mugs. End mug madness by sorting through the mug shelf, tossing battered or broken mugs, and putting every too-big, too-small, too-ugly, and even too-boring mug in the Goodwill box. In 5 minutes, you can cut your mug collection in half (or more, if you're really ruthless).

If it's chipped or cracked, throw it out. This is a *really* hard one. You have a matched set of glasses, dishes, or crystal. And one or more pieces are chipped or cracked. But hey, it's part of the set, right? So back on the shelf it goes. Now, it's true that every time I attend the local antiques extravaganza, I see a booth where someone is smoothing the chips on crystal and glassware. But tell me three things: (1) Are you really going to take your stuff to get it smoothed out? (2) If you do, would you give a guest a glass with a dip in the rim? (3) Would you want to drink out of it? Same with cracked plates. Unless you're talking about a priceless antique, why look at those ugly cracks a minute longer? Sure, it hurts to throw them out. (If you have a friend who makes mosaics out of broken china, you can see if he or she wants them. But don't *you* hold onto them in case some day you might decide to make mosaics!) And yes, it leaves you with fewer pieces in your set. But please don't tell me you actually use those cracked and chipped pieces now, anyway! Throw . . . them . . . out. You can use the space. And you can find intact replacements if you really want to via specialty services like Replacements, Ltd. (Find them on the Web at www.replacements.com.)

Buy just one. (Or two.) We're so conditioned to buy whole sets of china and glassware that it's almost an automatic response—yet most of us have neither the space nor the budget to indulge ourselves this way. Instead, indulge yourself by buying one or two pieces of china, mugs, or glassware you really love—or just enough for the immediate family. I was thrilled to see that Moss in New York had set up a registry that does just that—lets you get as few pieces as you want. (See www.mossonline.com's Me, Us, and Them Registry.) Or just tell yourself that it's really okay to buy just two glasses next time you see them at a store and fall in love.

Double up your bowls. I'll bet you're all already doing this, but just in case you've somehow overlooked this basic tip, stack 'em up, with the largest on the bottom and the smallest on top. Colanders usually fit nicely in a stack of bowls, too.

Remember to display and use. One great way to make the most of your kitchen display space without sacrificing storage is to choose "collectible" kitchenware that you can also actually use. Wonderful old (or new) crockery bowls, redware, yellowware, and many other kitchen items can either be bought new or still be used even if they're antiques. (Though I for one wouldn't want to use an old wooden spoon or wooden cookie mold unless it had come down in my own family and I could remember someone using it.) These evocative collectibles can be displayed to add a vintage or homespun look to your kitchen, but you can use them as you would any modern piece, so they do double duty.

Hide the big stuff in plain sight. My mother kept her gigantic silver and fine-china turkey serving platters—with their still more gigantic domed lids—and covered soup tureens on display in the dining room all year. The silver turkey platter and tureens were displayed on a sideboard with silver candlesticks, while the lovely white-and-gold china platter sat proudly in the center of the dining-room table, flanked by silver candlesticks and soup tureens at either end. The display looked great, and it freed up a world of storage space for other things. Remember, it's not clutter if it looks intentional!

[It's not clutter if it looks intentional.]

Hang your cutting boards, part one. Wooden cutting boards can make a really attractive wall display—as long as they actually look good and you hang only a few of them. Hang them over the counter where you'll be using them.

Hang your cutting boards, part two. You can hang more weather-beaten wooden cutting boards and plastic cutting boards from the insides of your lower cabinet doors. Again, hang them in the cabinets that are closest to where you'll use them.

File the plastic cutting boards. Buy one of those office organizer racks that have wire rungs to hold files upright (think of the reception desk at the doctor's office). Put your plastic cutting boards in one of these to hold them upright and ready to use. If you use plastic cutting boards, remember that old trick of using one color cutting board for meat, a second color for aromatic veggies like onions and garlic, a third color for fruits and veggies, and a fourth color for bread.

Minimize the plastic storage containers. I've seen whole cabinets in friends' houses devoted to plastic-container storage. In addition to containers that are intended for food storage, some friends who shall remain nameless even store empty yogurt, cottage cheese, and margarine containers. Yuck! Surely you can find better things to do with your space. I certainly agree that plastic containers are useful for storing leftover refrigerated food compactly and for packing lunchboxes. High-quality plastic containers can be relied on not to leak or break and are less likely than glass containers to slip out of your hands. The problem is not the containers themselves, but that people seem to hoard them like priceless collectibles.

So with that in mind, here are my six steps to a manageable plastic pile:

1. Throw out or recycle any plastic stuff not meant for storage.
2. Determine about how many containers you usually have in the fridge and send out in lunch bags at any given time.
3. Collect your best storage containers and set them aside, together, so you can see what you have once you've gotten rid of the rest.
4. Recycle any cheap storage containers, as well as any that are discolored, stained, smelly, bent, or broken, as well as any that have lost their tops (or bottoms).
5. See if you have enough left to meet your needs, and if not, write down how many replacements you'll need and in what sizes and shapes. (Don't exceed your limit! You can buy more later if you find that you really need them.)
6. Buy high-quality containers to fill your quota if you no longer have enough. Hopefully, you'll now have most of your plastic storage containers in use rather than taking up space in your cabinets!

Match up your plastic storage containers. If it's not obvious at a glance which tops go with which bottoms, there are several ways to avoid confusion. By now you should have a manageable number of plastic storage containers to work with (see the previous tip). So get them out and group all of the same-size tops and bottoms together. Then get an indelible marker and number the tops and bottoms. Start with a 1 on all the tops and bottoms of one size and shape, a 2 on the next group of matching tops and bottoms, and so on until you've numbered them all. Stack all of your 1s and store them together, and do the same for the rest. Now if the tops and bottoms get separated, you can match them up at a glance.

Store your picnic supplies in the hamper. Stash all the plastic or paper plates, utensils, straws, and cups—as well as napkins and picnic cloth—right in your picnic basket or hamper. You'll be putting that empty hamper to good use, and your supplies will be ready when you are!

Put your dish rack in the sink. If you depend on a stainless, wood, or plastic dish rack to hold washed dishes, glasses, mugs, and utensils, you probably keep it on the counter on one side of the sink (as I do). But if you have a double sink, you can buy specially sized stainless dish racks that will fit right in the sink. This frees up extra counter space and lowers the dishes' profile, reducing the visual clutter of a tangle of dishware at counter height.

Make sure you have this magnet. If you have a dishwasher, here's one magnet you can't do without: One of the ones that has "Clean" on one end and "Dirty" on the other. I, of course, hope that you put away your clean dishes as soon as they've cooled down, but even if you do, this magnet will prevent dirty dishes from being shoved in among the clean ones—or someone grabbing a dirty glass or mug and drinking out of it. (Ee-eewww!)

Sharp Advice for Knife Storage

Put your knives on the block. A wooden knife block keeps knives (and a sharpening file) upright, safe, and in easy reach. I put mine at the back of the counter under a cabinet and beside the stove, where it can't be tipped over. It's amazing how little space a knife holder takes up, and it will keep you and your family from cutting yourselves while rooting around in the utensil drawers. This is a must-have! (Too many knives for one block? Buy another one—it still won't take up much space and will be worth every inch that it does.)

Dispose of dull knives. People seem to have an awful time getting rid of knives—even wealthy people who could buy a knife company with pocket change and those of us with three generations' worth of hard-used knives spilling out of our drawers. Now, I certainly don't mean that you should toss perfectly good knives that just need to be honed. (Unless, of course, you know you'll never sharpen them.) But a dull knife is a bad knife. Not only is it dangerous, it also makes you work much harder for worse results. If you got a cheap set of knives when you started cooking and have since upgraded, keep that original wooden knife holder but give the knives it held to the local thrift store. Now you have a free knife holder for your new knives!

Store knives flat. If your counter cabinet has a shallow drawer, devote it to knives and store them side by side. They'll stay sharper if they aren't jumbled up with other utensils, and they'll be within easy reach.

Store knives in a tray. If you're afraid to just lay naked knives in a drawer, try an in-drawer knife tray. I saw a beautiful wooden one at Crate & Barrel that held steak and kitchen knives securely.

Kitchen Furniture and Furnishings

Match your space. When I bought my cottage home, I was lucky enough to acquire a recently renovated kitchen with a hanging bookcase that exactly fitted the wall between the refrigerator and the laundry-room door. I was thrilled—a place to put my, ahem, cookbook collection! But of course there was that open space between the bookcase and the floor. One day, I was driving past an antique store when I saw an oak dry sink (a sort of large hutch) in the display window. A bell went off in my head. The bookcase and my kitchen cabinets and woodwork were also oak. I pulled over, went in, eyeballed the dry sink, and decided it would exactly fit the available wall space. (I'm guilty of eyeballing rather than measuring things all the time, and for me, it seems to always work out. But as they say, don't try this at home.) I won't go into what it took to get that heavy old dry sink into my tiny Volkswagen Golf, or to get it out again and down to the house, but sure enough, once I'd wrestled it into place, it was a perfect fit. Whew! Now I had a place to put my good china, crystal, and silver where no one could disturb it, and I could use the top of the dry sink to hold my handmade ceramic canisters. If you need more storage and have an odd corner or space, keep alert. You never know when (or where) the perfect piece will turn up!

Shelve it. Bookcases aren't just for books. You can store plates, cups, bowls, and glasses in full view and easy reach in a bookcase—and the narrow shelves don't take up much precious floor space. Two things, though: Unless your shelves have glass doors, put only what you use every day on the shelves, or you're just creating dustables. And remember that it's easy to knock things off of open shelves—something to bear in mind if you have little ones. Lining the shelves with thin white rubber matting (it's easy to cut it to fit) will help keep the china in place. (You can put it between plates, bowls, and other pieces as well, if you're stacking them. But I think a better idea is to put cloth napkins between them—you'll be protecting your china *and* storing the napkins at the same time!)

Make your door work harder. Often, the space around the kitchen door is just that—space. But if you add tall, narrow shelving on either side and a connecting shelf over the door, you suddenly have a fantastic storage space for cookbooks, china, or cooking gadgets. Turn the space into an instant pantry by putting doors on the narrow shelves.

Go to Fantasy Island. If your kitchen is wide enough, an island in the middle of the floor is a real blessing. You can use the top as extra counter space when it's time to prepare food, and the shelves or cabinets below will hold appliances, pots and pans, bowls, a wine rack—whatever you need to keep within reach. Islands are especially great when you have several people cooking at one time—one can work on the island while others work at the stove and counters. Make sure there's good light over your island so it's a pleasure to work there, and make sure the top of the island is at countertop height so it's comfortable to work on it. Two things I don't like: Bar seating at an island, and pots and pans hung overhead (for some reason, designers tend to hang them over islands). Bar seating is always uncomfortable—the height is awkward, and the overhang is never deep enough to be really usable. If you want to eat in the kitchen and the only space you have is where you might put an island, go with a table instead. You can still prep food on it!

Make your island ambidextrous. While shopping at their local farmers' market, my friends Carolyn and Gary bought a kitchen island with cabinets that had doors on both sides and drawers that you could pull open from either side. I love this idea—you have total access to the drawers' and cabinets' contents from either side!

Block it out. A butcher-block top is a real luxury on an island, since it converts the entire island top into a cutting board. But if that's outside your budget, you can always get a nice freestanding butcher-block cutting board to set on top.

Cart it around. No room for a permanent island in the middle of your kitchen floor? Get a kitchen cart. These wonderful mobile furnishings come in all styles and price ranges and are readily available at DIY and housewares stores like Target. You'll probably have to assemble them yourself, but the tools and hardware are usually included and it doesn't take more than half an hour, even for the least experienced DIY-er. A butcher-block top is certainly a nice feature, and some come with hooks on the sides so you can hang utensils (nothing sharp, please), aprons, and pot holders. Just roll the cart to where you need it when it's time to make a meal, and store it out of the way when you're not cooking.

Be a basket case. If your island or cart has open sides, you can add handsome rectangular storage baskets to give it an uncluttered, attractive look while still providing plenty of storage.

Tuck in the trash. I saw a wonderful mobile kitchen island in the Improvements catalog (see page 48 or www.improvementscatalog.com) that took up only 18 square inches of floor space but had a granite top for cutting and food prep, three drawers, and a tilt-out compartment to hold a 13-gallon garbage can. It's really nice-looking, too!

Take your medicine. An attractive medicine cabinet that goes well with your kitchen's decor (say, an oak one in my oak kitchen) makes a good storage place for spices, herbs, and flavorings—it is dark and won't be located over the stove, where the heat would shorten the cooking life of your spices and herbs. The cabinet can also be a good place to stash keys, cell phones, sunglasses, and other stuff you might need to grab on your way out of the kitchen—and if it has a mirror on the front, you can even give yourself a quick check as you go by!

Add an armoire. If you can't afford a Hoosier cabinet or an expensive built-in storage system but you have the space for one, see if you can find an armoire at a flea market (or in your attic). These big old freestanding closets were all the rage before built-in closets became the norm. You can add hooks, shelves, drawers—whatever you need—inside, and store table linens, pots and pans, cleaning supplies (including tall tools like mops and brooms), or staples. You can paint or finish the armoire to match your kitchen's decor. Close the massive doors, and the content's secrets are safe with you!

Dress it up. If you don't have room for an armoire (or can't find an affordable one), consider using a dresser. These are readily available pretty much everywhere, from flea markets and yard sales to thrift and secondhand stores, and they come in all styles and sizes. (And again, you can always paint yours to match your other kitchen furnishings.) They're great for storing table linens; paper towels, napkins, and other paper goods; trivets; dish towels; cleaning supplies; pots and pans; and even cookbooks.

Try a wine tower. If you enjoy wine but don't have the space for a bulky wine rack, consider a wine tower. I saw a great one in the Crate & Barrel catalog; it took up only 16 square inches of floor space but stored 18 bottles of wine, had a drawer and two shelves, and had a top hanging rack that would hold 12 wineglasses.

Hang your wine on the wall. If you lack the room for a wine rack or like to keep only a few bottles on hand at a time, try this wonderful space-saving idea: Buy a hanging wine rack that attaches to the wall and holds four wine bottles securely on their sides in no more space than a cutting board. (The one I admired is from Ikea and costs less than a bottle of wine.)

Ditch the dish towels. If people know you cook, they'll often give you dish towels. And they're *so* pretty. You might need them. So into the drawers and under the sink they go . . . and go. Find them, drag them all out, and pick two (or four, or six). Put the chosen ones away, toss the worn-out rags, and put the new or good-as-new towels in the Goodwill bag.

Under the (Gulp) Sink

Unstuff the sink. Look around and under your sink and throw out any worn-out scouring pads, sponges, and dish brushes—and let's not forget that browning bar of French kitchen soap. Collect the remaining brushes (bristles up, please) in one of those mugs you just couldn't bear to throw out, and see if you can survive with a single sponge and scrubbing pad. Doesn't that look better?

Make the most of under-sink doors. Don't waste this valuable space. Attach hooks for dust cloths, dishcloths (not the one you're currently using, please), brushes, and other small cleaning tools. Screw on short, narrow wire bins to hold sponges, soaps, steel-wool pads, and other small supplies. You'll be surprised how easily this door storage can organize your under-sink area, making it a snap to find those small cleaning items when you need them. Now you can quit rooting around in the dark under there or digging through drawers!

Keep a flashlight on your under-sink door. Whether you hang it or put it in a hanging wire bin, make sure you have a small flashlight on the inside of the door.

[Tools of the Trade]

I think under-sink organizers are one of the greatest things around. Unlike some organizing tools that take up more space than they create, under-sink organizers instantly add two or three times the space of an "unimproved" under-sink area. That's because when you have just the open space beneath the sink, you can put in only one layer of cleaning supplies—all those spray bottles and cans of cleaning powder—or face a pile of unrecognizable junk in there if you toss in more stuff than will fit in a single layer. (And then you just buy new stuff because it's easier than trying to dig the old stuff out, right?) But an under-sink organizer gives you two, three, or even more deep shelves, and thus three layers, to keep everything upright and easy to find.

The organizers I use are made of sturdy plastic and snap together without tools. They're specially built to fit around sink pipes, and the shelves are adjustable, so you can space them just as you like and use as many or as few as you need. You can buy them from organizing catalogs and Web sites like www.allbrightideas.com, or look for them in your local home store. Highly recommended!

When you need to find something in the murky darkness under the sink, the flashlight is conveniently at hand.

Put what you use in front. You know how deep and dark it is down there under the sink. So make it easy on yourself. Organize the area so the supplies you use most often are in front and the ones you seldom use are in back. (And while you're at it, ask yourself if you really need those, anyway.) You'll save time and effort, and you'll also cut down on your bending, crawling, and cursing.

Junk the gunk. Gross, rusting cans of solidified abrasive cleansers. Spray bottles with a teaspoon of solution in the bottom. Jars with crusty gunk oozing out from under the lids. We've *all* (ahem) reached under the sink and grabbed hold of something we'd rather not see, much less touch. Since you're working down there now anyway, get rid of all that stuff. Once you've kicked out the clutter and put your small flashlight down there, you can easily see if something's getting into "it came from outer space" mode and pitch it ASAP.

Put in some plastic. Organize your under-sink cleaning supplies in plastic buckets, plastic pans, a plastic laundry bin, or a colorful plastic crate. (The plastic pans will fit neatly on under-sink shelves, if you opt to install them.) They'll make it easy to haul out the supplies when you need to use them, and if anything spills, well, it's a lot easier to clean a plastic container than your sink cabinet!

Recycle those sponges. Like toothbrushes, kitchen sponges should be given limited working lives—certainly no more than 3 months between replacements. But that doesn't mean you have to toss those "perfectly good" sponges right away. Instead, take a tip from my friend Chris and give old kitchen sponges a second career by using them to clean the bathroom before they're permanently "retired."

Corral compostables. I keep my compost bucket under the sink, where it's easy to grab when I'm preparing a meal or cleaning up afterward. I use a plastic bucket with a plastic lidded container inside—it's not fancy, but it's functional. I have seen many gorgeous ceramic and stainless compost buckets in garden- and home-supply catalogs. They've been designed to sit out on the counter, but ugh! I just can't stand the thought of that. To me, given what's going inside it, even the most elegant compost container should live under the sink.

Skip the poisons. Don't store poison baits, insecticides, flea sprays, or any other toxic pest controls in the kitchen. Period. Keep them locked in a cabinet in the garage or tool shed.

SANITY SAVERS

I love to cook and find it very relaxing, especially if there's some music on in the background while I'm slicing and dicing. I find music—whether it's jazz, Celtic, reggae, folk, or rousing rock—a real kitchen sanity saver. It helps make cooking time "my time." So a small boom box that will play my CDs is an essential part of my kitchen equipment. (They make really small ones now.) I keep my little boom box and CDs tucked away in a rustic little cabinet. With the door closed, it looks like it's always been part of my country kitchen. Swing the door open and plug in the boom box, and it's party time! You can also buy a CD player/radio that's made to attach under a cabinet—a real space-saving solution. Or get a little radio and tuck it away on the windowsill. If you don't mind wearing your music or don't want to disturb anyone else, grab your iPod, MP3 player, or Walkman and start rocking—I mean, cooking!

Lock it up. By the same token, if you store caustic chemicals like bleach and drain de-cloggers under your sink and you have small children, make sure you keep the cabinet locked. If you set a mousetrap under the sink, lock the cabinet to keep the unwary of all ages from sticking a hand in there in search of something. Put a big, scary-looking note on the inside of the door where it will get someone's attention (not outside, where it could scare off visitors). And don't forget to check the trap at least once a day!

The Fearsome Fridge

Manage the magnets. If you have more magnets, coupons, calendars, photos, take-out menus, kids' artwork, lists, and schedules on the fridge than the bulletin board at your favorite supermarket, it's time to take charge. A messy refrigerator door broadcasts visual (and actual) clutter into your kitchen, and with it a feeling of restlessness and loss of control—clutter chaos. But it's simple to fix. Put the need-to-know magnets on a magnetic board inside a kitchen-cabinet door (see the tip on page 93 for details) and keep the fun, decorative magnets everyone loves on display. (But not too many. If you have more than enough to make an artistic display, put the "extras" in your junk drawer and rotate them with the ones that are currently on display.) File the take-out menus in a hanging file on the pantry door (see the tip on page 95 for more on this). Frame the kids' art in the kind of clear plastic frames that allow you to simply slide the art in and out, so you can hang one frame for each kid and make a wall display. Change the art when new master-pieces come home. Keep your grocery lists inside a cabinet or pantry door. But do by all means keep one of those tiny magnetic calendars that show a month at a glance. Talk about a helpful at-a-glance tool!

Put up a memo pad or board. They now make magnetic memo boards and pads just for the fridge. Rather than covering the doors with sticky notes and layers of lists, memos, and other papers held precariously with magnets, try one of these and get rid of the mess. Everyone can leave messages where the whole family will know to look for them, and if it's a memo board, you can just erase or wipe it clean at the end of the day.

Print your grocery list. My friend Delilah has a checklist of the groceries and other supermarket items her household eats and uses most often. She keeps a set of printouts of the list on the refrigerator door. Before she goes shopping, she checks off the items on the list that need replacing and adds new items in the blank spaces at the end of the sheet. What a time-saver!

Hang a flashlight. If at least one side of your fridge is exposed, you can put it to good use by hanging a flashlight with a magnetic attachment on it. Make sure the batteries are always fresh, and everyone in the family will be able to find at least *one* working flashlight if the power goes off!

Don't waste the fridge top. The top of the fridge can provide valuable real estate for large pots and appliances. I keep my enormous pressure-canner, bread kneader, and heavy-duty nutcracker on mine—appliances I don't use every day and that would be a huge pain to try to store in my cabinets. Because this space is on view, you don't want to put anything unsightly (or unstable!) up there. You may also, like me, have a shallow cabinet over the fridge that only a contortionist could easily reach. This is a great place to store things that you seldom need but have to keep on hand in case your mom drops in and asks to see them.

Make your fridge top work harder. Because the top of the fridge stays warm—it has to do with the cooling process—you can use it to do quite a few ingenious things. Start seedlings, culture yogurt, set bread to rise—things that would ordi-narily take up counter or oven space.

Clean out the fridge before you shop. My friend Chris suggested this great idea. She cleans out the fridge and disposes of any lingering leftovers the day before she goes grocery shopping. Not only does this give you a first-hand look at what you need to get, it also, as Chris points out, means you're cleaning an emptier fridge, so there's less to clean up!

Organize what's in there. There are several ways to organize the contents of the fridge, but whichever you choose, the goal should be convenience and easy access. I try to put the stuff I use most often closer to the front, with the tallest bottles, cartons, and containers behind the shorter ones. My own goal is to be able to see everything that's in the refrigerator when I open the door—and as my boyfriend, Rob, could tell you, there's a *lot* of stuff in there!

Check your stuff weekly. Perishables can go bad faster than you can say, "Eeewww! What's that?" Make sure you check the contents of your fridge— including the crisper drawer—at least once a week and discard anything that's less than fresh. (My chickens love fridge-check time.) Force yourself to peek into those opened cartons of sour cream, cottage cheese, and yogurt. Smell the milk and half-and-half. Look inside the mystery containers. It may be only slightly less entertaining than cleaning the cat's litter box, but it won't take 5 minutes and it's for a great cause. Think how great it would be to know that literally everything in the fridge was fit to eat!

Don't keep your eggs in the egg rack. If you have an older fridge, it may have one of those open-air egg racks in the door. You're supposed to take the eggs out of the carton and pop them into the egg-shaped depressions so they're on full display. The problem with that—besides the fact that it's easier for them to get knocked off and break—is that the air around them will dry them out faster. Your eggs will last longest in a plastic egg carton like the ones sold in stores that carry camping supplies (check out Cabela's, Coleman, and L.L. Bean). But if you don't have one of those, store them in the carton in which you bought them.

Group perishables by type. My father's girlfriend, Alice, has three crisper drawers in her fridge. (Boy, am I jealous.) She keeps her cheeses in the shallow drawer on top, her veggies in the middle drawer, and her fruits in the bottom drawer. It's easy to see what's there and what needs to be replenished just by pulling open a drawer!

Put onions in produce bags. Onions won't make you cry when you cut them if you refrigerate them and cut them cold. But onionskin all over the crisper drawer, or worse, glued to the bottom of the crisper drawer, is just plain yucky. Avoid this mess by storing your onions in one of the clear or opaque plastic bags from the supermarket's produce section. (I keep the bulk of my onions in a dark lower cabinet with the potatoes and refrigerate just a few at a time to conserve precious crisper-drawer space. But even in the cabinet, I store them in plastic grocery bags to avoid footloose onionskins.)

Don't buy the big jars. Unless you go grocery shopping only once a month, you don't really need those giant bottles of ketchup and salad dressing, the huge jars of mayo, or the monster-size vat of pickles or jalapeños. Buy the small size and replenish them as needed.

Don't keep what you don't use, part one. The diet parmesan-peppercorn dressing seemed like a great idea. Trouble was, nobody liked it. But there's still half a bottle left! Wake up. Throw . . . it . . . out. Nobody's going to use it, and it's sitting there taking up space, along with the exotic shredded ginger–garlic sauce, the antibiotics you got for your cat 2 years ago, and the bottle of lemon juice you forgot was in the door (but suspect dates from your daughter's third birthday). Free up the space for stuff you really do use, or just free up some space so you can actually see (and reach) what's left.

Don't keep what you don't use, part two. This goes double for the freezer, whether it's part of the fridge or a freestanding model. Check the contents every month. Pitch any food that's iced over, is unrecognizable, is over 6 months old, or is unlikely to ever be eaten. If you bought three boxes of frozen lasagna on sale and the family hated the first box, I have a feeling they're not going to suddenly love the other two. Take them to work, give them to a neighbor, see if the local homeless shelter wants them, nuke them for the dog, or throw them out! Make room for the things you really eat.

Don't keep what you don't use, part three. If you have a hard time throwing out "perfectly good" food that just isn't very good, you'll probably have a *really* hard time with this: Your freezer is stocked with healthy veggies like spinach, green beans, and Chinese stir-fry mix. You feel virtuous because you've bought all these healthy foods for your family. But . . . you can't get anyone to eat them, including yourself. This goes for the fruits and veggies in the crisper drawer, too. Don't feel guilty. You really were trying. Instead, take them to work, give them to friends, or

Ask Claire DeClutter

Dear Claire,

Help! My wife insists on storing every dab and drop of leftover food in our refrigerator. But once they go in, these leftovers never come out. Our fridge is so crammed with plastic storage containers that there's no room for my beer! What can I do?

—Fed Up and Left Over

Dear Fed Up,

It sounds like your wife has a classic case of "waste not, want not" guilt. You need to recommend my "3-Day Rule for Leftovers." First, tell her that all the leftovers are taking up space that could be used for food the family really wants to eat. (I wouldn't mention the beer, if I were you.) Then, ask her if you can clear out all the leftovers for her. (Make sure you toss them!) Next, tell her that if leftovers haven't been eaten in 3 days, they probably will never be eaten, and that from now on she should throw out any leftovers that have taken up residence in the fridge for more than 3 days. (This is the 3-Day Rule.) Reassure her that it's okay to throw them out. Hopefully, one of two things will happen: Either she'll start using those leftovers and moving them out of the fridge on a timely basis, or she'll cook less food so she won't have to deal with leftovers anymore. Either way, there'll be no more guilt!

Good luck,
Claire

compost those babies and replace them with the healthy fruits and veggies your family actually enjoys. Who cares if they hate kiwifruit and papayas? Stock up on apples, grapes, strawberries, and oranges—they'll still get real health benefits.

Put up bamboo shelves. Shallow magnetic shelves and deeper magnetic bamboo file boxes attach directly to the doors or sides of your refrigerator. You can store spices or sticky notes, pens, grocery lists, and other small stuff in the shallow shelves. The deep file boxes can hold telephone books, catalogs, and magazines. They really stay put without scratching surfaces, and they're shallow—less than 4 inches deep—so they don't take up valuable room space. Check home improvement stores, housewares stores and catalogs, and online at ingenious-products sites like www.solutions.com (see page 48).

Eating In

Minimize your table. If your kitchen is small but it doubles as your dining room or your family just has breakfast and snacks there, you can save space by downsizing the table. Use a drop-leaf table and keep the leaves down when the family's not using it—it's amazing how a standard-size round table can suddenly turn into a tiny rectangle that fits snugly against the wall! Add candles and a bowl of fruit and you have an instant sideboard. Or get a table with removable leaves and add them when you need to (as long as you have a place to store the leaves when they're not in use).

Use a folding table. The ultimate space-saver is a folding card table (or two put together, if there are more than two of you). Keep it folded away when it's not needed, and put a tablecloth on it when you use it to dress it up. This option works best when the kitchen adjoins a garage or basement where you can stash one or more folded tables. Two pluses: Without the tablecloth, the kids can use the table for homework or projects, and you can use it as an extra work space, without any fear that it will get messed up!

Ditto for the chairs. You can now buy padded wooden folding chairs that are attractive (and comfortable) enough to use as everyday chairs. Or go for the metal standards. If you can't stand the look of them or want something fancier for company, dress them up with slipcovers that are made just for folding chairs, available from home stores and catalogs.

Nix the diner decor. Many older homes have a breakfast nook with wooden booths and a bolted-down wooden table. It's just like a diner, but not nearly as comfortable. The family is crammed together, which can lead to trouble, and the rigid seating can't be made comfortable no matter how many cushions you use. Plus, the booth benches tend to have high backs, blocking both the view of the diners and the view from the rest of the kitchen. Bad idea! Yes, it saves space, but at the price of comfort and attractiveness. There are better options. Tear it out and install a pantry, shelving, a second fridge or a freezer, or a kitchen island in its place.

Don't forget lighting. If your kitchen table is an afterthought, there may be no overhead lighting for it. Don't make your family eat in the dark! Food looks more appetizing when it's attractively lit (and you all will look and feel better, too). And good lighting is a must for the homework and projects that invariably get done at the kitchen table. No matter how bright the rest of the kitchen is or how many windows you have, it's worth hiring an electrician to hang a light fixture that matches your decor or install recessed lighting. Whatever you do, don't succumb to the temptation to just put a floor lamp or two by the table. The last thing you need in a place where people are constantly walking, standing, sitting, and moving chairs in and out is a clutter of cords!

Make the condiments convenient. Keep the napkins, salt, pepper, and other condiments you use regularly (that don't need refrigeration) on a tray or in a basket on or near the table. That way, they can be carried easily when it's time to eat or time to clear the table for homework or other activities.

Create a coffee corner. You can minimize morning chaos by dedicating a part of the countertop nearest to the table as your morning coffee station. Put the coffee machine, grinder, filters, and any other equipment you use to prepare your coffee together on the counter with a tray of mugs, sweeteners, spoons, and napkins. If you have tea-drinkers in the family, set out their tea as well, and position the kettle on the nearest burner. Now it's all ready when you are!

Reining in the Recipes

Clip 'n' save. My boyfriend's father was in the Foreign Service, so he knows a thing or two about staying organized. He also enjoys cooking and trying new recipes, so he subscribes to all the cooking magazines. But he doesn't just let them stack up. Each month, he goes through the magazines, chooses recipes he wants to try, and cuts them out. Then he can recycle the magazines and get all that paper out of the house. But he doesn't stop there. Once the recipes are clipped, they go into a special recipe notebook that has dividers separating types of recipes. The new recipes go in the front of each section, so that they can be saved or discarded once they've been tried. Can't face setting up your own notebook, or want something prettier than the classroom standard? Bookstores now sell attractive notebooks just for recipes, and you can get self-stick notebooks just for clipped recipes at sites like www.solutions.com (see page 48).

Read at the library. Save money and space by reading cooking magazines at your local library instead of subscribing to them. If you see a recipe or article you just have to have, make a photocopy while you're there.

Hang a magazine rack. The kitchen is a great place for a magazine rack because it lets you keep your favorite cooking magazines in easy reach. If you don't have room for a floor rack—or are afraid that you, your pets, or your family will crash into it—there are specialty wall-mounted magazine racks that are very attractive. Check home improvement stores, home decorating stores like Pier 1, and catalogs like Improvements (order online at www.improvementscatalog.com)—they're really easy to install with the special grippers provided.

Get a magazine butler. If you can't bear to toss, recycle, or give away your favorite cooking magazines (shame on you!), at least keep them upright, compact, and easy to find and use. Clear acrylic holders store a year's worth of magazines and are available from home centers, organizing stores, and catalogs.

Limit cookbooks in the kitchen. After spending what seems like a lifetime trying to get all my cookbooks *into* the kitchen, it hurts to recommend this. But frankly, it makes too much sense to pass up. Think about how many cookbooks you have. And then think about how many you actually use. If you have the space to shelve all your cookbooks in the kitchen, great! But if you don't, make space for the few that you use most often and shelve the rest in the bookcase that's closest to the kitchen. They'll still be nearby when you need them, but they won't be taking up precious kitchen space.

Cull your cookbooks, part one. Ouch! Ouch! This one's probably harder for me than it is for you. While you're sorting through your cookbooks, see if you can donate some to the library book sale or the local thrift store, or pass them down to the kids (if and *only* if they want them!). You may have some that you were given as wedding presents and never liked, some that sounded great but proved disappointing, some that you bought when they were the rage or when you got a new appliance, some that you got while traveling, or some that no longer reflect the way you eat. If you can get them out, do it.

Cull your cookbooks, part two. What if you have a cookbook you never use—except for that one special holiday recipe or favorite cake? If you use just a few recipes from a cookbook, it makes sense to photocopy those recipes and give the book itself away. (Make sure you note on the photocopy what book you took it from; that way, you'll be able to find it again if the photocopy gets torn or stained.)

Keep the one you love. Here's where I'll give you a break. The kitchen is rightly called the heart of the home, and there's a lot of sentiment attached to it. If you

Tight-Space Solutions

My friend Delilah loves to cook, and she loves to watch cooking shows. She hit on the ingenious idea of putting a TV in the kitchen so she can watch the shows while she's puttering around in there. But she and her boyfriend, Chaz, didn't want to take up valuable kitchen space by putting the TV on a counter or even mounting one on a wall. Instead, they bought a small set that is specially adapted to mount under a kitchen cabinet. Some of these even include CD and DVD players! (Delilah put hers under the tall cabinet over the refrigerator, where it's out of harm's way and easy to watch.) Now she can watch her favorite cooking shows and learn new recipes and techniques while she works!

never, ever use—but really, really love—an old cookbook (perhaps your first-ever Betty Crocker kids' cookbook or your grandma's battered, splattered first-edition copy of *The Joy of Cooking*), keep it. Display it with pride. You might want to hang it in a shadowbox on the kitchen wall. But I have to say it again: Make sure you're not using sentiment to justify keeping *all* your cookbooks.

Check out the library's collection. Let the library come to your rescue again by looking over their cookbook selection. You can check out the ones that interest you (one at a time, please), and put sticky tags on any recipes you think you'd like to try. Photocopy the tagged pages at home or when you return the book to the library. If you really fall in love with a library cookbook, you can buy it for your own collection next time you go online or to the bookstore. Meanwhile, think of all the so-so cookbooks you'll get to test drive without buying!

Get your recipes online. Lots of online sites offer extensive collections of free recipes. Try www.epicurious.com and www.recipes.com to start. Your favorite cooking products will often feature recipes on their Web sites, too, so use a search engine to find one—say, King Arthur Flour—and check it out. Enjoy comparing recipes online, then print out the one you want to try. If you like it, save the printout for the next time you want to make that dish.

Save your recipes on your computer. You can also keep recipes you enjoy or plan to try in a file on your computer (or on a disk) and print them out or refer to them as needed. If you have Martha Stewart- or Mary Engelbreit-like tendencies, the Internet has many sites that let you create beautiful recipes to print out with gorgeous borders and charming typefaces. (A quick Google search for recipe cards yields www.razzledazzlerecipes.com, www.graphicgarden.com, www.nextag.com, www.recipecards.net, www.countryclipart.com, and www.freeprintablerecipe cards.net, to name just a few.) Otherwise, just head for the copy paper.

Don't forget the faithful recipe file. It's not so great for clip 'n' save recipes, but if you write down your own, that old card file with the 3- by 5-inch (or 6- by 8-inch) cards is still a workhorse, holding a lot in a small space. You can find attractive wooden card files (or decoupage a metal card file, if you're handy). And you can get colored file cards, so you can use different colors for different types of recipes. And of course, you can keep them in alphabetical order with those handy dividers. Just be sure you write new cards to replace the ones that are wearing out (keeping a computer backup is a good idea), and go through the file at least once a year to clear out recipes you've never used or no longer use.

Go back to school. My friend Anne uses a three-ring loose-leaf binder for recipes. Recipes she clips from cooking magazines can be glued to the pages, and she can also write down her own. It's easy to get rid of recipes she doesn't use, too. She uses colored index tabs, just like kids use in school, to divide the notebook into sections.

Set up a cooking station. If you love cooking and spending time in your kitchen, it's a great place for a specialized mini-office. I call it a "cooking station." Rather than setting up your laptop on the kitchen table or counter, dedicate a space in the kitchen to this mini-office so you can have it set up all the time (and will therefore actually use it). Create an "office nook" with a computer desk and comfortable chair. Not enough space? You can find "roll-around microstations" at home centers and catalogs like Improvements (online at www.improvementscatalog.com), with an adjustable top, drawer, and two adjustable shelves for your printer and other essentials. It's on casters, so it rolls easily to where you want it or out of the way, and it comes in attractive wood finishes so it's as handsome as it is functional. Add a chair and a basket for necessities like your cell phone, pens, and paper, and you're in business! Now you can search for recipes online, exchange recipes with friends and family via e-mail, input your favorite recipes— and print out what you need, where you need it. If you have room for a permanent

Pet Alert!

My back door opens out of the kitchen, so I keep my golden retriever's, Molly's, leash hung on a hook on the wall beside the door. (You could also hang a leash on a hook on the side of a kitchen cabinet, if that side of the cabinet is near the door.) I have doormats both inside and outside the door, to give muddy paws maximum wiping time. And I keep a "Molly towel" neatly folded on a stool just inside the door if more paw-drying (or coat-drying, if it's raining and she gets drenched) is needed.

cooking station, you can hang bookshelves over it for your cookbooks, add a hanging magazine rack for your cooking magazines, and hang a TV under the shelves so you can watch favorite cooking shows (see "Tight-Space Solutions" on page 122).

The Door to the Great Outdoors

Use two mats. If, like me, your door to the great outdoors is in your kitchen, you already know that lots of the outdoors seems to get tracked in. (My house's previous owners, who in general did a great job decorating, put white tiles in the kitchen. Consequently, I can see every dab of mud. Ugh!) Fight the mess by using two doormats—a heavy-duty one outside the door and a decorative (but still functional) one indoors.

Get a second stand. You may recall that I recommended that you put an umbrella stand by the front door. Get a second one of these super-helpful stands for near the kitchen door. They take up a tiny amount of room but will keep everyone from dumping dripping umbrellas on the floor. I recommend a ceramic stand, since wet umbrellas won't rot or rust them. You'll be surprised by how many umbrellas they hold—all upright for easy grabbing. They also neatly contain other upright objects like baseball bats and brooms.

Box up your boots. With everyone tramping in and out through the back door, your kitchen is likely to accumulate a pile of wet, muddy, or otherwise grungy footwear. Not to mention all the mud, melting snow, grass, and other tracked-in stuff all over the floor. Fortunately, some ingenious companies have come up with wonderful rectangular shoe-and-boot organizers that will keep that footwear in line (literally). They are durable, come in several sizes, and even feature optional rubber inserts so water can drain right through and your boots and shoes can dry faster. Some of them even have two levels. You can find them in mail-order home catalogs and stores.

Add a bench. If you have room, put one of those ubiquitous benches that have storage under the seat by your back door. Whether they're the kind with a seat that lifts up to reveal a storage compartment or the type with rectangular storage baskets that fit neatly in place under the seat, these convenient benches serve double-duty as seating and storage. And they make it easy for everyone to pull off their shoes before they track gunk from outside all over the kitchen floor.

ONWARD!

Whew! You've conquered the kitchen and kicked the clutter out of every drawer, cabinet, and even the fridge. Now it's time to take on that other clutter-sink (so to speak)—the bathroom. Take a deep breath, turn the page, and plunge (those puns just keep coming) in!

Chapter 7

Bathroom De-Cluttering Basics

Bathrooms are usually small. Everybody uses them. And everybody's shampoos, cosmetics, lotions and potions, towels, dirty clothes, hair dryers, razors, medicines, toothbrushes, and you-name-it end up falling off every available surface. Then there's the issue of people slipping, tripping, and otherwise injuring themselves on the clutter. Try the tips in this chapter to kick out that clutter and organize what's left without causing a palace revolt.

PRIORITIES FOR BATHROOMS

Start the de-cluttering process in the bathroom by setting some clutter-kicking priorities. First, focus on what matters most to you about the way each bathroom (if you have more than one) looks. Next, consider your other concerns about the bathroom's appearance and make a list of everything that bothers you. Eventually you will rank your clutter concerns in order until you get to what matters least. The first step in setting clutter-kicking priorities for the bathroom is to take a good, hard look at the "before" state of the room, and then to visualize the "after."

A Bathroom Visualization

To get to your "after," you need to start with the "before"—the way things look right now. So get out some paper, or use the "My Bathroom—Before" form on page 128 (or make a photocopy of it) and write on that. Write down every place there's clutter in the bathroom, and note what that clutter is. Are there piles of unread magazines and newspapers? Towels tossed in a corner and getting smelly from dampness? Uncapped toothpaste tubes leaking on the counter? Scuzzy soap dishes? Maybe there are trailing toilet paper rolls and wadded-up tissues escaping from the trash. If there are, write 'em down.

Remember, the bathroom may be cluttered, but it's probably a small room. It won't take but a few minutes to finish your list!

Once you've jotted down a quick description of your bathroom's "before" state, it's time to move on to the "after"—how you want the room to look when you've kicked the clutter. Write it all down on a piece of paper, or in the "My Bathroom—After" form on page 128 (or on as many photocopies of it as you need to do it justice). To make sure you're being realistic, look at the room every few minutes while you're doing this.

Your description can be short and to the point: "I don't want to see tubes, bottles, hair and makeup accessories, nail polish, and spilled gunk from all of the above on the vanity top. I don't want to slip on one of the 17 bottles of shampoo and other hair and body products on the bathtub floor. I'd like to be able to organize the space under the sink, so I can see and reach everything. I'd like to see all the towels hanging up neatly instead of falling off the towel rack and onto the floor." Or you can create a detailed portrait of exactly how you'd like the room to look if it were perfect (for you). You can picture the colors of the walls, towels, and shower curtain; whether there would be tile, and if so, what it would look like; describe your ideal sink, vanity, and mirror—everything.

Getting There

Now that you have captured your bathroom's "before" condition, listing all the specifics, and you've imagined its "after" appearance, you can finally prioritize the

My Bathroom—Before

_____
_____
_____
_____
_____
_____
_____
_____
_____
_____
_____
_____
_____

My Bathroom—After

_____
_____
_____
_____
_____
_____
_____
_____
_____
_____
_____
_____
_____

My Bathroom Priority List

_____

_____

_____

_____

_____

_____

_____

_____

steps you'll need to take to get there from here. Again, bearing both "before" and "after" in mind, I'd recommend starting with what bothers you most about the "before" condition and working down the list from there.

Maybe you're concerned that soggy towels and washcloths on the bathroom floor are not just unsightly, they're also mildew and tripping hazards, and you want them picked up and hung up where they are easy to reach and will dry out quickly. Make that your top priority. Or perhaps you think you'll scream if you see another uncapped tube of toothpaste or all-but-empty shampoo bottle. Put that high on the priority list, too.

Write down whatever's driving you to distraction on the "My Bathroom Priority List" (or photocopy it, if you'd prefer), in descending order from most to least maddening. Now you have your priorities straight! Once you've finished, you can turn to the tips below to find ingenious ways of dealing with each problem.

THE BATHROOM TIPS

Take care of the towels. One great "Tool of the Trade" for towels is a towel rack that fits over the shower curtain rod, giving you a towel rack that extends the entire length of the tub. This is a great way to create space for everyone's towels if all you have now is the typical one-towel rack that several family members have to share. Get one of these, and keep those towels dry and off the floor.

Tone down the towels. For a guest bath, or if you have your own bathroom, keep the bath towels, hand towels, and washcloths all the same color. (If it's your bathroom, you can obviously have several sets in different colors and rotate them when you need a new look.) It will make things look less busy, and thus, less cluttered. Plain towels without patterns or contrasting colors will also give the room a cleaner, less cluttered look.

Give each his (or her) own. Then again, if several people share a bathroom, giving each person his or her own color of towels, washcloths, and the like will simplify things. In this case, a plain bath mat is a necessity. But you can liven things up by getting bath mats that match everyone's towel colors and rotating them.

Throw in the towel. Take the towels off the shelf and sort through them. You love that shade of peach, but there's a worn patch on the front and . . . yes, that *is* a little hole. Throw . . . it . . . out. Do you ever really set out those snowman guest towels? Has your child stopped using the Scooby-Doo beach towel? The "his and her butt" towels that seemed so funny at the time? What about those horrible velour towels that looked so gorgeous but don't absorb any water? Put all the worn-out towels in one pile, the "don't like 'em, don't use 'em" towels in a second pile, and the "still-good, still-used" towels in a third. Toss the worn-out pile; pack up the don't-use pile for Goodwill, the Salvation Army, or the Society of St. Vincent de Paul; and put the rest back. Whew! Look how much more room there is in your linen closet now! And maybe you can find a new peach towel on sale.

Stick with one mat. I've been in bathrooms where there was a bath mat or rug in front of the tub and another one in front of the sink. Even the toilet had its own fitted rug—and there was a fuzzy covering on the toilet lid, too. This polka-dot rug approach adds visual clutter—not to mention actual clutter! It creates tripping hazards, provides plenty of places for germs to collect and hide, and adds to your mountain of laundry. If you have multiple mats, clear them out! One per bathroom is plenty—surely people can move the mat to the sink if they need to. Or you could compromise: Splurge and buy a bigger mat that covers more of the floor.

Keep the mat on the floor. I see a lot of bath mats hanging over the sides of tubs. This looks messy and adds to the visual clutter. Make sure your bath mat or rug looks clean and presentable; keep a backup to rotate in so you won't have to do without when you're washing one; and keep that mat on the floor, where it belongs.

Simplify the shower curtain, part one. A child's bathroom with zebra, moose, or seashell shower-curtain hooks is cool. In an adult's bathroom, they just add to the visual clutter. Don't draw attention to your shower-curtain rod with elaborate hooks. Do you *really* want people looking up there?

Simplify the shower curtain, part two. You can guess what's coming next: Donate your busily patterned shower curtain to Goodwill and replace it with a plain one. A plain shower curtain in a pale or neutral color will make your bathroom look bigger and less visually cluttered. Save the fun shower curtains for the kids' bathrooms.

Simplify the curtains, period. What goes for the shower curtains goes for your window treatments, too. Curtains with busy patterns close in a room visually—especially when it's a small room like a bathroom. And all those little design elements just add to the visual clutter. You'll notice the same effect if you look at wooden or bamboo blinds that are a single pale color versus the ones that have darker spots and splashes patterning them. Whatever window treatment you choose for your bathroom, keep it light, bright, and simple.

Nix the naked shower-curtain liner. By this, I don't mean that you shouldn't use a liner without a shower curtain. If that's your choice, that's fine. Just don't use a *clear* shower-curtain liner. After all, you can see things through a clear liner. Things that look like clutter. Instead, opt for a solid liner and keep what's in the tub your secret.

Say "it's curtains" for the shower. This goes for the tub, too. Keep your shower curtain and liner fully drawn across the tub or shower stall at all times. It will look so much neater than a full view of the tub—even if it's the cleanest, least-cluttered tub in creation. The blank canvas of the curtain reads like a clean, spacious, uncluttered wall. And there's an added bonus—an extended curtain and liner will dry out faster, which really helps to keep germs and mildew at bay.

Hang it up. If you need a mirror in the shower, buy one of the fog-free versions (available in home catalogs and home improvement stores) that you can attach to the wall.

Add a shelf. I think a shelf in the shower stall or tub looks neater and less cluttered than razors and the like hanging on the walls. A mirror is one thing—people

5-Minute Fixes for Bathrooms

Here are six quick fixes for the bathroom. See what a difference you can make in just 5 minutes?

Stash the shampoo. Buy a shampoo holder rack that fits over your showerhead and put your shampoos, conditioners, detanglers, and other hair-care products on its shelves. You'll get rid of all those bottles lining the sides of the tub (or sitting in the tub, for that matter). Put the almost-empties in the front and tell everybody to use those first. Or, if you don't think they will, bag the full bottles and stash them out of sight until the others are used up.

Switch to liquid soap. This one's easy! No more dirty bars, slimy soap dishes, or slippery showers. (Confess: How many times have you dropped a bar while showering and then had to grope around trying to find it? Ugh!) You'll save space on your vanity, and you can put the tub bottle in your new shower-head rack with the shampoos.

Do one drawer. Pick any drawer in your vanity, then sort through it and toss anything you don't use—no matter how "good" it is or if it has never been opened!—and anything that's broken (including worn-out ponytail holders and broken barrettes). Wipe down the drawer, replace the in-use items, make a note of any broken stuff that you want to replace, and you're done. There! Doesn't that feel better?

Chuck old cosmetics. Yes, you loved Raven Red lipstick in high school, but that was 20 years ago. Yes, there's still a smear of blush in the case. And yes, that glitter nail polish was a lot of fun to wear three Christmases ago, but now it's separated into six sticky layers. Some people may not believe it, but many of us

expect to see mirrors on walls, after all, and a hanging one frees your hands. But a bunch of little stuff hanging all over sure says clutter to me. If you have more bits and pieces than a single shelf will hold, put up several, or put attractive waterproof containers on the shelf and group the objects in each container by type so you can quickly find what you need. (Of course, the shelf should be waterproof, too.) Don't put it any higher than you can comfortably reach.

Add a bookcase. One great way to add narrow bathroom storage, if you have the space, is to put a bookcase in the bathroom. You can run one from the floor to have sentimental attachments to our old cosmetics because of the memories they inspire—of a special date; of our mom (isn't that her French Blue eyeshadow?); or just of a time when we were young, thin, and carefree. And some of us can't stop trying the latest and greatest that we read about in a women's magazine—while, of course, not throwing out any of our other makeup. But please. The bathroom isn't a cosmetic museum or The Body Shop. If you must keep Mom's French Blue shadow or your Twiggy nail polish, tuck them into a keepsake box. Then toss your old makeup and any new makeup that doesn't look or feel good on you—unless the kids want it and will really wear it. (I don't care how much it cost or how new it is, if it doesn't look and feel good, you know you're never going to wear it.)

Pitch the perfume. Perfumes go bad. You know that, right? So why is that stinky old bottle of Love Potion Number Nine still taking up shelf space? Collect all those bottles and smell them right now. Toss any that smell "off," making a note to replace any you really love. Next, toss any perfumes you've never liked and never wear. (The sales clerk probably made him buy you that bottle of Shalimar, anyway.) If anyone asks what happened to the Evening in Paris, just inform them that hey, perfumes go bad!

Make sure your meds are current. You knew I'd get to this one, didn't you? Just do it. Open the medicine cabinet and check those expiration dates. Toss the old stuff in the toilet and flush. (Not the bottles, though, please.) Make a note of anything you need to replace. And don't self-medicate—if there's a prescription medicine in the cabinet for an old illness, even if the medicine hasn't expired, throw it out (unless it's for a recurring illness).

the ceiling, or you could use a two-shelf model and use the top for storage or display. Make sure the color suits the room—paint it to match or buy a neutral color or natural-wood case. Voilà—you've just doubled or tripled your storage space while taking up only a foot of floor space!

Buy some baskets, part one. A bookcase is a great bathroom storage solution. But because bookshelves are open, it's easy for them to look like a chaotic jumble of clutter once you start storing things on them. One way to avoid that is to buy a set of square or rectangular wicker, grass, or other woven baskets that are the

Dear Claire,

My mom is trying to de-clutter our bathroom. She's told me and my sister that we have to share the same shampoo, detangler, conditioner, gel, mousse, body wash—everything! And she says *she* wants to use the same ones, too! Eeeewwww! How gross is that? How can we tell her that we each want to use our own without getting in trouble?

—My Shampoo

Dear My Shampoo,

I suggest a compromise. What if you and your sister could agree to choose just one of each product to use at a time? You can keep the rest in a plastic bin in your drawer or closet and rotate or alternate as you please. And maybe in return for being allowed to use your own stuff, you could also agree to cut down on the number of cosmetics, curlers, ponytail holders, brushes, combs, perfumes, nail polish bottles, and all the other indispensable stuff you keep in the bathroom? (The rest of it can go in another plastic bin, if there's no room left in the first one.) Out of sight, out of (your mom's) mind, right? Show her that now there's plenty of room for *her* shampoo and conditioner, too.

Good luck,
Claire

right size to fit your shelves. You can stash your stuff in them and still have a beautifully neat, uncluttered look. Baskets are great holders for extra toilet paper rolls, feminine hygiene products, bars of soap, guest or hand towels, and washcloths—you name it. Out of sight but not out of mind!

Buy some baskets, part two. Large round wicker, grass, or other woven hamper-style baskets are beautiful storage solutions, too. You can put one at either end of your bathroom bookcase, cluster a trio of different sizes in a decorative grouping, or situate one as a focal point. Use them as traditional laundry hampers, roll towels and stash them inside, or use one to keep a plentiful supply of toilet paper or diapers at hand.

Table it. Need some counter space in the bathroom? Try a nightstand or bedside table. These are readily available at flea markets and secondhand shops—and probably in your or a relative's attic, too. Paint one to match the bathroom's decor and you'll not only gain a space-saving dressing table, you'll get a storage drawer, too!

Don't forget the trash. Talking about a bedside table reminds me that the area underneath it is the perfect size for a wastebasket. And we all know how important it is to have a wastebasket in the bathroom, right? I'm always dismayed to walk into someone's bathroom and see no wastebasket and no facial tissues. To me, these are every bit as vital as toilet paper. What are they thinking?! So please, make sure you have a wastebasket in every bathroom. No reason to buy revolting plastic or industrial models, either (unless your bathroom has an intentionally industrial look). Mine is a cranberry red tin bucket. A basket or hamper makes a great trash can, too—just tuck that ugly plastic one inside to keep the basket fibers from getting yucky. It goes without saying that, if your wastebasket isn't covered, you need to keep it extra-tidy and empty it regularly.

Keep it clean. Some of the most necessary things in your bathroom are also the ugliest: the cleaning supplies. You've got to have cleansers, brushes, sponges, a plunger, drain openers, squeegees, and all that other fun stuff accessible and at hand. But talk about something that needs to be out of sight! Now, please don't buy a cutesy doll or other plunger cover, I beg you. That just adds more clutter while still reminding everyone of what's under there. If you add a bookcase or other storage solution, you can free up the under-sink area and use it exclusively for cleanup items. Buy a colorful bucket for brushes, scrubbers, and sponges and tuck it inside; put hooks inside the door and hang cleaning rags on them. Don't store cleaners in the same space with shampoos, cosmetics, and other family items—the cleaners will get lost, spilled, or worse. Give them their own space. And keep them behind a childproof latch or lock if you have young kids.

Tools of the Trade

I told you about how great under-sink organizers are in Chapter 6, and the bathroom's another place where they're superhelpful. These organizers make it easy to store cleaning supplies or other things under the bathroom sink. I highly recommend them. See page 112 for the lowdown.

Make a cleaning basket. Yes, one of those tall, round hampers will work beautifully to hold the plunger and two buckets of cleaning supplies, too. Stack the buckets beside the plunger, put the lid on the hamper, and voilà!

Dress it up. Mix your furniture to suit your needs. If you have an outgrown child's dresser (or have or can find a suitable used dresser at a flea market or secondhand shop), see if it's a good size for your bathroom. If so, transform it with an appropriate coat of paint and move it right in. Drawers can hold tons of towels, toilet paper, and toiletries. If the dresser has two small drawers on the top, they're a great size for holding bandages and other first-aid supplies.

Put a skirt on it. We didn't have vanities in the Colonial home I grew up in. In fact, we were lucky to have bathrooms, which generations of former owners had to do without. With tiny add-on bathrooms and storage at a premium, my mother had to get creative. Using elastic and curtain fabric, she created "sink skirts" to go around the bathroom sinks, each skirt matching the curtains in that particular bathroom.

Skirt the dressing table. If you're short on bathroom storage, you can create additional storage space if you have room for a narrow dressing table. My mother had taken a marble-topped hallway table and turned it into a dressing table in my childhood bathroom by putting a "skirt" on it in a fabric that matched the sink skirt and curtains. (See the previous tip for details on these.) She hung a mirror over it, and voilà! Suddenly there was a pretty, useful dressing table that took up only a foot of valuable floor space (of course it was longer—probably 3 or 4 feet). And there was that long, high space beneath for much-needed storage.

File it away. Still on the lookout for tall, narrow bathroom storage? Try a file cabinet. A four-drawer file, or four-high, has nice, deep shelves for towels, linens, and cleaning supplies. If you have oak accessories in your bathroom, try to find an old oak file cabinet at a flea market or secondhand store. Otherwise, get a modern white one that looks less like office-supply stock than the typical heavy-metal versions, or paint one to match your decor.

Peg it. What to do with all those bathrobes? Remember those Shaker peg strips we talked about in Chapter 5? They're perfect for hanging bathrobes, too. Buy a short peg strip and paint it to match your bathroom woodwork or the color of the wall.

Hook it up. For a two-for-one punch, use decorative metal hooks—they have a

Pet Alert!

Aren't cats great? There's just one bad thing about cats (not counting hairballs, of course)—the litter box. If you don't have a basement or porch where you can stash the litter box, you may end up—like me—sharing your bathroom with the family cats. In this case, it's essential that you keep the litter box presentable—clean, odor-free, and preferably out of sight but not out of the cats' reach. If your bathroom is big enough, you can screen off a corner of the room and hide the litter box behind the screen. If it's small like mine, you may end up stashing the litter box in the only available space—the bathtub.

Wherever you put the litter box, keep it cleaned up, swept up, and covered up. I use clumping litter and add both an enzymatic deodorizer and a product called Ammo Cat that removes ammonia odors—and I clean the box every morning! Here's a hint, though: You may like the way scented litter smells, but cats don't. They may boycott a scented litter box. So stick with unscented litter and your cats will thank you!

One more thing while we're on the subject of pets: If you have pets, make sure everyone in the family and all guests know to keep toilet lids down at *all* times. Dogs like to drink toilet water and cats have been known to jump or fall in when the lid is left up. If you use toilet fresheners with bleach and other additives, be aware that they are toxic to pets. Your beloved furry friends could die from drinking toilet water or licking themselves after landing in it. Don't let this happen to your pets!

larger hook for your bathrobe, and a smaller hook at the bottom for your pajamas or nightgown. If you have little ones, put their hooks where they can reach them easily, and make sure those hooks have ceramic knobs on the ends. Wooden hooks are also a good option.

Don't forget the door. Make the most of bathroom door space by hanging a full-length mirror, available at home and DIY stores, on the back of it so that it faces you when the door is closed. These mirrors are inexpensive and supereasy to attach—you just hook them over the top of the door. Before I got one for my bathroom, I had to wait until I got to work to see what I looked like from the waist down. Yikes! Mirrors make rooms look bigger, too—a definite plus. If you don't like the color of the frame (mine is white), paint it to match your decor.

Don't forget the toilet. You're bound to have some space over the back of your toilet, so don't let it go to waste. If there's a window behind your toilet, put a small cabinet (like a jewelry cabinet) on top of the tank to hold hair accessories, odds and ends, and even jewelry. (Not your good jewelry, though—what if somebody tipped it over?) I prefer a closed cabinet to a wicker or openwork stand, even though the shape of the wicker toiletries stand is perfect for the toilet back. But wicker collects dust, which tends to gum down in a humid bathroom, and the open style lets you (and everyone else) see all the stuff on the shelves, which then looks like . . . clutter. If you have a solid wall behind the toilet, you can install a cabinet or étagère specifically designed to fit around and over the toilet. They're available from home centers. Or you can hang a second medicine cabinet, perhaps with a decorative framed mirror on the door, or a set of shelves. Just remember: If it sits on the toilet tank, it has to be easy to lift off without creating an object avalanche. And if it sits over the tank, the bottom has to be high enough so you can lift off the top of the tank and get in there easily.

Don't read in the bathroom. This one seems like a no-brainer to me. There's enough stuff in the bathroom without bringing in a bunch of magazines, books, catalogs, and newspapers. Besides, unless you live alone, other people are probably waiting to use the bathroom. And even if they're not, there are better places to read!

Keep appliance cords out of sight. Reserve one drawer, cabinet shelf, or covered basket for blow-dryers, curlers, electric razors, electric toothbrush chargers, and other electrical equipment. Cords are unsightly and hazardous. Use the appliances when they're needed and keep them out of sight when they're not.

Store toothbrushes upright. I have an ingenious handmade ceramic toothbrush holder with semicircular holders for four toothbrushes and a cup in the center that will hold two or three tubes of toothpaste upright. An ordinary glass or cup would work fine, too, as would a short vase or (new, please) flowerpot. Just make sure everyone's brushes are different colors!

Put it under glass. Funny how clutter doesn't look like clutter when it's cleverly contained. If you store your cotton balls, swabs, emery boards, bath salts, little soaps, and bath oil beads in matching glass apothecary jars, they suddenly look not only organized, but also pretty enough to display on open shelves. Can't face the expense? Try canning jars. But if you have little ones who might tip a jar over, opt for unbreakable plastic and file the jar idea for a future bathroom makeover.

Magnetize your medicine cabinet. Steal this great tip from Martha Stewart: Have a sheet of galvanized steel cut to fit the back of the medicine-cabinet door and caulk it in place. Attach a magnetic notepad holder (available at office-supply stores) to hold combs and brushes and magnetized hooks for lightweight tools like eyelash curlers.

Add more cabinet space. Make the most of tall medicine-cabinet shelves by adding acrylic risers to double the shelf space.

My friend Skye Alexander, feng shui master and author of several great feng shui–flavored clutter-control books (including *10-Minute Clutter Control* and *10-Minute Clutter Control Room by Room*), has a bathroom tip I really like. Skye suggests creating guest bath baskets with decorative soaps and personal-size toiletries like shampoo, conditioner, lotion, bath oil, toothpaste, and the like. Add a nicely rolled washcloth and hand towel. Skye points out that if you keep a couple of these baskets on hand, you'll always be ready when guests arrive.

Dustables

I know you see them in every magazine—certainly I do—those fascinating bathrooms with shelves or cabinets of decorative objects adding interest and beauty to the room. They look great—in the magazines. But in reality, they collect gummy dust and dirt faster than the dog. The heat, dampness, and humidity make bathrooms a bad place to display dustables—especially ones with porous surfaces like crystals and shells. If you want to feature a natural theme in your bathroom, add some plants, which will love the humidity and oxygenate the air. Then hang photos of seashells, rocks, a woodland scene, or whatever you find delightful—in waterproof, easy-to-clean frames.

Choose your cabinet carefully. If you're shopping for a new medicine cabinet, make sure it works as well as it looks. I saw a wonderful one just today that had a divided shelf under the cabinet. It was beautiful and provided extra storage or display space!

Stash the scale. What's most likely to trip you up when you stagger groggily toward the bathroom in the dead of night or rush in, thinking of something else? The scale. It lies there, low to the ground and usually in bathroom-ready camouflage, like a coiled reptile ready to strike. (This is also true if you're trying to weigh yourself.) If you have a bathroom closet, put the scale in there. Otherwise, keep it out of harm's way—under the lowest shelf or under a piece of bathroom furniture. It's easy to pull it out when you want to check your weight, and keeping it under there will be added incentive to vacuum frequently.

Beautify the facial tissues. I don't know which is worse—a naked cardboard tissue box (no matter how colorful the design is) or a frilly tissue holder that looks like a dust storm waiting to happen. A box of tissues is a bathroom essential, but it can also be an eyesore. Make your tissue box work for your bathroom rather than against it by matching it to the bathroom decor. If you store your bathroom staples in decorative baskets, buy a tissue box–cover in a matching basket style. Oak bathroom? Get an oak tissue box to match. (I did.) Lots of chrome? Get a chrome box. Unique bathroom style? Buy a standard plastic box and cover it to match your decor.

Watch for rust and rot. There are lots of gorgeous styles of modern and antique metal and paper canisters, and also canisters of all kinds with decorative paper labels. I see them featured in lush magazine shots of bathrooms all the time, and they're supposed to be for storing cotton balls, cotton swabs, makeup squares, soap balls, and the like. But unless you have a guest bathroom that's used infrequently or a half-bath without a tub or shower, I'd advise saving these containers for a drier room. Glass, stainless steel, ceramic, wood, breathable basketry, plastic— there are lots of bathroom options that can stand up to the splashing and humidity better than metal and paper.

Add a little vanity. My bathroom's barely big enough to turn around in—and that's the *big* bathroom, not the half-bath in the laundry room. But I still needed more space—basically, space to set down clothes or put down small stuff on the way in the door. A dressing table or any other sizable surface was out of the question, so I stopped at a local antiques store that had an assortment of tiny children's vanity tables out front. These tables had three legs and were flat in back so they could butt up against a wall. The smallest was about 2 feet long and 1 foot wide at its widest—perfect! And it was already white, so it would blend into the bathroom wall. Best of all, it was on sale for $15!

Let there be light. In no room is a nightlight more essential than the bathroom. People need to be able to find the door and the light switch quickly and easily. Choose one that's attractive but not fussy, and put it where it will be out of reach of water.

Keep lamp cords off the floor. Yes, it's important to have lots of good light in a bathroom. But floor and table lamps, with their hazardous cords, are especially out of place here. Instead, use wall sconces, ceiling fixtures, and light strips to provide enough light.

ONWARD!

These tips will help you kick your bathroom clutter. But *keeping* the bathroom de-cluttered requires a combination of cunning, incentives, discipline, and threats. You're on your own with those! (But I know you can do it.)

Meanwhile, let's turn to some rooms that are easier to keep organized once you've cleared them out—the living and family rooms.

Chapter 8

Livable Living Rooms, Functional Family Rooms

Can't find any of the remotes under all the bags and magazines? Did Grandma sit on Jen's iPod last time she came over, buried as it was under the cushions? Wonder where your favorite mugs wandered off to, not to mention the cat? Formal living rooms that aren't used can become storage rooms when a family's accumulated clutter creeps into them. And any room with an entertainment center can become not a rec room but a *wreck* room as everybody's snacks, papers, and assorted projects pile up. But never fear—in this chapter, you'll learn how to clear out these rooms without making them into sterile showpieces.

PRIORITIES FOR LIVING AND FAMILY ROOMS

The first thing to do is to determine whether your living room *is* your family room (in which case you have only one room to worry about), or if you have a formal living room (it used to be called a parlor) where you would entertain guests, as well as a family room where your family actually "lives." In this case, decide which room needs your attention first, and then focus on it.

There's a third possibility, too—that you have only a formal living room that's supposed to be the "good room" for guests, but it either never gets used at all because you want to keep the furniture looking new (or protect your priceless antiques), or it's turned into a clutter repository, an upscale storage room, because it was never really used for anything else.

In this last case, the family has no relaxing place to get together and play, talk, read, watch TV, and entertain friends, so everybody probably either holes up in their bedrooms or piles into the kitchen. I'd like to suggest that, while a formal room like this works fine in a large, spacious house with plenty of other rooms for the family, or for households where formal entertaining is a frequent occurrence, if neither of these is the case, it's a waste of valuable living space. Who are you preserving it for?

Your family would be happier with a cheerful, comfortable gathering place. Or you could turn the living room into a home office, library, or craft room. Just because your parents, in-laws, and grandparents all had these formal rooms is no reason to continue the tradition if your lifestyle doesn't require it and the room isn't giving you and your family pleasure.

I have two friends whose cheerful, sunny front room is actually sealed off from the rest of the house in winter to conserve heat, since no one ever goes in there. Its many windows, hardwood floors, and serene views are completely wasted, a museum for unused furniture. Meanwhile, this couple spent quite a lot of money retrofitting a windowless basement that floods in very rainy periods to turn it into a family room. That's where they (literally) hole up, watching TV in the semidarkness while the sun streams in upstairs. And it's where they entertain their guests!

Mind you, this is not a tirade against antique furniture or beautifully crafted modern pieces. I love both and have both in my own home. But I *use* them—they're my everyday furniture. As a result, I get pleasure from them each and every day. In the case of the antiques, I can picture past generations lovingly using each piece just as I do, and in the case of the modern pieces, I enjoy thinking about the artisans crafting them. I refuse to live in a museum! Museums are beautiful, but they're not livable.

Hopefully, your family also lives in its space. Now you just have to make the most of it!

What Do You Use Your Room For?

Because a lived-in living or family room gets such a lot of use and foot traffic, before you do more than pick up the floor or straighten the cushions, you should give some thought to your layout. After all, the living/family room is the ultimate multitasker, performing some of the functions that go on in almost every other room in the house (except, hopefully, the bathroom!).

The first thing to do is to take this book into your living or family room. Look around and ask yourself what usually goes on in there. Does the family watch TV and movies, play video games, listen to music? Do the kids do their homework in there? Do people eat in there? What about reading, knitting, and other activities? Does the family play board games or work on crosswords, sudoku, or jigsaw puzzles? Do you or the kids entertain friends in this room? Do your kids and pets play on the floor? Is this where you pay your bills? Does it double as a music room, with guitars, keyboards, and a piano? Do you have a minibar in one part of the room? Do overnight guests sleep there?

Once you've thought about what you do in the room, think about exactly where you do it. Where is the activity taking place? What furniture is used for each activity? Is it convenient, comfortable, and well lit for its purpose? Is there enough or too much of it? Is it appropriate for the activity? What about walk-through space? Is it easy to move through the room, or are people always crashing into things? Try to look at the room as though you were an efficiency expert seeing it for the first time. What "works" in the room? What needs to be changed?

Make some notes about what's working and what's not as you look things over. It might help to sketch out the room as it looks now, just roughly blocking out and labeling furniture, and then sketch some alternative arrangements that might work better. If you'd enjoy using something more attractive than a rough sketch, there are plenty of room-design kits available in bookstores and online from sources like Amazon, including the *Home Quick Planner,* with reusable, peel-and-stick furniture, the *Room and Furniture Layout Kit,* and the *3D Virtual Reality Room Planner* CD-ROM.

Your goal is to make this room really work well for everyone who uses it (including your pets). Note what furniture needs to go into other rooms or out the

My Living Room—Before

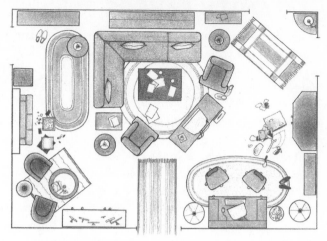

This living room is so cluttered that it isn't welcoming. There are no clear paths through the room. The furniture faces away from the fireplace. Furniture is in here that belongs in other rooms, and the furniture that does belong here isn't placed well.

My Living Room—After

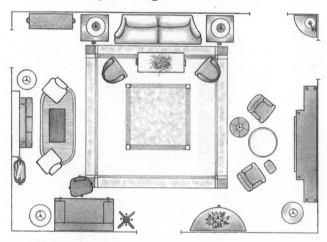

Same living room, different plan. This time, the furniture is arranged for comfort and use, the "stray" furniture has been relocated to rooms where it's more appropriate, and all piles have been picked up. Areas for reading and talking, watching movies or television, and relaxing in front of the fire have been created. An aquarium adds interest and helps family members relax. The room is easy to navigate without crashing into randomly placed furniture or clutter.

SANITY SAVERS

If your living or family room just doesn't meet your family's needs, it's time to get creative. Designing the space *you* want is a great sanity saver—and as my friends have found, everyone else will probably love it, too! Here's how some of my friends created the perfect space for their needs.

Let the light shine in. After flirting for years with the idea of a possible move to Maine, my friends Carolyn and Gary decided to remain in their Pennsylvania home. But rather than settling for less, they decided to reward themselves by adding on their perfect living/family room where they'd had a deck off the side of the house. Their new family or great room is wonderful—it has floor-to-ceiling windows that let in tons of light, ceiling fans to keep the air moving, and a propane "wood stove" that adds warmth and a romantic glow to the room. They also added floor-to-ceiling shelves on the wall that adjoined their existing home, so there's now plenty of room for beloved books, CDs, DVDs, and the occasional object or picture. Their new room is so welcoming that it's hard to get friends and family to abandon it, even for dinner! And it freed up space for them to create a real dining room in their home for the first time.

Indulge yourself. My friend Rudy inherited his present home, and its living room was small and dark. Rudy, who loves plants and birds, decided to add on a sunroom and make that his new living room. The result is a marvelous, light-filled space that lets him display his indoor plants and enjoy the colorful birds that flit around outside the windows. It's not a conventional living or family room, true, but it suits him and his needs, and it's so inviting visitors can't stay away.

Choose your own space. My friends Delilah and Chaz bought a house with a conventional living room—and they hated it. Instead, they converted a space they loved—their screen porch, with a fabulous view across their property to the mountains—into their living room. They sealed the screen windows and door with custom-made acrylic panels to keep the cold out, added a propane wood stove for warmth and atmosphere, set up a music system, hung gorgeous plants from Delilah's greenhouse, put down colorful Southwestern rugs, and added a comfy sofa and cushy armchairs around their wood stove. Given a choice of where to be in their beautiful home, I—and pretty much everybody else, including their Boston terrier, Duke—would opt for the porch-cum-living room. It's perfect!

door, what furniture you should move in from other rooms or buy, and how to group the furniture to make the best use of your space.

Many designers recommend clustering furniture by use—around the entertainment center, for example. I can't say I agree with this approach, though it's certainly practical. To me, clusters of furniture bunched around a room add up to clutter. I'd rather create a restful, open, multipurpose space, even if it means rearranging a chair to watch TV. But if the activity-based approach appeals to you, go for it! It may be the perfect solution for your family. And even I will admit that this design approach works well in a huge, cavernous room like some of today's great rooms, where furniture around the walls would get lost.

Once you feel comfortable with the big picture, it's time to take on the clutter. As you did in the previous chapters, start your de-cluttering process by setting some clutter-kicking priorities. The best way to begin is to take a good, hard look at the "before" state of the room, and then to visualize the "after."

A Living Room/Family Room Visualization

To get to your "after," you need to start with the "before"—the way things look right now. So get out some paper, or use the "My Living Room/Family Room—Before" form on page 148 (or make a photocopy of it and write on that). Write down every place there's clutter, and note what that clutter is. Things may look like a mess, but the clutter in these rooms is usually superficial, as you'll see when you start working on your list. It's not like dealing with the kitchen! Check each area of the room. Are there piles by the doors? Can you see the cushions on the sofa, much less sit on them? What about the coffee table?

Once you've jotted down a quick description of your living or family room's "before" state, it's time to move on to the "after"—how you want the room to look when you've kicked the clutter. Write it all down on a piece of paper, or in the "My Living Room/Family Room—After" form on page 148 or on as many photocopies of it as you need to do it justice. To make sure you're being realistic, look at the room every few minutes while you're doing this.

Your description can be short and to the point: "I don't want to see stacks of newspapers, catalogs, magazines, and mail all over the tables, floor, sofa, and chairs. I don't want dirty dishes, bags, crumbs, and drink rings all over the place.

My Living Room/Family Room—Before

_____
_____
_____
_____
_____
_____
_____
_____
_____
_____

My Living Room/Family Room—After

_____
_____
_____
_____
_____
_____
_____
_____
_____
_____

My Living Room/Family Room Priority List

I don't want to hear one more person whine that they've lost one of the several dozen remotes, their phone, their MP3 player, or anything else. And I don't want to break my neck on one of the kid's (or cat's) toys. I'd like to see all the CDs and DVDs in their cases and shelved in the entertainment center."

You can even create a detailed picture of exactly how you'd like your room to look if it were perfect (for you). You can picture the colors of the walls, woodwork, and window treatments; what the floor would look like; what furniture would be in the room, and how it would be arranged; whether there would be a fireplace; what art would be on the walls—everything.

Getting There

Now that you have captured your living or family room's "before" condition, listing all the specifics, and you've imagined its "after" appearance, you can finally prioritize the steps you'll need to take to get there from here. Again, bearing both "before" and "after" in mind, I'd recommend starting with what bothers you most about the "before" condition and working down from there. Focus on what matters most to you about the way your living room or family room looks, and make that your top priority. Then work your way down your list of concerns until you get to what's least important.

For example, you hate the big, ugly television and desperately want either one that hangs on the wall or an attractive entertainment center you can hide it in. If you want the sofa to be clutter-free so you and others can actually sit on it but right now it's piled high with magazines, empty potato chip bags, and other junk, one of your priorities will be to clean off the couch. Choose the most important thing you need to do, then make it Priority #1. Take your Before list and spell out what you need to do to arrive at the After state you want. Rank all the items on your list in order of importance and you're ready to get started.

Write down whatever's driving you to distraction on the "My Living Room/Family Room Priority List" on page 149 (or photocopy it, if you'd prefer), in descending order from most to least maddening. Now you have your priorities straight! Once you've finished, you can turn to the tips below to find ingenious ways of dealing with each problem.

THE LIVING ROOM/FAMILY ROOM TIPS

Just as in the kitchen, because so much goes on in the living or family room, I've divided the tips in this chapter into sections and grouped them by topic so it will be easier for you to find what you're looking for. Skim through the pages until you find where you want to start, and then get going!

Get the Big Picture

See what can go. Do you have furniture in the living or family room that's just taking up space? Maybe you have pieces nobody actually uses but that have somehow found their way in by default or because you felt at one point that you "needed" something there, but never thought about getting a more suitable piece once something was occupying the space. By now, you may have amassed a lot more furniture than you need—or you may need furniture you don't have room for because of all the "wrong" furniture that's in place. Take a hard look at each piece and see if it really belongs—if it's really serving a purpose now, if it's loved and used. Maybe it's a great piece but would work better someplace else in the house. Or maybe it's just time to send it to another home. (See Part Four: Trash [Yours] to Treasure [Theirs], beginning on page 349, for lots of ways to do that.)

A Cautionary Tale

One of my relatives was notorious in our family for the inhospitable nature of her home. Guests entered the house through a narrow corridor with boxes of unidentified stuff piled high on either side, slipping and sliding on a plastic sheet laid over the carpeting between the box barricades. It was like negotiating a landing strip. This hallway opened into the living room, which also had plastic not only on the carpet but also encasing every piece of furniture so guests couldn't somehow damage the upholstery by actually sitting on it. Trying to stay upright on any piece of furniture without sliding off on the slippery plastic was a feat few yoga masters could manage. (And mind you, this was department-store furniture, not priceless one-of-a-kind museum-quality stuff.) As a result, family visits were few and far between!

The moral of this story is: If your furniture and rugs are *that* valuable, auction them off at Christie's or Sotheby's, donate them to a museum, or lock them away in a room guests never see. Do your entertaining in an inviting room that everyone can enjoy. And get rid of those boxes!

Fill in the blanks. Now that you've evaluated what you have, you may realize that you're missing a few key pieces. Before you head to the store, think about the other rooms in your house and take a quick house tour with a notepad in hand. On the pad, write down what you need for the family or living room, then, as you take your house tour, see if a piece that's currently in another room would be a perfect fit for one of the items on your list. Be open-minded: Furniture doesn't have to serve the use it was made for (see the other tips in this chapter for more on that). As you're taking stock, think about furniture from the family room that might be better off in the room you're in now and if it would make sense to swap. Only when you've examined the options that are free and at your disposal should you consider heading off to the store or consulting a catalog.

Grow up. Does your living or family room look exactly like it did 20 years ago, when the kids were toddlers? Is it still displaying the furniture you moved in from your first apartment? Do you have very formal furnishings because you used to do a lot of entertaining for work, but now you're semiretired and would rather just kick back? Your life and needs may have changed while your furnishings stayed

5-Minute Fixes for Living Areas

Sometimes a list of clutter-cleaning priorities can seem so long and overwhelming that you wonder how you'll ever get through it. If that's how you feel, or if you're itching to get started but don't have much time, try one or two of these 5-Minute Fixes to get your feet wet. They're some of the easiest ways to start de-cluttering your living or family room. You'll be surprised by what you can accomplish in just 5 quick minutes, so get going!

Find the food. Nothing makes a room look messier, dirtier, or more cluttered than glasses and plates of forgotten food. Empty or otherwise, if the dishes are in the room and the diners aren't (unless, of course, they're in the bathroom), take those dishes to the kitchen and find a home for them in the dishwasher. Then tell the perpetrators you'll be finding a home for *them* if they don't start picking up after themselves!

Pack up the paper. Go into your family room, den, or living room—the place where you all actually sit and spend time when you're relaxing—and take a good look. See a bunch of magazines, newspapers, mail, and catalogs lying all over the place, spilling off tables, stacked on the sofa? Right. Get an empty copier-paper box from an office supply store, or a grocery bag, and stuff it all in there. Then tell everyone they have 24 hours to collect their stuff and put it in their respective rooms or where it actually belongs, or else it will go out with the recycling. This goes for your stuff, too.

Unstuff a shelf. If you're a bookaholic like me, your shelves are probably overflowing with books behind books and on top of books. Pick a shelf, any shelf, and try to find a few books to donate, consign, or give away. See if you can't get five books off the shelf (though even two would be a lot, in my experience). As you

the same. Think about what you and your family need *now*, and make sure your furnishings are supporting your needs.

Create a wall storage system. If you cover an entire wall with cabinets and shelving, all designed as a unit, you'll gain maximum storage space while keeping a uniform, uncluttered look. Put the most dominant element—usually your entertainment center—in the middle, with a row of cabinets below and shelves all around and over it.

sort, picture me jumping up and down while waving shredded-paper pom-poms and screaming, "Rah! Rah! Hurrah!"

Deck the dustables. If your shelves look like mine, they display a glorious array of little dustables in a neat line in front of the books. Yes, of course you love them. But remind yourself of the magic word: rotation. Put them in a shoe box or plastic storage bin (labeled with the contents, naturally), and choose one or two (okay, three) objects from the hordes within to actually display. Don't worry, they're still in there! Promise yourself you'll change the display every month.

Rein in the remotes. Sheesh! No wonder obesity is such a problem in America, with clutter hard on its heels. I'm always stupefied by the number of remote controls in any given household, and even more stupefied by the reluctance of pretty much everybody to drag themselves over to the actual appliance to push a few buttons. But then, I feel that way about drive-thrus at banks, fast-food chains, and pharmacies, too. Get out and walk, people! But I know I don't stand a huge chance of getting you all to give up your remotes, so here's an alternative suggestion: Get a box, tray, basket, or other container to put all of your remotes in. Mail-order catalogs carry tidy stand-up containers, but anything that corrals them so they're not spilling over every available surface works for me. What about labeling them while you're at it, so you know at a glance which appliance goes with which remote? Or get one universal remote and put the rest away.

Change your coffee table. This is an oldie but a goodie: Use a blanket chest as a coffee table so it can double as storage space. Chests are an especially convenient place to store afghans and lap robes so everyone can grab one if they get cold while sitting—but only if you don't pile so much stuff on top of the "coffee table" that no one ever opens it to get them!

Make sure you can move. Being able to move comfortably through the room—whether you're just passing through with a big box or basket of stuff or you're moving from the sofa to the bookcase or entertainment center—is essential, both to create a feeling of uncluttered openness in the room and to enhance your family's and guests' pleasure in being in it. If you have an open floor plan, with furniture spread around the walls and a rug in the center, make sure you don't block the doors by placing jutting furniture too close to them. If you cluster your furniture to create different sections within the room, leave plenty of space for navigation around each cluster. Picture two kids running through the room. Could they do it without hitting anything?

Let there be light. In a room that's used as much as your living or family room, lighting is at least as important as room to move, comfortable furniture, and ample storage. I actually decided to buy my cottage home based on the marvelous amount of natural light that streams through the living room and kitchen (and this despite the deep yellow of the living-room walls). This was especially important to me because where I live, there are seldom overhead lights. I've never understood why this was—where I grew up in the South, every room in every house had a ceiling light. But the lack of a ceiling light can make rooms really dark and shadowy, so make sure your room has enough usable, pleasing light to be inviting and to make it easy to actually use every part of the room for its intended purpose. A ceiling fan with lights can add welcome air circulation, as well. And wall sconces add light without taking up floor or table space.

But not too much light. Or I should say, not too many lights. Lots of little lamps all over the place look junky and become dustables, not to mention adding endless cords that can become tripping hazards. Choose a few good floor or table lamps that suit your decor and give off good light, and pack the rest up for Goodwill, a consignment shop, or the antiques store. (Or maybe you could use one in another room.) If you have a lamp you can't bear to get rid of but have no place for, remember that you can rotate lamps just like you do collectibles. If you have floor lamps that aim up rather than down, I'd get rid of those first. Yes, they're trendy, but they're also useless. Why would you want to spotlight your wall and ceiling? Good grief. Make all your lamps work as hard as you do. Keep the ones that light the space where you are!

Watch your head. If you have a chandelier, make sure it's high enough so it's not a head-hitting hazard for you or the tallest person in your family. Ouch! If a fixture hangs down low enough to hit someone, it's hanging in your eye space and creating visual clutter, too. Raise it or get a different fixture.

Keep it clean. Speaking of chandeliers, avoid those with zillions of multicolored fruits, flowers, or other assorted whatsits. More visual clutter! Clear crystals in a simple pattern are best.

Add life and light. I can't resist putting this in because it's so dear to my heart. Few things add as much quiet, fascinating entertainment to a home as a large, diverse aquarium, with colorful fish, plants, frogs, snails, shrimp, rocks, and branches. (Note that word "large"—a small aquarium is more clutter, unless it's in a kid's room.) The family and pets will watch for hours—but only if the aquarium is placed where it can be seen. And the bright, filtered aquarium light adds enormous ambiance. I love creating gorgeous naturalistic aquascapes, then sitting back and enjoying "fish TV" with my cats. But location is everything—if you can't find a place to display your aquarium where everyone can see it but no one can knock it over, it's just another maintenance chore.

Pick Up the Pieces

Keep a carry-all handy. Keep a decorative basket in the living or family room so it's easy to centralize things that have strayed in by mistake. You can take the basket with you as you go from room to room, replacing things in their rightful places. Or designate the basket as the family "Lost and Found" and make it a rule that everyone must collect his or her own stuff from the basket before bed (or before guests arrive) and take it away with them—or else! Let them know that anything that's not claimed will be tossed or given away.

Keep it moving. My friend Chris has a clutter philosophy we could all use. "Never walk empty-handed into another room in your home," Chris says. "Chances are, there's something you can take along to put away." This is especially true of the living or family room, and it's also true in reverse: Try to never walk *out* of the family room without taking something with you to put away.

Straighten your stacks. Neaten up those piles of magazines and catalogs on the coffee and side tables as you pass through the room and before bed. Not only will this simple act make the room look cleaner and less cluttered, it will also help you avoid the hateful paper avalanches that pitch magazines, catalogs, and the like all over your floor and tables in slippery slides.

Rack it up. Okay, a magazine rack is a more organized-looking way to store magazines and catalogs. But outdated magazines are not just going to vaporize on their own as new issues arrive. To mangle a phrase from the real-estate industry: rotation, rotation, rotation. Recycle old catalogs and put old magazines in the local library's giveaway pile (after cutting off the mailing labels). If you really, *really* want to keep something in either one, cut it out and toss the rest of the catalog or magazine.

Put up your puzzles. Cabinets with shelves and doors are the perfect storage places for board games and jigsaw puzzles. They're out of sight but within reach of even the smallest hands.

Tin your toys. Toys like Lincoln Logs, Tinkertoys, and Legos can have a billion little pieces. Corral them in decorative tins—you probably have some left over from candy, cookies, fruitcake (yikes), or popcorn that you received as Christmas gifts. If not, thrift stores and yard sales are always good sources. Needless to say, store just one kind of game per tin!

Be a mad hatter. Decorative hatboxes have made a comeback—but for storage, not hats. They're not as durable as tins, but on the plus side, they're quieter. If you need to store multipiece games on open shelves, hatboxes are an attractive solution.

Get a game center. No, I don't mean a PlayStation or an Xbox! In this case, I'm talking about an attractive wooden end table that has drawers that double as game boards and, of course, hold all the various game pieces. (Find them in catalogs like Solutions; see page 48.) If your family's wild for games like dominos, Chinese checkers, backgammon, chess, and the like, this is a great way to keep them at hand but out of sight.

Show it off if you can't hide it. My boyfriend, Rob, is a chess fanatic, always poring over the board (and trying to trick me into playing—and losing). Rather than pull the chess board out and set it up every night, we've made it a design feature by using a table with a built-in chess board inset in the top (also good for checkers) and a decorative chess set (Rob favors "Pirates versus the British Navy") on display.

Tote your yarn. If you enjoy working on knitting, crochet, quilting, or other yarn- or fabric-related projects while relaxing in the family room, tuck your supplies into a tote. You can find beautiful padded totes at yarn stores and quilt shops, but any sturdy, roomy tote, including the canvas boat-and-tote ones made famous by L.L. Bean, will work fine. I keep the yarn, needles, and other necessities for my current project in the tote and store my other yarns and supplies in boxes on a closet shelf, where they peacefully wait their turn. Bring your tote out while you're working on the project, and tuck it away out of sight in a cabinet or closet when you're not.

Take your plants to new heights. I love houseplants, but it takes only a few cat-induced disasters or guests reaching for a cactus to make you think twice about keeping them in easy reach. Instead, install hooks in your ceiling and hang plants in view but out of reach. You'll add life, interest, and more oxygen to the room. But again, don't block your light, don't dot the ceiling with a clutter of plants, don't hang them where they'll become head-banging hazards, and do rotate them when they're no longer looking their best.

Don't pile on the pillows. If you can't see your sofa and chairs because of all the throw pillows, you have too many pillows. Follow the three-pile rule to sort them out: Put the ones you love in the keepers pile; put the torn, stained, beat-up ones in the trash pile; and put the ones you don't like, need, or want anymore in the donation pile. If your favorite comfy pillow is battered but you can't bear to part with it, give it a facelift with a new cover. And what about the handmade pillow from Grandma Rose, the moose pillow from your spouse's co-worker Bob, the designer plaid pillow from your best friend—those sacred cows that no one likes or uses but that you're afraid to throw away? First, make *sure* no one likes them— if your son turns out to love the moose pillow, he can take it to his room, after all. Otherwise, take them to Goodwill, the Salvation Army, or the Society of St. Vincent de Paul. (Note: If you're really afraid that some day you'll wake up hating yourself for tossing out Granny's handiwork, you can always take it off the pillow and store it flat—maybe in your new blanket-chest coffee table. (See "Change your coffee table" on page 153.)

What about the Walls?

Don't clutter up the walls. I often see groups of a dozen or so paintings hung from ribbons over a mantel in design magazines. My own parents devoted a wall in their library to a museum-style display of art. But if you think back to your experiences in museums, or antiques shows, or galleries—anywhere a lot of art is displayed cheek-by-jowl on a wall—you may recall becoming exhausted. That's because seeing such a visual barrage tires the eyes, and that tires us. It's also why savvy museumgoers focus on a room or display per visit, savoring the experience and then getting out before they're worn out. And bear in mind that in a museum, there's nothing competing with the art for our attention—unlike a home full of furniture and other distractions! Avoid visual clutter. If you have more art than you can display in a spacious, focused manner, rotate your pieces. Don't show them all at once!

Hang pictures at eye level. Put your art where you can appreciate it. If you're very short and your spouse is very tall, or vice-versa, you have two choices: Hang the art midway between your eye levels, or hang each person's favorites at his or her eye level.

Showcase unusual art. If you have a striking quilt, a fantastic dream catcher, or a woven masterpiece, remember that you can display it as wall art. As long as the object is fairly flat—you don't want anyone to crash into it!—it can make a striking centerpiece or unusual accent. And if it's on the wall, you'll not only get to enjoy it, you won't have to find a place to store it!

Put up a mirror. A mirror can make your room look more spacious, and it can increase the amount of light. But note that little word "a." Multiple mirrors create a funhouse effect, as people moving through the room catch fragmented glimpses of themselves (or others) and flashes of passing objects. Instead, use one large mirror and position it carefully. If it faces windows it will bring in natural light and make it seem that both sides of the room open into the great outdoors. But if it faces a messy, cluttered view (say, a chaotic bookcase), it will double the clutter a viewer sees!

Hang the television. Even your TV can function as wall art if it's a flat-screen, wall-mounted unit. Not only does this save floor space, it also looks much better than a bulky television, and it makes the room more open and easier to navigate.

Show off with shelves. Wooden display shelves are small, ornamental, individually mounted shelves that will hold a single vase, potted plant, or three-dimensional piece of artwork or collectible. Attached with molly bolts (had to mention this because of my dog, Molly), they're a sturdy way to get breakables off tables and shelves and up to eye level. But use them sparingly to avoid a cluttered look.

Branch out. I had to mention this one because it's so unusual and interesting. My friend Edith, one of the most creative people I know, collects ornaments. But she also collects cats. To avoid the inevitable breakage, she displays her ornament collection by hanging groups of ornaments from branches, then mounting the branches on her wall so the ornaments hang at eye level.

Don't trash the mantelpiece. If you're lucky enough to have a fireplace, don't junk up the mantel with unsightly, distracting, and potentially flammable clutter. Except at Christmas, candlesticks are probably enough, especially if you have an impressive painting over the mantel. You can always add interest by creating unusual groupings of candlesticks. And you can add a bowl, vase, basket, or sculpture if you don't have a strong painting to hold the space.

Books and Bookcases

Think of books as art. If you have a bookcase full of colorful books, it has the same visual effect as a major piece of wall art. That's why white or neutral-colored walls are a smart choice if you have a lot of books. And no patterned wallpaper, please!

Take your books to new heights. For the same reason, give your books maximum space and visual impact by choosing a floor-to-ceiling bookcase. Put the books you read or refer to most often where they're easiest to reach, placing less-used books on higher shelves. Put the kids' books within their reach on the lower shelves.

Add built-in bookcases. Nothing adds class to a room like an entire wall of built-in bookcases. And they hold so much! Match their style to your room's decor. Make them deep enough to hold big books and LPs, but not so deep that they waste space (18 inches is about right). Fixed shelves that are the same height across the width of the bookcases add a unifying quality and aren't as chaotic-looking as randomly spaced shelves. But some of the shelves can be taller than others, as long as all the shelves across that row are tall.

Shelve books upright. Books shelved horizontally look messy, like they've fallen over. And it's harder to extract a book from a horizontal pile than to simply pull one from the shelf.

Use bookends. Speaking of books that have fallen over, keep that from happening to your books by inserting bookends every couple of feet. The flat metal ones available from office-supply stores are thin enough to be almost undetectable.

Shelve magazines in acrylic cases. These durable cases, available from housewares stores and catalogs, hold a year's worth of magazines organized, upright, and together, making them fit on a shelf like a dictionary. You can read the spines at a glance through the clear plastic. Remember to go through your shelved magazines at least annually to see if you can finally bear to part with them.

Show off your bookshelves. You don't have to just store books, magazines, DVDs, videos, video games, and records on your shelves, either! Save some shelves to showcase favorite crafts or collectibles. But remember, less is more here. One piece of beautiful pottery or a striking basket or sculpture is a lot more dramatic than a clutter of dustables. (And remember, you can rotate them.)

Glass-in the good stuff. If you want to showcase a collection of valuable breakables, such as pottery or glass, put it in a glass-fronted bookcase. Choose the most impressive pieces to display, and arrange them in the most attractive manner. No overcrowding! You can dress up a shelved collection with complementary staging—for example, displaying Southwestern Pueblo pottery on hand-woven Navajo horse blankets, which are small enough to fit on the shelves. Remember: If it looks intentional, it's not clutter. And if it's safe behind glass doors, there's no dusting, either. If you have kids, lock the case—just in case.

Light up your treasures. Install under-shelf lighting over the shelves you plan to use to display collectibles. They'll look gorgeous!

Make beautiful music. CD players are now made to attach under shelves. Choose a shelf, attach the CD player, and add the small speakers to other shelves to create gorgeous stereo sound. What a space-saver! You can store CDs on the shelf below the CD player.

That's Entertainment!

Entertain in an armoire. Use an armoire—those huge, antique, freestanding closets, also called wardrobes—to house your entertainment center. They're readily available at antiques stores and flea markets. Add extra shelves for DVDs, CDs, video games, and videos, and you're ready to go!

Downsize the TV. I know this is blasphemy in these days of room-size televisions that turn your living or family room into a home theater, but you'll save space if you get a smaller TV. It can fit more unobtrusively into a cabinet or on a shelf. And you have to admit, TVs are ugly! Your room will look a lot better—and bigger—without that monster machine squatting in the middle of it. But make sure the smaller, sleeker model is big enough for everyone to watch comfortably and that it has a high-quality picture.

Make it mobile, part one. No room for an entertainment center? Get a rolling cart, available from any home store or housewares catalog. At my house, the TV, DVD/VCR, remotes, and to-be-watched DVDs (or videos) are all on a small rolling cart. When Rob and I want to watch a movie or program, we roll the cart over and plug everything in; when the show's over, the cart rolls back against the wall, out of the way until it's needed again.

Make it mobile, part two. Make it easy to watch TV wherever you are with a swivel turntable. These handsome stands or unobtrusive flat turntables are sized to fit your TV and let you turn it 360 degrees for easy viewing wherever you are—without having to move furniture. Great idea!

Stash the CDs. CDs need to be upright and easily accessible, not piled horizontally in an avalanche-prone skyscraper or spawning orphan jewel cases. Buy a CD

Dear Claire,

My family room is like a minefield because of the CDs and DVDs that are all over the floor. I've tried picking them up and nagging everybody else to pick them up, but to no avail. They seem to multiply faster than dust bunnies. Yesterday, I stepped on a jewel case and skidded clear across the floor! This has to stop before someone gets hurt. How can I get my floor back?

—Musically Challenged

Dear Musically Challenged,

Gather your family. Explain that *their* cluttering almost broke *your* neck and that you can't enjoy your family room with trash all over the floor. Both conditions are unacceptable. Then announce that everyone has exactly half an hour to put all their CDs and DVDs in their designated places, and after that time, any and all CDs, DVDs, and cases found on the floor will be taken to Goodwill. Three "make sures" here: 1. Make sure they know you mean it. 2. Make sure your spouse is apprised and on board before you hold your meeting. 3. Make sure there *is* a designated place for CD and DVD storage. Then stick to your guns! After the kids have to buy a replacement CD or DVD with their own money, they'll be less likely to play fast and loose with your floor.

Good luck,
Claire

rack and use it. You can get handsome wooden models that store 1,000 CDs (in their cases) from mail-order catalogs, CD "bookcases" in numerous styles, a CD pedestal, wire and plastic towers, CD-holding apothecary cabinets, and CD holders made to look like pretty much anything else you can think of, so get something that appeals to you and matches the rest of your furnishings. You can also find some very interesting CD racks for a few dollars at thrift stores. I'm very proud of the ultra-modern one I found at Goodwill! Don't want the CD racks on view? Buy shorter ones and hide them in the cabinet that houses your entertainment center or stereo.

Book your CDs and DVDs. Want to ditch those jewel cases once and for all? Store CDs and DVDs and their booklets or artwork in specially made notebooks with sleeves. The Herrington catalog (see page 48) has leather-bound CD and

DVD notebooks that look just like high-end books. They even feature labels for the spines, so you can group all your rock, country, comedy, or action discs together. Set them on your bookshelves with pride!

Consolidate your stereo equipment. Still clinging to your clunky, battered, space-eating stereo from the seventies? Give it up. Play your LPs on one of the many styles of Crosley turntables, widely available through mail-order catalogs. They're like a boom box for records—the speakers and player are all contained in an attractive retro wooden box not much bigger than a hatbox. The sound is good, and what a space-saver! You can buy models with CD and cassette players, a CD burner, and a radio, too, if you like an all-in-one. And you can buy a matching stand to hold the player and your records, CDs, and cassettes. It's an attractive, affordable, space-saving solution!

Make your furniture work harder. Choose furniture for your family room based on how hard it will work for you and how well it fits in with the room's decor. You don't need high-tech furniture to store high-tech stuff. If your family room has a country theme, look beyond the purpose the furniture was intended for and see what it can actually do for you. Can that quaint little drop-front cabinet hold the family's collection of videos and DVDs? Will the country pine cupboard double as a place to hold Dad's vintage collection of LPs?

Make Room for Guests

Get a sofa bed. Sofa beds can be lifesavers if you have frequent sleepovers or, like me, you don't have a designated guest room. Try it before you buy it—get a comfortable one you wouldn't mind sleeping on yourself. Of course, if you already have a less-than-comfy model, you can always add a featherbed or even an air mattress on top. But even without the added softness, it's still bound to be more comfortable than a futon!

Take to the air. Inflatable air mattresses are wonderful ways to add extra sleeping space. The thick ones available now are incredibly comfortable, and with plug-in pumps, it's a minute's work to set one up (and to deflate it, too, if your pump is reversible). Some of the beds have fold-out legs to accommodate those who'd rather not sleep on the floor. You can also use an air bed, as noted in the previous tip, like a second mattress on top of a sofa bed; that will make it really cushy.

Quick Fixes

Guests arriving on short notice? Grab a box, a hamper—even a trash bag!—and quickly toss in everything that's cluttering the floor, chairs, sofa, and coffee table. Stash the bag in a closet or room your guests won't go in. Your living room will look guest-ready in a flash! (Just don't forget to sort through that bag once they're gone.)

Try a fold-out. Some sofas and chairs are made of connected cushions that unfold to create a single (chair) or double (sofa) bed. They're available from home catalogs like Plow & Hearth (see page 47).

A Place for Everything

Add an ottoman. Ottomans, those big square cushioned footstools, can turn practically any chair into the equivalent of a recliner. But they have other uses, too. Not only can one function as additional seating, but many catalogs and stores now carry hollow ottomans with tops that lift up to reveal hidden storage. It's the perfect size to hide an afghan and pillow for an afternoon snooze on the sofa, knitting and crocheting supplies (safe from the cats), or linens for the sofa bed.

Get a sofa table. Sofa tables are high, narrow tables made especially to stand behind a sofa, basically creating a full-length "sofa shelf." This is a useful place to stash reading materials, reading glasses, and other supplies, as well as a plate and glass or cup, all within easy reach. (Just make sure you take dishes to where they belong when you leave the room, or you'll leave clutter behind.) If your sofa doesn't back up against a wall but the back is out of sight (say, angled against a corner), the sofa table can also be a good place to stash toys in baskets or colorful plastic tubs (sold in garden catalogs for carrying weeds, soil, and plants, and in housewares catalogs for a multitude of uses). Just make sure there's easy access to the back of the sofa for both you and the kids.

Work your windows, part one. Don't let the space beneath your windows go to waste. It's the perfect place to put an organizer bench with a cushioned seat and storage cubbies or a lift-up seat with storage beneath. If you can see the storage area, as is the case with cubbies, use attractive square wicker or rattan baskets to contain and conceal what you're storing.

Work your windows, part two. The space beneath windows is also perfect for a low bookcase or bookcase table.

Work your windows, part three. Don't limit yourself to the obvious! I have a roomy hanging sideboard under one of my living-room windows.

Don't forget your doors. Put the space above and around your doors to work with an above-door shelf and narrow shelves or cabinets on either side.

Screen it out. A decorative screen can hide a multitude of sins (from the TV to a folded card table) when they're not in use. A screen can even hide a workstation when you want it out of sight for more formal entertaining. Find one to suit your decor, either new from a housewares store or catalog or from a flea market, thrift store, consignment shop, or antiques store. (Thrift shops often have screen frames with damaged or missing covers available for practically nothing. If you're handy, you can cover them with cloth or heavy ornamental handmade paper to match your room's look.)

Use your fireplace year-round, part one. If you have a fireplace, it's unlikely that you use it in the warm months. This is the perfect time to turn it into "found" storage space! Put whatever you need to keep out of view in the (cleaned and swept, please) fireplace, then conceal it behind one of those decorative fire screens or chimney boards until it's needed.

Use your fireplace year-round, part two. You can also turn an unused fireplace into a display area. Besides the massive dried flower arrangements you often see in fireplaces in design magazines, I've seen awesome candle groupings, ornaments piled high in glass vases and hurricanes, even a gorgeous poinsettia or striking houseplant (these will need lighting or frequent rotation to better-lit areas).

Put your tables to work. The coffee table and sofa table aren't the only things you can use for storage. Instead of simple end tables, use nightstands or small chests with lots of drawers. Bedside tables have drawers with plenty of room for reading glasses, coasters, remote controls, pens, and other necessities, and antique versions are handsome enough to display in the living or family room without apology.

Choose bookcase tables. Mail-order catalogs carry handsome end tables called bookcase tables because they're skinny (just 12 inches deep) like bookcases and have shelves for books, magazines, tissues, and other chair-side necessities. If your family loves to read, these are the perfect end tables for you. They're sized so the top comes just to sofa-arm height. Nestle one against each side of the sofa, set a coaster and glass or mug on top, and you're good to go!

Table your collection. You can display a prized collection without worrying about it becoming a bunch of dustables if you house it in your coffee table. Mine is a rectangular cherry table with a type drawer (from the days when printers set type by hand and stored it in shallow drawers) on top and a cherry-framed glass top over that. The type drawer displays prized fossils, seashells, and buttons, safely shown off under glass where everyone can admire them. It's quite a conversation piece! Mine was custom-made by my great-uncle Max, but I have seen gorgeous coffee (or "cocktail") tables available commercially with glass tops and drawers that combine display, style, *and* storage.

ONWARD!

Are you excited about your living or family room now? I hope so! It's the most fun room to transform. And how satisfying it is to watch a chaotic, cluttered, uncomfortable mess turn into the most delightful and best-loved room in the whole house. It warms my heart to think of you sitting in your clutter-free family room, relaxing and enjoying yourself.

But now it's time to travel to one of the most neglected and least-loved rooms in most homes: the dining room. In the next chapter, you'll find tons of tips on transforming your dining room from wasteland to wonderland. Let's eat!

Chapter 9

De-Cluttering the Dining Room

So *that's* where the table went! Like a formal living room, the dining room can become a storage center, especially if the family eats in the kitchen, in their rooms, or in front of the TV. And there's that nice big work space just begging to be used for homework or bill-paying. In this chapter, you'll find solutions aplenty for restoring order to dining-room chaos, and you'll learn how to make the most of the space when you're not using it for meals.

PRIORITIES FOR DINING ROOMS

As in the living room/family room chapter, the first and most important step here is evaluating what you actually use your dining room for. Does your family eat there? My mother served us three meals a day at the dining room table. But your family might eat at the kitchen table or in the family room, instead. Do you entertain in your dining room? My friends Delilah and Chaz love to have guests in their dining room, and they pull out all the stops to make the meal unforgettable. And my friends Carolyn and Gary are kind enough to host a group of us every week for the "Friday Night Supper Club" I organized (I cook, they host, another friend brings wine, another dessert, everybody enjoys themselves). But you may find that you really only use that big, imposing table to serve meals at Thanksgiving and Christmas.

So what's the room doing the rest of the year? Do the kids do homework at the table? Do you pay bills? Is it your default craft room? Has it become a museum room, sealed off and unused? Is it a storage room, full of boxes and bags? Does anybody ever really go in there?

If your family still eats their meals in the dining room, congratulations! But if they don't, it's no cause for shame. Instead, look at it as an opportunity—a "free" room waiting to be reclaimed. You can use that space. This chapter will help you see your dining room with new eyes and make the most of it no matter what you use it for.

As I suggested in earlier chapters on other rooms, start your dining room de-cluttering process by setting some clutter-kicking priorities. You can do that by focusing on what matters most to you about the way your dining room looks and then working your way through a list of clutter issues until you get to what matters least. Then you're done! But before you can set priorities, you first need to assess the current state of the dining room and see what needs to be done. Take a good, hard look at the "before" state of the room, and then visualize the "after."

A Dining Room Visualization

To get to your "after," you need to start with the "before"—the way things look right now. So get out some paper or use the "My Dining Room—Before" form (or make a photocopy of it and write on that). Write down every place there's clutter in the room, and note what that clutter is. In the dining room, one of two things is usually going on: Either things that don't belong are crammed in there, so it's a cluttered mess, or it's a sterile, underused, and obviously unloved space. In either case, you can fix the problem and transform the room into one that works for you and your family.

So take a minute now to write down your "before" so you can get to your "after." Is the table piled with mail or catalogs? Are craft or school projects spread over the table? Are there coats and hats plopped on chairs? Are the houseplants dead from lack of attention? Is that wheeled serving cart or silver chest creating an obstacle course rather than serving a useful purpose? Write it all down.

My Dining Room—Before

_____
_____
_____
_____
_____
_____
_____
_____
_____
_____

My Dining Room—After

_____
_____
_____
_____
_____
_____
_____
_____
_____
_____

Once you've taken a quick inventory of your dining room's "before" state—its existing clutter problems—it's time to move on to the "after"—how you want the room to look when you've kicked the clutter. Write it all down on a piece of paper or on the "My Dining Room—After" form on page 169 (or on as many photocopies of it as you need to do it justice). To make sure you're being realistic, look at the room every few minutes while you're doing this.

Your description can be short and to the point: "I'd like to actually see the surface of the dining room table! I'd like to open up the room and put it to use. I'd like to be able to open the doors of the china cabinet without unleashing an avalanche. I'd like a room that's open and bright, with white walls, lots of wicker, and plants—almost a sunroom—rather than the dark paneling and big, heavy old mahogany dining room set that's in there now."

Or you can create a detailed picture of exactly how you'd like your room to look if it were perfect (for you). You can picture the colors of the walls, woodwork, and window treatments; what the floor would look like; what furniture would be in the room and how it would be arranged; how the room would be lit; what art would be on the walls—everything.

Getting There

Now that you have captured your dining room's "before" condition, listing all the specifics, and you've imagined its "after" appearance, you can finally prioritize the steps you'll need to take to get there from here. Maybe you really want to clear out the antiquated furniture you inherited from Aunt Ethel and have always hated and put in pieces that are more functional and that suit your family better. Or perhaps you want to create a space where it's easy to transition from eating to homework or crafts. Or you'd like to add a china cabinet on the back wall for much-needed storage.

Write down whatever's driving you to distraction on the "My Dining Room Priority List" (or photocopy it, if you'd prefer), in descending order from most to least maddening. Now you have your priorities straight! Once you've finished, you can turn to the tips on the next page to find ingenious ways of dealing with each problem.

My Dining Room Priority List

_____

_____

_____

_____

_____

_____

_____

_____

THE DINING ROOM TIPS

Add a centerpiece. Set out some candles and flowers or a beautiful bowl. People will be less likely to trash the table if it's decorated. And a clean, uncluttered table says, "Welcome!"

Store your dishes in the dining room. If you eat in the dining room, that's where you should put your china, glasses, cups, silverware—whatever you use every day. If you keep your dishes in the kitchen cabinets, someone will just have to carry them into the dining room two or three times a day. Instead, keep them where you use them.

Corner your china. A corner cupboard is a great piece for the dining room. It's space-saving and handsome, with closed cabinets below and shelves on top. You can use the shelves to display prized dishes or bigger or awkwardly shaped pieces—pitchers, the teapot, the turkey platter—and keep your plates, cups, and saucers dust-free down below.

Try the pie. A pie chest—one of those old-time cupboards with patterned tin fronts—makes a wonderful dish cabinet if it suits your dining room's decor.

Go for the buffet. A buffet or sideboard not only holds dishes, but also provides a long, showy surface for candlesticks, silver, and bigger pieces that would be awkward to fit into cabinets.

5-Minute Fixes for Dining Rooms

Jump-start your clutter-kicking process with these fast, easy tips.

Table the trash. Dining rooms tend to be trash magnets, especially if they're used for things besides eating—like doing homework and crafts projects. Crumpled papers, yarn ends, broken beads, napkins, a half-eaten cookie (she doesn't really like that kind), an empty pen, peeled-off crayon paper . . . they all end up scattered all over the table. Ugh. Rather than trying to stop the trash flow, contain it. Make sure you keep an attractive but functional wastebasket in the room, encourage everyone to use it, and empty it often. Don't forget to check the floor and chairs daily to make sure that none of these objects—especially round ones like beads and crumbs—have escaped captivity. Unsightly problem solved!

Clean your plates. Get the plates off the table unless it's set for a meal or you keep fine china out as a display. (My mother kept her gold-rimmed serving platters on our large antique dining table, with candelabra on each side—but that was all she had on the table so it looked impressive, not cluttered.) Don't let dishes—even clean dishes—pile up on the table between meals. Besides inviting breakage, it looks cluttered.

Check the chairs. It's amazing what can end up on dining-room chairs, from the dog's leash to that bill you couldn't find last week, spare change to a stack of CDs. Don't use your dining-room chairs for storage. Clean them off and then

Add an armoire. Need lots of storage space? An armoire or wardrobe fits the bill nicely. And if the dining-room table's your main crafting area, an armoire is an ideal place to store your craft supplies. There's plenty of room for tons of supplies for beading, knitting, quilting, egg-painting, scrapbooking—you name it!

Dress it up. A handsome dresser can be a perfect piece for the dining room, holding plenty of linens, everyday tablecloths, table runners, napkins, placemats, trivets, and napkin rings. Just make sure it's a good fit with the rest of your furnishings.

Box it up. Seasonal dishes, like a set of Christmas china or Valentine mugs, take up a lot of cabinet space. If you really can't bear to sell them or give them away, store them in labeled boxes in the attic or an out-of-the-way nook until it's time to set them out. Use your dining-room storage for dishes and glasses you use more often.

check them daily. You'll feel better every time you sit down on a clean chair for a meal—or a visitor pulls out a chair and doesn't find a surprise on the seat!

Watch the rug. If you have a patterned rug in your dining room, it can amass camouflaged clutter—clutter that's easy to step on or trip over but that remains almost invisible against the pattern. Kids' toys, cat toys, coins, food, pens, paper clips . . . find it before it finds you.

Ditch the dishes. Are you holding on to chipped, cracked, or broken china and crystal? Have you gotten tired of some of your dishes but haven't gotten around to getting rid of them? Toss the broken stuff and box the rest for the thrift store. If your cracked or broken pieces come from your good set or just a set you love, check Replacements, Ltd. (www.replacements.com) to see if you can find replacements in good shape. They carry more than 200,000 china, crystal, and silver patterns, some of them more than 100 years old.

Clear the sideboard. Has your sideboard turned into a drop-off zone for keys, glasses, backpacks, and papers? If the answer is yes, take a wastebasket in one hand and a decorative basket in the other and make a clean sweep. Trash in the wastebasket, stuff that belongs in the hall (or in someone's room) in the other. Set the decorative basket in the hall with a "Lost and Found" sign, and tell the family to leave your sideboard alone!

Wrap it up. If you have a full set of sterling silverware, tuck it on a shelf in the cabinet in its own tarnish-resistant box. No box? Buy tarnish-resistant cloth silverware holders. They're sized to hold each type of silverware, from dainty shrimp forks to large knives. Each cloth has slots to hold individual forks, spoons, or knives. When you've inserted all your pieces, you simply roll up the cloth and tie it into a bundle. Put the bundles in a drawer and they'll be ready to wash and use. No more tedious polishing!

Divide it up. Store your everyday silverware, or flatware, in a utensil organizer or in one of your dining-room storage pieces. There are some really attractive ones out there these days, so get a nice one—don't use a kitschy molded plastic model in the dining room. (Unless, of course, you have a fifties retro dining-room theme!)

Shelve it. Built-in shelving can create a gorgeous wall perfect for dining-room dish storage. If this look works for your room, go for it! I suggest that you put the shelves against one of the end walls, though—preferably the one at the "back" of the room, away from the windows. This will maximize the wall space without the shelves seeming obtrusive or overwhelming the room. A reminder: Glass doors keep dishes clean and dust-free.

Add music to your meals. Specially designed CD players fit under a shelf, taking up no valuable storage space. Tuck one into your dining-room shelves, and enjoy romantic or relaxing music while you dine.

Don't forget the door. If you need extra space for display or storage, don't overlook the option of a shelf over the door. This kind of shelf looks best when it's attached to narrow sets of shelves or bookcases that run down one or both sides of the door, but it can be as effective as a wall unit, especially where space is at a premium. Just don't overload it with dustables!

Hide it in a hutch. Antique hutches and dry sinks are also great places to store dishes. They're usually deep, so they can hold two layers of china and half a dozen goblets or glasses from front to back. As always when stashing dishes, put the ones you're most likely to use in front and the ones you're least likely to use (those finger bowls, for example) in back.

Get crafty. Don't think for a minute that a hutch, dry sink, buffet cabinet, cupboard, or any other storage piece has to be used for dishes or table linens just because it's in the dining room. If you already have enough storage for your dishware and your dining room doubles as your "crafts studio," any of these pieces will hold an absolute ton of crafting supplies. The only caveat is that the piece has to have doors. Looking at myriad craft supplies is looking at visual clutter, and that can be disturbing when you're trying to eat.

Put it in plastic—or a basket. Sherry, one of the most creative people at my local Curves, is a highly skilled basket maker. She's so good, she teaches basket making in her home. And, you guessed it, her studio is her dining room. Since Sherry's always working on at least one project and needs to prepare for classes, the dining room table is buried under basket-making supplies. This makes eating there a nonoption for her and her husband and causes panic when she has to clear the table to entertain. I say, enjoy the crafting space but keep your supplies contained. If you keep them in the sturdy plastic carriers available in any home improvement center, drugstore, or grocery, it's a snap (literally, if you get the ones with lock-on lids) to put your supplies back in the containers and put them away in your armoire, hutch, or wherever you stash your stuff. These plastic storage containers come in all different sizes and are very affordable. I like the ones with locking lids and handles that lift up for carrying but flatten for stacking. And you can just look through the side to see what's in each one. Another option is to store your supplies in baskets. Just make sure they have handles so they're easy to carry when it's time to clear the table!

Skirt the issue. Do you remember the "sink skirts" I told you about? (See page 136 for details.) You can also use the skirt idea to create an instant sideboard from a low bookcase or even a pair of wall-mounted shelves. Cover them with a slip-cover that opens down the center, in a fabric that matches your dining-room curtains or table treatment, and you can store dishes inside, convenient but out of sight. Attach the skirt around the top of the shelves with Velcro, elastic, or discreet staples (if the fabric pattern will conceal them).

Skip the mirrors. Mirrors are great for making rooms look bigger and more open. But in the dining room, they're great for giving the family members sitting opposite them a clear view of themselves eating. Talk about visual clutter! Choose a picture for the wall, instead. (This is the right room for a still life of fruits and vegetables, after all!) But whatever you display, make sure it's tranquil. This is *not* the room for disturbing or distracting art.

Ban the busy wallpaper. A busy little (or big) wallpaper pattern can create a cluttered feeling in any room, but in the dining room it can have an especially bad effect. After all, you want to create a soothing, relaxing atmosphere at mealtimes. And of course, dark or brilliantly colored walls, even if they're a single color, are anything but appetizing. Choose soothing, warm-toned pastels, such as a very pale peach or bisque (cool shades like blue and green have been shown to be unappetizing), or go with a classic warm white or cream. (A rosy cream is especially inviting, and it's pale enough so the "rosy" part is almost subliminal.) If you want to dress it up, add a simple stencil pattern around the top of the wall.

Clear the decks. People are constantly coming and going through the dining room with food, dishes, drinks, and other stuff that can be dropped, spilled, or broken. Make sure there's plenty of room to move around between the furniture around the walls and the table and chairs. Don't put furniture, art objects, or anything else out in the middle of the floor. Make sure toys and other items are picked up off the floor before mealtimes. And while you're at it, make sure your table isn't too big for the room—people need to be able not just to walk around it, but also to sit around it comfortably.

Don't recreate Camelot. If there are just two or three of you, a small round table can be a nice, cozy place to eat. But the bigger the round table, the farther apart diners are. The center of a large round table is wasted space, since no one can reach it, and a table that large makes you feel like you're continents away from the people sitting across the table from you. Instead, choose a rectangular or oval table—it makes for better conversation and makes much better use of tabletop space.

Spread your wings. Crate & Barrel (see page 46) is a great source for furniture and furnishings for the dining room, but they've outdone themselves in the ingenuity department with their Pivot Table. Not only does it open out from the center to double in size when you need extra room for guests, but if you turn the top, it reveals a hidden storage compartment for linens!

Check the height. Spilled food is the worst kind of clutter, and when it comes to spills, kids are often the culprits. But if the table's not the right height, *it* may be the culprit instead of the kids. Imagine having to reach up over a table that's too high while trying to navigate food and utensils you can barely see! You already know how important it is to have your computer table at the right height to prevent wrist strain. To make sure even the smallest family members are comfortable when they're eating, look everyone over when they're at the table and adjust their chairs with comfy cushions if you need to. (That goes for your chair, too.) If the table's too low or too high for *anyone* in the family to eat at comfortably, I don't care what you paid for it, get rid of it and sit down as if you're going to eat at the next one before you buy it.

Take two. What if there are only one or two of you at the table most of the time? Rather than sit in regal isolation at a giant table, why not place two small, intimate tables in the room? If you have guests or kids (or grandkids) visiting, you can put the tables together if they're square and cover them with a single tablecloth or, if they're round, simply cover them in matching tablecloths and serve at both tables.

Fold it up, part one. Folding chairs can be lifesavers when you need extra seating. Some stores and catalogs now carry wooden folding chairs with padded seats;

these are attractive enough to display without hiding them under slipcovers. If you already have metal folding chairs, you can dress them up with slipcovers specially designed for folding chairs, available from housewares stores and catalogs.

Fold it up, part two. What if your dining room's full of big, awkward furniture—inherited or purchased when you married because, well, you had a dining room, after all—but your family always eats at the kitchen table? Rather than leave the dining room to languish for the rest of your days, why not sell that furniture, donate it, or pass it along to a relative who could really use it? Then get furniture that will give the room a much-needed makeover. Need a home office, a craft or sewing room, a game room, a music room? Presto—now you have one. But what if guests are coming or the extended family's descending for the holidays? A drop-leaf table is a handsome, space-saving solution. Fold the leaves down and it takes up almost no floor space as a side table against the wall. Move it to the center of the room and open it up, pull out the folding chairs, and you're ready to entertain. (Of course, it helps if your office furniture or sewing machine will roll out of the way!)

Pull up the covers. I remember my mother putting protective panels, or pads, on our dining-room table to save the surface from spills, stains, and scratches. She'd cover these panels with a decorative tablecloth. You may not want to go this route today, but the panels can still protect your table from craft-related accidents. (Think mashed crayons, overturned bottles of paint, or even hot wax that splashed when you were designing a Ukrainian egg.) Protective panels will also save your table surface if you need to use it to make a big, messy cooking project like a gingerbread house or (shriek) fruitcake, or if you need an extra surface so you can set down hot canning jars to cool.

Go for broke (or Baroque). Nobody's head will be in the middle of your dining room table, unless your cat gets up there or you're serving a roast suckling pig. So above that table is the perfect place to put a chandelier. No cracked skulls! Pick a fixture that fits the room's look—brass for a classic Colonial style, wood and wrought iron for a country room, crystal for an elegant feel, funky and floral if you want to add a whimsical note.

Light it right. Okay, this isn't about clutter, but because I feel so strongly about it, I just had to add it in this chapter. If you're like me, you love reading cookbooks and cooking magazines. But isn't it amazing how food can look so appetizing in one book or magazine and so cold, lifeless, or downright revolting in another? Here's the scoop: It's probably not the food, it's the photography. Good food photography depends on good, warm lighting. Take this to heart when you plan the lighting for your dining room. Candles (dripless, of course) are wonderful in the dining room because they're not just romantic, they also make food look great. You can mimic candlelight by installing "warm" (pinkish or purplish) light bulbs in your fixtures, not "cold" clear or blue-white bulbs. The dining room is not the place for glare! If you need brighter light for homework or projects, get an Ott-Lite or other bright, focused table light developed specifically for detail work. (I use mine for beading and it's fabulous.) When not in use, stash it in the cabinet with your other project supplies.

Sell the silver plate. Silver plate doesn't just refer to plates. Instead, it's a technique in which a thin coating of silver is applied over a baser metal. It's cheaper than sterling and worth a lot less. And the cheaper it is, the faster the silver wears

When professionals stack dishes, they don't just pile them up or separate them with paper towels or paper napkins. Instead, they baby the china by layering it with cut-to-fit pieces of soft flannel, fleece, or nonslip rubber matting. (For all of these cut-to-fit options, there's no need to cut round pieces to match the plates; square pieces are much easier to cut, and they work just as well.)

Pet Alert!

Pets plus food (yours). Not a good combination! Even if your pets go with you into every other room of the house, exile them from the dining room when you're eating there. (You can always give them a treat for "being good" or share the leftovers later—in their bowl, please, not from your plate!) Your guests will thank you. There's nothing more disturbing than a dog prowling around the table in search of a handout or a cat trying to jump up while you're eating. Every moving animal seems like 10 of them at mealtimes. Talk about clutter!

off, revealing the unsightly metal below. As if that weren't enough, silver plate requires as much maintenance as sterling. All that polishing! Unless you have a very special piece that's come down in your family, take it to an antiques store and unload it. You can probably buy at least one piece of sterling with the proceeds. It'll be a better investment and less to store!

Make it a piece of cake. You don't have a centerpiece for your dining-room table, but you do have a tiered set of cake stands? No worries. One hot trend is to set a two- or three-tiered stand in the center of the table and fill it with something decorative—fresh flowers, fruit, Christmas ornaments (in season), gourds and bittersweet (for autumn or Thanksgiving), collectibles (like colorful tiny teacups), a collection of African violets, petite party favors—or, of course, muffins, cupcakes, petits fours, or other treats. By collecting the items on the cake stands, you're not cluttering the table with them—and by displaying the cake stands, you're saving your storage space for other pieces.

ONWARD!

Whew! You've made it through the first floor of your house—or most of it. Congratulations! Now it's time to tackle the bedrooms. Turn the page to find out how to reclaim your bedroom, make the most of a guest room, and confront your closets.

Chapter 10

Bedrooms, Guest Rooms, and (Shudder) Closets

Think about it: Could you really show your guest rooms to a guest? Or are they auxiliary attics? Can you find your clothes in the morning, or are you fighting with the not-so-mythical monster that lives in your closet? And would you really call your bedroom restful, or is refuse-full more like it? The tips in this chapter will help you restore order to chaos; clear out your closets without causing yourself pain; and create beautiful, uncluttered bedrooms for yourself and your guests—without "wasting" any precious space!

Because bedrooms, guest rooms, and closets each have their own distinct clutter issues, let's take them one at a time.

PRIORITIES FOR BEDROOMS

Once again, start your de-cluttering process in the bedroom by setting some clutter-kicking priorities. The first step is to focus on what matters most to you about the way your bedroom looks. One way to focus is to decide what bothers you more—the exposed areas of the bedroom (like the bed, floor, chairs, and dresser tops), or the hidden areas (like the closet and dresser drawers). Once you start thinking about the kinds of clutter that really drive you crazy, you'll be able to rank your bedroom's clutter problems from most to least aggravating. The best way to do this is by taking a good, hard look at the "before" state of the room and then visualizing the "after."

A Bedroom Visualization

To get to your "after," you need to start with the "before"—the way things look right now. So get out some paper, or use the "My Bedroom—Before" form on page 182 (or make a photocopy of it and write on that). Write down every place in the bedroom that there's clutter, and note what that clutter is. Are there volcanic piles on the bed? On the floor? Do you have a feeling that something's living under the bed . . . and it's not the dog? Are you afraid to open the bottom dresser drawer? Write it all down. After all, no one will see this list but you!

Once you've taken an inventory of your bedroom's "before" state, it's time to move on to the "after"—how you want the room to look when you've kicked the clutter. Use the "My Bedroom—After" form on page 182 (or make a photocopy of it and write on that) to describe the room's "after" state. To make sure you're being realistic, look at the room every few minutes while you're doing this.

Your "After" description can be short and to the point: "I'd like more dresser space. I'd like attractive bedside tables with room for books and magazines and a great reading light. I'd like less fussy curtains that don't collect dust. I'd like more hidden storage space so the bedroom looks less messy and more romantic. I want soft lighting to give the room a romantic glow. I'd like to add some mirrors to open up the room and bring in more light without sacrificing privacy."

Or you can create a detailed picture of exactly how you'd like your bedroom to look if it were perfect (for you). You can imagine the feel you want the room to have (restful? romantic? playful?). Think about the wall treatments—paint, wallpaper, stenciling, texturing, paneling—and colors; the woodwork and window treatments. What would the floor look like—plush carpet, gleaming wood, handmade rugs, rush matting? What style furniture would you prefer, and how would it be arranged? Would there be a fireplace, and if so, would it be real or a gas or electric model? What would be on the bed; what art and mirrors would be on the walls—everything.

My Bedroom—Before

_____

_____

_____

_____

_____

_____

_____

_____

_____

_____

_____

My Bedroom—After

_____

_____

_____

_____

_____

_____

_____

_____

_____

_____

_____

_____

My Bedroom Priority List

_____

_____

_____

_____

_____

_____

_____

_____

_____

Getting There

Now that you have captured your bedroom's "before" condition, listing all the specifics, and you've imagined its "after" appearance, you can finally prioritize the steps you'll need to take to get there from here. Again, bearing both "before" and "after" in mind, I'd recommend starting with what bothers you most about the "before" condition and working down your list of clutter issues until you reach what's least important to you.

Maybe your bedside is piled with books and magazines and you're lusting after a floor-to-ceiling bookcase to stash lots of bedtime reading in. Or you'd love an elegant armoire to hide the TV, DVD player, stereo, and all the movies and music that are covering every flat surface. Or you have clothes piled everywhere and you're wondering about options for under-bed storage.

Write down whatever's driving you to distraction on the "My Bedroom Priority List" (or photocopy it, if you'd prefer), in descending order from most to least maddening. This is the order in which you'll tackle your bedroom clutter problems. Now you have your priorities straight! Once you've finished, you can turn to the tips beginning on page 184 to find ingenious ways of dealing with each problem.

5-Minute Fixes for the Bedroom

If you are intimidated by the prospect of transforming your bedroom into a clutter-free zone or just want to get your feet wet, try these quick fixes. They're some of the easiest ways to start de-cluttering your bedroom.

Pick up your clothes. Or his clothes. Nothing makes a room look messier than clothes on the floor, draped across the bed, tossed on a chair, flung across the top of the door . . . you get the picture. But fortunately, nothing's easier to fix!

Make the bed. Rumpled bedclothes and tossed-around pillows create a chaotic, cluttered look. But it takes only 5 minutes to put things right. You'll thank your-self every time you walk into the room for the rest of the day!

Take out the trash. Sometimes weeks can go by before that bedroom waste-basket gets emptied, and an overflowing wastebasket really adds to a room's cluttered look. Just emptying it will make the room look better—and make you feel better! Don't have a wastebasket in your bedroom? Unless you're compul-sive about carrying every Kleenex, renewal card, and clothing price tag to the kitchen trash can, invest in one next time you're out. That's 5 minutes well spent!

Nix the night-table pileup. Bedside tables are a huge convenience—I wish I had one!—but they can also become clutter magnets. Shovel off the magazines, cata-logs, bills, mugs, jewelry, and everything else that's accumulated on there. Now that you can see the surface, dust it. Then put back one book, one magazine, and

THE BEDROOM TIPS

Look under the bed. Send the dust bunnies packing and put that big space under the bed to good use as free storage space. I use those big, flat plastic storage containers, available pretty much everywhere, because they hold a lot and slide easily under the bed. Because I have an antique bed that sits high off the floor, I can stack the containers two deep or use taller ones to make sure I fit as much as possible in the space. I recommend storing bedroom-related stuff under the bed— bed linens, sweaters, out-of-season clothes—rather than stuff like Christmas orna-ments and canned goods. But if you have enough closet and dresser space (don't tell me—I'm already jealous!), you can put whatever else needs storing under the one catalog for nighttime reading (remember, you can rotate them as you finish), the box of tissues (if you must), a coaster for your mug or glass, and the alarm clock (if that's where it lives), and you are done. Your reading glasses, diary and pen, pills, and cell phone can go in the drawer; put everything else back where it belongs. Ahhhh . . . that's better!

Don't wait for laundry day. Unless you can fit a laundry basket in your bedroom closet (is that laughter I hear?), make a point of taking the dirty clothes to the laundry room every night before bed. (I'd say, "as soon as you take them off," but let's just say that all family members may not be too cooperative about that.) Just as in the case of picking up flung or fallen clothes and putting them away, you'll feel much better about going to bed in a dirty-clothes-free room. It may even put more romance into bedtime!

Do one dresser drawer. Pick a drawer, any drawer—pull hard now, you can get it open!—and sort through the overflowing contents. Make one pile for stained, holey, stretched-out, and "what *is* this?" items—that's the trash pile, of course; one pile for way too small or way too big (lucky you), I hate that color/pattern, and I never wear that—that's the donation pile; and one pile for still fits, still looks good, and still wearing it. That pile goes back in the (now much roomier) drawer. You can finally see what you have in there, so you can get to it that much faster and easier. And you have room to treat yourself to a new piece or two!

bed. And I confess, this is a "do as I say, not as I do" recommendation—I also have my guitar cases under my bed!

Roll it out. I have seen designs for wonderful homemade under-bed storage contraptions. Basically rolling wooden storage trays, they're shallow boxes on casters that either were sized for the bed or—much easier to maneuver, in my opinion—sized to fit under half the bed and used in pairs. If you or your spouse is handy, measure the space under your bed (leaving plenty of headroom, several inches to clear the bed's legs, and several more between boxes), and build a set of shallow storage boxes (to me, three would be easier to deal with than two). You can paint them to match the woodwork if you don't enjoy the sight of bare plywood, even under wraps. Or cover the boxes with old sheets—you can buy some fun, colorful ones at thrift stores if you don't have extras. Cut or fold the sheets to fit and staple or tack them down on one long side. And don't forget to add sturdy handles so you can pull the boxes out!

Skirt the issue. Under-bed storage is great, but *looking* at under-bed storage is another matter. If you use the space under your bed for storage, make sure you conceal it with a bed skirt or dust ruffle.

Invest in a chest. A blanket or "hope" chest is the perfect place to store, well, blankets. (Hope is another matter.) Quilts, sheets, extra pillows—they all tuck right into the chest. Put it at the foot of your bed, or put it under a window and add some flat pillows on top for an instant window seat.

Buy a bench. Speaking of window seats, those benches with lift-up tops for storage are perfect for blankets and bed linens and usually come with a comfy cushion on top.

Build it in. I love window seats—they're so romantic. One of the most ingenious ones I ever saw had been custom-built with a lift-up seat and a built-in storage bin underneath. Somebody was thinking!

Try a table. A long, narrow table can create additional storage at the foot of your bed. Get one that's the right length and height for your bed—you don't want it to be taller than the mattress! The Shakers designed a variety of tables that are perfect for this. Their Sabbathday Lake tailoring counter (available from Shaker Workshops; see page 47) is just 21 inches deep and has four drawers that are ample enough to act as a second dresser. Two-drawer worktables, serving tables, and Shaker sideboards are other options. Check local flea markets to see what you can find. Add attractive baskets under the table to create even more storage.

Don't treat your bed like a table. Maybe your problem is that you make the bed, but no one could tell under the mound of stuff that you/he/they have thrown on top of it. Under-bed storage is a great idea, but the same can't be said of *on*-bed storage! Clear that stuff off and put it where it belongs.

Don't pay bills in bed. My friend and feng shui guru Skye Alexander would say that using your bedroom as an office is very bad feng shui. It's also a fast way to clutter the bedroom with envelopes, receipts, and other easy-to-lose odds and ends. We'll talk about how to corral bills in Chapter 12—The Home Office (see page 242); for now, just collect any finance-related material, rubber-band it together, and take it downstairs.

Add an armoire. Before there were built-in closets, freestanding closets that were massive pieces of furniture were the norm. Called armoires, wardrobes, garderobes, or chifforobes, these capacious "closets" held the household's clothing. They still can. If you need extra space for clothes and have enough wall space for an armoire, look for one at a flea market or antiques store. There are modern versions, too, in furniture stores. Try to find one that fits with your bedroom decor, bearing in mind that you can always paint it. Add hooks for clothes, a rack for coat hangers, or shelves for sweaters, jeans, tee-shirts, and the like. Or use your armoire as a giant entertainment center and stash all that equipment in there, along with the videos, DVDs, CDs—even cassettes and albums—that you enjoy.

Capture a corner. When space is tight, a corner cupboard can be a lifesaver in the bedroom. Just as you can use an armoire or dresser in the dining room, a corner cupboard will give you handsome "found" storage space in your bedroom. If yours has open shelving or glass doors on top, use those shelves for your brightest, most ornamental quilts and coverlets. Stash the extra pillows, jeans, sweaters, and tee-shirts down below, where solid doors can hide a multitude of less-attractive sins.

Choose a quilt rack. Display your fine quilts and coverlets year-round on a quilt rack, which will show off three to six bed coverings (depending on how you fold them). You can find a rack to match just about any decor.

Put up a ladder. My friend and editor Karen has a great idea for storing afghans, lap rugs, and throws without wasting drawer or closet space. "Find a new or antique ladder and lean it against the wall as a decorator piece," says Karen. "Fold throws in thirds or quarters and hang them over the ladder rungs. I painted my ladder to match my country decor, and it's as decorative as it is useful."

Make a statement. The bedroom is a great place to display your fabric art. Use a quilt hanger to hang a quilt, coverlet, or weaving on the wall. Even full-size quilts make great bedroom art—and save storage space by hiding in plain sight!— but smaller wall quilts look wonderful, too, if you don't have space to hang a bed quilt. Make sure your display is out of direct sunlight to avoid fading your textile treasure.

Belt it out, part one. If your dresser has two shallow drawers on top like mine does, dedicate one to belt storage. Roll up the belts individually and tuck them beside each other in the drawer. This will keep them safe; make them easy to find, see, and reach; and keep them out of the way.

Belt it out, part two. The Shakers have contributed so many ingenious ideas to our culture, but I think my favorite is the oval Shaker wooden box. A shallow Shaker box is a great place to store belts. Roll them up and tuck them into the box side by side. Display the box on top of your dresser or on a side table.

Tackle those ties. If the man in your life has a collection of ties, you can store them in exactly the same way as you would belts: Roll them up and tuck them in a shallow dresser drawer or a Shaker box. If your guy loves gadgets, he might go for the clear plastic cylindrical "tie caddies" that each hold a tie and come with their own tie-winding mechanism. They're available from mail-order catalogs like Herrington and Solutions (see page 48). If your guy's on the go, he can just grab the ties he needs and toss them in his suitcase—no wrinkling, no worries.

Add a jewelry box. Whether it's a beautiful handmade walnut or bird's-eye maple chest; a Shaker oval box; or a jewelry chest that stands on the floor, has eight drawers, and doubles as a night table, if you have jewelry, you can find a beautiful way to store it. Choose a storage piece that matches your taste and budget (and, of course, the size of your jewelry collection).

Tray your treasures. Turn that shallow dresser drawer into a jewelry box with stackable, sliding jewelry trays, available from organizing catalogs, stores, and Web sites like Solutions and All Bright Ideas (see page 48). You can buy specially designed velvet-lined trays with compartments for necklaces, bracelets, earrings, rings, and brooches, then combine them into a compact, easy-to-use jewelry box in a drawer.

Get a jewelry mirror. Don't scoff—here's a brilliant idea for making the most of your bedroom space. Catalogs such as Improvements (see page 48) sell wall mirrors that open to reveal a long, capacious, two-sided jewelry cabinet. Wow! You can choose your jewelry for the day (or night), then use the mirror to put it on and see how it looks.

Don't forget the guys. What about *his* jewelry, watch, and cufflinks? Leather and guys—they seem to go together. As a child, I was fascinated by the small leather box my father kept his cufflinks and watch in. Now you can buy a leather organizer for your man with room for his wallet and cell phone as well as his watches and other accessories. Display it proudly on the dresser with your jewelry box, or tuck it discreetly into one of those shallow dresser drawers. But a guy's treasure chest doesn't have to be leather. I have a beautiful, ornately carved wooden box with velvet-lined compartments on my dresser just for Rob's things. (He picked it out himself.) And I've seen gorgeous wood dresser-top "valets" in catalogs like Solutions (see page 48).

Table it. Bedside tables, or nightstands, are infinitely useful, and not just by the bed. They come in myriad styles, so you can match your decor with new tables or find old ones at antiques stores and flea markets. They're just the right size for a lamp, mug, book, magazine, newspaper, and tissue holder. Choose a style with a drawer (or two) for storing reading glasses, coasters, pens, remotes, cell phones, sticky tags, hand cream, and anything else you find essential. Put a matching one on each side of the bed, with a decorative wastebasket tucked discreetly underneath. (Remember those tissues!) I don't have room for a bedside table beside my bed, but I do use one on the wall across from the bed; I piled beautiful wooden boxes on top to create a focal point, so it's functional as well as attractive.

Dress it up. Dressers are essential bedroom furniture for good reason—they can hold a lot of clothes. Get one or two you like, new or used, and divide the drawers according to use—nightgowns and PJs, underwear, jeans, tee-shirts, socks. Put the stuff you use most often in the highest drawers, the less-often-used items in the lowest drawers. If you must share your dresser drawers, give the highest to the tallest of you, then alternate on down. Make sure at least one of your dressers has a mirror so you can check hair, clothes, and jewelry before heading out. (Besides, the cat will love it.)

Deal with the drawers. Linda Koopersmith, the Beverly Hills Organizer and organizational expert and co-host of Style Network's series *Clean House* (see

"The Pros Know" on page 204) is a big believer in folding clothes and setting them end-up in drawers rather than laying them down horizontally. She points out that folding clothes and stacking them upright, with the smooth, rounded sides facing up, not only lets you pack more clothes into each drawer, it lets you have a "bird's-eye view" of everything in the drawer. No more lost or forgotten clothes! Need help keeping those rows upright? Linda recommends spring-loaded partitions called tension dividers to divide a drawer into sections and sock, bra, and brief boxes to keep your underthings in place.

Cache it in a cupboard. At a flea market many years ago, I found some cheap, colorfully painted old cupboards with doors that had once been glass-fronted but now were simply framed, and I brought them home to house my textile collection. The brilliant colors of the cupboards and textiles look smashing, and I thought I was being really creative and clever—until I saw the same idea in a home decorating magazine about 10 years later. Yikes! How humiliating that anyone else had my brilliant idea. But it's still a great idea!

Pack up the papers. I know one dad (who shall remain nameless) who is so sure he's going to get around to reading the entire *New York Times, Wall Street Journal,* and local papers that he saves them . . . and saves them . . . until he "can get to them." As if! The result is a mountain of papers under his bed. If you or your spouse falls into this category, even if you're not *that* extreme, make sure that all papers are recycled weekly. That gives everyone a full week to read the papers— and if they haven't read them by then, they're not gonna.

Hide it in a hatbox. Attractively covered hatboxes (or "nesting hatbox organizers" as I've seen them called) have been a design trend for more than 10 years. They're ornamental enough to display on shelves or on top of a dresser or table, and they're spacious enough to hold pretty much whatever you want to stash in them, up to blankets and clothes. I confess, I actually use mine for hats, which I stack on top of each other to maximize hatbox space, and costume-party wigs (Sweet Potato Queens, anyone?). Fun!

Find a folding screen. Create a dressing nook behind a folding screen in a corner of the bedroom. Add hooks and a full-length mirror on the wall, tuck a little bench back there, and you're good to go!

Add a low bookcase. A low bookcase along one wall not only gives you storage and display space, the top also acts as a table for a vase of flowers, candles (how romantic!), a bowl of potpourri, a lamp, an incense burner, or anything else you'd like to put in the bedroom to add beauty and atmosphere.

Or hang it high. A hanging bookcase or cabinet is also a wonderful way to add storage or display space in the bedroom. If you opt for a dresser without a mirror or a low bookcase, add a hanging cabinet or bookcase above and double your space.

Frame the door. Put narrow bookshelves around the door and a connecting shelf over the door to create a space-saving place for books, magazines, and treasures.

Don't junk up the walls. Your bedroom should be the most restful, soothing, romantic room in your home—a room that's just begging you to come in and kick back, park your cares by the door, and relax. Don't spoil the mood by jamming photos, paintings, and knickknacks on the walls. A few restful paintings, family photos, or nature scenes, plus a large mirror that captures a lovely outdoor scene, are plenty. In this room, excess quickly becomes wretched excess. Choose your artwork with care, leave lots of wall space, and remember that you can rotate your art and photos—you don't have to display them all at once.

Add some life. Plants not only add beauty to a room, they also remove pollutants from the air. But as always, your goal is to add beauty, not clutter. Choose single plants as accents or focal points, and then take good care of them so they look good—not dead. (Tip: Overwatering is as likely to brown up a plant as underwatering. Feel the soil before you water!) If you hang a plant near the window, it won't take up table space but will add beauty. Just don't hang it in front of the window and block your light—slightly to the side is fine. If you have a deep windowsill, a trailing or blooming plant in a lovely pot can add a burst of color and life. (But don't put a trailing plant over a heat source, and do keep after shedding leaves.) Choose a natural or single-color pot, not one with a busily colored pattern, so it accents the plant rather than fighting with it for attention and creating visual clutter. Finally, steal this great trick from my friend Delilah: She keeps plants in her greenhouse until they reach the peak of blooming perfection, then brings them inside to display, rotating out the ones that are past peak. You don't need a greenhouse to do this—just keep plants in a bright, sunny area where they're not in the spotlight when they aren't on display. Finally, do *not* keep more plants than you'll take care of! If one's your limit, better to have one beautiful plant than a dozen half-dead sufferers.

Light your fire. If you've always dreamed of a romantic firelit bedroom, there's no better time to get one than the present. I grew up in a Colonial home with a working fireplace in every room, including my bedroom. I can tell you straight out that there is *nothing* more romantic than a fire flickering away as you're falling asleep. But if you're not that lucky, that no longer means that you have to invest in major masonry to add a bedroom fireplace. Thanks to the wonders of modern technology, you can buy a plug-in electric fireplace with an attractive mantel or a gas fireplace or "woodstove" with wonderful warming flames. (I have two sets of friends who've opted for these pseudo-woodstoves, one in their family room and one on their porch, and I can attest to how warm and wonderful they are.) Many of the new models require no venting to the outside, so they can fit wherever you want to put them. All I can say is, "Wow!"

Add a mantel shelf. Gorgeous freestanding mantel shelves are available from home stores and catalogs like Plow & Hearth (see page 47). Dress up a fireplace or create the illusion of one with these easy-to-hang wooden mantels.

Feel the glow. Wall sconces are a great choice for the bedroom. They give the room a muted, romantic glow, and they don't occupy precious surface space!

Add display shelves. Rather than cover the surfaces of your dressers and bedside tables with your collection of crystals, shells, or other collectibles, show them off on a lighted wall shelf. These wonderful inventions, available from home catalogs like Solutions (see page 48), are made of wood and look almost like miniature mantelpieces. They range from a wall "sconce" (just over 10 inches long) to a "ledge" (just over 2 feet long), and are as easy to hang as a picture frame. The top of each display shelf is an acrylic panel that's lit from below by battery-operated LEDs. Because the light comes up from below, these shelves are especially good for showcasing transparent and translucent objects.

GUEST ROOMS

Okay, let's talk about guest rooms for a minute. In my view, unless there's a really good reason for setting aside an entire room for guests, you're wasting valuable space. Here are four good reasons for having a designated guest room that serves no other function:

1. You have partial custody of one or more kids. (In which case, hopefully, it's

 # Pet Alert!

If you have pets, chances are that they share your bedroom with you. If you give them their own space to relax in, chances are better that they won't try to take over yours. My golden retriever, Molly, has her own plush plaid dog bed at the foot of my bed. It's one of those cushy foam-filled dog beds from L.L. Bean or Orvis (see pages 46 and 49), and she sleeps on it every night (unless the cats push her off). My cats enjoy spending time on the tall "cat castle" that's tucked into a corner of the room and has three tiers of lushly carpeted sleep stations, as well as a sisal rope scratching post. I've added a variety of toys, and the cats alternate between spending time on the cat castle, curling up with Molly, and sunning in the picture window. Tripping over cat or dog toys en route to the bathroom at night is no fun, so I'd recommend that you keep an attractive basket or hamper in the bedroom to stash their toys in, too.

What about other kinds of pets? I think a bedroom aquarium is about the most relaxing, romantic accessory of all—the soft light, the soothing sounds of water cascading over the filter, the brilliantly lit fish swimming peacefully among the plants. But if you have parrots, parakeets, or any bird that can speak, keep them in another room! Birds tend to quickly pick up on any unusual or emotional words or noises, and you don't want your private affairs broadcast to the UPS man or your in-laws!

not a "guest" room, but your kid's room! See Chapter 11—Clutter-Free Kids' Rooms, for more on this.)

2. Your grown kids or grandkids come to stay almost every weekend.

3. Your house is a "vacation destination" for your friends and family because of its location near the ocean, lake, mountains, or Disney World, or just because of your famous hospitality.

4. You have more than one magnificent set of bedroom furniture and it's worth the space to display it. (If I'm lucky enough to inherit the fabulous Colonial cherry furniture in my childhood bedroom, I'll consider converting my music room back into a bedroom!)

Otherwise, sell or donate your guest room furniture and turn that space into something you want and need! Crafts room, exercise room/home gym, music room, home office, playroom . . . you can probably picture the room of your dreams right now. But what if you need the space for the occasional overnight guest? Here are some tips to help you be prepared to make guests feel welcome without sacrificing your precious square footage.

Set up a sofa bed. No matter what you decide to use your erstwhile guest room for, you're probably going to need some seating in there. Home catalogs like Plow & Hearth (see page 47) feature tons of options for seating that pulls out to convert into bedding. You can get a sofa, loveseat, chair, or ottoman, and some of them are quite lightweight—a real boon if you have to move them around to set them up.

Blow up the bed. As I've mentioned before, air mattresses are my all-time favorite guest bedding; they are supercomfortable. Some even feature double-depth mattresses, and others have foldout legs and frames, so guests don't feel like they are sleeping on the floor. But even standard on-floor air mattresses are more comfortable than most beds, and you can adjust the level of inflation to exactly match a guest's firmness requirements. With today's electric pumps, it takes less than 5 minutes to inflate or (if the pump is reversible) deflate the mattress, and the whole thing tucks away in a storage bag that's half the size of a sleeping bag. It doesn't

👍 Love It *or* Lose It? 👎

In the interest of saving space, you may be tempted to get a hat rack for your guest room, with the thought that guests can hang their clothes on the rack and you won't have to provide closet space. I've even encountered this arrangement in expensive inns. Ugh! Who wants to look at their clothes heaped on hat-rack hooks or coat hangers slung haphazardly on the hat rack? I travel light—I never take more than will fit in a small carry-on bag—but even I have more clothes than a hat rack can accommodate. Resist this temptation! Give your guests dedicated closet or armoire space, even if you have to temporarily move some of your own clothes to provide it. And make sure they have an ample supply of sturdy, presentable coat hangers—not twisted, wimpy dry-cleaner leftovers.

Verdict: Lose it!

get better than this! Incidentally, a full- or queen-size air mattress is the most versatile, since it can accommodate one or two guests.

Keep it close to the chest. A blanket chest isn't just attractive; placed in a guest room, it can hold the blankets, pillows, and bed linens for the guest bed. If you use an air mattress, the chest can hold the bed itself, as well. Add a flat cushion on top and you have seating, too.

Provide lots of pillows. Nothing says "welcome" like a whole pile of soft, cushy pillows for the guest bed—and nothing says "afterthought" like one pathetic, flat pillow. Keep plenty of extra pillows on hand for your guests and provide enough blankets so they can have all they want (which may be more than you'd use). Store pillows on the bed itself, so guests can use as few or as many as they like without feeling that they have to ask for extras. (And that way, the pillows don't use up extra storage space.) Same for the blankets—just fold them and pile them at the foot of the bed. Both pillows and blankets could also go in a blanket chest or trunk at the foot of the bed. That's hospitality!

Take a tip from hotels. My father's girlfriend, Alice, has fold-out luggage stands in all her guest rooms, just like hotels do. I love this—I can set my suitcase on the stand and have easy access to the contents whenever I want, without having to drag the suitcase in and out of the closet. You can get the stands from home stores and catalogs like Improvements (see page 48).

Make a guest kit. Another wonderful thing my father's girlfriend, Alice, does is to create a toiletries kit for every guest. You can do this by setting out a basket in the guest bathroom (or, if you don't have a separate guest bathroom, on a dresser in the guest room). Put a travel-size soap, shampoo, conditioner, lotion, toothbrush, toothpaste, emery board, razor, and talcum powder in the basket, along with anything else you think would give your guests a luxurious treat (bath oil balls or bubble bath, for instance). In these days of restricted carry-on toiletries, your guests will be especially grateful!

Bring out the rack. No closet space for guests? Instead of resorting to a hat rack (see "Love It or Lose It?"), get a rolling clothes rack. Yes, it will be right there in the room, but it will provide plenty of room for all your guests' clothes. And if you provide plenty of sturdy, attractive hangers, rather than a few bent, inadequate orphans, your guests will really appreciate it. Trust me on that! You can roll the rack back out of sight in the basement, garage, or other storage space when it's not in use, or make it part of the room when guests aren't there. (For example, it can hold quilts in a quilting studio, knitwear or crocheted sweaters in a yarn studio, or exercise clothes in a home gym.)

Make sure there's light. Guests need to be able to see to navigate in the dark, so put a nightlight in the guest room and make sure it's on when you have visitors. And don't skimp on the guest-room lighting—a dark room looks soulless and unwelcoming. Again, it's important here to keep lamps and cords where they won't become tripping hazards for unsuspecting guests. Ceiling fixtures and wall sconces are great options.

PRIORITIES FOR CLOSETS

I'm going to ask you to do a quick closet visualization exercise, too. "What?" you say, "Visualize a closet?" But think about it: Have you ever actually looked at your closet in an analytical way, at what the space might offer and how you're using it? Or have you, like most of us, been far too busy trying to cram things into it and pull things out of it (if you can find them) to really see the space itself? Bear with me here. It's just a closet—it won't take but a minute or two to look at the way it is now and then think about how it *could* look, probably with just a few quick changes.

As usual, start your de-cluttering process by taking a good, hard look at the "before" state of your closet, and then visualize the "after."

A Closet Visualization

Before you can visualize the closet you want to have after the clutter is gone, you have to start with the "before"—the way things look right now. So get out some paper, or use the "My Closet—Before" form (or make a photocopy of it and write on that). Write down the location of every bit of clutter in that closet, and note what that clutter is. Are there things in the closet that don't belong there? Is there enough rack space, or is everything crammed in so tightly that extracting a piece of clothing feels like a wrestling match? Do you have enough shelf space? Are shoes spilling out in an avalanche every time you open the door, or does it take so long to find a matching pair that you've started leaving the pair you actually wear

My Closet—Before

_____
_____
_____
_____
_____
_____
_____
_____
_____
_____
_____

My Closet—After

_____
_____
_____
_____
_____
_____
_____
_____
_____
_____
_____
_____
_____

My Closet Priority List

_____

_____

_____

_____

_____

_____

_____

_____

_____

_____

by the front door? Take a minute now to write down your "before" so you can get to your "after"!

Once you've jotted down a quick description of your closet's "before" state, it's time to move on to the "after." On a piece of paper or the "My Closet—After" form on page 197 (or a photocopy of it), describe how you want the closet to look when you've kicked the clutter. If you have any home magazines or catalogs that show fabulous closets, look through them now to get ideas. Make sure you look at your closet while you're doing this, too, as a reality check. There's no point in mentally creating the walk-in closet of your dreams when your real-life closet has barely enough room for the cat to walk in!

Your description can be short and to the point: "I'd like for all the shoes to be on a rack where they're easy to see and reach. I'd like plenty of light so I can see what's in there. I'd like floor-to-ceiling shelves on each side."

If you're lucky enough to have a walk-in closet, you can create a detailed image of exactly how you'd like your closet to look if it were perfect (for you). You can picture the colors of the walls and woodwork, what the floor would look like, whether there would be room for a chair and vanity, what the storage areas would look like, how it would be lit—everything.

Getting There

Now that you have captured your closet's "before" condition, listing all the specifics, and you've imagined its "after" appearance, you can finally prioritize the steps you'll need to take to get there from here. Again, bearing both "before" and "after" in mind, I'd recommend starting with what bothers you most about the "before" condition and working down from there.

Write down whatever's driving you to distraction on the "My Closet Priority List" (or photocopy it, if you'd prefer), working in descending order from most to least maddening. Now you have your priorities straight! Once you've finished your priority list, you can turn to the tips below to find ingenious ways of dealing with each problem.

THE CLOSET TIPS

Kick out the old clothes. Nobody wants to, but if you're looking at a closet revamp, you might as well start by de-cluttering your wardrobe. You'll have to take the clothes out anyway before you can do anything else. Here's how to pare down your wardrobe in seven stages:

1. Start with the stuff that's obviously beat—hopelessly stained, torn, shrunken, burned, and so on. Put it in a trash bag and get it outta there! If one or more of the damaged goods is a key wardrobe piece—something you actually need to have and wear often—write down what it is so you can shop for a replacement. (Assuming you don't find another one hidden in the closet somewhere.)

2. Tackle the clothes that no longer fit. Can I hear you screaming "But they're almost new!" or "Really—I'm going to lose the weight!"? Not to worry. If you can't bear to donate them or take them to a consignment shop, pack them up in a suitcase (see page 205) or plastic storage box, label it, and tuck it under the bed or in the guest-room closet. Maybe you *will* be able to wear them one day, or maybe you'll be able to part with them when you haven't seen them for a while and realize that you haven't missed them. (And might I gently suggest that styles do change!) In any case, at least you'll have

removed the clothes and freed up much-needed space for clothes that you *can* wear.

3. Now it's time to get tough with the clothes you don't like. Maybe that blouse cost a fortune, your mom or your husband gave that sweater to you, or that dress was the most gorgeous one you'd ever seen (just not on you). Whatever the case, whatever the reason—it's uncomfortable, it never fit right, you think it's ugly, it's last year's color or style—get it out of the closet and out of your life. Goodwill (or that high-end consignment shop) is waiting! If you're afraid your spouse will suddenly wonder where that gorgeous purple leopard sweater he gave you last Valentine's Day has gone, tuck it in the storage container with the clothes that don't fit. You'll have it within reach just in case. But don't be surprised if it doesn't come up! And now you have even more closet space.

4. What about clothes you love but no longer wear—your prom dress, wedding dress, first-date outfit, hand-embroidered hippie jeans? I have one question: What are those doing in your closet, anyway? Pack them away tenderly and put them where you can get them out and look at them when you're feeling nostalgic, but they're not taking up closet space you need now. Or, if you're a quilter or sewer, you can always photograph each garment, then cut it up and use the pieces to make memory quilts for yourself and the kids, make patchwork skirts or jackets for your kids, or add patches to their jeans. Keep the photos in a memory album, and put that quilt out on display where you can enjoy it!

5. While you're going through your clothes, see if any pieces need to be cleaned or repaired. Don't put them back until they're fixed and clean.

6. If you share the closet with your spouse or partner, you can go through this with his clothes, too. Just don't actually get rid of anything without his consent! I'll bet he'll be more willing to part with his ratty clothes when he sees how much of your stuff is going.

7. Repeat the process with your shoes, purses, hats, and other accessories.

Finally, you can see in there! Now it's time to start on the closet itself.

Let in the light. It's essential to have enough light in your closet to see what you're doing. My all-time favorite closet lighting is in my father's girlfriend's house: When you turn on the lights in a bedroom, the recessed lighting in the bedroom

the *Pros* Know

There are more specialty closet companies than you can shake a stick at. California Closets, EasyClosets.com, All Bright Ideas, Contemporary Closets, Closet Factory—the list is endless! If you want to go with the pros—many of which offer complementary consultations—turn to page 45 for contact data, or look in the local Yellow Pages for closet consultants in your area. Check out their offerings and pricing online, order a few catalogs, then give them a call. Decide on your needs and your budget beforehand, then find the best fit.

closet goes on automatically. Great idea! But whatever lighting system you opt for, make sure it's bright enough and is easy to turn on.

Color me beautiful. Too often, we view closets as afterthoughts—plain storage spaces that are painted white or another unremarkable color. But some of the most wonderful closets I've ever seen were painted vibrant colors or papered in fabulous prints. Use some imagination and spice up your space.

Use your door. Don't waste the inside of your closet door! Hang a shoe rack or a full-length mirror, both of which will hook over the top of the door comparatively unobtrusively. Some of the more heavy-duty over-door shoe racks can hold up to 36 pairs of shoes! Companies also make purse hangers for closet doors. And of course you can get those accordion racks with pegs to hang lightweight things like jewelry, scarves, and handbags, or a Shaker-style peg rack or decorative hooks for heavier items like purses, tote bags, or bathrobes.

Double up. You'll have a lot more space to hang clothes if you add a second clothes rod in part of your closet. (You'll want to leave part of the closet with a single rod for dresses, bathrobes, long coats, and other full-length garments.) But be prepared to raise up the top rod: A single clothes rod is usually attached at 66 to 72 inches, but double-hung rods should be spaced at 42 inches for the lower rod and 82 for the higher one. Hang blouses and shirts on the top rod and skirts and pants on the bottom one.

Add more shelves. Shelving can really add storage space to a closet. You can install standard wood shelves, painted to match your closet, or use plastic-coated wire shelf units (such as those sold by Closet Maid). Both ready-to-use wood and

5-Minute Fix for the Closet

Here's one of the easiest ways to start de-cluttering your closet!

Shed some shoes. Okay, it's not fun. But if you can't see your closet floor because of all the shoes—or you have a hard time finding a match for any shoe in the Mt. Everest of other shoes on the floor—it is time to unload. Just dive in there and pick two pairs of battered, stained, stretched-out, broken, you-name-it shoes and trash them. (Or donate them, if you think someone might be able to wear them.) You can do it! If you loved them back in the day, you can always take a photo of them in their current condition and write on the back what they meant to you. Hopefully, after a few viewings of the photo, you'll wonder why you took it and toss that, too—but if not, at least a photo takes up zero room in your clothes closet.

wire shelves are available in most home centers. (California Closets has an entire line at Target.) The wire shelving comes in all lengths and is designed specifically for closets, so it's sized to fit a standard-size closet. And it's durable, attractive, and easy to install.

Save the high shelf. Unless you're tall enough to reach that long, over-the-clothes-rod shelf, use it to store plastic containers with clothes that are out of season. You can see what's in them, but you'll have to take them down only a couple of times a year!

Use multihangers. Skirt hangers that have four or five cascading hangers can save a lot of space on the closet hanger bar. But now catalogs like Improvements (see page 48) also have ingenious hangers that allow you to hang five hangers for shirts, sweaters, or whatever you'd like from a supercompact "hanger holder." Instead of groping around for the one you want, you can simply reach in and remove the appropriate hanger. No fuss, no muss!

Hang clothes by color. If you hang all of your black skirts, gray skirts, khaki pants, and white blouses together, it's easy to see what's in the closet and what's in the laundry or at the dry cleaner's. It's also easy to see if you have wardrobe gaps! And it might be a bit easier to part with those ancient black slacks if you can see that you have five other pairs that still look good.

Sort through each season. I keep the current season's clothes in my bedroom closet and the off-season's in my office closet. When it's time to switch, I always take a critical look at both sets of clothes to see if some have finished their useful lives and others are out of style or out of shape (mine). Since I have to move them all anyway, it's the perfect time to review them.

Rack 'em up. Shoe racks—available in cedar, chrome, and any number of other materials—let you stack shoes vertically rather than leaving them piled at random on the floor or stashed in shoeboxes where you can't even see what you have. If you don't use your closet door for shoe storage or you have more shoes than an over-the-door rack can accommodate, shoe racks are the greatest thing going.

Hop on the carousel. An alternative to a shoe rack is a revolving shoe carousel, which holds two or three tiers (up to 18 pairs) in the floor space of two pairs of shoes. Give the carousel a spin and select your day's pair.

Corral some cubbies. Shoe cubbies are an attractive and durable way to keep shoes neat and accessible. Put them against the back of the closet wall for easiest access.

Dig out a dresser. Take this piece of good advice from Linda Cobb, the Queen of Clean: If you have space for a small dresser in your closet, you can store sweaters, tee-shirts, jeans, and other clothes that would just take up rack room (or, as is the case with sweaters, that keep their shape best if folded rather than hung). Get one at a thrift store, flea market, or yard sale. I'd suggest a child's dresser, since they're smaller and would fit more easily but are still big enough to hold lots of clothes. Paint it to match your closet and you're good to go!

Hang a medicine cabinet. If you have extra wall space in your closet and need shelves for purses, gloves and mittens, ties, hair accessories, and other small items, consider a medicine cabinet or other hanging wall cabinet. If it has a mirrored door, you have an instant closet mirror, too!

Hang up your ties. My boyfriend, Rob, has a tie hanger that looks like a short coat hanger with lots of stubby little arms. The hanger keeps his ties tidy and accessible—he can see them all at a glance—in an incredibly small amount of space.

Buy a belt ring. Another ingenious device in Rob's closet is a belt ring. It's like a giant circular key ring—the sort that latches open and closed—with a coat-hanger hook at the top. Rob flips open the latch, slides his belts on the ring (where they hang by their buckles), and hangs the whole thing on the clothes rack. He never has to wonder where his belts are!

Try a trouser rack. Compact wooden trouser racks can hold 10 to 20 pairs of trousers in an 18-inch space. The rack mounts to a closet door or wall and has swing-out wooden dowels to hold the trousers. Available from housewares stores and catalogs like Hammacher Schlemmer (see page 48).

Stop hanger hanky-panky. Have you noticed how those coat hangers seem to multiply every time your back is turned? Take a tip from my friend Chris and put an end to the population explosion. Chris has a designated spot to store hangers from the dry cleaner's, and she makes a point of returning them when the bag or box starts to fill up.

Use plastic hangers. Not the gross, brittle plastic hangers of old that would shatter as soon as you looked at them, but the smooth, sleek, colorful hangers available today in department and housewares stores. They're thicker than wire so they hold slippery and open-necked clothes better, and they don't bend. Don't want to pay full price? Thrift stores often sell them for pennies a bunch.

Book 'em. Add a bookcase to your closet (flea markets, thrift stores, yard sales, and secondhand furniture stores are all good sources). A low bookcase can add two or three shelves of storage for shoes, purses, sweaters, and so on, while not taking up more than a foot or so of precious floor space. Find one that's a good fit—again, a child's bookcase might be the best size because it's smaller—and paint it to match your closet. Put it against the back wall and fill it up!

Or bag 'em. I see a lot of really attractive square and rectangular fabric bags that are designed for storage. Some of them look fragile—the most beautiful ones I've seen are translucent and come in jewel colors—but they're up to the challenge when what you're storing in them is clothes. Because they're lightweight, they're good choices for that high closet shelf, and they have handles so they're easy to lift down.

Put your suitcases to work. Why let your suitcases take up precious closet space when you use them only a few times a year? Instead, make them earn their keep by using them to store out-of-season clothes like sweaters and flannel nightgowns or shirts in warm weather or tee-shirts and shorts in winter. Don't forget that you don't have to keep your suitcases in a closet at all—you can store them flat under the bed, instead.

Bring out the baskets. Those ever-useful square or rectangular woven baskets are great for closet storage, too. Put them on the floor or on shelves for a clean, tidy look. (Make sure they have lids to keep dust off your scarves, sweaters, purses, gloves, hats, or whatever you've stashed inside.) Print up attractive labels for them, since you can't see what's inside.

Hang up your hats, part one. Hanging shelves are suspended from coat-hanger hooks, so you just hang them on your clothes rod. Tuck hats, gloves, scarves, and handbags (not the heavy ones, please) into the shelf cubbies, where you can see them at a glance and keep them in easy reach.

Hang up your hats, part two. Hooks along one wall of the closet are perfect for hanging hats and purses. Put the hats on the high hooks and the purses on a second, lower row.

Get some wheels. If your closet is long but isn't a walk-in, getting to the far sides can be a challenge. A rolling cart makes it easy to store items like shoes and purses and to pull them within easy reach. Mine has three deep hanging baskets as well as a tabletop, so it holds a lot!

Use the one-for-one rule. Once you've gotten everything you don't wear and can't wear out of your closet and replaced the discarded pieces with clothes, shoes, and purses you really need, keep your closet in the clear with the one-for-one rule: When a new item goes in, an old one comes out.

Dear Claire,

My husband and I share a closet, and our clothes and shoes are so jumbled together we can't ever find anything. There must be a better way!

—Closet-trophobic

Dear Closet-trophobic,

Divide and conquer! I'm assuming separate closets are out of the question, so split your shared closet down the middle. Add shelving and double clothes rods on each side, as well as a section of single rod for long dresses and coats. Get yourselves two shoe racks and place one on each side. Buy some plastic storage boxes and divvy them up. Then pull out the clothes and shoes and divide them into yours and his. (I hope you can both dispose of some clothing and shoes at this point.) Put yours on your side and have your husband put his on his side. Problem solved!

Good luck,
Claire

ONWARD!

All right! You've conquered the clutter in your bedroom, given your guest room a makeover, and transformed your closet. Now it's time to tackle the kids' rooms. Read on to see how you can work with your kids to make their rooms clutter-free and fabulous!

Chapter 11

Clutter-Free Kids' Rooms

De-cluttering a kid's room presents its own challenges, since kids have their own ideas about how to use their rooms and all the stuff in them. Does this description sound familiar? Every available surface—beds, desk, dressers, the floor—is covered with a complete jumble of stuff: clothes, music, stuffed animals, chips and little cartridges for portable game players, toys, old gum wrappers, markers, crayons, toy figures—you name it. You may already have designated storage places for each kind of thing—clothes in the closet or dresser, books on the bookshelf, art supplies in one of the desk drawers, little toys in cubbies—but your kid simply doesn't put the things in them. In this case, you can still do a clutter-kicking visualization, to give yourself a clear picture of what you're trying to achieve. But then you'll still have to get your child to buy into your vision. (For help with that, see "The Pros Know" on page 216.)

PRIORITIES FOR KIDS' ROOMS

Start your de-cluttering process by setting some clutter-kicking priorities. First focus on what matters most to you about the way each child's room looks, then work your way through the clutter problems until you get to what matters least. The best way to do this is by taking a good, hard look at the "before" state of the room and then visualizing the "after." In the case of kids' rooms, the "after" part can really be a lot of fun, so go to it!

A Kid's Room Visualization

To get to your "after," you need to start with the "before"—the way things look right now. So get out some paper, or use the "My Kid's Room—Before" form (or make a photocopy of it and write on that). Write down every place there's clutter, and note what that clutter is. You'll be sharing the "after" visualization with your child (if he or she is old enough), but I'd recommend doing the "before" on your own—and when you can have the room to yourself so you can take a really good look.

Once you've jotted down a quick description of your child's room's "before" state, it's time to move on to the "after"—what you want the room to look like when you've cleared the clutter. In this case, if your child is old enough to have some concept of his or her own space, work with him or her to learn what they envision as their "perfect" room. (Make sure this is presented as imagining or "let's pretend," so they don't think you're making any promises!) Do the visualization with each child whose room you want to de-clutter. I promise, you'll learn a lot! If two kids share a room, get them both involved. Catalogs and magazines are great ways to jump-start everyone's imagination. Don't forget to take notes.

Next, keeping one eye on your child's vision and another on the actual room you're working with, describe how you want the room to look when you've kicked the clutter. Write it all down on a piece of paper or on the "My Kid's Room—After" form (or on as many photocopies of it as you need to do it justice). Your description can be short and to the point: "I want all the toys picked up off the floor and put away every day before school/every night before bed. Jamie wants a pink toy chest. I want the bed made neatly every morning. I don't want to see broken toys or bits and pieces of puzzles, Power Rangers, or anything else. I'd like a place to display some of Sam's drawings. He says he'd like to have a bulletin board." Or you can create a detailed picture of exactly how you'd recreate the room so it both meets your clutter-kicking needs and is perfect for your kid.

My Kid's Room—Before

_____

_____

_____

_____

_____

_____

_____

_____

_____

_____

_____

_____

My Kid's Room—After

_____

_____

_____

_____

_____

_____

_____

_____

_____

_____

_____

_____

_____

Getting There

Now that you have captured your kid's room's "before" condition, listing all the specifics, and you and your child have imagined its "after" appearance, you can finally prioritize how to get there from here. Bearing both "before" and "after" in mind, I'd recommend starting with what bothers you most about the "before" condition and working down the list of clutter issues from there.

Maybe you can't deal with the CDs and video games strewn all over the place. Or you're sick of tripping over clothes on the floor. Or you wish there were more space for books and toys. Or you want furniture that works harder and better for the space.

Write down whatever's driving you to distraction on the "My Kid's Room Priority List" (or photocopy it if you'd prefer), in descending order from most to least maddening. Now you have your priorities straight! Once you've finished your priority list, you can turn to the tips below to find ingenious ways of dealing with each problem.

THE KIDS' ROOMS TIPS

Chalk it up. If your child loves to draw, consider creating a chalkboard wall in his or her room. You can paint a wall (or section of wall) with chalkboard paint,

My Kid's Room Priority List

_____

_____

_____

_____

_____

_____

_____

_____

_____

available from home improvement centers, and provide a giant canvas for your kid's creativity while keeping the mess confined and paper from proliferating. Bear in mind, though, that this paint is chalkboard black, and choose a wall area where it won't darken your child's room.

Lighten up. Kids need lots of light. But their rooms also need to be safe—no cords to trip over, lamps to knock over, shades to crash into. Ceiling fixtures and built-in lights over desks, on walls, over the bed, and under tall shelves are all good options.

Choose furniture that works. My friend Karen has this to say about furniture for kids' rooms: "Give up traditional thoughts about children's furniture and go for the most storage possible in anything you buy, inherit, or refurbish. If it doesn't work for your situation or it's a space-eater, don't feel bad about passing it by. A feminine vanity would be nice, but most styles take up 4 feet of floor space and feature only a few drawers. A grand dollhouse is a beloved possession, but it's better placed in a room that has plenty of space—usually not a child's bedroom. The dollhouse furnishings inevitably spill onto the floor and gobble up even more space. A desk in a child's bedroom sounds like a great idea, but most children do their homework at the kitchen table, on their bed, or on the carpet. The desk becomes a space-waster and a catchall for clutter that could be tossed or given away."

On the other hand. Then again, says my friend Anne, older kids need a computer for homework (not necessarily one with Internet access, though, so you don't have that whole set of safety issues—computers with Web access should ideally be in a public part of the house for better monitoring). Since laptops aren't really

5-Minute Fix for Kids' Rooms

Here's one of the easiest ways to start de-cluttering your kids' bedrooms:

Don't overdo the animals. If your kids cover the bed—made or otherwise—with dolls, stuffed animals, or other toys, you have instant clutter. So ask each kid to pick one, two, or three toys to display on the (made-up, please) bed, and have them put the rest in the toy box, on the shelves, or in another designated location. (See page 215 for toy-storage tips.) Make it fun for them to choose each day's "bed toys" after they make their beds.

sturdy enough for kids, an older child might well need a desk and computer in his or her room.

Choose furniture that's stable. I guess it should go without saying, but before you put it in a child's room, rock and pull on all furniture to make sure your child can't climb on it and pull it over, with or without anything in it. If there's any doubt, as is the case with some freestanding bookcases, secure it to the wall. Better safe than sorry!

Head under the bed. Send the dust bunnies packing and put that big space under your kid's bed to good use as free storage space. Use those big, flat plastic storage containers, available pretty much everywhere, because they hold a lot, are lightweight, and slide easily under the bed. I'd suggest using the space for things that don't have to be pulled out too often, like out-of-season clothes and bedding. But as previously noted, I also use this space for my guitar cases. Your kid might want to do likewise!

Cover it up. Under-bed storage is great, but *looking* at under-bed storage is another matter. If you use the space under your kid's bed for storage, make sure you conceal it with a bed skirt. Try to find one that matches the rest of the bedding or the color of the room.

Check out a chest. A blanket or hope chest is a great place to store stuffed animals as well as blankets, quilts, sheets, extra pillows—they all tuck right into the chest. Put it at the foot of your child's bed, or put it under a window and add some flat pillows on top for an instant window seat. But remember that those wooden lids are heavy! Don't get one for your child until she's old enough to raise the lid with ease. Plow & Hearth (see page 47) has one just for children that you can have personalized with your child's name.

Add a low bookcase, plus. Putting a low bookcase along one wall of your kid's bedroom gives him tons of storage for books and toys—at his height. Add wooden storage cubbies and cabinets to match and create an entire wall of usable, kid-friendly storage and display space. You can even add a desk to this wall array if you use a board the same width as the other elements and attach it to the wall at the same height. Tuck a kid-size rolling chair under it and your child is set!

Make your own bookcase. No, I don't mean block-and-board bookcases, though I happen to love them and still have them out in my studio. Instead, you can make an appealing and interesting bookcase by stacking two wooden benches and bolting them together with a drill and wood screws. They're still low enough to be at the kids' level, and they're supersturdy. Paint them to match your child's room or taste.

Try shallow shelves. One of the most innovative room designs I've ever seen featured an entire wall covered with lengths of shallow shelving. The shelving, painted a color that contrasted with the wall behind it, was a design element itself, and the clever creator hadn't overburdened it with stuff, but merely accented it with the occasional starfish or bouquet. I immediately thought that this shallow shelving would be perfect for displaying small dolls and other toys, collectibles, and treasures in a child's room. But to keep from creating an entire wall of dust-ables, I'd suggest limiting it to the wall behind the bed. This will eliminate the

👍 Love It *or* Lose It? 👎

Armoires. Those big, tall, freestanding "closets" of old. Should you get one to add storage space for a child's room? I'd say that depends on the child's age. For a young child, opening the giant armoire doors is a real challenge, and it's impossible to reach the higher levels inside. (Trust me on this—I grew up with them.) But for a teen, it's a wonderful solution, especially if you add enough shelves and hooks to really maximize the space.

Verdict: Lose it for young kids. Love it for teens!

need for a night table, too—your child can put an alarm clock and a glass of water right on the lowest shelf.

Mix and match storage options. Look around for storage systems that allow you to mix and match different components. One of my friends swears by a storage unit with lots of little cubbies for her son's little cars, windup toys, card collections, sunglasses, swim goggles, and other disparate stuff. Another unit with a couple of dresser drawers fits on top, and there are several other mix and match pieces also available.

A tisket, a tasket, put stuff in plastic baskets. Kids—and those of us who remain kids at heart—love color. And parents love indestructible, convenient storage options. Put the two together and you have the big, colorful plastic tubs that garden catalogs like Gardener's Supply Company (see page 49) offer for hauling compost, weeds, produce, and the like around gardens. Capacious and inexpensive, these flexible tubs make perfect storage bins for toys, stuffed animals, and anything else you need to keep neat and off the floor, bed, and other surfaces—but in easy reach of small hands.

Or use bins. Plastic storage bins with snap-on lids are good storage options, too. You can stack them. You can sit on them when they're closed. Stuff doesn't spill out of them. And they are easy to wash out or wipe down when something leaks or spills in them.

Supply a stool. Remember what it's like to be too short. (Some of us still are, so we remember all too well.) Help your kids reach everything easily with a sturdy four-legged stool. Catalogs like Solutions (see page 48) carry sturdy, colorful plastic models that lock open for use, then fold up flat so they'll easily fit in a closet or under a bed.

Take time for trash. Kids generate trash, too (have you noticed?), and they need a place to put it. Make sure they each have a wastebasket (plastic ones that are scrubbable are good) in their rooms, and make sure they empty them weekly, or as often as is needed.

Box it up, part one. My friend Karen has her own way of handling her adorable daughter, Audrey's, art supplies. "The problem is too many tattered boxes of crayons, markers, glue sticks, and so on that kids stop using," Karen says. "The solution is to buy stackable plastic shoeboxes. They allow for the collection to grow as relatives bestow even more art supplies on the household."

Box it up, part two. Karen also has a way of dealing with what she describes as "the big shoe-toss on the bedroom floor." Her solution was to buy a large, unpainted wooden box at a craft store and paint it a bright color. She says, "You'll still have a jumble of sneakers, shoes, slippers, and flip-flops, but at least it's contained in the box (most of the time!)."

Get a rolling desk. If your kid has a laptop, consider getting a rolling laptop desk. I have a handmade one that lets me use a real keyboard and mouse and hook my laptop to a docking station (more on this in Chapter 12—The Home Office, beginning on page 227). But Improvements (see page 48) also carries one that is very attractive, comes in a variety of finishes, and takes up very little space—it's just 20 inches wide and 15 inches deep. The height is adjustable, and it has a drawer for screen cloths, sticky tags, and the like, as well as two shelves for textbooks, notebooks, and supplies.

Post a bulletin. Kids' rooms practically scream for bulletin boards; they let kids tack up anything from blue ribbons to art, homework assignments to photos. I think a wood-framed corkboard looks just fine. But if you want to dress it up, make your own by having a piece of Homasote board cut to fit a wooden frame, covering it with the fabric of your kid's choice (using your trusty staple gun), and securing the board to the frame.

Get a good hamper. One of my friends has a great place to put all the stuffed animals you're not displaying on the bed. "Buy a nice wicker hamper with a lift-top lid for your child's bedroom," she advises. "They come in lots of great colors now. Stash all the stuffed animals, dolls, and throw pillows in it every night. The clutter comes off the floor but is easily accessible when they wake up in the morning and want their favorite huggie bear or doll."

Then get another one. Get a second hamper for your kid's dirty clothes. Make sure it has a lightweight lid and is easy for small hands to open, so kids can corral their own clothes. And make it a different color from the stuffed-animal hamper, so there's no confusion.

Try tubular art storage. My friend and clutter expert Skye Alexander suggests storing kids' art rolled up in cardboard tubes. Use recycled tubes from wrapping paper, aluminum foil, and so on, matching the size of the tube to the size of the art. Roll up the drawing or painting and pop it in the tube (you can usually store quite a few in each tube). Put the child's name on the outside to avoid confusion.

The tubes keep the art safe and contained, and they're easy to store in a drawer, plastic storage container, or basket.

Check it out. Give children's books a trial run before you buy them by checking them out of the library. Once you see which ones are hits, you can buy just those and save some shelf space. That goes for DVDs, too!

Trap the trains. My friend Holly's son, Caleb, is crazy for Thomas the Tank Engine and his (seemingly) 500,000 friends. So her husband, Mike, built a train table for Caleb that's just the right height for him to play at. He sets up the tracks, equipment, and favorite train cars and engines on the table's ample top and stores the rest in drawers Mike built into the sides. No more trains on the floor! Your family might not boast a member with Mike's woodworking skills, but you can check around at thrift stores, flea markets, yard sales, and second-hand shops for tables that could fit the bill. (Don't forget about those drawers! You could also slide a plastic storage box or two under the table for easy train storage.)

Raise the stakes. Or tracks, in this case. Once your kids reach school age, their dad might want to start getting them model trains, especially if he himself is a train fanatic from way back. If this is the case in your household, try this space-saving tip, courtesy of my friends Carolyn and Gary. Gary has set up his model train track on narrow shelving that goes around the wall of his workshop. It takes up no floor or storage space, and his trains run happily around their elevated

If you want to not just kick kids' clutter but teach them effective ways of kicking it themselves, the best resource I know of for getting your kids to pitch in is a book called *Mrs. Clean Jeans' Housekeeping with Kids* (Rodale, 2004, $14.95). The author, Tara Aronson (aka Mrs. Clean Jeans), really knows how to get kids of all ages motivated to help with the housework and object control. Every chapter divides chores by age, so you can see exactly what you should expect your kids to be able to do. (Her own kids ranged in age from 2 to 13 when she wrote the book, and yes, there were chores for the 2-year-old!) Tara gives a lot of pointers on how to make chores more fun—more like family games. You may read this for help corralling your kids' clutter and end up getting them to help clean the house, too!

Ask Claire DeClutter

Dear Claire,

I have a baby and a toddler. But that's not all I have. I also have about 3,000 stuffed animals, all gifts from well-meaning friends and relatives. I don't want them, the kids don't want them, and I sure don't have any place to put them. But I don't want to hurt anybody's feelings! What can I do?

—Overstuffed

Dear Overstuffed,

I suggest that you take photos of your children with each adorable toy. On the back of each photo, note the date the photo was taken and who gave the animal to your child (or label the photos on the disk so you know what's what). Then donate everything you don't want to Goodwill or the Salvation Army, give it to a children's consignment shop, or send it to a home for unwed mothers, a shelter for abused families, or another suitable charity. If Aunt Martha asks about that fabulous stuffed rhino she gave baby Billy, show her the photo and tell her how much he loves it. Or loved it, before that unfortunate accident. I'm sure she'll understand.

While we're talking about stuffed animals, let me mention a lifesaver that's worth planning for. We all know how kids can latch onto certain stuffed animals and literally love them to death—until they're ripped, dirty, and generally abused beyond repair. If one of your children develops an obsession for an animal, rush out while they're still available and buy a duplicate. Then hide it. You can either alternate them while you're washing one or save the "twin" to use as a replacement when the original finally falls apart.

Good luck,
Claire

track, making all the train noises that enthusiasts find so endearing. His grandson, Jeremiah, and my boyfriend, Rob, can hole up in there with him for hours, watching the trains go round and round. Try it in your kids' rooms. Whoo-whoo!

Try hardware for hair accessories. Sick of picking (or sweeping, or vacuuming) up all the hair clips, bands, barrettes, scrunchies, and endless other little hair-related accessories your girls find indispensable? Head for the hardware store. Plastic tool trays and drawer sets are inexpensive and come with partitions or drawers in all sorts of sizes and combinations, so your daughter can pick just the right one to hold all her stuff. And since they're clear, she can see the contents without having to pull out the drawers or open the lid.

Ditto for doodads. Plastic tool trays and drawer sets are also great for holding beading supplies, puzzle pieces, marbles, tiny model cars, plastic animals, cosmetics, jewelry—you name it. If it's small and has lots of pieces, it's a match made in heaven. If your kid wants to carry his or her stuff around, choose a small plastic tool or tackle box with a handle.

Use pretzel logic. My friend Robin has a great solution for all those arts and crafts supplies. "In grocery stores, look for food containers that can have a second life after the treats are gone," she says. "Our family's particular favorites are those sturdy plastic bins of pretzel rods. Once the pretzels are gone, we recycle the containers to hold beads, foam pieces, chalk, and pom-poms. They're free, and since they're clear, it's easy to see what's inside."

Pull out the plastic. Donate some of those Tupperware and other plastic containers from your kitchen to your kids so they can easily store and find small toys, puzzles, Lincoln Logs, marbles, and other stuff with lots of bits and pieces. If you number the matching tops and bottoms with indelible markers—a trick I learned from Kathy, one of the members of my local Curves (see page 107)—the kids will be able to match them up quickly. Don't forget zipper-lock bags, either! They're great for containing little pieces and are ideal if kids want to store more than one batch of gizmos in one box.

Don't lose it. Give each kid a little cardboard or plastic "Lost and Found" box in his or her room. Then they'll have somewhere to store the odds and ends that inevitably turn up on the floor or in the bottoms of drawers until they eventually realize that they have the missing jigsaw piece (or their friend Mary's barrette) in their box.

Make a memory. Instead of preserving all your kids' bulky school projects for posterity, photograph them and keep them on a disk or in an album, one for each kid. Your kids may still want to save a few of the best, but the rest of the 3-D versions can be tossed, while the memories are there to look at anytime.

Box up outgrown clothes. My friend Jennifer tells me, "When my son outgrows a clothing size, I place the clothes into a labeled plastic tote. That way it's ready for the next child or to give away."

the **Pros** **Know**

Rose Kennedy knows a thing or two about kids and clutter. She's written a whole book on the subject—*10-Minute Kid Clutter Control.* Rose recommends cardboard "dressers" for pre-schoolers and kindergartners. You can buy them in cheerful patterns or cover them yourself. They're shorter than "real" dressers, and the lightweight drawers are much easier for small hands to pull open and push shut, so your children will be more likely to put stuff away themselves. Rose also recommends putting comforters on children's beds. Not only are they supercomfy, she notes that they're much easier for a child to pull up over the bed than a bedspread, which will help encourage them to make their own beds. Great ideas!

Don't sweat school art. My friend Chris has a super-sensible method for dealing with her son's artwork: "Prior to the beginning of the school year, purchase a sweater box or other large storage container for storing your child's papers and artwork that you want to save for the year," Chris says. "Each day, cull through your child's folder or backpack. Toss what you don't want and put what you want to keep in the box."

Send school art to boot camp. Lillian, another enthusiastic member of my local Curves, had another great way of dealing with her children's art, projects, and other beloved toys and possessions. As a young mom without a big budget, Lillian bought each of her children a metal trunk at the Army-Navy store. She painted each trunk that child's favorite color, then painted their name on top. Over the years, she stored their best or favorite artwork and projects, as well as photos, letters, stuffed animals, favorite outfits—anything that really meant a lot to them. She went through their trunks with them often, switching out anything that no longer had a lot of meaning and exchanging it with other things they valued. When the kids left home and set up their own places, Lillian sent their trunks along with them—treasured keepsakes that captured the best of their entire childhoods. Great idea!

Get stuff out of sight. My editor Anne has a time-tested tactic for cleaning out clutter from her son's room. "I sneak stuff that he doesn't play with anymore into a bin in the attic that he doesn't know about," Anne confesses. "If he doesn't miss it after a while, I can get rid of it. When I put junk in his wastebasket, he just pulls

Pet Alert!

Do your kids keep pets in their bedrooms? A parakeet, a hamster cage, maybe a little aquarium or terrarium for the lizard or hermit crabs? It's amazing how much clutter pets can introduce to a kid's (or anybody else's) room. There's the pet food, litter, toys, and dishes—not to mention the feathers, litter, fur, and unmentionables that are constantly being tossed out of cages. And then there are the free-roaming pets. One adorable little puppy or kitten can pull out every toy, book, and doodad in a child's room faster than you can get in there to see what they're up to. (And your furry friends will chew them up, too, if you're not fast enough.)

I admit, I think pets in kids' rooms are a great idea. They're fun, they're fascinating, they're friends. I'm sure growing up with pets made me a better and more caring person. But this is one case where the house rules must apply. If your child doesn't keep her pet's cage, tank, or aquarium clean, she loses her pet-keeping privileges.

Of course, you need to help her keep the area tidy by getting an aquarium/ terrarium stand with a cabinet to hold the supplies, a sturdy little table with shelves and a waterproof surface (even if you have to staple plastic cloth over it), or another sturdy piece of furniture with kid-friendly storage (drawers or shelves with doors—pet supplies are *not* attractive!). Help your child keep all the pieces in place with plastic shoeboxes or other plastic storage containers. And make sure you have a sturdy plastic trash can (with plastic trash-bag liners) either stashed inside the cabinet or right beside the pet's stand. You can't expect your kid to clean a cage or tank if there's no place to put the old litter or filter! A roll of paper towels in the cabinet is essential for spills and cleanup time, too.

it out again, so that doesn't work. I think he inherited his grandmother's pack rat gene!"

Scout for suitcases. Here's another unique tip from my friend Robin. "Scout for tiny suitcases (toiletry or carry-on size) to hold doll clothes and teeny, tiny, troublesome doll shoes," she says. "When you find a great sale, buy a few matching suitcases in the same size to make stacking and storing easier. It's great for kids

What about that kitten or puppy? Make it a rule that they can be in your kid's room only when he's there (and awake) to supervise. And make sure there's a basket or box of cat (or dog) toys in each child's room so the pup or kitten has something appropriate to play with—not your kids' stuffed animals and other stuff! At nighttime and nap time, put the little furballs where *you* can keep an eye on them.

Give adult dogs and cats cozy beds of their own if you let them sleep in your child's room. Catalogs like L.L. Bean, Plow & Hearth, and Orvis (see pages 46, 47, and 49) offer plush dog and cat "nests" in every conceivable size and a wonderful selection of colors and patterns. (Let your child choose the color or pattern for the one in her room.) Many have removable covers for easy washing.

One last thing: Resist any and all pleas, tantrums, and other attempts on your kids' parts to let them have age-inappropriate pets. If the family is sharing a pet and you're willing to be the primary caregiver, that's fine. But no matter how badly your 3-year-old wants a kitten of her own or your 5-year-old begs for a parrot, do not give in. Give her a stuffed kitten and have her care for it as a "trainer" until she's old enough for the real thing (or try a stuffed mechanical kitty that meows and purrs). Give him a parakeet—those colorful little birds have big parrot personalities without the complex requirements of parrot care (including the space requirements). Goldfish make great first-aquarium fish and require only a fraction of the care that a tropical aquarium does. (But they still need a bright, roomy tank with a filter!) Any reptile can escape from its tank, and so can those crickets (or, yikes, mice) you have to feed them. Ease your child into pet ownership and he or she will have a delightful—rather than dirty and overwhelming—experience. And so will you!

who are on the go: Now there's no need to gather up a tote bag of toys each time there's a play date or a visit to relatives."

Save your surfaces. Want to put a table, desk, or other crafts/eating/play surface in your kid's room? Of course you do. But look out! Spills and stains are a fact of life when you have kids (or, ahem, even when you don't). The solution is to cover that surface with an elasticized pad. You can get these in innumerable patterns and shapes (including one that adjusts to any shape) from housewares stores and catalogs like Improvements (see page 48).

Buy some sleeping bags. Once your kid's old enough to have friends come for sleepovers, get a couple of sleeping bags and stash them in his closet. You can store them on a high shelf where they're out of his way but easy for you to bring down when his friends are due over.

Or blow up the bed. Air mattresses are great fun for kids. They can jump, roll around, and wrestle all over them, and if they roll off, it's not far to the floor! A full- or queen-size air mattress can transform your kid's floor into a super sleepover space. With an electric pump, it takes less than 5 minutes to inflate or (if the pump is reversible) deflate the mattress, and the whole thing tucks away in a storage bag that's half the size of a sleeping bag. Stash it on a high shelf in your child's closet between overnights.

Camp out. Make that underused tent do double-duty when your child has over-night guests. Set it up in his bedroom and put his friends' sleeping bags inside for a fun "camp-over." Don't forget the marshmallows! The high shelf of a kid's closet is also a good place to store the tent once it's folded up.

Go back to school. A metal locker is a great storage accessory for a kid's room. Get one in your kid's favorite color, or paint it to match his room. Hooks hold jackets and caps, and kids can keep sports equipment in the bottom of the locker. And because lockers are metal, you can hang magnetic hooks, a magnetic mirror, and a magnetic memo board inside.

Get a rolling cart. A great storage option for kids' rooms is a rolling storage cart, such as the GuideCraft Moon and Stars See, Store, and Take Along. These carts are designed especially for kids' toys, books, art supplies, and other trea-sures, and are widely available from stores and Web sites like www.amazon.com and www.babyage.com.

Bring out the big guns. I think this tip from my friend Karen is one of the all-time most ingenious! "Our old house without closets couldn't corral the coloring books, workbooks, packs of colored paper, lined handwriting paper, and craft kits our daughter, Audrey, uses," Karen confesses. "Then we happened upon an old gun cabinet in a secondhand shop. It was 5 feet tall but only about 10 inches deep, perfect for our small space. We gutted the inside, added fresh paint inside and out, installed new hardware, added a few shelves, and hung a pretty lace curtain on the glass door. Now we have a wonderful kiddy storage cabinet that's fancy enough to fit right in with our decor."

KICK THE KIDS' CLOSET CLUTTER

Closets can be scary for kids. (Isn't a monster hiding in there?) But even when no terrors lurk behind the door, a closet can be an awkward, hard-to-use, hard-to-reach space for kids. In this section, let's look at ways to make your child's closet both kid-friendly and less cluttered.

If you'd like, you can use the same before-and-after visualization exercise for each child's closet that you did for your own closet. (See page 196 for directions and worksheets.) Or you can skim through these tips and just plunge in!

Let in lots of light. A dark closet not only makes it hard to see and find things—it makes it even scarier for kids. Make sure your child's closet is brightly lit, and put the switch low enough for them to reach it easily. (A pull-on light in a child's closet is *not* a good idea.) If you can't wire in a new fixture, you can use a battery-operated push light.

Add color and fun. Your child's closet should be an extension of their room. Add paint, wallpaper, stencils, stickers, and other design elements from their bedroom, or treat it like a separate room and brighten it up with whatever colors, patterns, or decorations your kid wants. Multicolored stripes? Big, goofy flowers right out of the sixties? A beautiful nature poster (or NASCAR or movie poster)? Get your kid in on the act and enjoy yourselves! But remember that a lot of the wall surface will be covered with clothes and storage units, so don't get *too* carried away or you'll be disappointed when that glorious decor isn't on view.

Make it easy to get dressed. Here's a great tip from my friend Betsy. (I've got to pass this one along to my brother and sister-in-law!) "It's important for kids to plan out clothing ahead of time to avoid the morning rush and frantic search for matching socks or gym sneakers," Betsy says. "Buy a weekly clothes organizer that hangs over the closet rod. It usually features sturdy fabric shelves with five to seven slots (in boy and girl colors). It's ideal for planning out a week's worth of school clothes, undergarments, shoes, socks, and baseball caps or hair accessories. And it keeps the daily clutter off the dresser top, off chairs, and off the end of the bed." Betsy got her daughter's from Lillian Vernon (www.lillianvernon.com; see page 46).

Use the door. Don't waste the inside of your kid's closet door! Hang a shoe rack or a full-length mirror, both of which will hook over the top of the door comparatively unobtrusively. Bear in mind that you don't have to use the shoe rack for shoes. Plastic shoe racks with pouches for the shoes will hold toys, socks, mittens, hats, and accessories just as easily.

Hook it up. Another alternative is to add big hooks on the back of the closet door for backpacks, bathrobes, and purses. Again, put them low enough for kids to reach easily, and make sure they have big knobs on the ends so nobody gets hurt!

Clip it on. For some reason, sports equipment is hard to store in a closet. It seems to immediately work its way to the very back of the space or to just disappear entirely, which doesn't make it easy or fun to play with! Keep it where it's easy to see and reach with the sort of door clips that housewares stores and catalogs sell to clip brooms, mops, and other cleaning implements to the pantry or basement door. When it's time to practice or play, your kids can grab what they need off the backs of their closet doors.

Stand 'em up. Another way to keep baseball bats, hockey sticks, and other sports equipment together is to tuck an umbrella stand inside the closet door. (Unlike the one in your hallway, though, you want this one to be wood, metal, plastic, or another unbreakable material—not ceramic. And make sure it's sturdy enough not to topple over when it's full of bats and sticks or when somebody's trying to pull one out.) Or use one of the metal umbrella racks you often see in offices and restaurants, with a grid of square openings on top to hold the umbrellas—or, in your case, sports equipment—upright.

Lower your sights. Make it easy for your kids to reach their own clothes by installing a clothes rod at their level. Then do as you should in your own closet and hang similar clothes (jackets, dresses, pants, skirts, tops) together so they're easy to find.

Put a case in the closet. Help bring your child's closet down to a more comfortable size by putting a kid-size low bookcase in there. Set it against the back wall and your child can walk right up to it—something her own height—to put things in or take them out. Pick up one at a thrift or secondhand store or a yard sale, paint it a cheerful color, and put it to work!

Move in a module. Customized closet modules, available at home improvement stores, let you get great use from your kid's closet space. You can get a module with dresser drawers under open shelves, attach two levels of clothes rods from either side, and add open shelving at the top, then paint it all whatever color your child desires.

Add more shelves. Shelving can really add storage space to a child's closet. You can install standard wood shelves, painted to match the closet, or use plastic-coated wire shelf units (such as those sold by Closet Maid). Both ready-to-use wooden and wire shelves are available in most home centers. (California Closets has an entire line at Target.) The wire shelving comes in all lengths and is designed specifically for closets, so it fits standard-size closets. And it's durable, attractive, and easy to install.

Save the high shelf. Store stuff that kids need but won't be tempted to try to get down themselves on that long, over-the-clothes-rod shelf. Blankets and other off-season bed linens, plastic containers with clothes that are out of season, sleeping bags, and other "occasional" items are the best choices for this shelf. You can also display beloved but no-longer-played-with stuffed animals and toys up there so the kids can visit with them when they open the closet door but they aren't taking up bedroom space that's needed for the "now" toys.

Corral some cubbies. Shoe cubbies are an attractive and durable way to keep shoes, purses, scarves, hats, caps, mittens, sweaters, umbrellas, and baseball gloves neat and accessible. And they sit on the floor, where even the smallest child can get to them without asking for help. Put them against the back of the closet wall for easiest access.

Use plastic hangers. Avoid the old, brittle plastic hangers that can snap and break. Instead, choose the smooth, sleek, colorful hangers available today in department and housewares stores. They're thicker than wire so they're easier for little hands to hold—and not nearly as tempting to use as weapons (and not as harmful if they are)! Don't want to pay full price? Thrift stores often sell them for pennies a bunch.

Clear out old clothes. Use the same techniques to sort through your kids' clothes that you use for your own (see page 199). If your child hangs on to favorite outfits like grim death, no matter how beat they are, suggest that you turn them into doll clothes (or bear clothes). Or save the best patches to use on their skirts, jeans, or jackets. If you're crafty, make them into a quilt for the kid's bed. Or put them in a plastic storage container and move them to a high shelf. (You can always move them to the attic or basement later, and eventually out the door once your child's wardrobe interests have moved on. But meanwhile, he or she will know they're there.) If you're dealing with a teen who refuses to relinquish any of her outfits, no matter how many there are and how squashed into the closet, the best approach is to divide them up by season and pack up the out-of-season clothes in plastic storage boxes to stash under her bed. When the next season rolls around, pull out the appropriate box and switch. Once she takes the clothes out and really looks at them, she may decide they're so out of style she'd be happy for you to take them to Goodwill. The exception is too-small clothes: If they're outgrown, unless it's a favorite outfit or two she wants to save, they go *now*.

ONWARD!

Okay, we've tackled all the bedrooms and all the (gasp) closets. Now it's time to move on to one of the scariest rooms in the house—the one you use as a home office. (And you thought the kids' rooms would be bad!) But it's not going to be as awful as you fear. Believe me, a home office can be organized, efficient, and functional—even all those files and bills—and once you've set it up right, it's easy to keep it that way. Mine is, and yours will be too. Promise! So read on and let's start shuffling papers.

Chapter 12

The Home Office

Bills. Files. Records. Research materials. Can you say "clutter"? In this chapter, you'll find tips that show you how to set up your home office most efficiently and make it a space where you truly want to spend time. Whether you just use it to pay bills and check e-mail or you actually work from home full- or part-time, and whether you have a whole room to yourself or just a computer desk tucked in a corner, kicking office clutter will make your office work harder. These tips will "work" just as hard at any other type of office, as well!

PRIORITIES FOR OFFICES

As I've recommended for all the other rooms in your home, start your office de-cluttering process by setting some clutter-kicking priorities. Do it by focusing on what matters most to you about the way your home office looks and functions, and then following the chain along to what matters least. The best way to do this is by taking a good, hard look at the "before" state of the room and then visualizing the "after." Once you've finished your visualization, you're ready to start tackling the clutter. Start with the most bothersome clutter problems, and work down your list of priorities until you get to the minor irritations. Then you're done!

Paper Escapers

When it comes to bills and the mounds of mail that pour into our homes every day, there seem to be two kinds of people—the ones who deal with it and the ones who don't. You'll find tips from the ones who deal with it throughout this chapter. But right now, let's focus on the ones who don't. Hopefully, they'll both reassure you that you're not as bad about dealing with the mail as you think and also inspire you to keep it under control.

I have a dear friend who, to hear her talk, spends every spare moment of her life "doing her paperwork." It's what she does every day after work and every weekend, or so she says. (Perhaps her husband and kids would tell a different story.) She pulls out the boxes of bills and other paper, pours them onto the dining room table, and . . . fade to black. I honestly can't say what happens then, because I have a terrible feeling that they're always the *same* papers. When Rob and I went to my friend's house for a cookout this past summer, she was frantically shoveling papers off the table while her husband fired up the grill. Six months later, she e-mailed to say that she was about to sit down once again with the same paperwork she'd been doing when Rob and I came over that long-ago summer day! She calls it "avoiditis." She e-mailed me today to say that she was still working on the pile and had just unearthed an unopened birthday card (to her) from last May and a wallet she'd bought a couple of years ago! Mind you, this is not someone who works from home. Presumably, she has no more paperwork to do than anyone else with a spouse and two kids. I don't know about you, but having the same bills, tax forms, and so on looming over me month after month would drive me insane.

Speaking of which, if you think my friend's story is scary, listen to this one: Years ago, I knew a woman who had a very responsible corporate job, where she managed a staff and a deadline-laden schedule and made quite a good salary. You'd have thought that if anyone could stay on top of bills and other paperwork, she'd be the one. But one night, I went over to her house for supper and saw the entire dining room filled with large cardboard boxes and bags. She'd been living there for 9 months at that point, so I was surprised that she hadn't gotten the boxes unpacked or at least stowed out of sight. But it turned out they weren't moving boxes. Instead, the boxes and bags contained all the mail she'd received for the past 9 months, unopened, unread. I frankly don't know why she still had heat, running water, and phone service when I arrived. I do know that, eventually, she hired someone to get it all sorted out. She has since married, and all I can say is, I hope her husband takes care of the mail!

An Office Visualization

To get to your "after," you need to start with the "before"—the way things look right now. So get out some paper, or use the "My Home Office—Before" form on page 230 (or make a photocopy of it and write on that). Write down every place there's clutter, and note what that clutter is. Are your files exploding? Has your desk disappeared under a pile of stuff that really belongs in other rooms? Is your computer comfortable to use, or is it perched precariously on a heap of telephone books? Try to think about where you get hung up when you're trying to get things done, where you lose things, and what distracts or irritates you. Take a good look. Take your time. Because the home office is usually a small room or part of a room, it won't take as long as you think to finish your list.

Once you've jotted down a quick description of the "before" state of your home office, it's time to move on to the "after"—how you want the room to look when you've kicked the clutter. Write it all down on a piece of paper, or in the "My Home Office—After" form on page 230 (or on as many photocopies of it as you need to do it justice). To make sure you're being realistic, look at the room every few minutes while you're writing your description.

Your description can be short and to the point: "I don't want light from the windows blinding me while I try to work on the computer. I want a better organizing system for my files. I want to get on top of my appointments, bill-paying, and birthday cards. I want a better-looking file cabinet and a comfortable office chair."

Or you can create a detailed picture of exactly how you'd like your office to look if it were perfect (for you). You can picture the colors of the walls, floor and floor coverings, and window treatments; imagine every piece of furniture, including where it would be, what it would do, and what it would look like; and try to see where the books, files, paperwork, equipment, and supplies would go. Think about what you don't have now but need in order to work well. Lots of magazines feature home-office makeovers, and catalogs such as Solutions and Improvements (see page 48) are full of furniture and accessories for the office. Look some over for inspiration. Visit your local Staples, Office Depot, or Office-Max store.

My Home Office—Before

_____
_____
_____
_____
_____
_____
_____
_____
_____
_____
_____

My Home Office—After

_____
_____
_____
_____
_____
_____
_____
_____
_____
_____
_____
_____
_____

Getting There

Now that you've captured your home office's "before" condition, listing all the specifics, and you've imagined its "after" appearance, you can finally prioritize the steps you'll need to take to get there from here. Again, bearing both "before" and "after" in mind, I'd recommend starting with what bothers you most about the "before" condition and making that your first de-cluttering priority. Then organize the rest of your "to do" list in descending order of importance.

Maybe you're sick of losing bills and getting overdue notices. Or you can't ever find your clients' addresses, no matter how many times you write them down. Or you've stopped even looking in your file folders because you're too scared to go into the file cabinet. Or your computer desk puts the keyboard and mouse at the wrong height and it makes your wrists, shoulders, neck, and back hurt to work there. Or you can't even find your computer among all the accessories that have colonized the desk.

Write down whatever's driving you to distraction on the "My Home Office Priority List" (or photocopy it, if you'd prefer) in descending order from most to least maddening. Now you have your priorities straight! Once you've finished, you can turn to the tips beginning on page 232 to find ingenious ways of dealing with each problem.

My Home Office Priority List

_____

_____

_____

_____

_____

_____

_____

_____

THE OFFICE TIPS

Since there are so many aspects to home offices, I'm going to divide up these tips by topic to make them easier to find and use. Whether you're trying to improve your home office setup, figure out a better way to pay bills, or determine how long to keep those #@!%$** records, scan the pages that follow and you'll find what you need.

Office Furniture, Files, and Other Necessities

Get a shredder. And use it. Not just to cut down on paper clutter—though it does a good job at that—but also to protect yourself from identity theft. The finely shredded paper is great for your compost pile, or you can use it in shipping boxes, or you can recycle it.

Build in portability. I love my home computer setup so much that I'm going to share it with you. Rather than having a desktop computer with a huge hard drive, I have a laptop with a "docking port." The docking port lets me hook up everything I need to operate comfortably—Internet hookup, printer, speakers, keyboard, and mouse. (When you work with words all day, as I do, that laptop keyboard and mouse just don't cut it.) When I travel and need to take my computer, I simply detach the laptop from its docking port and depart. It couldn't be easier, and it takes up so much less space. I don't know why anyone would want a clunky desktop computer!

Rack it up. Okay, I know this tip isn't clutter-related, but I want to share it anyway because it works! If you already use a laptop in your home office or I've convinced you to get one, you'll want to keep it from overheating. Despite the fact that it's vented, it can get quite hot after a while (ever heard that ominous buzzing when the fan kicks on?). To help my laptop keep its cool, I set it on a cooling rack—the kind you'd cool cookies, cakes, or bread on. Mine is coated wire with legs that hold it about an inch off the desk and allow air to circulate beneath the laptop while I work. It's just big enough to let me put my speakers on either side of the laptop. It brings the screen up to a better viewing height, too. Try it!

Go wireless. As the name implies, you'll avoid the clutter of wires, modem, and cables if a wireless network (wi-fi) is available in your area or you are technically savvy enough to install your own. But make sure the one you choose is protected from freeloaders (usually with a password), since the more people are using it, the slower it is. And if it's your own network that's wireless, be sure that the router you have purchased includes a firewall.

Get rid of old computers. If your home office is really more of a graveyard for your family's old computers—or it's simply time to upgrade to a laptop or better model—it's time to recycle the old ones. Have you been holding onto them because you don't want to throw them out and don't know what else to do with them? Go to www.earth911.org to find out how to recycle them.

Cart your work around. I find a rolling cart—the kind home stores like Target and Home Depot sell for kitchens—to be invaluable for my home office. I put my inbox, calendar, and address boxes on top and my projects in progress in each of the slide-out baskets. (Once the projects are finished, I go through the baskets and discard or shred anything I can, then put the rest in a labeled file in my file cabinet.) I can pull the cart up next to my computer workstation while I'm working, then stash it out of the way when it's not needed. It's a lifesaver!

Get a file cabinet. Whether you opt for a luxurious oak file cabinet or a metal version (they don't have to be ugly—I have turquoise and red file cabinets as well as the typical gray and beige), treat yourself to this essential office organizer. Then get hanging folders for bills (see page 242), projects, warranties (see below), health-related papers, tax forms and records, house-related information and services, school-related materials (one folder for each child), wills, living wills, powers of attorney, car-related papers (insurance, titles, manuals, repair and maintenance records), pets, take-out menus . . . the list is endless! Label each file with its contents so it's easy to find, and organize them in a way that makes sense to you. (Most people opt for alphabetical organization, but do what works for you.) To me, file cabinets are as essential as my computer, phone, and calendar—a vital piece of home-office equipment. I even keep my gardening catalogs in file folders in one of my file cabinets!

Make your desk do double-duty. No room for a file cabinet *and* a desk, you say? Consider turning your desk space into storage. Buy a flat door or a thick plywood sheet and put it across two file cabinets to make a roomy desk.

Cart your files around. You can also get rolling carts specifically designed for offices. These are designed for hanging file folders, so you can roll your files over

Linda Koopersmith, the Beverly Hills Organizer and co-host and organizational expert on the Style Network's hit series *Clean House*, specializes in helping clients get their offices under control. In her book *The Beverly Hills Organizer's Home Organizing Bible*, she shows you her step-by-step techniques for organizing files, addresses, checkbooks, and much more. One of Linda's great ideas is to replace your inbox with a desktop caddy. It's an upright container for hanging files that takes up about as much desk space as a shoebox. The advantage is that you can set up inbox files that will actually let you see what you have without having to pick up the whole slippery pile of papers and digging through it over and over—that time-wasting "I know it's in here somewhere" syndrome. Linda points out that the caddy needs to have sides so papers can't escape from the hanging files.

to your desk and then stow them away in a closet when you're not using them. They're a great alternative when a permanent file cabinet's not an option.

Organize your files. File cabinets and carts are not, repeat, *not* museum vaults. If they're not working for you, they're just clutter. Keep your files current. Shred or recycle material you no longer need. If you have files you aren't using but may want to refer to again at some point, store them in labeled printer-paper boxes in the office closet or a dry basement or attic. Make sure the files you keep in your file cabinet are clearly labeled and organized chronologically, with the most recent additions in the front of the file. If your projects are complex, divide the contents of your files into labeled folders and tuck them back in the file. Again, organize each folder chronologically. And make sure your file drawers aren't so overstuffed that you can't even remove the files! When you have to pull to get a file out, it's a sure sign that your drawer is overdue for cleaning.

Stand them up. My editor Anne keeps paperwork for active and ongoing projects in folders in a standup file rack where she can instantly put her hands on them. She reports that this method works for kids' school projects and reports, too.

Clear your desk. My friend and feng shui guru Skye Alexander says that, according to feng shui, an uncluttered office can increase prosperity. In her book *10-Minute Clutter Control Room by Room*, Skye says, "By putting your office in order, you demonstrate a willingness to deal with problems involving your finances and to increase prosperity."

Corner it. No good place to put your desk? Get a desk that's designed to fit in a corner, like Ballard Design's Winston Desk (see page 46).

Add an armoire. By now you're probably sick of hearing me recommend armoires—those freestanding closets so beloved of the Victorians. But they can really hold a lot of office supplies, especially if you add extra shelves. You can tuck in file and document boxes, too, creating a file cabinet that looks like furniture. Open the doors, and there's everything you need to work efficiently; close them, and it's all out of sight.

Or add an entertainment center. If you don't have room for an armoire but would still like to close up your files and supplies in a conventional piece of furniture, an entertainment center might be the perfect thing.

Get the right chair. You're probably either using a leftover chair from someplace in the house or a really cheap office chair in your home office. Stop! It's worth every penny to get a padded, supportive, adjustable office chair. Sell or donate the old one and treat yourself to a chair that will make it a pleasure to get to work. You may find that you're using your home office much more often—and no more aching back!

Make it like Martha. Leave it to Martha Stewart to create the perfectly organized, perfectly civilized office. Her perfect tone-on-tone files, boxes, and accessories are all decorated with ornamental floral moldings! This may seem like a bit much for us mere mortals, but her office did offer some other excellent take-away ideas. First, it was painted and accessorized in restful but attractive colors. Next, she'd installed a wall of shelves with a full row of storage cabinets at the bottom. But instead of filling the shelves with books (as in my office), she'd used rows of magazine boxes to neatly contain files in an accessible, easy-to-find manner. Because the spines of the folders face the office, the files are hidden from view but immediately at hand. No file cabinets for Martha! Finally, I was pleased to see that Martha had a laptop on her desk rather than a clunky desktop computer. Sleek and savvy!

Case the books. A small bookcase in the office is a handy place to keep phone books, a dictionary, home maintenance guides, and a family medical encyclopedia.

Hang your shelves. No room for an office bookcase? Hang a set of shelves or a hanging bookcase over your desk.

Don't forget the trash. (And recycling.) Because a home office generates so much paper, a wastebasket is as essential as a shredder. My corporate office had dual bins in each office—one for trash and one for recycling. Great idea!

Put your printer to work. Why have a printer, a fax machine, a scanner, and a copier cluttering up your office when you can buy a compact, inexpensive machine that does it all? Make your printer earn its office space.

Ditch the desk phone. Use your cell phone in the office instead. If you must have a regular office phone, get a wall phone that won't eat up precious desktop space.

Have one drawer for office supplies. Unless you use them constantly, there's no reason to clutter your desk with all the little office supplies that are essential when you finally do need them. Designate a drawer for sticky notes, paper clips, scissors, rubber bands, clips in various sizes, stamps and stamp pads, colored tabs, tape, and anything else you need.

Get yourself a tray. You can stash office supplies—pens, pencils, erasers, a calculator, glue sticks, a stapler, staples, liquid paper, map pins and tacks, magnets, and tape—in a utensil tray. Keep the tray in a drawer in your home office or out on the desk within easy reach. My boyfriend, Rob, has his office essentials in a desk organizer (a plastic tray with compartments for office supplies). He got his at OfficeMax but says they're available at all office-supply stores.

Hang an office medicine cabinet. Another good place to stash office supplies is in a medicine cabinet, where they're out of sight but within easy reach. When you upgrade your bathroom, donate your old cabinet to your office!

File your warranties. My editor Karen has some useful advice for the rest of us: "I keep a file folder of receipts, warranties, and instructions for appliances, electronics, and toys, roughly in alphabetical order," she says. "I go through the file once or twice a year to get rid of the information for things we no longer have or use."

Keep a file for the kids. Karen prefers to keep daughter Audrey's papers in an accordion folder with dividers. She puts Audrey's long-term school assignment instructions, absentee blanks, Scout handbooks, classroom lists, and other paperwork in the folder, so it's all together and easy to find. Karen recommends one accordion folder for every child in the family.

Tools of the Trade

Marla Cilley, better known as FlyLady, knows a lot about staying organized on the go. So she's created an "Office in a Bag" to help you get your stuff together when you need to take your home office away from home. You can buy it in the FlyShop on her Web site, www.FlyLady.net, or go for broke and buy the Office Pack, which includes the Office in a Bag and organizing tools to put in it: My Control Journal, FlyLady's inspirational desk calendar, The Comfort Zone, and her customized FlyLady mousepad.

Don't know FlyLady? Marla helps clutterholics fight the good fight to end CHAOS (Can't Have Anyone Over Syndrome), one baby step at a time. She calls her clutter-control system FLYing, and it's based on tackling clutter and housework just 15 minutes at a time. As she puts it, "We do what we can today and then we do a little more tomorrow. BabySteps." You can read all about it in her book *Sink Reflections* (Bantam, 2002, $15).

File your family papers. My friend Chris has a filing system worked out for all her household papers. She keeps separate file folders for receipts, tax information, warranties, car-related material, school papers, and insurance policies.

Bank on it. Unless you happen to have an indestructible, fire- and flood-proof safe at home, keep your important documents—birth certificates, Social Security cards, passports, wills, marriage and divorce papers, insurance documents, titles to vehicles, medical records, and the like—in a safe-deposit box at the bank. For your own use, keep photocopies in a labeled file folder in your file cabinet. Add a sheet with important addresses—your family doctors, accountant, attorney, and the like.

Put it on the board, part one. At the corporation where I worked, bulletin boards were standard issue for every office. There's no reason not to have one in your home office, as well. Keep only current materials on your bulletin board—business cards, your daily to-do list, outlines, appointment reminders, and so on. At the beginning of your workday, update the board and toss, shred, or file anything that you're not working on right now.

Put it on the board, part two. I love the way my friend Skye deals with her to-do list: She writes it on a blackboard! She uses different-colored chalks for different tasks and degrees of importance (red chalk for urgent projects, for example). At the end of the day, she can simply erase the list and start over.

Put it on the board, part three. A magnetic memo board may be more your style than a bulletin board. If you get one, though, the rules are the same: Don't overload it, keep only current items on it, and update it daily.

Do like the doctors. Those over-the-door plastic file organizers and hanging plastic magazine bins make great "in-and-out" boxes. You can find them at office supply stores. Rather than taking up desk space for your in- and out-bins, you can use the pockets in the organizer for incoming and outgoing mail, memos, and projects. Just make sure you check them daily and keep their contents moving in and out!

Hold pens up. Keep a stash of pens contained and upright on your desk. Here's the place for that beloved but no longer usable mug (or one that's gorgeous but really isn't big enough—or is too big—to use for coffee or tea). Years ago, a friend who knew how much I love gardening gave me a little vase shaped like a pair of green Wellington gardening boots. I couldn't imagine putting flowers in these Wellies, but I could instantly see their utility—and appropriateness!—as pen-holders. I don't know about you, but I've found that even new pens won't write if I wait too long before I use them, so I think the number of pens a mug, tumbler, or vase will hold is perfect. When they're gone, it's time to buy new ones! And meanwhile, penmakers, could you *please* work on making a pen that will keep forever? Thanks.

Dare to duplicate, part one. Back up your files! Keep backup CDs and zip disks in a disk holder (available from any office supply store) so if your computer crashes, *you* don't crash with it. Don't want to keep track of a bunch of disks? Then do what I do—e-mail them to your spouse or partner. As I finish writing a chapter or other important document, I send a copy off to Rob to store on his computer. If mine crashes, I'm still covered.

Dare to duplicate, part two. Try this tip from my super-organized freelancer friend Jennifer. What a time-saver! "I keep duplicates of often-used items in the locations where I use them," Jennifer says. "For example, I have scissors in the office, kitchen, and laundry room; nail files in the bathroom, kitchen, and car; and diaper-changing supplies in the nursery, living room, and office." No more time wasted looking for something, or losing it, or leaving it out (and creating clutter) so you can return it "later."

Reuse your paper. "I have a basket in my office to store paper that has printing

SANITY SAVERS

A lot goes on in offices, even in home offices, and it's hard to keep things spic-and-span. Rather than hold yourself to an impossible standard—that horrid old ideal of the spotless desk and bare walls with nothing but schedules, forecasts, and other business-only papers tacked at eye level on a bulletin board—take comfort from two books that take the opposite approach.

In the first, with the great title *A Perfect Mess* (Little, Brown and Co., 2007, $25.99), authors Eric Abrahamson and David H. Freedman contend that in business, "moderately messy systems can be more profitable and creative than their organized counterparts." They point out that working in disorganized, messy environments never slowed down the likes of highly successful folks like Einstein, Bill Gates, and Arnold Schwarzenegger.

Then there's *Yearnings: Embracing the Sacred Messiness of Life* (Hyperion, 2006, $23.95). In it, author Irwin Kula talks about how office mess is "never about the desk." "We have this dance between messiness and order, messiness and order," he says. "When it feels messy, that is the moment when there will always be some discovery. Even in the clutter of a messy desk, when you're looking for that one thing, you find something else."

I once saw a sign that said, "If a cluttered desk is a sign of a cluttered mind, what is an empty desk a sign of?" Good point. I despise sterility in any home or office surroundings and am a big believer in surrounding yourself with what pleases you wherever you are. My offices, at home and in the workplace, have always been full of color and life—books, plants, stones, art, even an aquarium. But the thing is, in less than a minute I could put my hand on anything I or anyone else wanted or needed because my actual work was well organized.

And that's my point: Having a rich, stimulating work environment is ideal, and yes, it does boost creativity. But having a cluttered, chaotic work environment simply means that you waste a lot of time trying to find things, duplicating work because you can't find what you're looking for, even avoiding certain kinds of tasks because you're not prepared for them. In your home office, strive to create a work environment that enhances your creativity and well-being without compromising your efficiency—an environment that "works" for you.

---

on one side," Jennifer says. "My son can draw on the other side, or I can print out nonwork things on the other side."

Save on ink. You might guess that Jennifer does a fair amount of printing (see the previous tip), so she's come up with ways to save on ink. "I always print on 'fast' and 'grayscale' to save on ink," she says. "This saves money and time on trips to the store, and reduces the need to store lots of extra ink cartridges."

Add a little life. An office shouldn't be a dull, lifeless space. Instead, brighten it with a hanging plant or two and some inspiring nature photos. Just make sure they're not *so* inspiring that looking at them makes you want to forget about work and head outside!

Keeping Up with the Calendar and Addresses

Put it in plain sight. If you don't see your calendar, you won't use it. I use one that has a two-page spread for every week—plenty of room to write down appointments, engagements, birthdays, and so on—and I keep it on my rolling cart beside my computer desk and telephone. It makes it easy to check, and I can write down appointments as soon as I make them via phone or e-mail.

Keep track online. If you have a program like Microsoft Outlook, which has a built-in calendar, use it! I used my Outlook calendar faithfully when I worked for a corporation, and it was great. But I'll admit, I always had a print calendar as well as a backup so I wouldn't miss any meetings if the computers were down. My Yahoo! calendar is versatile. If you use a different e-mail service, see if it has a calendar feature as well.

Get a perpetual calendar. I found this great device at a store that specialized in French housewares. A Victorian staple, the perpetual calendar is a small, circular device that lets you manually rotate the day of the week, date, and month. I change the date on mine every morning when I turn on my computer (and check my lottery tickets!). Mine is in French, so I can practice my French while I see what day it is. I love it!

Keep addresses up to date. Most of my colleagues keep their addresses in their computer's address system. (Microsoft Outlook has a good one, and my Yahoo! address book is excellent.) Some people use Rolodexes (see below). I keep my addresses on good old 3- by 5-inch index cards in a recipe file with alphabetical dividers. Use the system that works for you. But whatever system you use, keep it current. Go through your addresses at least every 6 months, culling any that are no longer relevant. If you receive a new address from someone in your address system, update the address immediately and delete the old one to prevent confusion. I like my cards because they give me room for each person's name, address, phone numbers, cell phone number, e-mail address(es), and spouse's name—plus their children's and parents' names, nicknames, e-mails, addresses, and birthdays. Follow my system and you won't lose anyone's address if your computer crashes. But you could put all that in your electronic address book, too.

Don't use an address book. The one kind of address system I wouldn't recommend is an old-fashioned address book. People—at least the ones I know—seem to move, change jobs, change phone numbers, and change e-mails constantly. I like to write addresses in ink so they're easy to read, and obviously, keeping an address book would involve a lot of crossing out. It's a lot easier (and less messy) to simply write out a new card or update your electronic address book. Besides, you can lose an address book if you take it on trips. (A friend lost hers when a thief stole her purse.)

File business cards. Tape the business cards you need to keep on hand to your 3- by 5-inch cards or Rolodex cards and alphabetize them. Make sure you remove and replace them when someone leaves a company or changes their address! If someone's name isn't pronounced the way it's spelled, I always make a note on the card of how it's actually pronounced so I can remind myself before I speak to them.

Work your Rolodex. My friend Jennifer has some fabulous ideas for keeping track of family and friends' data. "I keep a Rolodex in an office-supplies drawer," she says. "On each friend or family member's card, I write their name, address, and phone number. On the back I write directions to their home and the amount of time it takes to get there. Down one side I keep track of whether or not I sent them a Christmas card each year, and if I received one back."

Put it in your planner. "I keep a list of each family member's clothing sizes and doctor's names and phone numbers in my planner," Jennifer says.

Buy your birthday cards, part one. I write upcoming birthdays on my calendar so I don't forget them, but Jennifer takes her birthday record-keeping to a higher level. "I write friends' and family members' birthdays on my calendar," she says. "I go to the card store only a few times a year and buy as many birthday and anniversary cards as possible. Then I label them with the appropriate person's name and, in the space where the stamp will go, I write the date that I need to mail the card. Once I buy the card, I place a check mark next to their names on my calendar so I don't accidentally buy another one."

Buy your birthday cards, part two. While we're on the subject of birthday cards, my friend Chris has a different system. "At the end of each month, buy all the greeting cards you'll need for the next month," she says.

Cross-check your calendars. Jennifer also has a system in place to make sure family obligations and occasions aren't forgotten. "When an event includes both my husband and me—such as dinner at my parents'—I write it on my calendar and put a check mark next to it on my calendar after I've made sure it's on his calendar, too," she says.

Get a PDA. Palm is probably the best known of these electronic "personal digital assistants," but there are plenty of others out there, including Nokia, HP, and BlackBerry. (A quick Google search will give you a ton of info on the latest, greatest models by these and other makers. Do your homework before you go shopping.) Basically hand-held computers, PDAs allow you to connect with the Internet, check e-mail, check appointments and addresses, make phone calls, navigate, do math calculations, and much more. They are pricey—$200 to $400 or so, depending on the model—but if you need access to your home office's computer or to the Internet while you're on the road, they're certainly handy.

Bills, Bills, Bills

Bite the bill bullet. I hate paying bills as much as anyone. There's nothing like that sinking, pit-of-the-stomach feeling of watching your money drain away! But I make it as painless as possible by organizing the bills so at least I can pay them quickly and not have to worry about late fees. Here's my system:

- ❏ I have a file folder in my file cabinet labeled "Bills."
- ❏ In this folder, I keep the previous month's paid bills banded together with a rubber band. I also keep stamps, return-address labels, and a few envelopes in the folder.

An Ounce of Prevention

Starting out with a sensible approach to home office management can save you a lot of grief. Use these tips from Jaap van Liere, an art curator who works from his home in Berks County, Pennsylvania. He's renowned for having a home office that "never shows signs of clutter."

"The key is always order," says Jaap. "Deal with stuff as it comes in and file it or get rid of it." Here's what Jaap has to say about his approach to managing his paper piles:

✳ Adequately sized work surfaces allow you to see what has to be done next and allow you to spread papers out so you can actually see them.

✳ Important information and resources can disappear if your focus on keeping it orderly means that piles of paperwork are hidden on shelves and in filing cabinets.

✳ Anything that hasn't been looked at or worked on in the past 18 months can probably be thrown away.

✳ A lot of what you have to deal with probably comes in .pdf form, so even if it is absolutely necessary to print it out to have on hand so you can read it and have it in front of you for a meeting, that certainly doesn't mean that it has to be stored. The electronic version is already on a hard drive somewhere.

✳ Three-ring binders and legal-size file sleeves, paper or plastic, are great for keeping things organized.

✳ Filing boxes are really useful. The smaller vertical size can go onto a bookshelf for short-term stuff, and the bigger boxes with lids can go into storage in the closet or basement.

✳ Lastly, small office equipment helps. Laptops and little printers or all-in-one printer/scanner/fax/copier units are a big help. And wi-fi connectivity helps get rid of a lot of wires.

❏ When a new bill arrives, I open it and note the due date. I write the due date on the outside of the envelope and circle it.

❏ I also note if my previous payment was received, and if so, I take the previous month's bill out of the rubber-banded batch and shred it.

- Then I file the new bill with the other unpaid bills, putting them in order of soonest to be paid to latest. (Occasionally—but never often enough!—bills won't come due for 2 or even 3 months after they're sent.)
- I check the file weekly and pay any bills that are coming due.
- When I've paid a bill, I write "paid" and the date under the due date on the front of the envelope and circle it. Then I put the paid bill in the rubber-banded stack.
- I keep my credit-card receipts in the envelope with the credit-card bill.
- I'm a stickler for writing down everything I pay for in my checkbook as well, and I do that as soon as I write each check.

Because bills tend to dribble in one at a time, it takes only about a minute a day to keep up with this system. And when it's time to sit down and pay up, you'll be so grateful everything's in order and ready to go. No more lost bills and wasted time!

Pay upfront. My boyfriend, Rob, is the original absent-minded professor. To make sure he doesn't miss a payment, he pays his bills the day they come in. That way, he never has to worry about where they've gotten to or think twice about whether he's remembered to pay them.

Pay online. Sign up for online bill payment and avoid the paper problem, or use online banking software to schedule transfers.

Pay automatically. Many bills can be paid automatically each month through your bank. Sign up for these services and the bank will pay your bills for you!

Get a bill organizer. My friend Jennifer has a different version of my bill-paying system. "Whenever I receive a bill, I toss the extra paperwork and flyers and place the bill in the envelope," she says. "Then I write the date the bill is due where the stamp will go and put the bill inside a bill-paying organizer on my desk."

Pay and toss. My friend Chris also has a simple system for dealing with the clutter bills create. "Throw away phone, electric, cable, and similar invoices after you've paid them," she advises.

Consolidate your credit cards. The more credit cards you have, the more bills, clutter, and stress you have with them. Yes, store clerks are trained to try to talk you into getting a store card every time you check out, but don't let them! The "great deals" you'll get with the card aren't worth the bills that come later. Try to cut down to one general credit card per person and a gas card if you find it convenient. In addition to having fewer bills to deal with, you'll be able to see what you're actually spending.

Checkbooks and Bank Statements

Write it down and add it up. I write down every check I write or deposit and every ATM transaction I make in my checkbook's record section as soon as I've finished the transaction. Then I add or subtract the amount and balance my checkbook. When I'm using the ATM, I also compare the balance they show with the balance I've recorded. (Of course they don't always match up, since things clear at different times, but this gives me a way to see if I'm on track.) I know that some people have *never* balanced their checkbooks (think of that old joke about how there must still be money in the account, since there are still blank checks in the book). But unless you really enjoy getting overdraft notices (and charges), I don't understand this. It takes only a minute to bring the checkbook up to date. This is simple addition and subtraction, not rocket science! If you don't trust your math, use a calculator.

Do it online. My friend Jennifer swears by online banking. "I balance my checking account using the online statement, so I can just shred the statements when they arrive," she says.

Shred your ATM receipts. I used to hold on to all my ATM receipts—what if I was audited and the IRS needed them? But gee, they certainly piled up. Now I check my bank statement every month and shred the receipts as soon as I'm sure they're on there.

The Taxman Cometh

All those forms, receipts, and other tax-related documents may seem like the worst kind of clutter. But this is one type of clutter you'd better hang onto, and even accumulate before you need it. Here's how to get ready for Uncle Sam so you're not panic-stricken when mid-April rolls around.

Get it together. Keep each year's tax materials together in a file, accordion folder, or large envelope. I like to keep mine in one of those giant manila envelopes that offices use to route things in. They have ties at the top that hold the envelope closed securely. I write the year on the front, then include smaller envelopes to hold receipts for donations, tax receipts, W-2 forms, and other relevant data. When my federal, state, and local tax forms arrive, they go in the big envelope, too. When it's time to do my taxes, everything's right there. I keep the envelopes from previous years in a labeled printer-paper box, with the most recent on the top and the oldest on the bottom, so if I need to check my records, they're all in the box.

Keep your stuff for 7 years. You need to keep your tax records and supporting material for 7 years because the IRS has 6 years to audit your return. (You may have heard that it has 3 years, but that's true only if it thinks you made a good-faith error on the return! If it thinks you underreported your income, it has 6 years to go after you.)

Check your forms. Don't wait 'til the last minute to make sure you have all the forms you need to file your taxes. A lot of forms aren't included in the standard

Pet Alert!

Pets in the office? It certainly doesn't sound like a good idea. When I started telecommuting a couple of years ago and began using my home office full time, I was worried about what my pets would do. Would the cats jump up on the keyboard or onto my lap, yowling for attention? Would my golden retriever, Molly, make a nuisance of herself? I was prepared to shut the door and lock them all out, but I decided to give them a chance first.

To my surprise and delight, what happens is this: In the morning, when I settle down at the computer, the cats and dog follow me into the office. My kitten Layla curls up in the rocking chair and goes to sleep. My Maine coon cat, Athena, settles on the nearby desk and goes to sleep. My kitten Linus crawls under a chair and falls asleep. And Molly lies down behind my chair and goes to sleep! I was so relieved—companionship without chaos. They really just wanted to be in the same room. Admittedly, I keep the parrots and parakeet in the kitchen, where we can spend quality time together but they won't take it upon themselves to add raucous commentary to my phone conversations.

Come to think of it, though, perhaps I shouldn't have been surprised. One of my publishing friends, John Smallwood, and his colleague, Emma Stewart, both took their dogs to their New York offices at Smallwood & Stewart every day. The dogs were always well behaved (at least, after the scruffy Walter, John's junkyard rescue dog, leaped from the open window shortly after his arrival), and I'm sure their staff enjoyed the stress relief that pets can bring to a busy workplace.

If you have pets, I suggest that you give them a chance and see how they behave. They may turn out to be first-class office animals!

federal booklet they send you. If you need a form that's not there, check at the post office or download it from the IRS Web site's forms and publications page (www.IRS.gov).

Avoid the midnight rush. File electronically and avoid those long tax lines at the post office. Print out copies of the forms for your tax file or folder.

Be a copycat. If you mail in your tax forms, make sure you photocopy them (front and back) for your records before you send them off. My father the accountant always made me send mine in by certified mail, so I would have a record both that I sent them off in time and that the government received them.

Get help online. My friends who do their own taxes swear by programs like TurboTax (www.turbotax.com) and H&R Block's TaxCut Online (www.HRBlock.com). These programs are inexpensive ($14.95 to $29.95, depending on what you order) and include their own e-file, so you can mail your returns in electronically when you're done.

ONWARD!

You've chased down the last paper, finished organizing the last file, and gotten your bill-paying system in gear. Take a deep breath, and get ready to tackle those legendary clutter repositories: the laundry room, basement, and attic. But don't worry—you don't have to do them all at once! As you read through the next chapter, pick just one tip that appeals to you and start with that. You'll be on your way!

Chapter 13

De-Junking the "Junk Rooms"

LAUNDRY ROOM, BASEMENT, AND ATTIC

Maybe there are rooms in your house you don't even want to go into because of all the creepy piles of stuff; the basement and attic are often the prime suspects. But what a waste of potentially useful space! Then there's the laundry room, the last refuge of dirty clothes, ancient, half-empty containers of cleaning supplies, and heaven alone knows what else. In this chapter, you'll find out how to reform and reclaim these dreaded clutter-catchers.

PRIORITIES FOR LAUNDRY ROOMS

Let's start with the smallest of these problems—the laundry room. Since most laundry rooms are either very small rooms, are combined with a bathroom, or are part of the basement, I'm of two minds about including a visualization exercise for them. But I want this book to be a complete record for you of your clutter issues and control solutions, so I've included one. If, like me, you can take in your laundry room's current situation and potential solutions at a glance, you can skip directly to the laundry room tips on page 253. But if you'd like to take a good, hard look at the laundry room and see what's there and what needs to be done, here are the forms. Fortunately, this is one visualization exercise that should take less than 5 minutes!

Start your laundry room de-cluttering process by setting some clutter-kicking priorities. Begin by first focusing on what matters most to you about the way your laundry room looks and functions. That will become your top de-cluttering priority. Then you'll work your way through the clutter problems until you get to what matters least. The best way to do this is to take a good, hard look at the "before" state of the room and then to visualize the "after"—how you want the room to look when the clutter's all gone.

A Laundry Room Visualization

To get to your "after," you need to start by assessing the "before"—the way things look right now. So get out some paper or use the "My Laundry Room—Before" form (or make a photocopy of it and write on that). Write down every place there's clutter and note what that clutter is. Is dirty laundry heaped on the floor and spilling out of the laundry basket? Are there detergent boxes and bottles, some without caps, haphazardly sitting on top of the dryer or on the floor? Maybe you can't find the bleach, or there are used fabric softener sheets all over the place. Try to think about where you get hung up when you're trying to get things done, where you lose things, what distracts or irritates you. Take a good look. Take your time. Because the laundry room is usually a small room or part of a room, it won't take as long as you think to finish your list!

Once you've taken an inventory of your laundry room's "before" state, it's time to move on to the "after"—how you want the room to look when you've kicked the clutter. To make sure you're being realistic, look at the room every few minutes while you're doing this.

Your description of your de-cluttering goals can be short and to the point: "I want to be able to get to the machines. I want enough space to stash the dirty laundry and plenty of room to fold the clean laundry. I want a system that makes it easy for everybody to put their dirty laundry in the laundry-room hamper and put away their own clean clothes."

My Laundry Room—Before

_____
_____
_____
_____
_____
_____
_____
_____
_____
_____

My Laundry Room—After

_____
_____
_____
_____
_____
_____
_____
_____
_____
_____

Or you can create a detailed image of exactly how you'd like your laundry room to look if it were perfect (for you). You can picture the style of washer and dryer, the equipment in the room, any other furnishings, and what the room itself looks like. What sorts of storage, equipment, and furniture that you don't have now do you need to make the room more functional? What would make the laundry room a more pleasant space that you'd enjoy spending time in? Curtains, a mirror, a cheerful shade of paint on the walls, a comfortable chair or stool—once you know what you want, write it all down on a piece of paper or on the "My Laundry Room—After" form on page 251 (or on a photocopy of it).

Getting There

Now that you've captured your laundry room's "before" condition, listing all the specific problems, and you've imagined its "after" appearance, you can finally prioritize the steps you'll need to take to get that room cleaned up and functioning better. Again, bearing both "before" and "after" in mind, I'd recommend starting with what bothers you most about the "before" condition and making that your top priority. Work down your list from there and put it in descending order of importance.

Maybe you feel—especially if it's in the basement—that your laundry room is

---

My Laundry Room Priority List

just a dark, dank hole, and you hate going down there. Or maybe it's not designed efficiently, so you have to take the clothes to a different room to iron them. Or you're just sick of fighting stains and static—not to mention those mysterious disappearing socks.

Write down whatever's driving you to distraction on the "My Laundry Room Priority List" (or photocopy it, if you'd prefer) in descending order from most to least maddening. Now you have your priorities straight! Once you've finished, you can turn to the tips below to find ingenious ways of dealing with each problem.

THE LAUNDRY ROOM TIPS

Stack 'em up. You can save a lot of space with a dryer-over-washer arrangement. I have a tiny laundry room/bathroom, so mine's apartment-size, but I've seen some really attractive full-size models recently. Check them out!

Add some shelves. Shelves next to your washer and dryer add much-needed storage for detergents and other laundry supplies. My laundry room is also my "bathroom pantry," so I keep soap, sponges, tissues, toilet paper, and cleaning supplies—including those venerable standbys, vinegar and baking soda—on the shelves. I stash wash buckets with brushes and bottles of detergent under the lowest shelf. And to make sure they're there when I need them, I keep my household cleaning books on one of the shelves, too. If I need to handle a spill, stain, or other household crisis, I turn to the Queen of Clean, Heloise, Vicki Lansky, or another household diva for a fast solution.

Opt for utility. A set of those metal storage shelves that are more commonly found in basements and garages are perfectly fine for laundry-room storage. They're spacious and stable. If you can't find a color you like, buy some metal paint and get creative!

Get a rack. Drying racks are great—they expand when you need to air-dry clothes, then fold up accordion-style to tuck beside your dryer or into any tight space in your laundry room. I have an old-style wooden rack, the kind you hang the clothes right on, but I've seen sleek metal racks that let you air-dry clothes on hangers and that fold to just 2 inches wide! Look for them in housewares and hardware stores and catalogs.

5-Minute Fixes for Laundry Rooms

Want to jump-start your laundry-room clutter-kicking? Try these fast tips first!

Ditch dried-up detergent. If you have boxes of powdered detergent, borax, and bleach that have hardened to concretelike consistency, stop deluding yourself that they're still usable and throw them out. Make a note to replace the ones you actually use.

Let go of lost socks. If you have a collection of partnerless socks and gloves, now's the time to bid them adieu. (And no, I don't know what happens to the missing ones, either.)

Pitch yellowed paper products. If you're like me, you have a stash of "emergency" paper towels, toilet paper, napkins, and tissues in the laundry room, but somehow, you never get around to using them. If they still look good, vow to rotate them into use and buy fresh replacements as soon as you use them. But if they're warped, yellowed, water-stained, or otherwise unusable, throw them out.

If you can't get it out, throw it out. If you have a pile of stained clothing waiting to be cleaned—but you *have* cleaned it, tried spot-remover, bleach, and everything else you can think of, and the stains are still there—bundle it up and give it to Goodwill, the Salvation Army, the Society of St. Vincent de Paul, or a shelter. (Don't worry, these won't be sold to shelter residents as clothes. Shelters often sell these beat-up clothes as rags and get some money for them.) Those stains are there to stay! Then pick up a good spot-removal guide (see "The Pros Know" on page 257).

Circular-file the fabric softener sheets. I don't care how many times you've heard that there are 150 ingenious uses for used fabric softener sheets. If you're hoarding used fabric softener sheets, throw them out. If you use fabric softener sheets, trust me—you'll have one on hand when you need to soften the burnt-on food in that casserole dish.

String 'em up. You can still find outdoor laundry lines in houseware and hardware stores and catalogs. Look for the kind with a reel for the line so you can pull out the line, hook it to a wall or tree, then unhook it so it can automatically retract. And there's no reason you can't attach one inside the laundry room! Hook up the line to air-dry your clothes, then retract it when they're dry and swivel the case flat against the wall.

Cart it around. A great option for storing all your laundry supplies is a rolling laundry cart. Improvements has one with three sturdy shelves, and it's just 8¼ inches wide, so you can roll it between the washer and the wall when you're not using it. (See page 48.)

Put up a pole, part one. Housewares and home improvement stores sell tension poles for tubs and showers. You install the pole in a corner of the shower and adjust a group of organizer baskets to hold shampoos and other supplies. This kind of pole is a good idea for the bathroom, but it's also a great idea for the laundry room, where space is always at a premium. The poles will extend to 8 feet tall. Tuck one into a corner and put your laundry supplies in the baskets.

Put up a pole, part two. Hang a shower-curtain tension rod over the washer and dryer and use it to hang up clean clothes as you take them out of the dryer or off the ironing board. This will give you a place to hang all your clothes without wasting floor space. And it's great for wrinkle prevention!

Set it on the side. If you have the space, set a sideboard or hallway table against one wall of your laundry room. You can put baskets for darks, lights, and delicates on top, then stash the empty baskets under the table when the laundry's done— and you can use the tabletop for sorting and folding. These narrow tables are ideal for a narrow space like a hallway or laundry room.

Buy a bench. Again, if you have the space, a hallway bench is another good option for the laundry room. The kind with three square wicker baskets for storage underneath and cushions on top is ideal. You can use the baskets to sort darks, lights, and delicates for laundering and sit down when you need to repair a piece of clothing or just need a break! Look in home stores and catalogs like Plow & Hearth (see page 47).

Keep a sewing kit. You'll often first notice clothes that need repair—loose buttons, ripped hems, or the like—as you're getting ready to put clothing in the washer. A small, basic sewing kit can be a lifesaver here, since you can stick it on a shelf and grab it to make a fast repair when you see a problem. I keep mine in a plastic food-storage container—just a small pair of scissors, needles and a needle threader, a thimble, some extra buttons, spools of black and white thread, and one of those tiny sewing kits you can buy in the grocery or pharmacy with lots of colors of thread. Instead of putting all those clothes to be mended in a pile (clutter), fix them on the spot.

Brighten it up. It's hard to see stains, tears, loose buttons, and the like if your laundry room is dark and dingy. When a friend broke her leg, I did her laundry in her cavernous basement, and it was enough to make anyone swear off laundry for life! Get some bright lights for your laundry room. Use cheerful, colorful wallpaper or stencils to liven up the area. If you're dealing with a concrete basement floor, put a cheerful throw rug (or at least a big bath mat) in front of the machines. Your feet will thank you!

Throw it out. Keep a wastebasket in your laundry room for stray threads, dryer sheets, and—of course—dryer lint. Yes, I'm sure someone's written a book on knitting with dryer lint, and I don't care. Clean your lint trap *every single time* you use the dryer, and throw that darned lint out.

Get a sink. I've always envied people who have those old-fashioned galvanized wash sinks—the huge, square tubs on legs with a drainage hole in the bottom. I myself have a teeny, tiny sink in my laundry room, barely a foot wide. But whether you have a spacious stainless sink or a plastic bucket, you need someplace to pretreat stained and soiled clothing. Make sure you have one on hand, and if it's not attached to the wall or held up on legs, get a stool or bedside table to set it on. If there's no water source, keeping big filled bottles of water by the bucket or washbasin is a convenient solution.

Dry sweaters on a rack. Housewares and home stores and catalogs sell nylon-mesh racks that let you dry sweaters flat so you don't stretch them out of shape.

> ## Tools of the Trade
>
> One of the most ingenious laundry room gizmos I've come across is a handsome oak wall cabinet that opens to reveal a fold-down ironing board. It's just 4½ inches deep when it's closed, so it takes up hardly any space in the room. And the door can be attached to open to the left or right to suit your space. You could even attach a mirror or artwork to the door if you wanted to. It sure looks a lot better than an ironing board! Look for this dandy invention in home improvement stores and catalogs like Improvements (see page 48).

The racks are stackable, so you can dry multiple sweaters at a time, and they fold up and have a coat-hanger hook at the top, so you can hang them up when they're not in use.

Use a rolling rack. Use a rolling clothes rack in the laundry room to hang clothes fresh from the dryer or iron. Improvements (see page 48) sells one that folds up to just 5 inches deep for storage when it's not in use.

Put it in the pantry. Do you like to store a lot of staples like toilet paper, paper towels, paper napkins, tissues, soap, and, of course, laundry products in your laundry room? Well, if you do and you have the space, consider getting one of those tall kitchen cabinets that serve as in-kitchen pantries for your laundry room. They hold a ton—and there's room to stash the laundry basket, too!

Go over the appliances. Lots of organizers recommend putting a storage shelf over your side-by-side washer and dryer to make the best use of the space. That's a start, certainly, but I've seen whole wire organizing systems that surround the washer and dryer and create a wealth of useful storage space for all your essentials. Like most of these systems, they have a white plastic coating over the wires or are gleaming stainless steel and are very attractive. If I had side-by-sides, I'd be getting one!

Put it in a basket. No room for a pantry—or even a shelf? Store all of your laundry staples in a bucket or laundry basket where they're easy to find and use.

Put it in a bin. Housewares and home stores and catalogs like Solutions (see page 48) sell magnetic storage bins. They're advertised as an accessory that you attach to the refrigerator, but these shelf- and file-size bins work just as well on the washer and dryer. They're a great place to stash a stain-removal guide; laundry checklist; those small, easy-to-lose bottles of sweater washing fluid; and the like.

Put it in pull-outs. If you have a deep storage space beside your washer or dryer, install wire pull-out baskets on rollers so you don't have to grope around the backs of deep shelves to find what you're looking for.

Spring for some steel. You don't really know the meaning of the word "mess"—not to mention sodden, disintegrating clutter—until your washer hose bursts at 9:30 p.m. on a Sunday night, spewing scalding water all over the laundry room and its contents. (Take this from one who knows.) So do as I say—and as I (subsequently) did—and replace those old hoses with flexible steel-wrapped safety hoses that are guaranteed never to burst.

Put laundry on a pedestal. If you have a front-loading washer and dryer, you can buy pedestals for them with drawers for storage. Great idea!

Crown it with a countertop. Front-loading appliances also give you the option of adding a countertop (many colors and kinds are available at home improvement stores) over them to create a stable, attractive work space.

Use the door, part one. Hang or attach towel racks to the back of the laundry-room door. You can put clean clothes on the racks as you fold them, or hang clothes on hangers hooked over the towel racks.

Use the door, part two. Home improvement centers and organizing stores sell wire racks for pantry doors. Find the sizes and widths that work for you, and store your laundry products on your door.

Use the door, part three. Attach a fold-down ironing board to the back of the door for a space-saving ironing solution.

See? That wasn't so hard. Let's hope it's inspired you to go on to greater things, because now it's time to tackle the dark, the dank . . . the basement.

PRIORITIES FOR BASEMENTS

I remember the basement of my family home as a dark, dank space. There were jumping spiders leaping around when someone turned on the single bare lightbulb, boxes of ancient family photos, and papers that had warped, cracked, and moldered. That fifties-era bomb shelter became a playhouse for those of us brave enough to venture down there. But despite the dankness and creepy-crawlies, I always loved exploring the basement as a place of mystery and surprise. One of my great regrets about my cottage home is that it has no basement—it's beside a stream (which is otherwise a wonderful thing). But fortunately, I have lots of friends with basements that aren't dark and dank, and they've passed along some great tips to share with you all.

In this section, I'll talk about storage, crafts rooms, and other basement options. (There are so many great things you can do with a basement that it makes me jealous just thinking about it!) I won't talk about using your basement or part of it as a den or family room, though, since you can turn to Chapter 8 (beginning on page 142) to find tons of tips about that. I won't talk about using part of it as a laundry room, since we talked about that earlier in this chapter. And guys, I also won't talk about turning your basement into a workshop or "man cave"—you can read all about that in the garage chapter (Chapter 15, beginning on page 311). But that doesn't mean I think these options are bad ideas! For goodness' sake, go for it, if that's the space you want to use for any of these options.

But before you can use your basement for anything, you've got to get it cleaned up. First, let's begin by thinking about exactly what you want to use your basement space for. You're going to start your basement de-cluttering process by setting some clutter-kicking priorities. To do that, first focus on what matters most to you about the way your basement looks and functions—that will become your top de-cluttering priority. The goal at this stage is to list the basement clutter issues from most to least bothersome. The best way to bring your priorities into focus is to take a good, hard look at the "before" state of the room, and then visualize the "after."

A Basement Visualization

Start with the "before" of your basement—the way things look right now. Get out some paper, or use the "My Basement—Before" form on page 260 (or make a photocopy of it and write on that). Write down every place in the basement there's clutter, and note what that clutter is. Try to think about what you could be doing

My Basement—Before

_____
_____
_____
_____
_____
_____
_____
_____
_____
_____
_____
_____

My Basement—After

_____
_____
_____
_____
_____
_____
_____
_____
_____
_____
_____
_____
_____
_____

with your basement space and what you're using (or not using) it for now. Really *look* at your basement, as if you were the design team from *Extreme Makeover: Home Edition* or, say, Martha Stewart, and you just happened to wander down there. What do you see? (Assuming you can see through all the gloom.) Cobwebs? Shelves of dust-covered whatsits? Disintegrating cardboard boxes slumped haphazardly on the floor?

Once you've taken an inventory of your basement's "before" state, it's time to move on to the "after"—how you want the room to look when you've kicked the clutter. Write it all down on a piece of paper or on the "My Basement—After" form (or on as many photocopies of it as you need to do it justice). To make sure you're being realistic, look at the room every few minutes while you're creating your "after" description. Bear in mind that there are actually lots of things you can do with the space once you've shoveled it out. You may want to read through the tips in the section called "Options for Basements," beginning on page 274, before you complete your "after" description. I feel certain you'll be inspired!

Your description can be short and to the point: "I don't want to fight water in the basement. I want better lighting. I want lots of shelves. I want to turn the space into a cozy family room."

My Basement Priority List

_____

_____

_____

_____

_____

_____

_____

_____

_____

Or you can create a detailed picture of exactly how you'd like your basement to look if it were perfect (for you). Think about how you'd divide up the space. What sorts of rooms do you need that you don't have space for in the rest of the house? Then picture the colors of the walls, floors and floor coverings, and window treatments. Imagine every piece of furniture—where it would be, what it would do, what it would look like. Write it all down!

Getting There

Now that you have captured your basement's "before" condition, listing all the specifics, and you've imagined its "after" appearance, you can finally prioritize the steps you'll need to take to get there from here. Bearing both "before" and "after" in mind, start with what bothers you most about the "before" condition and work down your list of clutter problems and wishes for the de-cluttered basement.

Maybe you'd love to have a home gym. Or you'd like more storage space. Or you've been wondering if you could turn the basement into an in-law apartment and make it really inviting. Or you'd just like to think you could store things down there without worrying about whether they would rust, rot, or be eaten by mice.

Write down whatever's driving you to distraction on the "My Basement Priority List" on page 261 (or photocopy it, if you'd prefer) in descending order from most to least maddening. Now you have your priorities straight! Once you've finished, you can turn to the tips below to find ingenious ways of dealing with each problem.

THE BASEMENT TIPS

Let's talk about storage first—and protection from the elements. If you need a sump pump (or several) in the basement, there's not much I can tell you that you don't already know: Before you do anything, hire a professional to dry the place out! And seal any cracks and leaks while you're at it. *Then* turn to the storage tips. After those, we'll talk about all the things you can use your basement for. That's the fun part! I think you're going to see your basement space in a whole new (good) way.

Safe Storage

Solve the water problems. My friend Delilah's house is on the side of a mountain, and when it rains really hard for a long time, sometimes the water comes down the mountainside and heads through her basement on the way to a stream far below. While waiting to have her yard bermed to reroute the water, she hit on a great idea. Heading to her local Tractor Supply store, Delilah bought heavy-duty rubber mats—the kind sold for horse stalls—and covered her basement floor with them. They're, of course, waterproof, and they raised the functional floor surface about an inch, so nothing would get wet even if water came in. The water runs under the mats and ultimately out through the floor drain. The mats added great insulation and softness to the hard concrete floor, making it much more pleasant (and warmer) to walk around on. Delilah put rugs over the rubber mats, and voilà! Her basement was transformed into a welcoming living space.

Go for the high ground. Store stuff on shelves, not on the floor. That way, if the basement *does* flood, there's less chance that your things will be ruined.

Clear the stairs. If you have steep stairs going down to your basement, don't make them even more hazardous by leaving stuff on them—not even along the sides. Get a basket or hamper to carry things that need to go from the main floor down to the basement, but keep it on the house side of the door, not the basement side. A lot of people hang stuff on the wall alongside the stairs, but this can also be hazardous, since you or a box or laundry basket that you're carrying could

[Tools of the Trade]

If you think there's the least chance that water might pool on your basement floor, it's safest to store everything at a higher level. Fortunately, some inventive soul created rust-proof, rot-proof plastic Hi & Dri Storage Pallets to raise basement storage out of harm's way. They come in two sizes, can support 1,000 pounds, and lift your boxes 3½ inches off the floor. If water seeps in, it will just flow underneath the pallets while your stuff stays, well, high and dry. Look for them at home improvement centers and in catalogs like Improvements (see page 48).

crash into them and dislodge them. I feel this way about hanging things on the basement door, too. You don't want something swinging into or falling onto you as you're going down the stairs. Secure a flashlight to the wall by the door and leave it at that. You can always display the kids' art on the wall to brighten the space, but tack it up; don't put it in frames that could be dislodged. While I'm at it, make sure the stairwell is well lit and there's a strong, well-secured banister that will take someone's weight if they lose their footing. Better safe than sorry!

Park the paint. Keep paint cans together in a plastic storage bin on the floor or the bottom shelf of a storage unit. They'll be less likely to spill or get knocked over.

Park the paint permanently. One of the best clutter-control tips I've learned (from Martha Stewart, of course) is to create a decorator's folder. Get a small clear or translucent plastic accordion file from an office supply store. Mark each sectional divider with the name of a room in the house, then put paint chips, carpet samples, and fabric swatches from the curtains and upholstery in that section, with a card that gives the name of each, the date you bought it, and where you got it, as well as the dimensions of the room and the room's door. No need to keep paint cans lying around now—if anything needs refurbishing, the data is at your fingertips and the folder is small enough to take to the store with you! Stash it where you're sure you can find it—in your home office, on a shelf in the basement, or in a drawer in your craft room.

Pint-size the paint. One cool gadget I've found is a paint bottle with a sponge applicator top. If you need to touch up a surface, you just pour leftover latex paint into the 4-ounce bottle, press the sponge applicator against the surface, and dab on the paint. Wash the sponge applicator in hot water between uses and cap the bottle. (Label the bottle with the paint color and the room and surface you used it on.) Look for them in home improvement centers and catalogs like Improvements (see page 48).

Pitch the paint. Latex paint spoils after 2 or 3 years, or if it's exposed to freezing temperatures (32°F or below). Dispose of any latex paint in your basement that's old or cold!

Work your walls. Maximize your basement storage with wall-to-wall shelving. Be creative—if you've upgraded your bookcases or a wall unit in the living room, move the old one to the basement. Don't be shy about using metal storage units, either. You can paint them more inviting colors than the usual black or gunmetal

Linda Cobb, the Queen of Clean, gets tough on basement box pile-up in her excellent book *The Queen of Clean Conquers Clutter*. She points out that boxes tend to pile up, unopened, in basements, especially after moves. And once there, they can malinger for years, keeping company with broken furniture and appliances, cushions that no longer go with anything, and other detritus that went down like a sinking ship, never to rise again. Linda's advice is simple: Open them. *All* of them. Go through them. Decide what you want to keep, and toss, sell, or donate the rest. (Not to mention all that other stuff.) Then get rid of the boxes themselves if they're no longer useful for storage or you don't need them. Listen to the Queen!

gray! And you can choose from a plethora of wire storage units from home improvement centers and organizing stores like All Bright Ideas (see page 48). I will say that using all one type of shelving looks a lot better than a hodgepodge of different sizes and materials—your basement will have a tidy, intentional look that will be much more pleasing.

Say "curtains" to pipes. If you have a wall of exposed pipes, you can cover them by putting open storage shelves in front of them, but that makes it a bit challenging to get to them if you need to make repairs. An alternative is to hang floor-length curtains in front of them to cover the entire wall. Choose a color that complements or matches the wall paint. (You *did* paint the walls an inviting color, right?) Turn that part of the room into an entertainment center with a TV and DVD or video game player, some comfy chairs or a loveseat, and a bright rug, and suddenly your hideous wall becomes the attractive backdrop to a cozy retreat.

Hang some cabinets. If you have old kitchen cabinets left over from a renovation or can find some at a flea market or yard sale, put them to work in your basement. (Remember, if they're dark or ugly, you can paint them to match or complement the walls.) They'll look best if you have a set of them, so they look intentional, and they'll look even better if you install the matching counter and storage cabinets below them. As in the kitchen, you'll gain a wall of storage space and a big surface for projects.

Add a door. Another way to add useful work and storage space under hanging shelves or cabinets is to get a flat door or thick piece of plywood and use it as a table or work surface. Put it on two two-drawer file cabinets (you can find these in neutral or cheerful colors or paint them to suit), paint it if you like, and you're ready to go.

Get your freezer in gear. If you're lucky enough to have a chest freezer in the basement (can you tell I'm jealous?), don't let it become the final resting place for a bunch of frost-coated body bags. (*How* long has that been in there?) Date your food, eat your food, and replace it regularly. If someone gives you something you don't think your family will eat, don't throw it in the freezer, throw it out. (The same holds true for unpopular leftovers. If they didn't like it the first time. . . .) How to tell what you have in there? Use this technique from my friend Jennifer. "I always keep food in my freezer in roughly the same location so I can see at a glance what I have and don't waste time, money, and space buying extra things," she says. Super-organized Jennifer puts the same technique to use in her refrigerator, pantry, bathroom, and office.

Dress it up. An old dresser or two can add much-needed storage in a basement and can look especially good grouped with chairs and a sofa in a seating area. If you don't have any extras hanging around, keep your eyes open; sometimes you can find perfectly good old dressers set out at the curb for the trash, or you can pick one up at a thrift store, flea market, or yard or estate sale. And—let me say it one more time—if you don't like their color, you can always paint them! As with any furniture, if you use more than one, they'll look best if they match.

Make a wall for wire. I don't think pegboard is great for basement walls—hanging stuff all over it creates visual clutter, unless you're using the space as a workshop or crafts room. But you can make an attractive wall display with wire shelving (the kind sold for pantry and cabinet doors in home improvement and organizing stores and catalogs). If you can't mount shelves directly to your wall because it's concrete block, mount a large plywood sheet, paint it to match or complement the wall color, and mount the white-coated wire shelving to the plywood in a pleasing and functional pattern.

Minimize cord clutter. Anywhere you use a lot of electrical devices, including the basement, you can accumulate a lot of cord clutter. Confine it to one place with a Squid Power-Outlet Multiplier, which lets you run five electrical devices off one grounded outlet, even if each device has a large transformer plug or timer. This ingenious contraption (which does look rather squidlike) is available from home improvement stores and catalogs like Improvements and Herrington (see page 48).

Put it in plastic, part one. My boyfriend, Rob, absolutely swears by those plastic storage units, such as the ones made by Rubbermaid. He points out that they're waterproof and indestructible—both advantages in a room that can take a lot of abuse. And they have doors, so you can hide your boxes out of sight.

Put it in plastic, part two. Speaking of Rubbermaid, if your basement is home to an ever-expanding collection of sports gear, contain it in the Rubbermaid Sports Station Organizer, which has compartments and hooks for racquets, bats, and hockey sticks, as well as storage space for balls and helmets and a mesh bag for storage or carting off to the game.

Put it in plastic, part three. Plastic storage containers, available from groceries, pharmacies, hardware stores, home improvement stores—pretty much anywhere!— in a wide range of shapes and sizes, are ideal for basement storage. You can see what's inside so it's easy to find things, and you can buy whatever size you need to fit your shelves or your stuff. No more bits and pieces raining down when you're trying to find something! And, of course, they provide great protection from water and dust.

Get a folding stool. Use a step stool to stay safe while reaching for stuff on high basement shelves. If you get one that folds, you can tuck it almost anywhere when you're not using it—you'll just need a 2- or 3-inch-wide space.

Raise your water level. If you store 5-gallon water bottles in your basement, you can stack them for easy retrieval and get them up off the floor with a three-tier water-bottle rack, available from housewares stores and catalogs like Improvements (see page 48).

Store your wine. One thing the cool, dank conditions of a basement favor is wine storage. (They don't call wine cellars "caves" for nothing!) Set up your wine rack where no one will crash into it, and enjoy!

Store your cleaning supplies. My friend Jennifer wanted to free up her kitchen storage space. "We built a huge storage closet in our basement in which we store the vacuum, rug scrubber, and all of the cleaning supplies," she says. "The only cleaning product we keep under the sink is the dishwashing detergent. This frees up the cabinet so we can keep the trash and recycling containers under there, safe from the baby, behind cabinet locks."

Use common sense. Basement conditions are tough on fragile things. Whether it's mildew and damp or just wear and tear, life in the basement makes the Damage Rule a necessity:

$$\Big[\text{ Damage Rule: If you can't stand the thought of it getting damaged, don't put it in the basement. } \Big]$$

This goes for everything from antiques and supersensitive electronics to photos and books, and, of course, art and clothes, quilts, and other fragile textiles. (If your quilting studio or sewing room is in the basement, it should be climate controlled.)

Lighten and Brighten

Add some flash. A basement's a bad place to be if the lights go out. Hang a flashlight on the wall by the basement door and put another on a shelf where you can reach it easily if you're working down there when the power fails. Check both regularly to make sure the batteries are working.

Brighten it up. A dark, dingy basement can look even smaller and more cramped and cluttered than it really is. And yet many older basements are painted horrific colors like brown or dark green. Time to lighten up! Give the basement a facelift with white paint (on the ceiling, too) or a soft primrose yellow, cream, or other pleasing color. Add plenty of bright light (preferably ceiling lights or wall sconces, to keep cords off of the floor) and put a durable rug, grass matting, or laminate flooring on the floor. Make your basement a place you want to be!

Fire it up. If your basement has a family room, den, or entertainment area with a big, blank wall, make it warm and welcoming with a fireplace. You can now buy a fireplace—complete with a mantel in any number of styles—or a faux wood-stove and install them anywhere. It's amazing! They're available at hardware and home improvement stores and catalogs like Plow & Hearth (see page 47) and Improvements (see page 48). Whether you're burning fuel-gel cells or just plugging in, the soothing flames will cheer and relax the whole family and bring warmth and life to the room. Put bookshelves on either side of the fireplace for storage (some fireplace models even have bookshelves built in), add a wall-mounted TV screen over the fireplace, and cuddle up.

Craft or Hobby Rooms

Dedicate the space. Whether you have a corner of the basement for your quilting, sewing, scrapbooking, dried flower crafting, beading, basket-making, knitting, painting, or pottery, or you have the luxury of an enclosed basement room, dedicate the space to your craft. In this space, functionality should reign supreme. The worktable, chairs, wall space, lighting—*everything* should contribute to your comfort and convenience as you work. And you shouldn't have to be distracted by toys, bills, home storage, and other clutter intruding on your space. Banish everything else to other parts of the basement.

But make it appealing. There's no reason your craft room should look like a workshop—unless you just happen to like that bare, functional look. Brighten your work space with color and art. Add a music system—even if it's just a boom box—so you can relax as you work.

Make your walls work. In this room, inspiration should edge out my usual injunctions against visual clutter. You need open, uncluttered work space, but your walls can be a rich collage of ideas. Put up bulletin boards, magnetic boards, pegboards—whatever works best for you. On them, display photos, fabric scraps, yarn, patterns, works-in-progress—whatever will boost your creativity. Don't overlook the value of synergy—sometimes something totally unrelated can spark your best work. A pattern in an oriental carpet or a close-up of a bird feather could turn into

(continued on page 272)

[Tools of the Trade]

"If you haven't seen a Big Board yet, you're in for a treat," says my friend (and avid quilter) Karen. "It's a huge rectangular ironing board that sits atop drawer towers. You get a great ironing surface (without the pointy end) and loads of storage space underneath, rather than the space-wasting X design of a traditional ironing board." Visit www.bigboardenterprises.com and see for yourself!

Pet Alert!

If you have both a basement and cats, chances are that you keep at least one litter box down there. You may have a cat door cut into the basement door or just leave the door ajar so they can come and go. (Hopefully you don't choose the latter option if you have little kids!) But just because the litter box is out of sight doesn't mean it should be out of mind. Nobody's going to want to go down to the basement if they'll be confronting a reeking, overfilled litter box—and that includes your cats! Here are some tips to keep the litter box bearable:

❋ **Put up a screen.** A decorative screen will keep the litter box out of sight, but you and the cats will still have easy access.

❋ **Make sure the box is big.** Make sure the box is big enough to accommodate your cats.

❋ **Have enough boxes.** Ideally, you should have one box for each cat.

❋ **Use the right litter.** Besides preferring a clean, fresh litter box, cats also have different litter preferences than their owners do. For example, many people use scented litter in their cats' boxes. But cats can't stand those perfumy smells and may boycott the box as a result. Some people line their cats' litter boxes with plastic liners to make them easier to clean. But if you don't clean the box and change the plastic liner every day—thoroughly drying the bottom of the box—urine can build up under the plastic and smell to high heaven. Finally, not all litters are created equal. Clumping litter is by far the best option—it won't get smelly, and you can simply sift out the used clumps and leave the rest. So skip the plastic liner and put that money toward better litter. (I'm a big fan of EverClean, which was recommended to me years ago by the cattery owner where I got my Maine Coon cats. Trust me, it works!)

❋ **Add some deodorizers.** Not perfumes, remember! But there are some highly effective additives you can sprinkle on your litter to help it stay

fresh-smelling. The ones I use are Ammo Cat, which removes ammonia from the litter, and Nature's Miracle Litter Treatment enzymatic powder, a powerful odor-eater. Since I don't have a basement, my cats' litter box shares the bathroom with me, and I'm not about to tolerate even the faintest smell!

❋ **Clean every day.** Make it a point to clean your litter boxes at the same time every day—first thing in the morning's my time. It will be a lot easier to remember (and do) if you make it part of your routine.

If your family has dogs, cats, parrots, bunnies, or any number of other pets, you may store their food in the basement. Ditto if you set out birdfeeders. Keep it safe from insect pests and rodents by storing it in decorative tins. You can sometimes find them at pet stores for free—pet food manufacturers use them as giveaways—and stores that cater to wild birds often have gorgeous ones for sale. These are not only pest-proof and stackable, they look a lot better than most storage options—certainly better than opened sacks of feed!

I see wooden barrels and bins offered for pet-food storage, but I don't trust them to keep out insects or mice. And I see recommendations to store large amounts of feed in metal garbage cans, but I wonder about how pest-proof they are, as well. And of course, you do have to look at them! I'd rather look at a decorative tin than a plastic container, too. To me, metal tins are the gold standard. I just tuck a scoop inside, and I'm ready to dish out everybody's dinner.

Finally, if you and your pets spend family time in your basement, remember that the floor gets awfully cold for your furry friends. Whether you put down a braided rug in front of the sofa or add a dog or cat "nest" (available from catalogs like L.L. Bean, Plow & Hearth, and Orvis; see pages 46, 47, and 49), make sure your pets have someplace warm and comfortable to lie.

a beaded masterpiece; a leaf or machine part could become the basis for a pair of earrings. Let your mind fly!

Find functional furniture. Open your eyes to the possibilities around you. Besides the obvious shelves, cabinets, and filing cabinets, consider a hutch, dry sink, buffet cabinet, cupboard, dresser, or armoire. Any of these pieces will hold an absolute ton of crafting supplies.

Put it in plastic—or a basket. If you keep your craft supplies in the sturdy plastic carriers available in any home improvement center, drugstore, or grocery, it's a snap (literally, for the ones with lock-on lids) to put your supplies back in the containers and put them away on your shelves or in your armoire, hutch, or wherever you stash your stuff. These plastic storage containers come in a myriad of sizes and are very affordable. I like the ones with locking lids and handles that lift up to carry but flatten for stacking. And you can just look through the side to see what's in each one. Another option is to store your supplies in baskets. Just make sure they have handles so it's easy to carry them when it's time to clear the work table.

Tackle the small stuff. I like to store small supplies like beads in compartmentalized plastic cases, which you can find in any hardware or craft store. But I know plenty of people who store small supplies in tackle boxes!

Shelve the small stuff. My friend Karen has her own smart system for craft-supply storage. "Make or hang shelves over doors and windows in your hobby room," she says. "Plan ahead and find storage containers that can be stacked two or three deep between shelf and ceiling. Use them to organize all your notions (elastic, zippers, ribbon, variegated thread, needles, knitting and crochet supplies) in a dust-free environment."

Don't forget totes. I love roomy totes for carrying my in-progress projects. I have padded totes specifically designed for crafts projects, with lots of inside pockets and attractive patterns; I have woven African basket totes with handles and bright designs; I even have a tall rectangular Shaker basket with leather handles. And I admit, I love them all. Whether I'm working on my knitting, quilting, or beading, I have my supplies in the appropriate tote and can "tote" it along with me from room to room. If you're working on a lap project in the family room, you can take it upstairs in your tote, then stash it back on its shelf in your craft room until you have another chance to work on it.

Share your supplies. If you share your craft room with a child, take a tip from one of my friends. "I finally merged my collection of fancy craft scissors, decorative hole punches, and fancy scrapbook papers with my daughter's," she says. "She constantly borrowed them, and I constantly gathered them up and stored them safely away after she was done. Once I realized that she wasn't damaging the 'good' stuff, I gave up the ghost on 'hers' and 'mine.' A few quick lessons on caring for things, and she's benefiting creatively from access to the higher-end art supplies."

Put patterns in plastic. Here's another great tip from Karen, who's also an accomplished sewer. "Instead of stuffing pattern pieces back into the envelope, get plastic sleeve pockets for a 3-ring binder," she says. "Store the pattern envelope, tissue patterns, and any special notions that you purchased for the project in the sleeve pocket." Then put the sleeves into a labeled binder and it will be right there on your shelf when you need it.

Get a grip on gift wrap, part one. If you spend a lot of time wrapping presents, cut down on the clutter of wrapping paper and ribbons with a gift-wrap organizer. Get a big plastic under-bed storage box that is long enough to hold long rolls of wrapping paper but shallow enough to fit on a shelf in your craft room, and tuck smaller plastic boxes inside to hold ribbons, tape, gift tags, and scissors. Or buy the "official" version, a gift wrap case that has flip-down legs to turn it into a wrapping station, clips to hold wrapping paper in place while you work, a lift-out organizer bin, a lid compartment for flat sheets, and special sections for ribbons and bows. (You can find this marvel at Solutions; see page 48.) You can get portable plastic carriers that organize and dispense up to 16 spools of ribbon and padded, heavy-duty polyester gift wrap and bow organizers and gift bag organizers that are as well built as suitcases and have carry handles and hooks for wall mounting (from Improvements; see page 48).

Get a grip on gift wrap, part two. Don't feel like buying a gift-wrap holder? Do as my friend Chris does and store your wrapping-paper rolls upright in a clean trash can. (Crafty Chris also saves the Christmas cards she receives each year, then cuts them out and uses them as gift tags the following year.) I keep my tall wrapping-paper rolls upright in a tall tin flower bucket like the ones vendors use in French open-air markets, and I stash my flat wrap and gift bags in a labeled printer-paper box, both tucked away in my crafts closet where they're easy to reach.

Options for Basements

Go for a gym. My friend Delilah has set up a home gym in part of her basement. She's made sure the space is bright and inviting, and for inspiration, she put up posters of Marilyn Monroe working out with barbells. Make sure you have a good selection of music or a TV on hand to make the time go by faster. Delilah has a rack on her stationary bike that lets her read magazines while she cycles.

Build a plant paradise. My ex-husband is an orchid enthusiast. He created a fabulous basement setup with rows of plant-laden tables (actually called "benches," but trust me, they're steel-and-wire tables), fluorescent lights, and a type of aerial sprinkler system that misted, watered, and fed his plants on a regular basis. Going into the basement and seeing the exotic orchid blooms—and the sea of green leaves—as you descended the steps was incredible, especially in winter when the garden was buried in snow.

Start some seeds. Creating a plant room in the basement may be too ambitious for you, but if you enjoy gardening, you can easily set up a seed-starting area. Garden catalogs sell "light gardens," tiers of shelves with fluorescent lights suspended over them, that are ideal for starting seeds. You can buy special seed-starting setups and heat mats that will give your seedlings the best possible growing environment. Check out the Gardener's Supply Company catalog (see page 49) for an introduction to all the possibilities. If you don't want to invest in a light garden, you can always buy a table at a yard sale or thrift store and string up a couple of shop lights.

Spruce up houseplants. Light gardens are also good "sanatoriums" for exhausted or past-peak houseplants. Give them light and TLC while they revive, then bring them back up to show off in other rooms of the house while you move other tired houseplants from upstairs back under the lights to recover.

Add a potting shed. My friend Delilah uses part of her basement as a potting shed. Again, you can buy a potting bench (really a table) setup from garden catalogs like Gardener's Supply Company and Charley's Greenhouse & Garden (see page 49). These benches are made of wood or metal with shelf space below for pots and potting soil, racks to hang tools, and lots of other neat features. Or you can head to a thrift store or flea market and buy a table you wouldn't mind spilling dirt and water on, then set up shop with a plastic tub to hold the soil, a trowel, and some pots.

Make some music. My friend Tom and his sons have turned their basement into a music room, complete with guitars (electric, acoustic, and bass), drum sets, a piano, keyboards, and recording equipment. They all compose, play, and record together, just for the fun of it.

Play Ping-Pong. I love Ping-Pong (aka table tennis), and the basement's a perfect place to set up a table, because Ping-Pong takes up a lot of floor space. Also, unlike when you play Ping-Pong outside, the balls won't get lost, and unlike upstairs, they won't hit anything they shouldn't (except maybe your opponent).

Set up a snack center. If you have a den, family room, or TV room in the basement and your family spends a lot of time there, it makes sense to set up a basic snack center. Get a cabinet, table, or kitchen island and place it against the wall of your entertainment area. Put a microwave or an electric popcorn popper, a hot plate, and a blender on top, tuck a mini-refrigerator inside or underneath, and stash some small pans, bowls, mugs, glasses, straws, napkins, paper towels, and utensils inside. Stock popcorn, pretzels, chips, crackers, cookies, candy, and other family favorites in glass jars or ClickClacks (see page 92), and put drinks, fruit, cheese sticks, yogurt snacks, and butter in the fridge. Add a slow cooker to keep soup and hot drinks like cider and hot chocolate warm. If you don't have a sink in the basement or if it's across the room, make sure you have a plastic dishpan so you can carry the dirty dishes to a sink or dishwasher and bring them back clean.

Add another bathroom. A feature of older basements in the area where I live is a basement bathroom. These older houses often had only one bathroom, so they took advantage of the plumbing to create a second bathroom underneath it. Some of these are no more than a toilet on a pedestal with a sink nearby—not good for your decor or your privacy!—but it's certainly a good idea to add a little basement bathroom, especially if your family spends much time down there. But wall it off, please!

Add a retro rec room. It's your basement—why not have some fun there? If you have an enclosed room in part of the basement and you have a favorite decade, make a retro hideout for yourself. An Elvis lounge? Seventies love nest? Hippie hideaway? Flapper speakeasy? Eighties disco? Shop flea markets for retro fabrics, fixtures, and furnishings for your chosen era. Look for accessories in your parents' attic (or your own) and at yard sales. Make it fabulous! My friend Candyce even painted her formerly dingy basement stairs in a beautiful spatter pattern of purple, black, gold, and red—positively psychedelic!

Put in a playroom. If part of your basement is enclosed, you can create a playroom for your children. My brother, Ben, and his wife, Julie, created a wonderful play space for my nephew and niece, with twirling swings anchored securely to the ceiling, a trampoline, a bookcase full of games and children's books, and lots of beanbags and other kid-size cushioning. It instantly became their favorite place to be—you were sure to find them down there the minute they got out of bed. Kids too big for a playroom? What about a clubhouse or pirate's lair?

Put in a pantry. My friend Rudy's house was built in the forties, when victory gardens were the norm in backyards across America. His home has a wonderful setup of open wooden shelves that his grandmother kept filled with jars of glistening jams and jellies and home-canned fruits and vegetables, as well as bottles of his grandfather's home-brewed beer. If you enjoy preserving your own food, a cool, dry basement is a great place to store it.

Add a root cellar. Another old-fashioned essential for food preservation was a root cellar—a cool, moist area of the basement where folks stored bins of home-grown apples, onions, potatoes, carrots, cabbages, and other long-keeping staples. If your basement has a damp corner, you might want to try this yourself. (I've always fantasized about having a root cellar, so you can imagine how jealous I was when my friend Delilah bought her house and there was a big one in a separate room in the basement!) If the idea appeals to you, the classic book on root cellaring is Mike and Nancy Bubel's *Root Cellaring*. It's no longer in print, but you can look for it used on www.amazon.com, www.barnesandnoble.com, and other bookselling Web sites.

Build a bomb shelter. Duct tape and plastic, anyone? Those Cold War–era basement bomb shelters don't seem so farfetched in today's post-9/11 world. They don't take up much space, and you can always use them to store staples. But if you do, remember the three rules of long-term food storage: 1. Make sure what you buy will keep. 2. Don't buy what your family won't eat. 3. Rotate your stored food (which means, go down there, bring it up to the kitchen, cook it, and replace what you took out of the basement on a regular basis). And don't forget to store water!

Can you believe you've made it out of the basement alive? Congratulations! Now it's time to take on the biggest clutter-catcher of all (except, possibly, the garage)—the attic.

5-Minute Fixes for Attics and Basements

Save the art and photos. Art and photos don't belong in attics and basements, where they'll be exposed to temperature swings, dampness, and possible pest problems. Get them out of there! And once you've gotten them out, go through the art and see what you really want to keep. As for dealing with photos, turn to Photo Finish on page 450 for tips on conquering photo clutter.

Kick the cobwebs. Wrap an old rag around the head of your broom and make a clean sweep of the cobwebs cluttering your basement and attic. You'll start to feel better the minute they're gone, and the room will look bigger and brighter, too.

Throw out the trash. Take a quick survey of your attic or basement and see what's in there that's obviously trash. Pitch the rusty nails, the moldering box of wrapping paper, the moth- or mouse-eaten blanket, and the stack of decomposing newspaper someone forgot to put out for recycling.

Clear the walks. If there are no clear paths through the basement or attic, or the stairs and the area around the stairs are blocked, clear them first for safety's sake. Even if you have to temporarily put stuff down in another part of the room, you really *must* make the area navigable or you'll never succeed in clearing the clutter. After all, you can't clean it if you can't reach it!

Take five. Fast, grab five things in your attic or basement that you can take to the thrift store. Duplicates, old toys, an appliance or piece of furniture that's past its prime—take them to the car right now. It's a start!

PRIORITIES FOR ATTICS

I think attics can be the most eccentric, individualistic areas in the whole house. They can be wonderful or just bizarre. (In my house, the previous owners built their addition over the roof of the original summer cottage, so the original roof comes up through the attic floor!) But attics can also be repositories for generations of castoffs and other clutter that's exiled there to die slowly in obscurity, like Mrs. Rochester in *Jane Eyre*.

If you have structural problems in your attic such as leaks or a lack of insulation, deal with them first. If your attic overheats, add vents and an automatic fan that comes on (and opens the vents) when the thermostat directs it to. If you have exposed ceiling joists instead of a safe, solid floor, install flooring or at least put down heavy plywood sheets (and insulate under them). Make sure your stair or pull-down ladder is secure and will take not just your weight, but your weight hauling up heavy stuff, and make sure it has a secure, weight-bearing railing or banister so you can steady yourself while climbing it. Install plenty of lights so you can see into every corner, and keep a flashlight handy on a wall or shelf where you can reach it fast if the power fails.

Get an exterminator or wildlife specialist to come and remove any lurking critters, be they squirrels, bats, pigeons, mice, snakes, or ominous spiders. (My friend Edith had a raccoon—a very large, very angry raccoon—trapped in her attic at one point, and my sister Liz had a very large, very stinky opossum crawl into her attic and die. Don't let this happen to you!) You want your attic to be a safe, dry, well-lit place in which to store your stuff.

Once you have dealt with any basic problems, you can start your attic decluttering process by setting some clutter-kicking priorities. To do that, focus first on what matters most to you about the way your attic looks and functions and take a good, hard look at the "before" state of the room. Then you'll go on to visualize the "after"—how you want the attic to look when all the clutter's gone. Then you can set your priorities.

An Attic Visualization

To get to your "after," you need to start with the "before"—the way things look right now. So get out some paper, or use the "My Attic—Before" form (or make a photocopy of it and write on that). Write down every place in the attic where there's clutter, and note what that clutter is. Be frank here—you may have no idea what's in some or even most of the boxes up there. Note those areas for special attention later. Can you see where you're going? Is the roof cracking you in the skull unless you stand right in the center of the attic? Can you get to everything— or anything? Put it all down.

Once you've taken an inventory of your attic's cluttered "before" state, it's time to move on to the "after"—how you want the room to look when you've kicked the clutter. Write it all down on a piece of paper, or in the "My Attic—After" form

My Attic—Before

_____
_____
_____
_____
_____
_____
_____
_____
_____
_____

My Attic—After

_____
_____
_____
_____
_____
_____
_____
_____
_____
_____
_____
_____

(or on as many photocopies of it as you need to do it justice). To make sure you're being realistic, look at the room every few minutes while you're doing this.

Your description can be short and to the point: "I want to be able to see where I'm going. I don't want to run into cobwebs. I want to have clear paths so I can actually get to everything. I want sturdier storage boxes. I want to be able to find the Christmas ornaments without looking for an hour. I want to use the space under the eaves."

Or you can create a detailed picture of exactly how you'd like your attic to look if it were perfect (for you). You can picture the lighting, types of storage containers, built-in shelves and cabinets—everything.

Getting There

Now that you've captured your attic's "before" condition, listing all the specific clutter issues, and you've imagined its "after" appearance, you can finally prioritize the steps you'll need to take to get there from here. Again, bearing both "before" and "after" in mind, start with what bothers you most about the "before" condition and make that your top priority. Then order the other items on your list.

If it's the clog of clutter—no clear path through the piles—that's driving you

---

My Attic Priority List

_____

_____

_____

_____

_____

_____

_____

_____

crazy, list that first. Or maybe it's the dust that's coating all the broken-down furniture and giving it a ghostly (or just ghastly) air. Or maybe it's the disintegrating boxes and trunks of old clothes. Or your grown kids' "priceless" possessions that they don't want but don't want you to toss.

Write down whatever's driving you to distraction on the "My Attic Priority List" (or photocopy it, if you'd prefer) in descending order from most to least maddening. Now you have your priorities straight! Once you've finished, you can turn to the tips below to find ingenious ways of dealing with your attic's clutter problems.

THE ATTIC TIPS

Come back from Neverland. First, look at what you can actually see and identify—the stuff like furniture that's *not* in boxes. Then ask yourself what it's doing there. Did you save all your kids' baby furniture, strollers, bassinettes, and so on for *their* kids? Well, get a grip. A lot of that stuff's no longer considered safe, and a lot of parents have objections to using grimy attic relics in their babies' rooms. If you have a real heirloom—say, a baby rocker that's been used by six generations of your family or a Victorian wicker stroller—see who wants it. They can display it even if they don't actually use it and so, for that matter, can you. Ask around and see if any of the kids want any of the rest of the stuff—with the stipulation that if they want it, they have to come get it *now*. Otherwise, donate it, take it to a kids' consignment shop, or trash it.

Fix it or toss it. Still checking out the furniture, see if you have any broken (or just broken-down) chairs, lamps, and other furnishings lying around up there. If you do and you want them *and can use them*, get them repaired now. Otherwise, toss them.

Just say no to other people's boxes, part one. If you have boxes of your grown kids' clothes, toys, sports equipment, or high school yearbooks taking up space in the attic, invite each child to come over and sort through his or her stuff. (Remember how I told you about Diane (see page 11), who hauled all her kids' boxes and other clutter down from the attic to the guest bedroom and gave them 2 weeks to come and get it? Great idea!) Have a plan in place to donate, sell, or trash what they don't want, and make sure some or all of those things happen before they leave. Naturally, they can take their stuff and sell it themselves if they want. The point is to get it out of *your* house.

Just say no to other people's boxes, part two. Are Great-Aunt Ethel's alligator suitcases moldering in your attic? Do you still have a pile of unwanted wedding presents up there in their original boxes? Did you inherit Grandma's hideous china, and is it tucked away in yet another box in the attic? When you helped your parents move to a retirement home, did all of their stuff also move—right into your attic? It's time to say good-bye. It's your house, and it's your space. It's time to keep what *you* want. Here's how:

- ❏ Go through the stuff, and make "Keep It," "Shop It," "Sell It," "Donate It," and "Toss It" piles.
- ❏ If you put something in the "Keep It" pile, make sure you have a good reason. Is there someplace in your house you could use it? Can it replace a less-good appliance or piece of furniture you're using now? (And no, you should not then turn around and put *your* stuff in the attic!)
- ❏ The "Shop It" pile is for stuff you think other family members and friends might be interested in. Ask them, and if you don't find a taker, move that piece into the sell, donate, or toss pile.
- ❏ And then do it! Get that stuff out. Put it out for the trash. Call a hauler to take it away. Make a trip (or several) to Goodwill or the Salvation Army or the Society of St. Vincent de Paul. Drop by an eBay store, consignment shop, or antiques store. (They'd probably love Aunt Ethel's suitcases.)
- ❏ You don't have to do it all at once—this is potentially a Herculean task! But do a little each day or each weekend. Keep at it until it's all gone. If the job starts to seem overwhelming, stop, take a break, and focus on what you'll be able to do with all that space. Then go back in an hour or a day or a week and pick up where you left off.

Just say no to unfinished projects. Recently, my father presented me (with great ceremony, I might add) with a large box. Inside was an unfinished cross-stitch quilt that my grandmother had worked on perhaps 40 years ago. Now, my grandmother made a number of lovely cross-stitch quilts in her day, but I think she gave up on this one because it was so ugly. And it was also stained from its long life in storage. Perhaps you have a few projects of your own that fall into this category, all sitting in the attic waiting for that mythical rainy day. Or half a wall is taken up with your kids' ancient science projects. Or your Uncle Max's attempts at woodworking, or the model car kits your spouse collected when he was 12 but somehow never managed to put together (or throw out). You know how it goes. Now it's time for that stuff to go. If somebody wants one of the projects, they have to take it. Away. (Preferably far, far away.) And if it's a project you or said spouse really want to take up again, take it up—somewhere out of the attic. If you take it to your work-room or garage and it just sits there, you'll know it really is time to say good-bye.

Consolidate the kid stuff. This time I'm not talking about the stuff your kids dumped on you—I'm talking about the boxes of baby clothes, stuffed animals, school art, and the like that you kept because you couldn't bear to throw it out. Sweet memories are made of this! But you can keep the memories without keeping all the stuff. Make a video for each kid, showing each item and recording your memories of the happy times they bring to mind. Or photograph them and make a scrapbook for each child, including swatches of clothes and samples of art, school papers, and so on. Or make baby quilts for the grandchildren out of scraps of beloved baby outfits, blankets, and so forth. Get out the digital camera and record it all on a CD for each kid. Or pick a piece or two of each child's art that you'd like to frame and display somewhere in the house, then ask them to sort through the rest and choose what they want to take. Don't feel guilty! It's theirs, after all. And you'll still have the memories!

Stash what you can't trash. When you're de-cluttering the lower floors, you may find things you just can't bring yourself to part with, even though you can't find a place or think of a good use for them. Hey, that was Aunt Tillie's cameo! Put them in a "Review" box, label and date it, and tuck it in the attic. Then review it—check out what's in there once a year. If several years go by and nothing's migrated from the box back into the house, it's time for it to go. This is also a good way to wean kids (including rather large kids) from toys and other things they've outgrown. Move the stuff into the attic in a labeled box, either with their cooperation if they're eager for more space in their rooms or clandestinely if they're still clinging like grim death to toys or accessories they haven't actually played with in 6 months. If you don't hear any kicking and screaming for a year, get rid of it.

Clear out the clothes. A warm, dry attic is a fine place to store clothes, as long as they're well protected from moths and other hazards. But what if your attic is packed with boxes of moldering clothes—Grandpa's fine wool suits that were "too good to throw out," your college jeans and bikinis that you're sure you'll wear again, Tammy's high school outfits, your too big/too small clothes? Wake up and smell the mildew! Storing off-season clothes in the attic is one thing. Storing really sentimental clothes—your wedding dress (or your mother's), a Flapper outfit that belonged to your great-grandmother, your husband's uniform from his glory days as a high school quarterback, your daughter's christening gown, your mom's coolest tie-dyed shirt and hand-embroidered hippie jeans—is fine, as long as they're properly stored and there aren't dozens of them. But take stock of all the too big/too small/too torn/too stained/whose was this?/out of style clothes, and chuck them. If they're still wearable, donate them. If they're classics, like Gunne Saxe dresses from the seventies or original Diane von Furstenberg wrap dresses, take them to an eBay store or vintage clothing store. (As long as they're in good shape.) You'll finally have room for the clothes you need to put up there!

Store clothes with care. Let's assume that you have kicked all the old, moldy, unsuitable clothes out of the attic and are ready to put the still-good, still-in-style, still-the-right-size clothes back in. If you have lots of clothes and other hangables, you can put up a clothes rod in the attic (where it's accessible but no one will crack their head on it); otherwise, choose a rolling clothes rack (or two). Put clothes in heavy-duty plastic zipper bags with cedar inserts and hang them up.

Box your clothes. You can also box up out-of-season clothes like corduroy pants, sweaters, turtlenecks, hats, gloves, and so on—things that will still look good and keep their shape after being folded for a whole season—and store them in plastic storage boxes with tight-fitting tops. No toxic mothballs, please! Store them with cedar or lavender sachets to keep them smelling fresh. Label each box and stash them on sturdy shelves or under the eaves (as long as you can get to them easily and it doesn't get damp and humid under there).

Box the kids' clothes. If you have growing kids and want to keep their best clothes around to hand down to the younger ones, box those items the same way you'd box your own out-of-season stuff, but sort it by age or size. Label each box with the contents and appropriate age or size, and store it securely away.

Watch out for mice! If you have problems with mice and squirrels getting into your attic, be extra-careful about storing clothes up there. Mice in particular can get into the smallest opening, and squirrels are ferocious chewers. You don't want

My friend Skye Alexander is a wonderful artist, as well as a mystery writer, feng shui master, interior designer, and clutter-control expert. (And I'm sure she can do lots of other things I don't even know about!) So you can trust her when she says that the attic is no place to store photos, paintings, and other artwork. Anywhere it's damp or there are temperature swings can be very bad news for paper and canvas—not to mention what's on it. So keep your art, including art photos, in a climate-controlled closet when you're not displaying it in the house. (We'll talk more about family photos on page 450.) And take Skye's advice to store artwork upright rather than stacked flat. She recommends putting each piece between sheets of acid-free paper and then taping foam boards on each side to prevent damage and breakage. But then how do you know what's in there? Skye takes a photo of each piece and tapes it to the foam board.

to go up in the fall and find that your lovely sweaters have been making a family of baby mice or squirrels very comfortable all summer! If your attic has pest issues, heavy-duty hanging plastic zipper bags are probably a better choice than plastic boxes. Better yet, store your clothes, paperwork, and other temptations downstairs and put less-perishable items in the attic.

Add some storage. Too often, attics are nothing more than open rooms piled with boxes. Putting in wall-to-wall shelving, old dressers, and other storage options will really help you make the most of your space.

Don't let yourself be limited. I actually have recurring dreams about exploring wonderful, endless attics full of hidden treasures. An attic can be a wonderful space! When my friend Fern bought a twin home in Emmaus, Pennsylvania, she found that the previous owners had converted the attic into a fabulous bedroom and playroom for their two sons. I saw this transformed space—with lots of built-ins, good lighting, and color—and was incredibly inspired. If you buy an old home, you may find that the attic was divided into rooms for maids or a nursery for the children of the family. Individual rooms are always full of possibilities! I'm reminded of Jo March, the heroine of the children's classic *Little Women,* who turned her family's attic into her secret retreat and writing studio. Look at your attic space with fresh eyes, and you may be amazed by what you can do with it!

Don't overfill the attic. This is probably the most important tip in the whole chapter: Do *not* overstuff your attic! Make sure there are roomy corridors running both the length and, periodically, the width of your attic so you can not only see what's in there, but you can also get to it easily. The whole point of kicking out your clutter is to make it easy to get the most from your space.

The Ornament Issue

One thing that usually finds it way into (and, hopefully, back out of) the attic is the avalanche of holiday ornaments and paraphernalia that's become an intrinsic part of the season. With the ever-increasing popularity of faux Christmas trees, wreaths, and swags, there's a lot more to store than the ornaments and stockings. And that's just the indoor decorations!

Where I live, every year brings more elaborate displays to neighborhood yards. Outdoor lights, net lights, rope lights, and icicles; illuminated reindeer, giant candles, candies, elves, Santas, Rudolphs, and crèches; entire sleds, complete with a full team of reindeer and Santa in the driver's seat, perched on top of roofs; and now, those gigantic inflatable snow globes, Grinches, snowmen, polar bears . . . yikes!

Fortunately, along with all the stuff has come a range of sensible storage options. You're no longer limited to wrapping up ornaments and putting them in cardboard boxes or storing the tree in a big plastic garbage bag. (Though both of these options still work.) Read on for better storage solutions.

Decorate it once. My friend Delilah gets a real tree for Christmas, but she has the most gorgeous faux swagging for her fireplace and banister I've ever seen, with beautiful tiny amber lights and red, gold, and silver ornaments that exactly match the decorations and lights on her live tree. How do they look so perfect? Ever-ingenious, Delilah and her boyfriend, Chaz, decorated the swags and railing greenery *once*. Since then, they've carefully wrapped each piece—lights, ornaments, and all—and tucked it away in the attic at the end of each season. And there it sits, perfectly decorated, until the following season. All they have to do is unwrap the swags, attach them to the mantel and railing, and voilà!

Store extra bulbs in a box. Keep a collection of replacement bulbs for all those light strings and ornaments in a labeled plastic box with the rest of the Christmas ornaments, so they're at hand when you need them.

Ditto for hooks. Give ornament hooks their own labeled, lidded box. When you bring everything down from the attic, you'll be able to see at a glance if you have enough or need more.

Roll up the lights. You're probably familiar with those garden hose rollers that keep hoses wound neatly around a cylinder and prevent kinking. But did you know they're available for holiday lights, too? Each compact (just 8½- to 10½-inch) Wrap-N-Roll reel holds two or three 100-bulb minilight strands, two 150-bulb icicle light strings, or one 50-foot extension cord. They're sold in sets of four, and you can buy a convenient nylon storage bag to keep your rolled-up lights safe and dust-free in the attic when they're not in use. Say good-bye to tangled lights! Look for them at Christmas shops and catalogs like Solutions and Improvements (see page 48).

Bag the tree. No, I don't mean a body bag like the kind sold for disposing of poor live trees. (It still practically makes me cry to see once-beloved real trees tossed out for the trash.) Instead, buy a suitcase-quality padded poly bag to hold your faux tree from year to year. It's water- and stain-resistant, with plenty of carrying handles to make the trip to the attic easier. Some of them are like long duffel bags and others have wheels to help you roll them to their final resting place. They also have wall hooks, so you can use your attic floor space for other things. They're designed to hold trees up to 7½ feet tall. Look for them in Christmas shops or catalogs like Improvements (see page 48).

Bag the wreath. If you have a faux wreath, you can buy a cylindrical padded bag for it to match the one for your tree and lights, from the same source. A convenient feature of these storage bags is that—in addition to protecting your Christmas adornments from dust and damage—they all match, so you can find all your decorations in seconds.

Bag the big stuff. Sure enough, there are even padded poly holders for all those outdoor ornaments like the inflatable snowmen and the lit-up wire-and-twig ornaments, giant candy canes, and reindeer. Look at your local Christmas store or a catalog like Improvements (see page 48) for a variety of sizes and shapes.

Buy an ornament box (or two). I still store my Christmas ornaments—and trust me, I have zillions, including fragile breakables and heirlooms—in tissue or their original boxes inside labeled copy-paper boxes. Shame on me! There's no excuse now not to buy plastic or padded storage containers designed expressly to protect

Christmas ornaments. They have individual compartments for up to 60 orna-ments, or partitions for big ornaments like those Santa and moose statuettes you just had to buy. The rigid plastic boxes are stackable, with handles for easy stor-age; the cushioned boxes store ornaments just as you would fine china. If, like my mother, you have several themed trees, you can label each box with the kind of ornaments and which tree they are for. And, of course, you can store them with their hooks still attached, since they'll be safe from entanglement with other orna-ments. What a time-saver! Look for ornament cases at your local Christmas shop or in catalogs like Solutions or Improvements (see page 48).

Or put them in cardboard. Linda Cobb, the Queen of Clean, advises against storing ornaments in plastic and comes down squarely in the cardboard-box camp. She's concerned about moisture buildup ruining ornaments, not to mention mold and mildew. Gee! Maybe I'm not as big a slacker as I thought.

Store stuff by season. If you love decorating for every holiday, as everyone does in my part of Pennsylvania, you'll appreciate this tip from clutter-control expert Skye Alexander: Store all your decorations by season. Keep separate labeled boxes for Valentine's Day, St. Patrick's Day, Easter, the Fourth of July, Halloween, Thanksgiving, Christmas or Hanukkah, and so on. Skye recommends storing the boxes chronologically in the attic so they're supereasy to find.

Store eggs in the carton. I had to mention this because I collect Easter eggs—everything from traditional Ukrainian pysanky (wax-resist eggs) and Colonial-era dyed-onionskin eggs with pin-scratched designs to my Araucana hen's naturally robin's-egg-blue eggs and eggs I've watercolored myself. If you keep Easter eggs—mind you, not the hard-boiled kind!—keep them safe in egg cartons stored in a labeled cardboard box. If the cartons don't fit tightly, pad them with tissue, crum-pled newspaper, or bubble wrap for a snug fit, and tape the lid.

ONWARD!

Whew! We've tackled the whole house now. Congratulations! Take a break, and reward yourself with something wonderful. Now . . . are you ready to take on the great outdoors? In the next section, you'll find clutter-kicking tips for decks, porches, patios, the garage, and, of course, the yard and garden. Let's take a walk outside.

PART THREE

Clutter-Kicking
Outside the House

Chapter 14

Clear the Decks!

(AND THE PORCHES, PATIOS, AND DOORSTEPS)

That outdoor kitchen seemed like a great idea. But now there's no room for anyone to walk out there, much less sit on the deck or patio and enjoy a meal. Pots of plants are all over the place; decaying furniture and boots, volleyballs, and other outdoor gear have taken over the porch. And the pileup of umbrellas, backpacks, roller blades, and racquets has made doorsteps walks of shame. Save these great outdoor living spaces with the wealth of clutter-kicking tips and techniques in this chapter.

PRIORITIES FOR DECKS, PORCHES, PATIOS, AND DOORSTEPS

Decks, porches, and patios are wonderful "outdoor rooms"—extensions of your living space into the outdoors. Few things are as enjoyable as sitting in a porch swing, enjoying a meal hot off the grill on the deck, or sitting around the patio fire pit on a crisp night with friends. But unfortunately, these are all spaces that lend themselves to clutter accumulation. And few things are as trashy looking as a porch crammed with so much battered furniture and other family detritus that it looks like it's ready for an estate sale, or a deck or patio littered with tricycles, playground balls, baseball bats, toy trucks, rusting or collapsing lawn furniture, half-dead plants, and overturned pet food bowls. Then there are the doorsteps— the entries to your home. Do they say "welcome" or "watch your step"? (Or even, "abandon all hope, ye who enter here"?)

As you did inside the house, start your de-cluttering process by setting some clutter-kicking priorities. Before you can establish your priorities, you need to focus on what matters most to you about the way your deck, porch, patio, and doorsteps look. The best way to do this is to take a good, hard look at the "before" state of the space. Then you can go on to visualize its "after" condition.

A Deck/Porch/Patio/Doorstep Visualization

To get to your "after," you need to start with the "before"—the way things look right now. So get out some paper, or use the "My Deck/Porch/Patio/Doorstep— Before" form (or make a photocopy of it and write on that). Write down every place there's clutter, and note what that clutter is—a sagging lounge chair, a rusted wrought-iron table, a broken planter. I'm giving you only one form here, but it has enough space for you to note down the current state of the deck, porch, patio, and doorsteps. Mercifully, it shouldn't take but a minute or two to size up the present state of any of them.

Once you've taken an inventory of your deck, porch, patio, or doorstep's "before" state, it's time to move on to the "after"—how you want the space to look when you've kicked the clutter. Write it all down on a piece of paper, or in the "My Deck/Porch/Patio/Doorstep—After" form, or on as many photocopies of it as you need to do it justice. To make sure you're being realistic, look at the area every few minutes while you're creating your description.

Your description can be short and to the point: "I'd like to have a place to put the grill when we're not using it. I'd like to be able to walk easily across the porch. I'd like to be able to use the deck year-round. I'd like to make the front doorsteps look welcoming, not junky."

If you're more ambitious, you can envision a more detailed picture of exactly how you'd like your deck, porch, patio, and doorsteps to look if they were perfect (for you). Picture the layout of the space. If it's a patio, what would the surface be?

My Deck/Porch/Patio/Doorstep—Before

My Deck/Porch/Patio/Doorstep—After

My Deck/Porch/Patio/Doorstep Priority List

Does the deck have railings, multiple levels, a built-in hot tub? Is the porch screened in or enclosed? What furniture and accessories are in the space? What are the doorsteps made of, and what is the color and design of the door? Is there a lighted path leading to it? Are there plants? Write down everything.

Getting There

Now that you have captured your deck, porch, patio, and doorstep's "before" condition, listing all the specifics, and you've imagined their "after" appearance, you can finally prioritize the steps you'll need to take to get there from here. Again, bearing both "before" and "after" in mind, start with what bothers you most about the "before" condition—that will become your top clutter-kicking priority. Then rank the clutter issues in descending order of importance.

Maybe you have been using the same battered hand-me-down porch furniture since you got married and would like to graduate to a lovely matched wicker set. Or the cracked, stained, too-small surface of your patio makes you ashamed to

5-Minute Fixes for Decks, Porches, Patios, and Doorsteps

Bring on the blooms. Few things make a better impression than a couple of large pots of blooming plants. Set them on either side of the front door (after clearing off any toys, dog bones, and newspapers) or the deck door, at the entrance to the patio or on the patio tables, or on either side of the porch door or in front of the porch windows.

But clean up the pots. If you have broken pots, spilled potting soil, dying plants, or dropped leaves or flowers on your deck, patio, or porch, clean up the mess for an instant improvement.

Clean off one table. Pick one table on the porch, deck, or patio, and clear off the clutter. Then give the surface a quick wipe-down and put a centerpiece on the table—fresh flowers, an attractive bowl, some candles. See how much better the area looks already!

Put out a magazine rack. Corral magazines, catalogs, and papers in an attractive magazine rack by the seating area on your porch, patio, or deck. (Just remember to move it to safety when it rains!)

Pick up sticks. One fast way to kick the clutter and improve your outdoor living spaces is to pick up any fallen branches, twigs, and leaves on or around your doorsteps, deck, patio, or porch. While you're out there, deal with fallen nuts, fruits or berries, and flowers, too.

invite guests out there. Or you'd like some plants on the deck and need a safe place to display them where the dog and kids can't knock them over. Or you'd like to finally do something about your overgrown foundation shrubs so the family can use the front door again.

Note down whatever's driving you to distraction on the "My Deck/Porch/Patio/Doorstep Priority List" (or photocopy it, if you'd prefer) in descending order from most to least maddening. Now you have your priorities straight! Once you've finished your priority list, you can turn to the tips beginning on page 296 to find ingenious ways of dealing with each problem.

THE DECK, PORCH, PATIO, AND DOORSTEP TIPS

Because decks and patios, porches, and doorsteps each have their own challenges, I'm going to group the tips for each one so you can find the one that interests you without having to look through every tip in the chapter. But because decks and patios share so many functions, I'm going to combine their tips together. And I'm going to give you the doorstep tips first because that's usually the first close-up view people have of your house. Let's get started!

Doorsteps

Like the front yard (and I will have plenty to say about that in Chapter 16), the door where guests arrive—usually but not always the front door—sets their expectations for what they'll find inside your home. It also gives them a few impressions about you! Make sure they're good impressions by creating an attractive, inviting doorstep. Some of these tips may not seem at first glance to be about clutter, but I believe that the approach to the front door, if it's well maintained, clutter free, and attractively lit and planted, practically screams, "This is an organized, on-top-of-things household!"

Make it easy to arrive. Is there a clear (and cleared) path to your door? Does it have in-ground lighting so people can navigate at night? Is it paved, and if so, is the surface even, or are bricks or concrete edges sticking up? Are the bricks or concrete chipped or cracked? Are stepping stones smooth and secure in the ground? If it's a mulch path, is the mulch clean and thick, or weedy and uneven? If it's a grass path, is it neatly mowed and raked? Help people reach your door easily and safely with a smooth, uncluttered path.

Put out the welcome mat. Okay, you loved the "Warning: Dog Can't Hold Its Licker" mat when you saw it in the catalog. But now it's faded and dilapidated, creating visual clutter. And it never looked quite right with your Colonial home, anyway. Make sure your doormat is clean, new, and functional (especially if you want your floor to be clean once people walk in!). Replace it regularly. A simple doormat will go with any style of home and will encourage people to look at your house, not at the ground. If you just love a doormat with a funny message, why not put it by the back door? Or do what I do when I'm tempted by one of those humorous sayings catalogs offer on doormats, pillows, and plaques: Tear the page out of the catalog and keep it in a "Humor" file. Flipping through the file will always cheer you up without cluttering your home. (I keep favorite funny greeting cards and cartoons in the file, as well. It's so much fun to pull it out and page through it when I need to laugh out loud!)

Watch the steps. There's nothing like stained, cracked, sagging, or broken steps to give people that Bates Motel feeling as they approach your home. Why not just hang a big "Condemned" sign on the door and get it over with? Of course replacing steps or a stoop is a huge pain. But it's nothing compared to the cost of a lawsuit if someone falls and gets hurt on the way to your door. And just think of how much better it will feel to arrive at a welcoming entrance when you get home! It's too easy to stop seeing things when you see them all the time (just ask your spouse what outfit you were wearing yesterday). Get a fresh perspective by approaching your door as if you were a realtor planning to sell the house. *Now* what do you see?

Paint the door. If your door is falling apart or the paint is peeling off, that's the first impression people will have of you and your home. And some doors are just plain ugly. You may have disliked your door from the moment you bought the house but just never got around to doing anything about it. Get a door you love, paint it a color you love, and suddenly coming home will feel better than ever!

Clean the door. My friend Anne points out that a dirty front door—especially one painted a light color—looks messy. Clean the doors, and the windows in them, when they look dirty—screen doors and storm doors included.

Light the door. In addition to lighting the way to the door, make sure the door itself is well but not blindingly lit at night. Not only will this make guests feel welcome and get them safely down the path, it will save you time and aggravation groping for your keys (and then the lock) in the dark!

Ring a bell. Help people alert you to their arrival by making sure you have some sort of bell, knocker, or other device in place; that it's easy to see and use; that it's attractive (if it's a knocker); and that you can actually hear it throughout the house and out in the backyard.

Clear the way. Trikes on the path. Sports equipment at the door. Umbrellas. Shoes. Trash bags (God forbid). All kinds of stuff can materialize in front of doors, on the path to the door, and on the doorsteps. After a while, nobody even sees it—except people who are tripping over it on their way to see you. Get everything out of the way and contained somewhere else—boots and shoes on a shoe mat, umbrellas in a stand, sports equipment in the garage or hall closet, and so on—and make sure they're inside, not outside, the door.

Fix the foundation. A cracked, stained, grimy foundation is every bit as repulsive—though not as dangerous—as cracked, stained, and grimy steps. Seal it and paint it or cover it with low trellising or fencing, but make it look neat and tidy.

Prune the plants. Overgrown foundation plantings are unwelcoming. In fact, they're just plain creepy. Too many homes have contractor-selected plantings that looked good when the house was new but should never have been planted anywhere near a house. Why? Because they get too big, obscuring the windows, crowding the doors, and making the house look dank and neglected. And I don't know which looks worse, foundation plantings that have swallowed the house or sheared-off plantings with rigid rectangular shapes and bare branches exposed everywhere. Ugh! If you don't already have a foundation planting (they were originally created to cover up ugly concrete foundations), think about what your foundation looks like. Is it ugly? If so, select a low-growing evergreen shrub or a mass planting of evergreen ferns, hellebores, and other perennials to conceal it without consuming the house itself. If your foundation is not an eyesore, choose a low bed of evergreen perennials like vinca (periwinkle) and a changing display of flowers— daffodils and tulips in spring, bleeding-hearts and peonies in late spring, daisies and salvias in summer, mums and asters in fall, and so on—will create a lovely display without taking over. The key is to keep the plantings simple and symmetrical. This is *not* the place for a busy mixed garden!

Add a decorative element. Yes, you want to keep the entry to your home clutter free. But that doesn't mean it has to be bare or boring (unless "bare" in your home's case translates as "stately"). I have a pair of handmade wrought-iron "shepherd's crooks" in front of my house, one on either side of the entryway. During the growing season, I hang trailing plants from the hooks; in winter, I set out lanterns and light the candles when I'm expecting guests. A pair of planters, one on each side of the door, would look great as long as they're well composed *and* well maintained. What about statuary? I'd keep that pair of dogs with the baskets in their mouths for the front entry gate. If it suits your home's style and the size of the doorstep, try a single statue at one side.

Give guests the boot. The boot scraper, that is. You can find boot scrapers in hardware and home improvement stores and catalogs like Plow & Hearth (see page 47). Setting or installing one outside the door will not only be a courtesy to your guests, it will help keep mud and snow out of your house.

Decks and Patios

Time spent on the deck or patio should be the most pleasurable, relaxing part of your day. But for too many of us, decks and patios are more like obstacles to be crossed on the way out to the yard—one more unpleasing, unmanageable space. And cluttered decks and patios invite tripping, especially when wet. If you're lucky enough to have a deck or patio, it's time to claim (or reclaim) that space.

Know what you want. Hopefully, if you did the "after" visualization on page 292, you'll have a clear idea of what you really want to do on your deck or patio. Having a plan in mind is the key to a restful, uncluttered deck or patio. Do you want a serene transition between yard and house, with flowering plants, a mini-water garden, and a seating area where you and friends can relax and enjoy your colorful, fragrant surroundings? Do you want an outdoor entertainment center, with a grill and dining area? Or a hot tub and lounge chairs for sunning? Or a place to set up the Ping-Pong table, card table, or puzzle boards? You can achieve any of these goals and a dozen others. But unless you have a really huge space, if you try to achieve more than one of them, you'll probably end up with a cluttered, overwhelming mess. There are ways around this—my friends Delilah and Chaz have a patio for grilling and entertaining that's surrounded by beautifully land-scaped gardens, for example. And my friends Barbara and Peter had a massive wraparound deck that had a seating area with plants on one side of the house and a hot tub on another side of the house. Each area was out of sight of the other and both had plenty of room. But for the most part, the simpler your plan, the less cluttered and more satisfying the results.

Unify the furniture. Your deck or patio will look planned, cared for, and cared about if the furniture matches. You can buy incredible teak, metal, or wicker sets with loveseats, chairs, dining and side tables, huge umbrellas, and more from home stores and catalogs (L.L. Bean, Plow & Hearth, Smith & Hawken, and Orvis are just a few companies with good selections; see pages 46, 47, and 49). But you don't have to go that route to get a unified look. When the wonderful folding wooden rocking chairs I received as a housewarming gift finally bit the dust, I decided to buy those heavy, super-comfortable vintage metal chairs for my deck—the ones with a curved tubular support that, thanks to their ingenious design, rock ever so slightly while you sit in them. I found two at an antiques store and a third at a flea market, and a friend gave me the gift of a round woven-metal table to put with them. So I had three colors and styles of metal furniture. I chose a soft moss-green metal paint and spray-painted them all. That's all it took to bring the group together. Another possibility is to buy matching cushions for your furniture—though if the furniture is made of different materials, this won't be as effective as if the pieces are all, say, wood or wicker.

Don't overdo the cushion patterns. Speaking of cushions, if you choose to put them on your deck or patio furniture, keep them simple. A single color for the cushions with a contrasting color for the throw pillows is pleasing without being busy. Cushions with busy, multicolor floral patterns can quickly become overwhelming, especially if there are lots of them and your deck or patio gets a lot of sun. If you add flowering plants as well as floral cushions, you'll create a whirlwind of visual clutter! Instead, if you'd like to use a floral pattern, use it on the throw pillows and choose a pattern that includes the color of your cushions. There are exceptions: If your deck or patio happens to be very shaded, a floral pattern might help brighten it, and if you have a huge space, patterned cushions will make it seem smaller and more intimate. Stripes are also popular on outdoor cushions, and they form something of a middle ground: You can use striped throw pillows, or have a couple of chairs with striped cushions and solid throw pillows in a group of furniture with solid cushions and striped throw pillows. In either case, the stripes should echo the solid color of the other cushions to unify the grouping and minimize visual clutter. But generally, solid colors work best in modest spaces.

Get some backup. If your deck or patio is a modest size, don't overdo the furniture. Set out as much as you and your family normally use, then get some comfortable folding chairs and tables that you can set out if you have a deck or patio party. Stash the extras in the basement or garage until they're needed. Here's a case where getting extra cushions that match the ones on your permanent deck or patio furniture would really pay off in terms of helping blend the temporary furniture in with the rest.

Organize with accessories. Judiciously placed small tables or cup holders can prevent the clutter of a sea of glasses sitting next to all the chairs on a deck or patio, according to my editor Anne. Just make sure they don't become tripping hazards.

Direct deck traffic. Make sure it's easy to get across your deck or patio and around the various groups of furniture and plants. Guests, kids, and dogs should all be able to move freely around the deck or patio without knocking anything over, hurting themselves, or going up in flames from a too-close encounter with the grill or fire pit.

Don't get busy. Patio surfaces composed of a mosaic of different-colored tiles, busy brick or stone patterns, or combination materials (like brick and stone) create

Tools of the Trade

Fire pits—those wonderful metal "bowls" on legs that hold wood for fires—are the greatest outdoor accessory since the grill and the half-barrel water garden. If you have a patio, you can put a fire pit on it and sit around it. Even if you have a deck, you can put the fire pit in the yard where you can watch the flames from the comfort of your deck chairs. (If it's in the yard, make sure you wait for wet grass—like the day after a rain—to light it.) Setting it on a stone slab or fireproof mat like the ones made to go under grills on decks can also help prevent runaway fires. Fire pits come in a wide variety of styles and sizes, from gorgeous hammered copper to basic black, and most have protective screens and grilling racks, too. They're available at home improvement stores and catalogs like Cabela's (see page 49), Improvements (see page 48), and Plow & Hearth (see page 47). (Plow & Hearth even has a propane-fired model that they recommend for safe on-deck use.) Or you might like to have a chiminea instead of a fire pit—they look like ceramic potbellied stoves on short legs, with a tall chimney to vent the smoke. They're widely available at garden centers and home stores.

But I'm not just recommending fire pits because they look wonderful and it's fun to sit around a fire. They are phenomenal outdoor clutter-controllers. I don't know about you, but my worst yard clutter issue (besides weeds!) is falling twigs and branches. Every wind, every storm, every *day* I'm out there playing pickup sticks. With the fire pit, I can toss them in until it's full, then enjoy a lovely fire and start again. Paper grocery bags, crumpled newspapers, and other uncoated trash paper make ideal fire-starters, so the fire pit helps control that clutter pileup, too. Try one—you'll love it!

visual clutter. They aren't restful. The same could be said of decks that are made of crosshatched wood patterns like a parquet floor. Keep the surface simple, and make the focus of attention what you put on it (or can see from it), rather than making it compete for attention.

Watch the weeds. My mother had a thing for brick patios, and we had one at both my childhood homes. A brick patio is beautiful to look at, but she favored the kind where the bricks were tamped into sand rather than mortared, and as a result, I spent my childhood summers pulling weeds. If you've ever tried to pull a billion tiny but obstinate weeds out of hard-packed sand, I'll bet *you* don't have a sand-based patio! I know I wouldn't. This doesn't mean that you should dump toxic chemicals on your patio to kill the weeds (God forbid—think of your poor kids and pets, if not yourself, your spouse, and guests!), but it does mean that you should consider your patio surface carefully. A weed-covered patio looks cluttered and chaotic. Whether you're laying brick or stone, when it comes to patios, concrete is your friend. And well-maintained concrete (which can now be stained, painted, and even stamped to look like stone) is a low-maintenance, weed-free option. If you do want bricks or pavers in sand, install a weed barrier fabric first. It won't last forever, but it will help.

Unify your plants. A billion little pots of individual plants crammed around your deck or patio is a study in visual clutter—take it from one who knows. But it's great to have the color, fragrance, and softening effect that plants can bring to a deck or patio. To have your plants without the clutter, use the same style of container and plant large pots or planters with multiple plants, or buy them already planted from your local nursery or garden center. (As with the furniture, the pots don't have to be identical; you can have some plain and some patterned, for example, as long as they are all terra cotta, or different colors and even shapes if they are all from the same pottery and the glaze is the same type.) And limit the number of pots you set out—a group of three or one large pot in two corners and one as a centerpiece on the table is probably plenty for a small deck or patio.

Group pots together. If you're a plant collector or you just want to have lots of individual pots, group them on tiered shelves or other multilevel stands to keep them all together. Not only does this look less cluttered, you also get better visual impact that way.

Raise up the plants. If you have kids or pets crashing around your deck or patio, or you need all the "floor" space you can get, you can still enjoy beautiful plants. Just grow them off the ground. Hanging baskets with beautiful trailing plants, window boxes, or baskets or planters that are designed to sit on or hang over the deck railing (Kinsman Company, page 49, specializes in English-style moss-lined wire baskets) are all great options.

Protect your deck. If you have plants on your deck, make sure you have sturdy plastic or glazed ceramic saucers under them to prevent water leaks and the hideous rings they make on deck surfaces. (Check any garden center to find strong terra-cotta-colored plastic saucers with nice high sides to go with your real terra-cotta pots.)

Care for your plants. While few things are as lovely as well-grown plants, practically nothing's as unattractive as brown, dying plants or an overgrown jungle of neglected plants. If you choose to grow plants on your deck or patio, make a commitment to groom, water, and feed them as needed to keep them looking and blooming their best. Cut off dead flowers and any dead leaves and stems regularly. Let your plants be a feature, not an eyesore.

Keep your eye on the ball. This seems like simple common sense, but I've seen enough disasters in this area that I'll mention it anyway, so bear with me. Do not site a basketball hoop, volleyball net, driving range, or anything else involving projectiles where they could crash into the stuff (or people) on your deck or patio. If you already have a sports area that's too close for comfort, it's easier to move the hoop or net than the deck or patio, so do it before you're sorry you didn't!

Add a privacy screen. Sometimes you buy a house with a deck or patio looking right out on the road, into the neighbor's yard, or—gasp—at the McDonald's and gas station on the corner. (What *were* the former owners thinking?) Or the only place you can put one is where you look out at something you wish you didn't have to see. Your own clutter isn't the only kind around—there's also borrowed clutter, when a busy scene or a bunch of somebody else's stuff intrudes on your visual space. If this is the case at your house, screen out that unsightly view. A tall, dense evergreen hedge makes a great screen, since it also filters out some of the noise and pollution that may drift over from outside. But I suspect that you don't want to wait a few years until the hedge grows up—and hedges tend to be pricey and labor-intensive, to boot. Alternatives include attractive wooden privacy screens (Improvements sells a lovely one; see page 48) and, of course, fencing. One

👍 Love It *or* Lose It? 👎

Of course you want to protect your deck or patio furniture from the elements during the off-season. (Not only will it last longer, but it will also be in better shape, which reduces visual clutter just as shabby furniture increases the impression of clutter.) And of course it's a pain to haul all that stuff to the basement or garage—assuming you even have room for it in there—and then drag it all out again in spring. So it's tempting to buy protective covers for the furniture and grill, cover everything up for winter, and just leave it right there on the deck or patio. But this is one temptation you should definitely resist. A bunch of giant body bags out on the deck or patio is not just clutter, it's a major eyesore—and it's an eyesore you'll have to look at every time you go in or out of the house for months. There are better solutions! You can store everything in a special storage tent, or you can get furniture that will stand up to the elements. Stores and catalogs like Plow & Hearth (see page 47), Orvis (see page 49), and L.L. Bean (see page 46) sell very realistic-looking plastic "wicker" furniture that can take winter's abuse, and even metal furniture will hold up if you keep it painted.

Verdict on outdoor body bags? Lose them!

advantage of a screen over fencing is that you can arrange it just around the deck or patio rather than having to fence in the whole yard (or one side of it). Fencing works best when it's used as fencing, not screening, as I know firsthand. One of my neighbors tried to block his view of a busy corner by putting up a small angled section of palisade fence, but rather than looking planned, it just looks like someone walked off with the rest of it!

Aim for outdoor storage. Wouldn't it be convenient to store your outdoor furniture cushions right on your deck or patio? Well, you can, even in the worst winter conditions. But there's a trade-off: You have to store them in plastic. Home improvement stores and catalogs like Improvements (see page 48) sell heavy plastic resin benches with lift-up seats and hefty wheeled "deck boxes" with room to store your cushions, umbrellas, toys, and summer sports equipment. Can't face plastic furniture on your deck or patio? They also sell an attractive cushion storage bag that you can stash in the garage or basement in the off-season. Other good sources for outdoor storage are Frontgate and Plow & Hearth (see pages 46 and 47).

Store your stuff under the big top. Once it's too miserable outside to enjoy your deck or patio, if your furniture and furnishings aren't weatherproof and you don't have room for them in the basement, garage, or tool shed, you can put them in a storage tent. The tents are an unobtrusive gray and are made of weatherproof, triple-layer ripstop polyethylene, just like a real tent. Unlike a camping tent, however, they're made to stay up all season, with ground augers for anchoring, a tubular steel frame, and zippered doors at each end. Set up your tent in a part of the backyard where it will be at least partially hidden from view, and stash your deck or patio furniture, grill, equipment, and even the lawn mower inside. Unlike using individual furniture covers (see "Love It or Lose It?"), consolidating everything under a single cover that's away from the house reduces visual clutter rather than contributing to it. Look for storage tents at home improvement stores, stores that sell lawn furniture, and catalogs like Improvements (see page 48).

Thrill to an uncluttered grill. My friends Delilah and Chaz have the most wonderful outdoor kitchen on their patio, with a huge grill and an elaborate sink, fridge, and counter setup. It would be easy for a kitchen this size to overwhelm the rest of the patio, which they use for entertaining much of the year (at least until freezing weather finally drives them indoors). But they kept that from happening by careful planning—siting the kitchen setup against the wall of the house, where it would be least intrusive, and making all the elements match (the grill, fridge, and sink are all burnished steel). Because they put in lots of counter space, they have big under-counter cabinets where they can store all their outdoor dishes, condiments, and grilling supplies, all out of sight but in easy reach. And the refrigerator also tucks in under the counter so it fits seamlessly with the visual line—grill, sink, counter, and fridge are all the same height.

Put up the grill. It's no thrill to see a grill sitting abandoned through the winter. Around here, I can't get in the car in the winter without seeing grills half-buried under snow. This is *not* good for your grill, and it creates a junkyard effect in your yard. Please, when its season is over, put it away!

Go below deck. If your deck is off the ground and people can see under it, things can get ugly fast. A great-looking deck can be ruined by a bunch of unkempt weeds, half-eaten dog bones, or castoff junk lying under it. Conceal the space with lattice fencing, trellising, or shrubs that will not grow tall, and make sure what can be seen is clean and tidy.

Pet Alert!

If you put food, water, or toys for your pets on the deck or patio, make sure you use sturdy, attractive bowls, since they'll draw the eye, and have a basket or attractive box to stash the toys in when Maggie isn't playing with them. Most important: Do *not* leave food out overnight—at least, not unless you want a clutter of skunks, opossums, raccoons, and rats enjoying the all-you-can-eat buffet outside your door!

Out On the Porch

One of my all-time-favorite memories is of sitting with my grandparents in the porch swing on their open porch. Good times! And I love to see exquisitely designed and furnished porches in decorator magazines and catalogs. Unfortunately, people's porch reality is often more like a clutter nightmare: The porch has sunk out of sight under a mountain of discarded toys, junk furniture, whatsits, dust, and cobwebs. It's become the refuge of stray cats. (I've now known two people whose porches became stray-cat havens.) Between the mice and the spiders, you're afraid to go out on that porch. Reclaiming your porch may require a boot-camp mentality, but it's worth it. Read on to restore your porch from catchall to class act.

Take out the trash. Depending on what's on your porch, gather some trash bags and boxes and clear out everything that doesn't belong there. If it belongs somewhere else in the house, put it aside in a marked box or labeled bag (but in the house, not on the porch), and take it to its rightful home once you've finished with the porch patrol. Put anything you want to donate in a second labeled box or bag, and put everything else in the trash. Now, look at what's left (if you can see it under its shroud of dirt and dust). Ask yourself four questions: Do you like it? Do you want it? Do you need it? Can you replace it? If the answer to the first three is no, and the last one is yes, put it in the appropriate pile. That goes for ugly, battered porch furniture, too. Hose it off and take it to Goodwill or post it on Freecycle (www.freecycle.org) or craigslist (www.craigslist.org). By now, you should have a much smaller pile of porch-related items that will go back out there once they're cleaned up and refurbished.

Clean it up. Once you've emptied out the porch, it's time to clean it up. You can't really see your porch's potential until it's sparkling clean. So bribe the kids, hire a maid service, or just get out the mop and bucket and have at it. When it's empty and clean, take a good look at the space. What does it need? A new coat of bright, light-enhancing white or a soft cream or very pale pastel paint? (Wallpaper is a bad idea on a screen porch!) New screens or windows? A new floor? Better doors? Any TLC you can give your porch now that it's finally shoveled out will enhance your enjoyment every time you're out there from now on. And living space gained is worth some trouble and expense—it's still a lot cheaper than building a new room!

Choose furniture that fits your dreams (and needs). Whether you picture a row of white rockers on the veranda of a great Victorian resort hotel; a cozy, cottage-style arrangement of wicker furniture with chintz cushions and monster Boston ferns; or a porch swing tucked on one side, give yourself a reality check before you start rummaging around through catalogs and at flea markets. Don't forget the "needs" part. If you have kids, that row of white rockers isn't going to do them much good. You can still get a classic white rocker (or two), but make sure you also have kid-friendly furniture and activities planned into your porch's makeover. Try Ikea, L. L. Bean, and Pottery Barn Kids (see pages 46 and 47) for kids' furniture in a variety of styles.

Theme your furniture. As in the case of the deck or patio, your porch will look best if the furniture matches. This doesn't have to be true for all the furniture on the porch—your antique rocker or the kids' play table should absolutely have their place. But a room full of random furniture looks more cluttered than it is, while coordinated furniture makes a room look bigger. Again, it doesn't have to be an exact match—you can have a variety of wicker pieces, for example. But they'll work better if you paint them all the same color or the same intensity of color (all white; or all pale green; or one pale green, one pale blue, and one pale peach, for example) and give them matching cushions. You may recall that I railed against using floral cushions out on the deck or patio, but because of the subdued light and quiet colors of the porch, chintz cushions are not just appropriate, they're also traditional.

Warm it up with rugs. Whether you'd like to cover the entire floor with grass matting or toss some cheerful braided rugs (with nonslip backing, please!) around to contrast with the painted wood floor, your porch will be warmer (both in look and in fact) and more comfortable if you add some floor coverings. But keep them quiet—you want people to look out, not down, when they're on a porch.

Add some acrylic (and light a fire). My friends Delilah and Chaz turned their screen porch into a year-round retreat, thanks to acrylic window panels and a gas fireplace. They had a local window and door shop cut acrylic panels to fit the porch windows, and they had them framed in aluminum. Now when cold weather arrives, they screw the panels on; once it's balmy again, they unscrew them and enjoy the cooling breezes through the porch screens. It's their favorite place to enjoy steaming mugs of coffee or cocoa, curled up on the sofa in front of the comfy blaze of their propane "wood" stove.

Remember that less is more. Don't re-clutter your porch with furniture, games, and other stuff once you've finally cleaned it out. A porch that's open and inviting is a porch you'll want to spend time in. A couple of seating areas with side tables and baskets for magazines, knitting, and other diversions will entice people to bring their breakfasts out to enjoy in the serenity of the porch. Add music if you'd like to hear it in that setting.

Don't overdo the art. "Less is more" applies to art, too. You want people to look out, enjoying the view from the porch, so don't clutter walls and surfaces with art. A couple of pieces on the walls and a single *objet* on a table, or a trio on a shelf, are plenty. Remember: You can always rotate them!

Bring out a bookcase. A low bookcase against the porch's back wall or under the windows will hold books and baskets of magazines, crafts, and necessities like tissues and reading glasses. The top can be used for display or be cushioned as a window seat, depending on its placement.

Bank on a bench. As in your home's entryway or mudroom, one of the storage benches that are widely available in home improvement stores and catalogs is a great porch accessory. These benches have cushions for seating and storage space beneath, usually with woven square or rectangular baskets to hold necessities (from books to toys to outdoor gear, if your porch opens to the outside).

Consider a chest. A blanket chest or vintage trunk (painted to match your furniture) also makes a great porch accessory. Used as a coffee table in front of a loveseat, it can hold extra pillows and afghans for those chilly mornings (or evenings) or just to accommodate a soothing nap.

Try a tray. Carrying food and drink back and forth from the kitchen to the porch can be a challenge. If you get a few large wooden or wicker serving trays with comfortable handles, it will not only be easier to carry things around, but you can also set the trays on the table and serve from them without having to take all the dishes off the trays, put them out on the table, and then replace them on the trays when everyone's finished.

Or add a cart. A rolling cart can be a great addition to the porch. You can use it like a portable sideboard, to serve food, or use it to house books, toys, crafts, or anything else you'd like to have out there. Just roll it over when you need it and roll it out of the way when you're done. Carts come in a number of styles, from chrome and glass to wicker and wood, so you should be able to match your room's decor.

Add some life. Because a porch is a transitional area between the indoors and the outdoors, it's a great place for plants and animals. A hanging plant by a window, a cage of cheerful finches, a birdfeeder hanging just outside a window—all can enhance your family's enjoyment of the porch. Of course, the porch has to be enclosed and climate-controlled for birds, and you or your family must be willing to take care of any plants and animals conscientiously. Any hanging plants or cages must be well out of the line of traffic. (And caged birds must be out of reach of the family cat!) And you must resist the urge to clutter the porch with plants and animals—a few choice plants, pleasingly displayed and well cared for, and a single birdcage will be far more effective and aesthetic than a collection. And don't forget your four-legged pets! A cozy dog "nest" or cat bed will give them a place of their own where they can enjoy the porch with you.

ONWARD!

Let's sit a while on our cleaned-out porch, deck, or patio with a glass of iced tea and pat ourselves on the back for a job well done. Rest up now, because it's almost time to tackle that famous cave of clutter . . . the garage. Are you ready? Pull on those dirty sneakers and take a deep breath. (Better take that breath *before* you go in the garage!) Now, let's go!

Chapter 15

Cleaning Out the Garage

What do you mean, the cars go in there? For all too many of us, the garage has turned into just another place to stash our excess stuff. It's like the basement revisited. The garage sale "before." The heap of stolen (and unrecognizable) treasure on which Smaug, the dragon in J. R. R. Tolkien's *The Hobbit,* made his lair. But don't panic—whatever your garage looks like now, in this chapter I'll give you loads of ingenious tips to help you turn it into organized, usable space. I guarantee there's more room in there than you think! So read on to find out how to make the most of garage storage, turn your garage into a multipurpose space, *and* park your cars in there. It's all possible—really!

PRIORITIES FOR GARAGES

Before you start setting priorities, ask yourself what you use your garage for now—and what you'd like to use it for once you've kicked the clutter. Try to set goals that are realistic—if they're too pie-in-the-sky, they'll be overwhelming, and the clutter is already overwhelming enough!

Next, as in earlier chapters, start your de-cluttering process by setting some clutter-kicking priorities. To do this, you're going to focus on what matters most to you about the way your garage looks and functions now, and make that your top priority. The best approach is to take a good, hard look at the "before" state of the garage, and then visualize the "after."

A Garage Visualization

To get to your clutter-free "after," you need to start with the "before"—the way things look right now. So get out some paper, or use the "My Garage—Before" form (or make a photocopy of it and write on that). Write down every place there's clutter, and note what that clutter is.

Fortunately, the garage—however overwhelming it may look right now—is really just a room, and usually a room with no major appliances (if you don't count vehicles!), except maybe a second fridge. So even if it's crammed to the rafters with sports equipment, power tools, lawn mowers, and all the other yard equipment, boxes of old appliances, paint, projects, rags, ladders, bikes, newspapers, and mercy alone knows what, it can take only so long to get a good idea of what's going on in there. So back the cars out—if by some miracle they actually fit in the garage at the moment—and take a minute now to write down your "before" so you can get to your "after"!

Once you've taken an inventory of your garage's "before" state, it's time to move on to the "after"—how you want the garage to look when you've finished de-

My Garage—Before

_____
_____
_____
_____
_____
_____
_____
_____
_____
_____

My Garage—After

_____
_____
_____
_____
_____
_____
_____
_____
_____

My Garage Priority List

_____
_____
_____
_____
_____
_____
_____
_____
_____

cluttering it. Write it all down on a piece of paper, or in the "My Garage—After" form (or on as many photocopies of it as you need to do it justice).

Think about what you want the garage to _do_ when you've kicked the clutter. To make sure you're being realistic, look at your garage every few minutes while you're taking notes.

5-Minute Fixes for Garages

Stash your trash. Put a trash can by the door to the house and another one beside or under your workbench. The family can toss garbage as they head from the car into the house (rather than leaving it in the car), and you'll be more willing to toss workshop trash if there's a can right there waiting for it.

Put out the welcome mat. If your garage is connected to the house, keep mud and other gunk out of your house by putting a heavy-duty doormat on the garage side of your door.

Keep steps clear. If you have stairs going from the house down into the garage, the steps are *not* the place to keep newspapers for recycling, a spare bag of cat litter, or other clutter. You may not be able to see what's piled there because you're staggering along under a load of groceries or another bulky burden and kids are racing back and forth to get into or out of the car. It's the very definition of a hazard! Get a basket, bin, or hamper to hold things that need to go from the house to the car, but keep it on the house side of the door, not the garage side.

Hang sports balls in mesh bags. Keep basketballs, soccer balls, and volleyballs in sight but not underfoot by storing them in mesh bags hung from hooks on the wall or on a pegboard.

Park the paint. Keep paint cans together in a plastic storage bin on the floor or the bottom shelf of a storage unit. They'll be less likely to spill or get knocked over.

Move (or pitch) the paint. As I noted in the basement chapter, latex paint spoils after 2 or 3 years, or if it's exposed to freezing temperatures (32°F or below). If your garage is unheated and the temperature inside goes down to freezing, dispose of any latex paint you have on hand and find another place to store your paint in the future. (See page 316 for information on disposing of past-its-prime paint.)

Get a knife strip. The magnetic knife strips that are sold as kitchen aids are great in the garage. Use them to hold lightweight tools like screwdrivers, scissors, and pliers.

Your description can be short and to the point: "I'd like all the stuff to be off the garage floor, and I'd like the floor to be clean, not covered with oil spills and stains. I'd like to create a work space where I can create wreaths and other dried-flower projects. I'd like to walk through the garage just once without tripping over bikes and baseball bats. I'd like more wall shelves."

If you like, you can create a more detailed picture of exactly how you'd like your garage to look if it were perfect (for you). Visualize every detail—the storage systems, the work spaces, the floor and wall treatments, the lighting, the vehicles. Write down every detail.

Getting There

Now that you have captured your garage's "before" condition, listing all the specifics, and you've imagined its "after" appearance, you can finally prioritize the steps you need to take to get there from here. Bearing both "before" and "after" in mind, start with what bothers you most about the "before" condition and make that clutter-kicking priority #1. Then work through the clutter issues on your "before" list and use them to create a list of things you will do and in what order you'll do them.

Is your goal simply to fit the cars inside the garage? Or are those moldering piles of bags, boxes, and junk heaped around the walls driving you crazy? Do you dream of a well-lit workshop with a great work space and the latest power tools? Or is your ultimate fantasy of a clean, well-lit, fresh-smelling space with walls of shelves and everything stored neatly in its place?

Note down whatever's driving you to distraction on the "My Garage Priority List" on page 313 (or photocopy it, if you'd prefer) in descending order from most to least maddening. Now you have your priorities straight! Once you've finished the priority list, you can turn to the tips below to find ingenious ways to reclaim your garage.

THE GARAGE TIPS

Dig in. It's unlikely that you could clear out the entire garage all at once, even if you had a whole day (or weekend) to work on it. Instead, pick a wall, or the floor, or a particularly annoying pile, and deal with that one problem. You know the drill by now: Make piles of stuff that should go to the trash, items that need repair, things you want to donate or sell, and stuff that should go back into the garage. Box or bag anything that's not going back right now and label the boxes or bags "Trash," "Salvation Army," "Sale," "Fix," or whatever. Once the clutter is all sorted, stop and take anything that's going out to its final destination. Since your goal is first and foremost to make space, it's more important to clear the stuff out than to go through the entire garage. Schedule another part of the garage for a similar sorting-through on another day, and continue on until you've gone through it all. And as long as you stay focused and tackle the garage in manageable bites, you *will* go through it all! Then the fun can really begin, as you make the garage truly work for you.

Haul off the hazards. Don't let your garage become—or remain!—an accident waiting to happen. Get rid of oily rags; dried-up paint; gunked-up cleaners, oil, solvents, and other fluids and chemicals that have passed their useful lives; old batteries; moldering stacks of old papers and magazines; woodshop leftovers and sawdust; construction scraps; and anything else that could pose a fire or poison hazard. (Call your trash-collection company or municipal waste-disposal office to find out how to dispose of hazardous materials.)

Clear out the tripping traps. While you're at it, get rid of any tripping hazards, too—clear the floor of obstacles. (There are better places for that skateboard or scooter!)

Light it up. Most garages are dimly lit with just one fixture (or—shriek!—bare bulb), contributing to their cavelike atmosphere. Brighten yours up by installing track lighting (available from home improvement stores) so you can finally see what's going on in there! You may want to add shop lights, under-shelf lighting, or even spot lights to give you good working light for your work spaces, but it's a good idea to add bright general lighting as well, and track lighting gives you maximum flexibility, since you can position the lights wherever you need them. Another good idea is to install a motion-sensing light on the wall where you park your car, so you won't have to fumble for a light switch when your arms are full of groceries.

Fix the floor. Once you can actually *see* the garage floor, you may be horrified by its dingy, stained, and generally disgusting appearance. Clean it up! (And see "Love It or Lose It?" for a great way to keep it clean forevermore.) Use a cleaner specifically designed for concrete, such as Quikrete Concrete & Asphalt Cleaner or Behr Concrete Cleaner & Degreaser. Once the concrete's clean, patch any cracks with a concrete patch (available in squeeze-tube and caulk-tube formats). Then give it an upgrade with a concrete stain, concrete paint, or durable epoxy coating like the Rust-Oleum EpoxyShield Garage Floor Coating system (which comes with its own concrete cleaner, decorative chips, and an instructional video). For a fancy floor, you can get durable colored and patterned high-impact copolymer tiles from RaceDeck (www.racedeck.com), and snap together the stain-resistant floor of your dreams by combining tile colors and patterns.

Clear the paths. If you have an unattached garage, make sure you pick up equipment, tools, garbage, and any other clutter that's lying around along the outside walls. Keep visual clutter minimized by making sure you mow the lawn around the garage and trim the weeds. And maintain walks and entries connecting the garage to the house.

Cart it off. Make it easier to bring things from your unattached garage into the house, instead of letting them pile up, by getting a dolly or upright grocery cart. These make loads easy to move without lifting.

Park smart. Contain slush, snow, mud, water, oil, and other yucky spills with an Under-Car Garage Mat. It's a heavy-duty vinyl mat with snap-on rims that can contain up to 50 gallons of liquid. (But let's hope you don't have to deal with *that* much fluid!) Besides keeping the garage floor tidy and preventing tracking into the house, these mats clearly show where to park so nobody accidentally hits the garage wall. They're available from auto parts and home improvement stores and catalogs like Improvements (see page 48).

Stow the shoes and other wet stuff. The door that connects the garage to the house is also a great place to put one of those rubber "boot trays" to keep wet, muddy shoes on the garage side of the door. They're available at hardware and home improvement stores and from catalogs like Plow & Hearth (see page 47). And don't forget an umbrella rack to keep dripping umbrellas from crying a river on your kitchen floor!

Hang a flashlight. As in the basement, make sure you have a flashlight on hand if the lights go out. Hang a flashlight on the wall by the door into the house. Check it regularly to make sure the batteries are working.

Work your walls. Maximize your garage storage with wall-to-wall shelving. Use metal storage units, or try the vinyl stacking units my boyfriend, Rob, swears by. His are from Rubbermaid and are easy to assemble—you simply snap them together. He put them along an entire wall of his garage and points out that they keep everything dry and off the floor and, despite the fact that they're vinyl, they're extremely strong and durable. (Another friend uses them to store wreath bases and other supplies for her dried-flower business in her garage, and she swears by them, too.) You can also choose from a plethora of wire storage units like the ones made by ClosetMaid, available from home improvement centers and organizing stores.

Go on the grid. Schulte Activity Organizers feature attractive, heavy-duty epoxy-coated steel grids that mount to your garage walls. The 2- x 4-foot grid panels mount horizontally or vertically. Once you've put the basic grid in place, you can attach shelves and organizers to hang tools, sports equipment, even bikes—each grid will hold up to 75 pounds. Look for them at organizing stores and Web sites like All Bright Ideas (see page 48).

Go on the grid (iron). For a more industrial look, try a whole-wall storage system like the Grid Iron system (www.gridironusa.com). Grid Iron makes heavy-duty lipped metal panels that you attach to your wall; sturdy holders for equipment and shelves lock onto the panels' 1-inch rolled-steel channels.

Gear up with GearWall. If you don't want a full-wall covering but like the idea of panels, consider 1- by 8-foot GearWall panels from Gladiator GarageWorks (www.gladiatorgw.com). You can install as many of these heavy-duty plastic panels as you need onto studs or drywall, and their slot-wall system holds all Gladiator and GearBox accessories for tools and excellent, accessible bins for nails and other hardware.

Go with PVC panels. Another option along the same lines is storeWALL PVC panels, available in five colors and a variety of widths and lengths (www.storewall.com). Grooves in the panels hold shelves, cabinets, and other accessories including bike hooks. Look for components for storeWALL systems from The Accessories Group (www.theaccessoriesgroup.com).

Hang it up. For a cleaner look that still gets your stuff off the floor and onto the wall, choose one of the specialty hanger systems like the ones made by Racor (www.racorinc.com). They attach to WallDocks fasteners and will tidily—dare I say attractively?—hold and display everything from bikes, sleds, and golf bags to power tools and shop supplies. You create your own flexible (and easily changeable) storage system to meet your individual needs. Look for them at organizing stores and Web sites like All Bright Ideas (see page 48).

Get on the fast track. Another clean-looking wall-mounting system is FastTrack from Rubbermaid (www.rubbermaid.com). Wall-mounted FastTrack Rails hold numerous types of hooks, holders, mesh bins and baskets, cabinets, and shelves that snap on for flexibility or screw on for more permanent placement. They're durable enough to hold ladders and wheelbarrows as well as tools, power equipment, and sports gear—up to 2,000 pounds per rail.

Raise stuff to the rafters. Use your ceiling space for storage with help from heavy-duty galvanized steel racks, available in single and double widths and capable of holding up to 500 pounds, or the crank-operated Heavy Lift "Garage Elevator," a 4- by 4-foot steel platform that raises and lowers up to 250 pounds. Both are great for storing tires, ladders, lightweight lawn and patio furniture, and other seasonal storage. For lighter ceiling storage, consider Rafter Solutions, which attach to the rafters and have two shelves, each of which holds up to 75 pounds. All three are available from home improvement stores and catalogs like Improvements (see page 48).

Put up some pegboard. If you have a workshop area in your garage or just need a place to hang tools, a pegboard is an excellent choice. The good news is, you don't have to settle for boring brown hardboard pegboard—DPI (www.decpanels. com) makes metallic pegboard panels that will brighten up your work space. You can attach pegboard to furring strips, exposed wall studs, or a pegboard fastening system that provides spacers to hold the pegboard away from the wall so you can hang up the pegboard hooks to hold your stuff. Pegboard is great for tools because it holds them securely—no risk of anything falling off shelves—and all your tools will be displayed where they're easy to find, right where you're going to use them. To make sure you're not missing any, use this idea from my days as an editor at *Organic Gardening* magazine: One of our readers' favorite tips was to put up a pegboard and paint or draw the outline of each of their tools on the board. With a glance, they could see if any tools were missing.

Put it in plastic. Plastic storage containers, available from groceries, pharmacies, hardware stores, home improvement stores—pretty much anywhere!—in a

[Tools of the Trade]

Store tools in a mobile tool cart, which holds drawers for tools in a wheeled metal frame. Stash paintbrushes, measuring tapes, hand tools, and other essential stuff in the drawers, then just roll the cart wherever you need it. Or you can load it up for a particular project so you have everything you need in one (mobile) place, instead of having to search all over the garage every time you need another tool or piece of hardware to complete a project. Look for carts like this at home improvement centers and hardware stores.

wide range of shapes and sizes, are ideal for garage storage. You can see what's inside so it's easy to find things, and you can buy whatever size you need to fit your shelves or your stuff. No more bits and pieces raining down when you're trying to find something!

Cache it in cabinets. Garage cabinets should be tough, and some are specially manufactured to take abuse and still look great. Try Schulte's freedomRail garage system (www.schultestorage.com) or the good-looking, durable, ready-to-assemble garage wall and floor cabinets from Rubbermaid (www.rubbermaid.com).

Protect your walls (and car doors). Put thick polyethylene wall bumpers along your garage walls at car-door height to protect your car doors and garage walls (once you're actually able to get your cars in there!). They come with wall-mounting hardware for drywall, open studs, concrete, or brick and are available at home improvement stores and catalogs like Improvements (see page 48).

Put sports gear together. If your garage is home to an ever-expanding collection of sports gear, contain it in the Rubbermaid Sports Station Organizer (www.rubbermaid.com), which has compartments and hooks for racquets, bats, and hockey sticks as well as storage space for balls and helmets and a mesh bag for storage or carting off to the game.

Grook your gear. Or hang up your sports equipment on a wall-mounted Grook Tool holder, with rubber loops and hooks to hold gear securely. Find it at The Container Store (www.containerstore.com).

Hang up your bike. The Bike Hoist Pulley System lets you raise a bike into the air and lock it in place by pulling on a cord (just like you lift and lock blinds), and lower it the same way. Brackets hold the bike at ceiling height and out of your way until it's needed. The system is available from catalogs like Improvements.

Add shelves to your studs. For unfinished garage interiors, there's even a special shelving system designed to fit between exposed 16-inch on-center studs. The shelves, which attach with screws, come in 6½- and 11-inch depths, and the system also includes extension-cord hangers. Ingenious! Look for them at home improvement centers and catalogs like Improvements.

Or turn them into storage centers. The Improvements catalog also features two powder-coated steel storage centers designed to mount on 16- or 24-inch on-center studs. The Power Center holds power tools like trimmers, leaf blowers, and chain saws, while the Aqua Center holds garden and coil hoses, sprinklers, and nozzles.

Get creative with car parts. If you happen to have vintage car parts lying around your garage, there's an alternative to hauling them off to the dump or selling them on eBay: Turn them into wall art instead of clutter. I'll never forget how impressed I was when I went to nearby Emmaus, Pennsylvania, to see the home my friends Fern and Tom had bought. The house itself was a typical suburban home, but in the garage, the previous owners had hung a Corvette—or was it a Corvair?—grille with (working!) lights on the wall. You turned on a switch on the wall and the headlights came on. It was *so* cool!

Ban busted appliances. If your garage has become a graveyard for broken kitchen appliances, office equipment, bikes, electronics, and air conditioners, get real, please. Either get it fixed or get it out. Is it cheaper to get a new one, or have you long since replaced the old appliance but are keeping it out there "just in case"? Donate it or toss it. "In case" is never worth the space.

Have a hierarchy. Put the stuff you use most often where it's easiest to reach. Stash the seasonal or "once in a while" stuff higher on the shelves or walls, or hang it from the ceiling, where it's out of your way but easy to get to when you need it.

Group garage stuff. You'll save a lot of time and frustration if you keep like stuff together—sports equipment in one place, workshop supplies in another, auto supplies in yet another, garden equipment in another, and so on. No more endlessly looking for what you need! And it's easier to see if something is missing or needs to be replaced if you know exactly where it should be.

Rent what you don't use often. Why buy—and store—a tool or piece of equipment you use once or twice a year? Rent it instead and save the space (not to mention the upkeep)!

Keep recycling convenient. If you store your recycling bins in the garage, keep them near the door to the house to make it easier for the family to toss cans, bottles, newspapers, and other recyclables into the appropriate bins as they come and go.

Try a T-bar. T-bars hold skis and even lumber off the floor and out of the way.

Corral corrosives. If you keep potentially hazardous materials like pesticides, paint stripper, turpentine, solvents, cleaners, and pool and hot tub chemicals in your garage, lock them up behind closed cabinet doors to keep them from getting spilled and to protect family members and friends from them!

Clip it on. Use this tip from my friend Karen to collect all those to-do and materials lists, project plans, bills, and other papers that can cover your worktable (and

Tools of the Trade

Like basements, garages can flood, so I'm repeating this tip here: If you think there's the least chance that water might pool on your garage floor, it's safest to store everything at a higher level. Fortunately, some inventive soul created rust-proof, rot-proof plastic Hi & Dri Storage Pallets to raise garage storage out of harm's way. They come in two sizes and can support 1,000 pounds, lifting your boxes 3½ inches off the floor. If water seeps in, it will just flow underneath the pallets while your stuff stays, well, high and dry. Look for them at home improvement centers and in catalogs such as Improvements (see page 48).

Pet Alert!

If your pets go into the garage for any reason—because the cat door's in there, because the dog gets into the car in there—it is absolutely essential that you protect them from antifreeze spills. Antifreeze is incredibly toxic to animals, but unfortunately, it's apparently also irresistible to them—sort of like Gatorade for pets. But one slurp of the lime-green or brilliant blue liquid and they'll be heading to pet paradise. I don't know why manufacturers don't add a scent or flavoring that's repellent to pets, but until they do, make sure you clean up any spills, pools, or splashes of antifreeze ASAP.

floor) or take up too much wall space: She uses a big spring-loaded clip with a magnetic back to hold everything in one spot.

Minimize cord clutter. Anywhere you use a lot of electrical devices, including the garage, you can accumulate a lot of cord clutter. Confine it to one place with a Squid Power-Outlet Multiplier, which lets you run five electrical devices off one grounded outlet even if each one has a large transformer plug or timer. This ingenious contraption (which does look rather squidlike) is available from home improvement stores and catalogs like Improvements and Herrington (see page 48).

Rack it up. Organizing catalogs and stores like All Bright Ideas (see page 48) also sell wonderful heavy-duty wire grid systems that hang on the wall and hold tools with a series of different hooks and clips made to fit each tool. They can hold anything from picks and sledgehammers to rakes and shovels, so you can customize the rack for the tools you need. The hooks and clips are coated to protect the tools and provide a secure grip.

Put up some clips. You can also clip your tools directly to the wall using the kind of metal clips sold in home improvement and organizing stores and catalogs to hold brooms, mops, and other cleaning equipment on pantry doors.

Hang some hooks. Put up single hooks or two-pronged hooks to hold tools, equipment, birdfeeders, scoops, leashes, and plastic bags you use to pick up after the dog. Hang them where no one will run into them or get their clothes caught.

Set up some shelving. Set up a metal shelving unit along a wall of the garage to hold bags, boxes, plant pots, birdhouses, plastic bins of hardware, and anything else that will fit securely. (It's best to hang hand tools and anything else that could hurt someone if it slid off a shelf.) My boyfriend, Rob, would advise you to get heavy-duty vinyl shelving (such as Rubbermaid's). If you'd like to set up a wall shelving system that's customized to your space rather than a freestanding unit, CabinetMaid makes wire shelving of all types and lengths just for this purpose. All three types are available at home improvement stores.

Bring out the tins. If your garage is where you store grass seed, birdseed, cat or dog food, or anything else that mice might think was tasty, put it in big, mouse-proof metal tins. Pet stores often give them away for free as part of pet-food promotions, and stores that sell wild bird supplies sell an assortment of sizes with beautiful bird-themed art on them. I know home and pet stores and catalogs sell beautiful wooden bins for pet food, but I wouldn't bet on them being mouse- or bugproof. Heavy-duty plastic might work, but tins are safe and convenient (and did I mention they're often free?). Label the lids with the contents so nobody accidentally gives your grass seed to the birds or feeds Clifford's food to Garfield by mistake!

Cars, Cars, Cars

Let's not forget the cars (trucks, SUVs, vans) themselves. Sometimes it seems like they've accumulated as much clutter as the garage! It's astounding how much stuff can be crammed into such a small space. These tips will help you get your car cleaned out and organized.

[Tools of the Trade]

Prevent gasoline spills with a Petro Pump, a 5-gallon gas container with its own pump. No more lifting the container to pour fuel into your lawn mower or other gas-powered equipment—or onto the garage floor! The 4-foot fuel hose gives you a good reach, and you can control the flow, from fast to a trickle. Good idea! It's available from home improvement stores and catalogs like Improvements (see page 48).

Clear out the glove compartment. Admit it: You have no idea what's in there, do you? Is your glove compartment an explosion waiting to happen—crammed with outdated road maps; ancient tissues; fast-food napkins, condiments, and other detritus; hand-written directions on scraps of paper to places you haven't been in years (or printouts to same); a few school papers; an old vet bill; and mercy knows what else? Take 10 minutes and a plastic grocery bag and deal with it. Pull out the stuff, trash everything you can, and try to find better homes for the rest. (You don't really need to keep the map of Virginia in your glove compartment if you go there once every year or two. Put it in a labeled plastic storage bin with your other maps and directions and shelve it in the garage!) Once you've cleaned everything out, treat yourself to a current road map and road atlas. You deserve it!

Empty the console. Consoles also accumulate all kinds of junk—broken sunglasses, dried-out pens, bottle caps. Get rid of all the trash, and leave just a few essentials: a notepad, pen, tire gauge, and flashlight—and maybe a *functional* pair of sunglasses.

Find the floor. Now it's time to tackle the car floor. Can you see it? Or is it buried under bags (what's in them, anyway?), shoes, cartons and other fast-food trash, soda cans, toys, sports equipment, umbrellas, a fleece jacket, tissue boxes, CD cases . . . good grief. You may need a full-size garbage bag for this one! But again, you should be able to clean it all out in just 10 minutes, no matter how trashed it is. Throw out what you can and find homes for the rest in the house or garage. For the stuff that has to stay in the car, get a large canvas tote (like the famous ones from L.L. Bean) or a Cargo Carryall (see "Tools of the Trade" on page 329) and store your stuff safely (and upright) in them. All done? Time for another treat—a trip to the car wash and a vacuum. Then sit back, relax, and enjoy that cleared-out, cleaned-up car!

Tackle the trunk. Do you know what's in your trunk right now? Take a good look. Your trunk should function as an emergency center, with a spare tire, jumper cables, and other auto emergency gear like flares and a "help" sign (see "The Pros Know"); supplies like motor oil, brake fluid, antifreeze, and windshield-washer fluid; a local phone directory; a travel snow shovel; a bag of cat box filler or sand (for traction on ice); and the like. It can also hold dog-walking supplies, picnic gear, car-washing supplies (in a plastic bucket), a tote for umbrellas and rain gear like ponchos, and Cargo Carryalls (see "Tools of the Trade" on page 329) to

One thing it definitely makes sense to carry in your car is a stash of emergency supplies. And who knows more about being prepared than that diva of domesticity, Martha Stewart? She recommends putting a large, rectangular, heavy vinyl catchall in the car and stocking it with supplies like a first-aid kit, auto fire extinguisher, jumper cables, flares, tire repair kit, paper towels, duct tape, and bungee cords. To be prepared for a breakdown, Martha suggests packing a separate bag with a blanket, warm clothing, bottled water, and granola bars.

hold grocery and other shopping bags upright. Everything should be neat and easy to find. If you're using the trunk as a mobile storage area for stuff that has no place in your car, clean out the junk, put the storage where it belongs, and organize what's left for easy access. Then, if there's something that *should* be in the trunk but isn't, you'll have room for it.

Be prepared, part one. Always keep a few essential tools in your car so you'll be prepared for an emergency. You can stash them in a plastic storage container (I like the ones with handles) and put them on the floor in the back or in the cargo area. New inventions have made it easier than ever to have what you need on hand. Besides a vehicle emergency kit (see "The Pros Know"), I recommend a Life Hammer (it can smash car windows and cut jammed seat belts so you can escape from your car; put this gadget where you can reach it if you're in a crash, don't store it in the trunk); a "Sputnik" 7-in-1 screwdriver with an LED flashlight or a 12-in-1 Hammer Tool; a portable Rescue Shovel for snow and a Rechargeable Ice Scraper that charges through your cigarette lighter socket to deal with windshield ice fast; a 4-in-1 Emergency Flashlight that's crank-powered and includes an FM radio, cell phone charger, and emergency siren; and the Car Charger, a battery charger that works through your cigarette lighter socket so you don't have to get out of the car or wait for another vehicle to help you. And, of course, I hope you have an LED miniflashlight (called a Clip-Light) on your keychain! Look for all these wonder tools at auto parts, home improvement, and hardware stores, and in catalogs like Plow & Hearth, Herrington, Solutions, and Improvements (see pages 47 and 48).

Be prepared, part two. My friend Jennifer isn't about to be stuck on the road without a few essentials of a different kind. "I keep my going-away toiletry bag packed and ready all of the time with extra toiletries and a hair dryer inside," she explains. "I keep it in the car just in case I'm ever stuck on the road someplace with car problems or bad weather." Sure beats getting unexpectedly stuck in a hotel without so much as a toothbrush!

Stash the stroller. Jennifer has another tip for making the best use of your car space. "I store my son's stroller in the trunk of my car, where it's handy if we're out someplace and need it," she says, adding the clincher, "and it's not taking up space in the garage."

Bag it up, part one. Jennifer's not the only one who knows how to make the most of her car's storage capabilities. My environmentally conscious friend Chris likes to reuse plastic and paper bags at the grocery store. She stores them in the trunk so they're readily available and she doesn't have to remember to bring some every time she goes to the store.

Bag it up, part two. Of course, Jennifer has her own solution to the bag issue. "I keep two big cloth bags in my car and take them to the grocery store," she says. "I can get most of the groceries into these bags, which makes it easier to get into the car and into the house than carrying a bunch of small bags—and then I don't have to store or get rid of all those plastic bags."

Bag it up, part three. Speaking of bags, make sure you always have a trash bag in the car to collect wrappers, tissues, cups, papers, CD wrappers, and the endless other detritus that seems to accumulate in vehicles. Keep some plastic grocery bags in the glove compartment and pull one out for each trip. When you get home, if there's trash in it, take it inside with you.

Make your cup holder multitask. Get organized with a Cell-Cup, a gray foam container that fits in your car's cup holder and has compartments to hold your cell phone, pen and pencil, change, or sticky notepad safely and in easy reach. It also has an opening in the bottom for your cell phone charger cord. Look for it at home improvement and auto parts stores, and from catalogs and Web sites.

Hang it up. Backseat passengers can stow books, magazines, water bottles, snacks, and other stuff in a pocket organizer that hangs over the back of the front seat.

Say bye-bye to bumper stickers. Don Aslett, in his wonderfully named book, *Clutter's Last Stand,* calls them "junker stickers." And you know he's right. How-

Keep grocery bags upright, recycling from scattering all over the trunk, and sports gear from rolling around in a Cargo Carryall. The sturdy rectangular nylon carryall folds flat when not in use, then expands to one, two, or three compartments to suit your storage needs. It has carrying handles and Velcro strips to secure it to the trunk floor's carpeting. Great idea! Look for it in home improvement stores and catalogs like Solutions (see page 48).

ever irresistible the message, a bumper sticker makes a car look cluttered. And a bunch of bumper stickers doesn't just create visual clutter—it distracts other drivers, making fender benders more likely. So do what I do—if you absolutely must have that bumper sticker with Chief Seattle saying, "The earth does not belong to us, we belong to the earth," buy it and tack it up on the garage wall as garage art. If you have a handful of favorites, rotate them. That way, you'll get a boost every time you walk through the garage—without trashing your car.

Ditto for dashboard detritus. I can't tell you how many times I've seen cars with their dashboards covered with bobble-head characters and the rear window completely obscured by stuffed animals. And some dashboards look like out-of-control file cabinets and wastebaskets, several inches deep in papers and paper coffee cups. This is clutter for clutter's sake. It restricts visibility, clutters the car, and could even hit you or your family in the case of an accident or sudden stop. (This goes for long things hanging off the rear-view mirror, too. If you want to hang up a rosary, dream catcher, or whatever on the mirror, keep it tightly wrapped so you don't lose an eye if you have to jump on the brakes.) Get . . . it . . . out.

ONWARD!

Wow! You've kicked out all that garage clutter. You probably feel that you deserve a medal—or a chestful! Instead, how about a little fresh air? If you stroll outside, you're bound to see the subject of our next chapter—the yard and garden. But don't worry: After taking on the garage, de-cluttering those outdoor spaces will seem like, well, a walk in the park! So turn the page and let's head on out there.

Chapter 16

Sprucing Up the Yard and Garden

Maybe you don't *really* need 25 birdfeeders . . . especially when 7 of them have fallen apart and you've positioned 14 of them where you can't even see them from the house. And okay, that garden gnome looked cute, but his accumulated siblings make your front yard look like the home of Snow White and the Seven Dwarfs. In this chapter, you'll find tons of useful tips to help you know when lawn art looks like art and when it just looks like junk; how to keep the yard and gardens looking tidy and inviting; how to tie it all together; and how to combat visual clutter. Plus "5-Minute Fixes" to give your yard that pulled-together look in a flash!

PRIORITIES FOR THE YARD AND GARDEN

At most houses, the front yard and backyard have different purposes. The front yard is a showplace, the part people see from the street. The backyard is the place where outdoor living happens. Because their functions are so different, I suggest you do two separate visualizations, one for the front yard and one for the backyard. You can adopt the "My Yard and Garden—Before" form to make space for both.

As in earlier chapters, you'll start your de-cluttering process by setting some clutter-kicking priorities. The first step in that process is to focus on what matters most to you about the way your front and backyards look by taking a good, hard look at the "before" state of each part of the yard. Then you'll go on to visualize the "after."

A Yard and Garden Visualization

To get to your "after," you need to start with the "before"—the way things look right now. So get out some paper, or use the "My Yard and Garden—Before" form on page 332 (or make a photocopy of it and write on that). Once again, it helps to look at your yard with fresh eyes. Pretend you're a realtor who's come to evaluate the property or, say, your prospective new boss arriving to see if you'd be a good candidate—based on the appearance of your yard. Write down every place on the lawn and in and around garden beds and borders where there's clutter, and take note of what that clutter is. In the case of a yard, untidiness—anything that makes the yard look unkempt—equals clutter, in addition, of course, to clutter itself. So take a minute now to write down your "before" so you can get to your "after"!

Once you've taken an inventory of your yard's "before" state, it's time to move on to the "after"—what you want the yard to look like when you've kicked the clutter. Write it all down on a piece of paper, or on the "My Yard and Garden—After" form on page 332 (or on as many photocopies of it as you need to do it justice). To make sure you're being realistic, look at the yard every few minutes while you're creating your description.

Your description can be short and to the point: "I'd like a lush, green lawn out front, not a weedy mess. I'd like to have something nice under my trees, instead of bare ground. I'd like a neat hedge or fence, not the leafless hedge we have now. I'd like to have a playground for the kids and a cutting garden for myself in the backyard. I'd like to cut down the tree that's shading the living room."

If you like, you can create an even more detailed picture of exactly how you'd like your yard to look if it were perfect (for you). Picture every lovely detail—the flowerbeds, the rose-covered arbor, the pool or water garden, the luxuriant kitchen or herb garden, the paths, the pergola—everything.

My Yard and Garden—Before

Front Yard: _____
_____
_____
_____

Backyard: _____
_____
_____
_____
_____

My Yard and Garden—After

Front Yard: _____
_____
_____
_____

Backyard: _____
_____
_____
_____

Getting There

Now that you've captured your yard's "before" condition, listing all the specifics, and you've imagined its "after" appearance, you can finally prioritize the steps you need to take to get there from here. Bearing both your "before" and "after" in mind, start with what bothers you most about the "before" condition and make that your top priority.

Unmowed grass, garden tools lying around, dog toys, balls, bikes, kids' toys, and hoses snaking across the lawn may be making a mess of your yard. Maybe you'd like to turn that unkempt, weedy brush pile in the backyard into a flowerbed or upgrade the falling-down playground equipment and set up a fantastic swing set and fort for the kids. Or turn that shaded bare spot in the back that's just collecting a clutter of sticks and your dog's favorite half-chewed bones into a volleyball court. Or you'd like to haul off the disintegrating compost bins and replace them with attractive new bins—and add some tidy raised beds for your veggie garden, while you're at it. Or you can't take another week with the rotting railroad-tie steps in the front and want to replace them with something that's both attractive and durable.

Write down whatever's driving you to distraction on the "My Yard and Garden

My Yard and Garden Priority List

_____

_____

_____

_____

_____

_____

_____

_____

_____

_____

A Dozen 5-Minute Fixes

You got held up in traffic and your guests are due within the hour. Your boss just called to say she'd be by to drop off some papers in a few minutes. You've been so busy housecleaning before your big date that you completely forgot about the yard. Or you're just intimidated by the size of the cleanup job you're facing. Yikes! What to do? Try these tried-and-true tips to make the yard look presentable fast.

Pick it up. Take a plastic garbage bag and rush around the front yard, collecting any fallen sticks, litter, and other debris. Get it out of sight!

Clear the drive. If there's anything in the driveway—toys, bikes, garbage bins—get them out. Bag the toys and put them, the garbage bins, bikes, sports equipment, and other stuff in the garage (for now).

Sweep the drive. Quick—sweep the drive so it looks its best. Do the sidewalk, too!

Clear the lawn. If you see toys, debris, or anything else on the lawn, get them out of sight ASAP.

Clear out your car. If your car is sitting out in plain sight, rush over there with a plastic garbage bag and dump the trash, random bags, bottles, books, CDs, gym bag, wrappers, and anything else you find into it. Nothing says clutter like a trashed car!

Clean around the mailbox. Weed around the mailbox with gloves, shears, or a weed-whacker. Make it look neat. If you have flowers growing around the mailbox, water them and deadhead (cut off any dead flowers). Pick up any newspapers lying around the mailbox and bring in the mail.

Clear the path. Sweep the walkway, while you're at it, and pull any weeds on the walk, tossing them into a plastic bag en route to the compost or trash. If

Priority List" on page 333 (or photocopy it, if you'd prefer) in descending order from most to least maddening. Now you have your priorities straight! Once you've finished your priority list, you can turn to the tips below to find ingenious ways of dealing with each problem.

you have an overgrown grass path, give it a quick mowing. Make sure there's nothing on the path—no toys or sports equipment, no fallen leaves, seedpods, sticks, or rocks.

Sweep the stoop. Next, sweep the front stoop and steps (if you have any) and shake out and sweep the doormat.

Add a feature. If it's not too cold and you have enough forewarning, run to your local nursery—or even a grocery store—and buy a blooming plant to put by the door. Make sure it's big and colorful enough to make a splash. If it's a hanging basket, set it by the door and tuck the chain discreetly underneath the pot or temporarily detach the plastic or metal hook. (You can always reattach it once your company leaves if you want to hang it up in the backyard.) Buy something you'll enjoy when your guests are gone, or give it to them as a guest gift when they leave.

Add more color. Front yard looking drab? Race around to the deck and see if you have any colorful container plants. Tuck them in beds in the front yard for a burst of instant color.

Light the way. If your guest or guests are arriving after dark, turn on the walkway lights and the light over your front door. No pathway lights? Consider making luminarias. (These are small paper bags with sand in the bottom to hold them open and stabilize them and tea lights or votive candles set in the sand.) When lit, they provide soft, lovely illumination.

Come out to meet them. It's much easier to distract guests from the less-than-perfect state of your front yard if you rush out to greet them, talking enthusiastically while herding them toward the front door before they know what's hit them. Just remember, if it's not dark when your guests leave, you'll also have to accompany them back to their car, chatting enthusiastically all the way.

THE YARD AND GARDEN TIPS

Now that you've gotten your feet wet, let's start in the front yard—the part people see first. Then we'll head around back.

The Front Yard

Manage the mailbox. The mailbox is the first thing people see when they arrive at your house, so take a good look at it yourself. Is it falling down, ancient, dented, rusting, or otherwise dilapidated? Are weeds or grasses reaching for the stars all around it? If so, it just screams to the world, "Slovenly people live here!" So come on, how hard is this to fix? Put up an attractive mailbox. Mow or weed-whack around it to keep the weeds and grass low. And add a decorative vine like a gorgeous clematis to grow up the post and spill over the top with its beautiful starry blooms. Or buy one of those clever planters that fit around a mailbox post and fill it with colorful marigolds, petunias, or other plants of your choice. But don't plant anything if you won't water and maintain it! Better a tidy but bare appearance than a display of crisp, brown, formerly living plants.

Handle the hedge. An overgrown hedge is dark, creepy, and unkempt. And a badly sheared hedge has that hideous fringe effect—a thin layer of leaves on the outside and bare branches inside. If you have a hedge, make it work for you. Keep it pruned and tidy. If you must shear it, shape the hedge like a pyramid, not a box, so light can reach the lower parts more easily. This will help avoid "bare-legs syndrome," where the top is green and the bottom branches are bare because they've been shaded out. If you don't have a hedge but are considering one, or you are ready to really renovate yours, consider a flowering hedge to add more interest and beauty to your yard. Rugosa roses are tough road-, salt-, and weather-resistant bushes. They have beautiful, fragrant flowers, showy red rose hips, and yellow fall foliage, creating a long season of interest. My favorite is 'Alba', with lovely single white flowers. You should also investigate hedge roses like 'Carefree Beauty', widely available from garden centers, nurseries, and plant catalogs like Carroll Gardens (444 East Main Street, Westminster, MD 21157-5540; 800-638-6334; www.carrollgardens.com) and the 'Simplicity' series from Jackson & Perkins (1 Rose Lane, Medford, OR 97501; 800-872-7673; www.jacksonandperkins.com). All of these roses are bred to be tough and disease-resistant, and they stay comparatively low—usually 3 to 5 feet tall—so the only maintenance they require is for you to mow around them to keep them from spreading and to prune out any dead branches. If you want an all-green hedge, two classic plants are privet and, in the Southeast, yaupon holly.

My friend Cole Burrell is a well-known landscape designer. Besides designing landscapes for clients, Cole also teaches landscape architecture, lectures around the country (and sometimes the world), and has written numerous books and myriad articles on plants and garden design. Need I say that he knows a thing or two about how to put a landscape together? Because one of Cole's specialties is designing gardens featuring native plants, his clients often want him to put a prairie garden or wildflower meadow in their front yard instead of a more traditional flower border.

Now, as you can imagine, one concern about putting a meadow in the front yard is the danger that neighbors and passers-by, instead of appreciating the ever-changing beauty of nature at work, might conclude that you'd simply forgotten to mow the grass for the entire season and call city hall to complain. But Cole has a solution for this. When he designs meadows for clients, he frames them carefully to make them look intentional. By surrounding them with a ribbon of very carefully maintained lawn, Cole makes it obvious that this is a garden, not a yard gone wild. And of course the beauty of the flowers and native grasses in bloom reinforces this impression.

So keep the idea of intentionality in mind when you create gardens and features for your yard. A tidy fence, a neat stone or brick edging, or a strip of manicured lawn or mulch can make the difference between perceived clutter and design brilliance!

Focus on your fence. Good fences may make good neighbors, but bad fences make clutter. If your fence is falling down, needs painting, or has weeds coming up around it, it's an eyesore. Unless your front yard faces a really busy street or a hideous view—say, a cluster of stores or your neighbor's junkyard—an open rail fence or a low picket fence is better than a high, impenetrable palisade or panel fence. If at all possible, you want to keep your view open in front, displaying your yard and home like a jewel. As for the weed issue, I'd suggest putting down landscape fabric and mulch in a narrow strip under and around your fence, then planting climbing roses and clematis or honeysuckle through it at regular intervals to foam over the fence, filling the air with fragrance and the eye with color.

Watch the walk. The front walk is one of the most important, and neglected, aspects of your front yard. It should be wide, smooth, and uncomplicated. No pointless meanderings allowed! Instead, it should curve gracefully from the parking area to the front door. If you have a formal landscape, opt for a nice straight walkway, instead. It should be obvious and easy to follow, cleared of debris, snow and ice, and toys or other clutter. If you edge it with plastic edging (which you pound into the ground so it's not visible) or narrow strips of mulch over landscape fabric on either side, it's easy to maintain a weed-free path. Add in-ground lighting so people can navigate at night. If it's paved, the surface should be even, with no bricks or concrete edges sticking up. Make sure you replace chipped or cracked bricks or concrete, and level stepping stones, securing them in the ground. If it's a mulch path, the mulch should be clean and thick, not weedy and uneven. If it's a grass path, keep it neatly mowed and raked. Help people reach your door easily and safely.

Ditto the driveway. A cracked, splitting, discolored, weedy driveway gives an awful impression of the family that owns it. And the same is true of a weed-filled, bumpy gravel drive, where most of the gravel has migrated into the lawn and vice versa. Keep your driveway maintained and picked up. Bikes, trikes, and toys should never be left in the driveway, unless you just happen to enjoy crushing them on your way in or out. And, needless to say, rusting vehicles or auto parts should be hauled off unless your family has an in-home junkyard business.

Love your lawn. An unkempt, weedy lawn tells everyone who sees it that you don't care what state your house is in—you're a slob. And a lawn full of bald spots is even more of an eyesore. Both create visual clutter, too. Keep your lawn mowed, but keep it from browning by setting the mower blades high—2 inches is the usual recommendation—so the grass won't dry out. Whether you have lawn surrounding lush shrub plantings and flowerbeds, a handkerchief-size lawn, or a vast sea of grass, it's important to maintain it. A nice lawn sets the tone for your whole property.

Tame your trees. So often, a tiny yard is dwarfed by giant shade trees. Years ago someone planted maples or weeping willows or looming evergreens in a small front yard, and now they've plunged the whole yard and house into shade, their roots have made it impossible to grow anything in the yard, and they've cracked the sidewalk (and are threatening the driveway). Yikes! You basically have two choices: create a raised walk, like a boardwalk, or have the trees cut down. (Use a professional service for this, both because of the hazards and because you want them to take out the stumps and roots.) Then you can regenerate the soil and start over with trees that will stay small and be decorative. (Remember that some of the showiest small trees, like Japanese maples and crabapples, can create a lot of landscape clutter when their fruit or seed drops—and seedlings start appearing everywhere—so consult a pro before choosing a replacement.)

Go to Fantasy Island. Speaking of trees, if you have trees and shrubs dotting the front yard, instead of fighting weeds beneath them all, why not connect them with island beds? These lovely free-form beds surround the trunks of the trees or shrubs and flow out from them in a naturalistic manner to connect with other trees or shrubs. Plant beautiful shade-tolerant flowering or foliage plants and groundcovers in your island beds (astilbes, hellebores, heucheras, bleeding hearts, ferns, pulmonarias, and hostas are just a few of the landscape choices for shady sites). To avoid a spotty, cluttered effect, connect small island beds into fewer, larger, contiguous ones rather than simply ringing your trees and shrubs. Echo the plant choices in all the beds, whether or not they are connected (though you can vary the flower and foliage colors, if you wish) to create a unified look with no visual clutter.

Go to bed. A flowerbed can brighten a small front yard, and a matching pair adds a low but attractive foundation planting to the front of the house. If you're siting it in the middle of a lawn, a round, oval, or kidney-shaped bed will look more pleasing than a rigidly rectangular bed. Plant groups of three, five, or seven of the same plant rather than one of each, and repeat groupings to avoid a chaotic, cluttered look. If you're choosing your own plants, select types that thrive in your conditions and grow well together. Need help choosing? Check out my friend Cole Burrell's book *Perennial Combinations* for some wonderful suggestions.

Patrol your borders. Flower borders are simply longer versions of beds. Depending on your energy level, enthusiasm, and free time, you can plant borders along your driveway, around the perimeter of your property, around your house, or in a formal garden. Borders are elegant landscape features, but they require a lot of maintenance to look attractive and not unkempt. Unless you're an experienced gardener, work with a landscape or garden designer to create a border that's right for your area, conditions, budget, and the amount of upkeep you're willing to invest in it. Start small—with a single modest border—and add on as your knowledge and enthusiasm grow. (If the plants don't grow well, you won't be looking at a major maintenance nightmare.)

Play ring around the rosy. Dress up light posts, mailboxes—even telephone poles and other vertical features—with a ring of flowers or groundcover plants. Garden centers and catalogs sell semicircular planters designed to fit around the base of a light post or mailbox. These cut down on digging but require daily watering if it doesn't rain. Cut weed cloth to fit beneath the planters, fill them with the annual flowers of your choice, set them on the weed cloth, and voilà! They'll protect your post from the mower and string trimmer, too. Just limit the varieties and colors of the plants so they don't end up becoming visual clutter. Don't forget to water, and remove dead blooms regularly to keep the plants blooming and tidy.

Limit lawn art. I have a friend whose lawn art outnumbers the plants in her yard. Everywhere you look—gnomes, statues, gazing balls, brightly painted tools, and a plethora of other lawn art are peeking at you, looming over you, or about to decapitate you. Or you're about to step on or trip over it. While most yards aren't quite *that* full of lawn art, it's easy to get carried away. Down the street from my house, one old gentleman has filled his driveway with a Mexican and burro with cart, a large Uncle Sam, several deer statues, a standing bear, and an assortment of other statuary. (You should see his Christmas display.) It looks for all the world like a low-end garden center.

Use lawn art where it will create an impact, not clutter. One birdbath, gazing ball, or large urn can make a striking focal point. Don't be afraid to try something different, too: nestling a gazing ball into a garden bed instead of putting it on a pedestal, using an old wrought-iron chair as a sculpture. One of the most magical effects I ever saw was a gazing-ball mobile hanging down from the branches of a huge tree (well above head height, of course); the small silver balls glittered like stars. So have fun and enjoy your lawn art, but use restraint and choose pieces that fit your garden and home style. An ultra-modern abstract sculpture in front of a serene Colonial home is jarring, while a pedestaled sundial is a lovely fit. (And that abstract sculpture would look great in front of an ultra-modern home.)

Don't fixate on feeders. Birdfeeders are delightful additions to the yard—the backyard. But don't put them in the front, where they look like clutter and the dropped seed creates an unsightly mess. The best place for a feeder is off the deck or kitchen where you'll be able to sit and enjoy watching all the birds. And remember—the more feeders, the more clutter, the more mess. Two—or at most, three—feeders are enough for any family, unless you've converted your backyard into a wildlife habitat with trails and viewing spots. Then feeders at intervals along the trail will add interest to your habitat. Maintain your feeders and replace any broken or battered ones immediately to avoid a run-down, junky-looking landscape.

Mulch it. Mulch gives gardens a neat, finished look. Use the same kind and color of mulch everywhere you use it, and remember that the point of mulch is to blend in, not to become a landscape feature in its own right—so for mercy's sake, avoid all those unnatural, screaming mulch colors, and don't mound it on like you're trying to create your very own mountain range.

The Outback

Create a nice view. Remember that you'll be looking into the backyard from the deck, patio, porch, or back windows (such as, in my case, the sliding glass doors off the kitchen). So create a view you want to look at, even if it is in the backyard. That doesn't mean the backyard can't be useful as well—a charming playground with a delightful playhouse you've painted with flowers; a beautifully laid-out kitchen garden full of vegetables, herbs, edible flowers, and berries; or a grouping of flowering shrubs that can be practical as well as beautiful.

Design destinations. Your backyard will work hard for you, and contribute the most to your household, if you design it by breaking it into areas. Think about what you want to put there—a grove of shade trees with gorgeous autumn colors; a greenhouse; the compost bins; a playground; a craft studio; an herb garden; a wildflower meadow; a water garden; a trellised gazebo covered with climbing roses; a mini-vineyard; a little chicken coop; a dog kennel; a raised bed of strawberries; or a few dwarf fruit trees.

Once you've narrowed the list to what you really want, lay out the area on paper, giving each area its logical location, and then do a reality check. Do you have the room, money, and time for all these things? If not, what can you most easily drop (for now)? If so, are the features arranged in a logical, easy-to-access manner that gives them the protection, structures, and lighting they'll need without interfering with other important activities? For example, a playground for the kids sited near a raspberry or blackberry trellis invites cuts and scratches; if it's located near a greenhouse, it could mean broken glass.

Once you've pared down your list to the best options for your present circumstances and income and have laid them out in the most logical and appropriate way for your family and site, you should think about how you, your family, and others will move around the backyard. Will someone haul water to the greenhouse, then feed the fish in the water garden and check the filter before swinging by the veggie garden to water and pick ripe produce, making a final stop at the chicken coop to drop off any spoiled stuff from the veggie garden, feed and water the chickens, and collect eggs? Will the kids engage in a fevered volleyball game, then jump in the pool?

Think about how you and your family will really use your space, and then lay out your paths accordingly. Don't waste time creating elaborate paths that no one will use as the family cuts across the yard instead. Plan paths that reflect backyard traffic flow. Unless your paths reflect real-life traffic patterns, you'll end up with bare-soil paths where people really walk, which creates unsightly visual clutter.

Tame your tools. Neglected, abandoned, rusting tools are landscape clutter—and they're also tripping hazards. Follow the good gardener's rule, and put each tool back in its place at day's end, cleaned and ready to use the following day. A good tip is to paint tool handles with bright fluorescent colors—orange, hot pink, chartreuse, yellow—so it's easy to find them in the yard or garden and bring them back inside. See Chapter 15 (beginning on page 311) for tips on tool storage in the garage.

Fence your vegetables. Many gardeners enjoy growing at least a few homegrown veggies in the backyard garden. But an unfenced vegetable garden invites dogs, cats, raccoons, and we won't even say what else into the garden plot to enjoy themselves, especially after dark. Don't get mad—get even. Bury a wire fence around your garden, sinking it a few inches into the ground to discourage prowlers. Make sure it's tall and secured well enough to discourage climbers like raccoons and jumpers like deer. Don't like the look of wire? Cover it with wooden latticing or grow vining plants like grapes, pole beans, clematis, and hardy kiwis over its surface to soften it.

Perfect your playground. There is no reason for your kids' playground to look junky, ugly, or cluttered. A well-built, well-secured swing set is a pleasure for the whole family. (Try it!) A gym set, slide and tube, merry-go-round, sandbox, tire or rope swing, and other toys can be every bit as much fun. The key is to think of the playground as a public park and to build it to last and to grow with your kids' needs. Check out what's in your local park or your kids' school playground—and which pieces of equipment in the park or school your kids love—before you buy your own playground equipment. Then site it where it's shaded and won't dominate the whole yard, but where you can still keep an eye on the kids. Replace rusty, falling-over playground equipment immediately or, if the kids have outgrown it, donate it, have the stuff hauled off, or place a classified ad and hope somebody will come and get it!

Oust awful outbuildings. Collapsing outhouses, leaning sheds, ancient doghouses—say good-bye to any structure that's no longer usable. Replace what you need with attractive, safe, useful outbuildings, but consign the hopeless cases to the flames or to trash pickup.

Reel in the hose. Don't just leave your hoses lying around the yard or across the driveway; they can be ruined by someone running over them with the lawn mower or driving over them with the car, or *you* can be ruined when someone trips over them and sues you. Put them on a reel cart that keeps them coiled and kink-free when not in use, can be rolled to where you want to use them, and tucks away in the garage or tool shed when you're through with the watering or ready to store the hoses for winter. You'll prolong the life of your hose, and maybe your own, as well!

Move the mowers. Repeat after me: Lawn mowers are *not* lawn art. Don't leave them out in the yard, where they're not just giant eyesores, but will also be wrecked

👍 Love It *or* Lose It? 👎

Faux stones. Know what I'm talking about? Those hollow plastic "boulders" a lot of catalogs and home centers sell to cover up unsightly things like septic pipes and utility boxes. Well, no one would deny that pipes and other metal objects sticking up out of the ground are unsightly. But so are these plastic atrocities! It's bad enough to see all the *real* boulders people toss onto their lawns in misguided attempts at landscaping (they always make me think of "The sky is falling!"), without us now having to stare at hideous plastic ones. (It takes a highly skilled landscape architect to use stones well in a landscape. My advice: Do *not* try this at home unless you have superb professional guidance.) A far better solution is to garden around the eyesore and hide it among the plants.

Verdict: Lose it!

by the weather. Take care of your investment and reduce yard clutter by storing your lawn mowers in the shed or garage when you're not using them.

Put a brake on the bikes. That goes for bikes, trikes, skateboards, and all other mobile devices that kids love but seem incapable of storing. These create visual clutter, get battered by the weather, and create tripping (and mowing) hazards. If the kids are old enough to ride 'em, they're old enough to put 'em away.

Fence the utilities. Garbage cans, central air units, and other large, useful, but unsightly objects are facts of life. But that doesn't mean you (and your guests) have to look at them. An attractive picket fence or lattice screen enclosing the trash cans or AC can make a world of difference. Paint it to match your house (or trim), and make sure one side opens easily for access. True, it won't make the eyesore disappear, but at least it won't be an eyesore any more!

Clear out deadwood. Few things are as unsightly as a brown, dead shrub or hedge—or as unsightly and dangerous as a rotting, fallen tree trunk or branch. Call an arborist and have them hauled away or stacked neatly under cover where they won't be an eyesore but are still convenient for stoking the fireplace or woodstove. Don't leave a hideous tree or shrub in place when it's beyond saving—it will ruin the whole yard, since it will be the first thing a visitor's eye goes to. ("What's that dead brown thing?") Cut it down and haul it off or burn it!

Watch the woodpile. Speaking of burning wood, if you have a woodpile, manage it. Don't ever put it out in the front yard to become an eyesore. Stack the wood neatly in a sheltered location in the backyard, and cover it with a brown (never blue!) tarp to protect it from the elements. Hardware and home improvement stores and catalogs like Plow & Hearth (see page 47) and Solutions (see page 48) offer racks to hold your cut firewood upright and stable, and they also sell tough, durable covers for the piles. These are great ideas. But the best idea is to *use* your wood, rather than letting it sit and rot while waiting for the next "Y2K" to strike. Instead, enjoy it! Replace your stack with more good wood every year, and you'll still be ready if disaster strikes.

Ditto for detritus. Okay, all. Bits and pieces of rusting metal, fencing, cardboard boxes, pallets, stacks of newspaper and tin cans, abandoned lawn mowers and other equipment, burst hoses, old tires, leftovers from ancient do-it-yourself projects, tools that look like they came from a Mayan ruin—gather them up and haul them off. Or have someone else haul them off. Do not leave them lying around the yard creating a tetanus hazard and transforming what could be a pleasant space into an amateur junkyard. There is *no* excuse for this! Get that stuff outta there.

Patrol the pool. Besides making sure your pool is kid- and animal-safe, make sure it looks as good as it can. Inground pools usually look great as long as they're well maintained (especially if they're landscaped), but no pool looks good if moldy towels, flip-flops, pool toys, plates and glasses, suntan lotion, and heaven knows what else are left out there to decompose at their leisure. Pick up all the pool debris after each swim session and put it back where it belongs. (And get your kids involved in dealing with their own pool stuff—taking away pool privileges can be a powerful motivator!) If you have an aboveground pool, try to site it as attractively as you can. Putting a deck around it and adding plants, lattice screening, and attractive deck furniture can help make the pool look like part of your yard, not something that fell to earth from a passing spaceship. If you can connect the pool decking to the house deck, so much the better—it will look more integrated and be easier to get to.

👍 Love It *or* Lose It? 👎

When I started gardening, I didn't have a lot of choice about what sorts of containers to use to haul soil, compost, and fertilizers around in. They tended to be ugly, awkward, and heavy. But these days there are some really wonderful options that are lightweight and colorful as well as capacious. Garden centers and home and garden catalogs like Gardener's Supply Company and Kinsman Company (see page 49) sell sturdy but flexible plastic tubs (called Trug-Tubs) in a variety of cheerful colors. They have handles so they're easy to haul around, and they're attractive enough to keep out on display on your potting bench or under your plant bench, full of potting soil, bulbs, or whatever you'd like.

But that's not all. These companies also sell collapsible, lightweight "pop-up bags" that fold down to 4 inches for storage but open up to 20 inches. They're made of water-resistant woven plastic and are strong enough to hold up to 45 pounds of leaves, soil, spent plants you want to haul from the greenhouse out to the compost, and so on. They also have cushioned handles for comfort and come in an array of cheerful garden-themed patterns.

Verdict: Love them both!

Pet Alert!

Dogs and yards go together. But dog-related clutter—be it a kennel of bare dirt, holes, bones, and scraps, a down-at-heels doghouse, or piles of poop and yellowed rings in the grass—still spells clutter. (And worse. "Neglect" and "disease" are both good words.) If you like to let your dog out unattended, consider putting in an invisible fence instead of a kennel or run.

Make sure your dog's house looks appealing and well maintained. Try to make it match your house's architecture style or color. If you're handy, you can have a lot of fun designing a custom doghouse. See the book *Barkitecture* by Fred Albert, or look to another doghouse style book for inspiration. The same goes for toys, bowls, and any other dog-related paraphernalia: Make sure they're in good shape, replace them regularly, and contain them when your dog's not playing with them. Two or three dog toys and bones are enough; don't litter the yard with them. As with anything else, rotate your dog's favorites instead of letting them all lie out there exposed to the elements. They'll last longer, hold your dog's interest longer, and keep your yard looking better!

Finally—and this should go without saying—pick up after your pet. No one wants to walk through a minefield of poop! And you can pick up parasites if you wander barefoot through a poop-filled yard. Of all the kinds of outdoor clutter, this is the very worst. As for those yellow lawn rings, if you take your dog to a new spot every day and make sure the grass is watered during dry spells, you should be able to avoid them.

Compost what you can. Make free, nutritious fertilizer for your gardens and lawn by putting vegetable and flower clippings, pulled weeds (minus seed heads), kitchen scraps (except for dairy products, oily leftovers, and meat scraps, which can attract vermin), leaves, shredded paper, and grass clippings in a compost bin. Contain the compost in a homemade pallet bin or a ready-made wood or plastic bin so it will look good and not perturb your neighbors. You can get rid of a lot of landscape, kitchen, and paper clutter this way, and feed your lawn and gardens at the same time!

Clean up your gardens. At the end of the growing season, gardens are brown, weedy, overgrown, and unkempt. They are, in short, yard clutter. Cut down the dead stuff and compost it, please. You'll thank yourself every single fall and winter day as you look out at an attractive landscape instead of a jungle of dead plants. And your garden will be ready to go in spring instead of still awaiting cleanup. Worried about sheltering birds and beneficial bugs? The bugs will be fine in the compost pile, which, after all, will hardly be cooking when it's cold outside, and you can put up feeders and houses for the birds.

Recycle plant pots. If you're like me, you buy lots of transplants and container plants every year, and after you set them out in the garden or pot them up, you have a wealth of plastic plant trays, pots, and seedling packs left over. Fortunately, I've discovered that most nurseries will be happy to take them back if you bring them over. If you have cracked and chipped terra-cotta pots, smash those suckers and use the pieces to add drainage at the bottom of good pots.

ONWARD!

Well, congratulations! You've made it through the indoors, the outdoors, and the gray areas where outdoors and indoors meet. You've kicked the clutter out of your house and yard. But now, what do you do with it? In the next section, Trash (Yours) to Treasure (Theirs), you'll find out about the myriad ways you can donate, sell, swap, or just plain get rid of every last piece of (ex-)clutter. Maybe all that stuff will finally pay off—or at least pay you back something for taking up so much of your life for so long.

PART FOUR

Trash (Yours) to Treasure (Theirs)

Chapter 17

Donations and Write-Offs

When you're kicking out clutter, Goodwill, the Salvation Army, and the Society of St. Vincent de Paul can be your best friends. So can homes for pregnant teens and abused families, homeless shelters, missions, and numerous other charities. Here's how to find them, how to tell in advance who'll want what, and how to get a tax break for your stuff without risking Uncle Sam's ire.

GIVING IT ALL AWAY

I don't know about you, but I find few things as satisfying as hauling a bag of stuff off to Goodwill or the Salvation Army. The thrill of seeing all that unused stuff moving out of my house! The thought that perhaps it will be sent to someone in need, or at least find a second home where it will be appreciated! I always have a "Goodwill bag" going, and as soon as I cart it off, I start another one. But these aren't the only places you can take your (former) clutter. Read on for plenty of ways to match your stuff with a charity or other worthwhile nonprofit agency. Just remember to donate responsibly—don't donate stuff that's in such bad shape that it really belongs in the trash.

Think Like an Angel

For the past 7 years, the local paper in my area, the Allentown, Pennsylvania, *Morning Call,* has held a "Be an Angel" campaign for 2 months, from the end of November through the end of January. Its purpose has been to match up nonprofit organizations and their wish lists with local donors. The program has been so successful that last year, the *Morning Call* had 407 organizations involved, each listing three wishes, from cars and cameras to diapers and craft supplies. They ranged from local hospitals, the Red Cross, and Easter Seals to the local ecumenical food bank, adult literacy center, Meals on Wheels, and Crime Victims' Council. Schools, pet shelters, historic societies, museums, churches, fire companies—the breadth of organizations involved was just amazing.

Your community may not have such an organized giving campaign, but you can still locate services and agencies in your area just like the ones where I live. I suggest that you call your favorite nonprofits and ask them if they'd accept donations and, if so, what they need. I was amazed at how many groups wanted things that are typically hard to get rid of, like computers and appliances. And, of course, lots of them wanted household items, clothing, books, toys, TVs, DVDs, video tapes, CDs, and players for those videos and CDs. It's certainly worth a few phone calls to find a *really* good home for your unwanted stuff!

SPECIFIC DONATIONS

Trying to get rid of something in particular? Check the list below to see where you can find an organization that needs your donation. If I haven't listed your item, try contacting the organizations in "The Pros Know" on page 354 for help.

Appliances. If you want to donate a (working) appliance that's no more than 3 years old, contact Habitat for Humanity (www.habitat.org). Or check out Excess Access (www.excessaccess.org) to be matched with a local charity that will come pick up your appliances.

Automobiles. JustGive's Web site has a lot of links to charities that accept cars and other vehicles in a variety of conditions. Check them out at www.justgive.org.

Books. See if your local library will accept donations. Check with your local veterans' home, senior centers, and assisted-living facilities to see if they accept

An Ounce of Prevention

Before 2007, it used to be easy to give stuff to places like Goodwill and the Salvation Army. You handed stuff over, filled out a form listing the items you'd donated and their value, and then pulled out your deduction lists at tax time. (The Salvation Army has a valuation guide for goods of all kinds on its Web site; go to www.salvationarmyusa.org and search for "valuation guide." Goodwill Industries also lists values as guidelines on its Web site at www.goodwillpromo.org.) But beginning with 2007 tax returns, the guidelines are different for taxpayers who choose to itemize their deductions rather than taking the standard deduction.

The IRS now requires that only "usable items" can be deducted—no broken appliances, torn clothing, and the like—and that any item valued at more than $500 must have an official appraisal submitted with the tax form. Should you wish to deduct a large item like a used car, boat, or RV, you may only deduct what the charity actually receives from the sale of the item, as opposed to the "fair market value" that was allowed in the old days. And unfortunately, the valuation guidelines posted by the various agencies are considered a conflict of interest under the new laws. So how do you know what it's legal to deduct? Though there are still no cut-and-dried guidelines as of this writing, you might consider the advice of the New Fairfield Community Thrift Shop in Connecticut, which suggests that its donors deduct 10 percent of the original value of their items. And make sure you check IRS publication 561, "Determining the Value of Donated Property" (www.irs.gov/pub/irs-pdf/p561.pdf).

What caused the change? A congressional study found that, in 2003, Americans who itemized their deductions were writing off pretty eye-popping sums: 4 million households wrote off an average of $1,440 each for clothing donations, and 2.4 million wrote off an average of $1,356 for donated household goods. Now, if you're going to itemize, you're going to have to provide proof that your donations actually measure up to your claims of their value. So make sure you have the receipts and valuations!

books. Local day care centers might appreciate a gift of children's books. You can also donate children's books to BookEnds (www.bookends.org), an organization that provides them to shelters, schools, family literacy centers, and youth organizations. There are also national specialty organizations that accept donated books. You can donate textbooks from elementary school through college level if they're

10 years old or newer, current editions of encyclopedias, and issues of *National Geographic* from 1985 on to Books for Africa (www.booksforafrica.org). Books for America (www.booksforamerica.org) donates books to community organizations, hospices, shelters, and prisons.

Calendars. Sometimes it seems like you can't turn around toward the end of the year without getting a free calendar in the mail, being handed one every time you walk into a store, and, of course, receiving half a dozen as holiday gifts. Don't throw them out or resort to "regifting." Follow my friend Chris's lead: She saves her unused calendars to give to assisted-living facilities.

Cell phones. Donate these to a national organization like Donate a Phone or Collective Good. Find them at Earth 911 (www.earth911.org). Used cell phones can be used to dial 911, and shelters for abused women and children often give them to their clients for emergency use.

Clothing. Make an itemized list and take your used or simply unworn and unwanted clothes to your local Salvation Army (which has receipt forms to fill out inside the drop-off door), Goodwill, or Society of St. Vincent de Paul. Or, if you don't want a receipt for tax purposes (see "An Ounce of Prevention" on page 353) and you don't care what happens to your clothes, simply look for a used clothing drop-off bin. Where I live, these are marked dumpsters located in corners of various pharmacy parking lots. Lillian, one of my fellow Curves members, admits that she always uses these but is a bit concerned because she has no idea what happens to the clothes once she drops them off. I've read that clothing in these bins is often sold by the pound to be recycled into rags for rag rugs and industrial purposes, with the proceeds going to charity, but who knows for sure? The bins always seem to be full, so I guess the convenience is worth the uncertainty for lots of local residents!

Not sure where to donate something? Luckily for us, some organizations specialize in matching donors with nonprofits. Check out the Web site of Earth 911 (www.earth911.org), the "ways to give" area of JustGive's Web site (www.justgive.org), or Excess Access (www.excessaccess.org), which will list your stuff so interested organizations can pick it up.

Other options are to donate clothing to a local homeless shelter or thrift store or to see if your church, temple, or other place of worship has a clothing drive or other suggestion for donating clothing. (Also see "Work clothing" on page 356.)

Computers. If your computer or its components still work and you're just upgrading, contact Share the Technology (www.sharetechnology.org). It will put you in touch with a nonprofit organization that needs computers. If it's fewer than 5 years old, you can also donate it through www.pcsforschools.org or www.techsoup.org/recycle; if it's older, try www.worldcomputerexchange.org. Or check the list of places to donate computers and related technology to at JustGive (www.justgive.org). Just make sure all of your personal information is completely removed from your hard drive—you need to do more than just delete it or put it in the recycle bin.

Eyeglasses. Donate these to the Lion's Club (www.lionsclubs.org). They put containers for donated glasses in local libraries, LensCrafters, Goodwill stores, community offices, and other places.

Food. Find a food bank near you by checking the Yellow Pages or America's Second Harvest (www.secondharvest.org), the national food bank and food-rescue network. Don't even think about trying to donate expired food, though, please! Or you can donate food to a local soup kitchen; look for them in the government section of your phone directory, or ask at your church, synagogue, or other place of worship if they know of a soup kitchen in your area.

Furniture. Your local Salvation Army, Goodwill, and Society of St. Vincent de Paul stores are all good choices for furniture donations, and they may even come pick up your stuff. They do expect it to be in saleable condition, not beat. Or check JustGive's Web site (www.justgive.org), which lists additional places that accept furniture. Or go onto Excess Access (www.excessaccess.org), which will match you with a local charity. Other options include local homeless shelters and shelters for battered women and families, which may be looking for furniture to help families that are starting over.

Gardening tools. Donate gardening tools, hoses, wheelbarrows, and other supplies to your local community garden. Check the Yellow Pages for a community garden in your area, or contact the American Community Gardening Association (www.communitygarden.org).

Hearing aids. Donate hearing aids to Hear Now (www.sotheworldmayhear.org/hearnow), a nonprofit program directed by the Starkey Hearing Foundation.

Pet Alert!

My friend Chris donates old towels and linens to a local animal shelter. Great idea! Some shelters need newspapers, too. If you're like me, well-meaning friends are always giving you pet treats and toys you don't feel are "good enough" for your precious furry friends. Pass them along to the shelter, too. And, of course, if you have extra grooming tools that are in good shape, I'm sure they'd appreciate those! Not sure where to give? Check out Pets 911 (www.pets911.com) for recommendations.

Musical instruments. Check with your local school district to see if they'd be interested in your family's cast-off musical instruments (assuming they're in good shape).

Videos, DVDs, and CDs. Many of the same organizations that accept books (see page 352) will also take video tapes, DVDs, and CDs. Also check with your local libraries, senior centers, assisted-living facilities, veterans' homes, shelters, hospices, blood centers, and childrens' homes and organizations to see if they'd be interested.

Work clothing. Help low-income people get and keep jobs by donating work clothing and accessories. For men, donate to Career Gear (www.careergear.org). For women, check out Dress for Success (www.dressforsuccess.org) or the Women's Alliance (www.thewomensalliance.org), which has the wonderful motto, "Someone's future is hanging in your closet."

ONWARD!

Well, I hope you've been inspired to donate useful items to deserving organizations, whether you choose to itemize your deductions for your tax return or simply enjoy feeling good about doing something positive with your clutter (for a change). But you might be tempted to try your hand at selling some of your stuff, as well. It can be fun and rewarding! In the next few chapters, we'll review the many ways to unload your clutter for cash or credit. In the next chapter, we'll start with secondhand shops.

Chapter 18

Secondhand Shops

From music and bookstores to consignment clothing stores, you can often sell your cast-off stuff for cash or store credit. The tips in this chapter will help you decide when to take the money and run, when to take the credit, how to find the right stores for your stuff, when to donate it instead of sell it, and, of course, how to get the most for each precious piece of clutter.

THE JOY OF SECONDHAND STORES

My mother would have as soon been dead as set foot in a secondhand shop, so it took many years and many miles before I began to patronize them. Admittedly, I had always been a huge fan of used bookstores—especially the giant barnlike ones with floor after floor of hidden treasures. And my whole family was addicted to antiques stores (see Chapter 22—Antiques in Your Attic, beginning on page 429, for more on this). But, thanks to enthusiastic friends like Delilah and Susan, I finally began to appreciate the charm of consignment stores, vintage clothing stores, and thrift shops. Then, when I read an article that pointed out that if no shirts were ever made again, there'd be enough shirts to clothe everyone in the world 'til the end of time, secondhand shops became my favorite clothing stores.

Not that I don't also succumb to clothes from the Orvis and Boston Proper catalogs and the nearest Coldwater Creek store! But for everyday, the thrill of the chase—finding that Laura Ashley, Calvin Klein, or Liz Claiborne piece for $3.50, good as new; or the absolutely best-fitting-ever jean skirt; or perfect, wonderfully colored tee-shirts for under $10 for a huge bagful—simply cannot be beat. I myself am afraid of used shoes—I dread the thought of bringing the fungus among us— but I've gotten wonderful belts and purses (not to mention Hawaiian shirts for my boyfriend, Rob, who has a weakness for them) at secondhand shops.

Then, of course, there are the amazing cooking supplies—pots, pans, dishes, silverware, glass, and appliances of all stripes and types—to be found at stores like Goodwill and the Salvation Army, pretty much all for under $5, many of them vintage and wonderful. (Check out these stores for astonishing heavy-duty cast-iron and grilling cookware at unbeatable prices.) I found a mini–slow cooker there for heating up dips; it cost less than $3 and worked like a charm. And Rob loves old-fashioned drinks like Manhattans, so I've amused myself by looking for interesting, old-fashioned cocktail glasses for him—not to mention actually elegant wineglasses for us. Secondhand stores are also great places to buy Christmas ornaments affordably, as well as linens, towels, bedclothes, and much, much more. (You may remember me raving in an earlier chapter about the wine racks and CD holder I found at the local Goodwill, all for under $5, and I've had equally good luck at the Salvation Army.)

Sometimes, you really can find hidden treasure at secondhand and consignment shops. I once found a Navajo Wedding Basket, worth at least $250, that had been stuffed into a bin of Easter baskets, all priced at $4, at a local consignment shop. And my friend Tom e-mailed me recently to ask if I'd heard that a man had found a copy of the Declaration of Independence worth $250,000 at his local thrift shop!

But wait, aren't we supposed to be talking about *selling* stuff, not buying it? Sorry, I got carried away. Let's head out to some consignment and secondhand shops and see what you can expect.

Consignment versus Secondhand

First of all, what's the difference between a consignment and a secondhand store, anyway? Basically, they're both "secondhand"—that is to say, both deal in previously owned if not previously used items. The difference is in the way they acquire

I Did It!

You'll get the most from your secondhand or consignment experience if you ask the store owner or manager these questions before you simply head over with a trunkful of bags or boxes:

1. Do you have a brochure I could look at?

2. What sort of items are you interested in?

3. How many years have you been in the business? (I was astounded by how many decades most area secondhand and consignment businesses had been operating.)

4. Do you offer cash up front or cash when the item sells (consignment)?

5. What percentage of the sale price will I get?

6. Do you offer a higher percentage in store credit?

7. (If it's a consignment shop) How long do you keep the item?

8. (If it's a consignment shop) Do you discount the price at intervals while it's on display?

9. Do I need to make an appointment to bring items in?

10. Do you have a limit on the number of items I can bring at one time?

11. Do you take seasonal items only, and if so, what are your seasonal time limits?

12. Do you pay in cash or by check?

13. (If it's a consignment shop) Can I pick up any unsold items at the end of the consignment period?

14. (If it's a consignment shop) Will you donate any unsold items to a charity for me?

15. (If it's a consignment shop) Will you give me a donation receipt (for tax purposes) for any items you donate to charity?

their merchandise. A secondhand store buys the stuff from you directly—if they want it, they offer you a price, and you take it, make a counteroffer, or pack it back up and move on.

At a consignment shop, you're basically asking the store owner to sell items for you on commission. Technically, the items are still yours and could come back to haunt you if they don't sell within the time limit the store owner typically sets. The majority of consignment shops, but not all of them, are used-clothing stores, but not all the clothing stores limit their sales strictly to clothing, or even clothing and accessories like jewelry, purses, ties, and shoes.

To add to the confusion, not all consignment stores sell the same way. I have patronized quite a few in my area and have noticed two distinct sales trends. One is the single-price item, which sells for the same price during the entire 90 days (or however long) it's for sale. The other (always enticing for bargain-loving buyers) is the sliding price scale, where an item has three prices on its sales tag—one for the first month, a lower one for the second month, and the lowest for the third month it's on sale in the store.

Though it's great news for patient buyers who are willing to take the chance that their prize may sell for a higher price to someone who's willing to pay it, the sliding scale may not be the greatest news for those of you who are trying to sell your stuff, since you still make a set percentage of the sale price, however low it goes. Still, if your primary goal is to get your clutter out the door and your secondary goal is to make a little money in the bargain, any of these options are exciting. Let's take a closer look at them.

STARTING OUT RIGHT

To get the most for your stuff at a secondhand or consignment shop, you need to do your homework. Once you do, you'll find stores that will take pretty much anything you want to consign, as long as it's in decent shape. (Not 5 miles from my house, the sign in front of the Eagle Arms proclaims, "Cash for Guns!") Taking the time to check out the secondhand and consignment shops near you is definitely worth it.

For example, if I had clothes to consign, I could take them to 20 shops in my area. But if they were designer clothes, I'd get more for them at Designer Re Runs, which specializes in higher-end fashions; if they were clothes for college kids, I'd get the best deal at the Attic, whose clientele is between 15 and 30; and if they were for little kids, Back Again for Kids would be the place to go. The closer the match between your stuff and a shop's specialty, the more you're likely to get for it.

Browse the shops in your city and in nearby towns (trying, of course, to resist bringing home yet more clutter!) and see what they offer. Many consignment and secondhand shops have excellent brochures that spell out their consignment and buying policies; collect as many as you can. Talk to the owners and try to get a feel for the place. Ask how long they've been in business. Ask if they also sell online, maybe on eBay. (Some stores sell the majority of their merchandise online, which can mean a faster turnover.)

Finally, keep your eyes open! What sort of person is shopping while you're in the store? Are there many people coming through? Are they buying? If you have time, go back in a week or two and see if the merchandise has changed noticeably. (I know one extremely busy shop whose merchandise changes daily!)

So find a place that's a good fit in terms of what's being sold and how well the store seems to be doing in terms of business and merchandise turnover. Then, if you're happy with their sales or consignment agreement and terms, make an appointment and bring in your stuff. You're on your way to kicking the clutter!

Above all, be realistic. You're not going to make what you paid for an item. You're probably not going to make half. But usually the store owner has a good idea what the item will sell for—especially if the shop specializes in that type of goods. And remember, if you get anything for your items, you're coming out ahead—doubly!—since you're getting stuff out and bringing cash in.

WHEELING AND DEALING

Let's take a tour of some typical consignment and secondhand shops so you can see the sort of arrangements you'll be likely to encounter when you bring your own stuff in.

Hitting the Books (and Making Music)

Brendan D. Strasser is the proprietor of the Saucony Book Shop in Kutztown, Pennsylvania. Like many used-book stores, the Saucony is a book collector's paradise, with buried treasure piled high to the ceiling in every room, shelves overflowing, and the occasional old map or print enticing you to come over for a closer look. But the Saucony is noticeably lacking the paperbacks that are the bread-and-butter of the used-book trade—the popular fiction, bestsellers, and romances that fill the back rooms of most used-book stores.

SANITY SAVERS

By now, you all have probably grasped that I really, really, *really* love books and music. So of course I take the store credit option when I bring books to the Saucony Book Shop and Young Ones in nearby Kutztown, Pennsylvania. But my goal is to pare down my collections, not haul home more stuff. So here's what I do: I get a store credit slip, and I indulge myself by wandering around the store and checking out what's in stock. Then I leave. When I'm desperate for a treat or I've heard about a book or CD that I think I simply must have, I'll go back and get it, then save the rest of the credit for the next time I need a little indulgence. That way, I spread out the pleasure and resist the temptation to reclutter my shelves. And it's a great feeling to walk into a store and get something you want for "free"!

But it's only a great feeling if you really want something a store has on offer. If you're selling something you have no real interest in, ignore the fact that a store offers a "better" deal if you take store credit because for you, the better deal is to take the cash. Remind yourself that getting real hard cash for something you don't want and can't use beats the heck out of getting nothing—and that you're already getting a bonus by freeing up space in your house.

That's because Brendan specializes in terms of what he sells, featuring local history, general history, cooking, art, music, and a range of other topics. So when you bring books in for Brendan to look at or you describe them to him on the phone, he's likely to know right away if he's interested. If he's not, he'll direct you to other booksellers who carry the type of books you have, or he'll donate them to a library if you'd just like to get rid of them. He'll also do estate appraisals or come to your home if you have a large collection; otherwise, you can make an appointment to bring books in.

Brendan prefers to buy books outright; he takes a book on consignment only if it's really valuable (as in, worth thousands of dollars). Like many store owners I spoke to, he'll give more store credit for a book than he will outright cash—50 percent of what he sells it for in store credit versus less than half that in cash, your choice.

Brendan prices books based on 20 years' experience in the business and on a sound knowledge of market value: He checks what books are going for on national and international book Web sites and on eBay. And, like many other businesses I checked out, most of Brendan's business—90 percent—is done online, on the six major book sites (like Alibris, which has 60 million books at its disposal); only 10 percent of the books are sold through his bricks-and-mortar store.

A few blocks from the Saucony Book Shop is Young Ones, a fabulously funky used and new music store with an original mural covering the outside wall. In brilliant color, it pays tribute to such legends as Bob Marley, John Lennon, and Jimi Hendrix, with eye-catching, larger-than-life figures of the fallen stars of rock and reggae. It's equally colorful inside, with a tremendous selection of new and used CDs and of used LP records, cassettes, DVDs, and video tapes. Like the Saucony, Young Ones will give you a much better deal if you take store credit rather than cash.

Clearing Out the Closet

Clothes are another thing we all seem to have too many of. Whether our clothes have gone out of style, we've worn them to death, or we just can't fit into them any more (maybe because we've *lost* weight, hooray), we usually find ourselves picking up new clothes and facing a closet stuffed with old ones every season. (And then, of course, those kids do keep on growing. And if you think *you're* style-conscious, ask yourself how many times you've hauled your teen to the mall in the past week!)

Finally, one too many fights with coat hangers, shoe avalanches, drawer volcanoes, or other overstuffed disasters makes you decide you really *have* to whittle down your wardrobe. And now you've taken the worn stuff to Goodwill and still have a bagful of stuff (or two or three) that's in good enough shape to consign. What are your options?

Designer Duds

At Designer Re Runs, an upscale consignment and resale boutique in Allentown, Pennsylvania, owner Kay Chrin provides a helpful brochure with extremely clear guidelines for potential consignees. Kay accepts brand-name women's and junior's apparel and accessories in sizes 2 to plus. She'll accept only seasonal items and advises everyone to "think what you would wear for the 8 weeks your articles will be on consignment" when deciding what to bring in. (She does provide broad seasonal guidelines, too—fall clothes after Labor Day, winter starting October 14, spring beginning February 14, and summer clothes starting April 14.)

Kay wants "gently used" clothing that's freshly washed and pressed or dry cleaned, and she reminds consignees to check zippers, pockets, and seams. She asks that you bring all items on hangers (which will be returned to you) rather than in bags where they could wrinkle. As she says, each item must be in excellent condition and in style—1 or 2 years old. (Her key question: "Would you purchase it?")

Unlike many stores, Designer Re Runs will let you bring in your consignment clothing and accessories without an appointment, 7 days a week, as long as you come in more than an hour before they close. Once Kay accepts an article, she'll keep it in stock for 8 weeks, then you can either pick up your items or Designer Re Runs will donate them to charity. Kay points out that it's your responsibility to keep track of the pick-up date and retrieve your stuff promptly if you want it back. Once the consignment cycle is over, Kay's clients receive 50 percent of the selling price; she mails a check within 15 days.

Across the Board

In the town of Emmaus, Pennsylvania (where my publisher, Rodale Inc., maintains its home office), Once Is Not Enuf has been going strong for 30 years. Once Is Not Enuf sells women's fashions across the board, from evening gowns to jeans, along with a wide selection of purses, scarves, shoes, jewelry, and other accessories.

Like Designer Re Runs, Once Is Not Enuf has a thorough, excellent brochure that spells out exactly what they expect from their consignment clients and what clients may expect from them. But unlike Designer Re Runs, Once Is Not Enuf asks that you call for an appointment and, when you call, indicate the number of items you're planning to bring in, with a limit of 25 per appointment. They accept seasonal clothing only and list their seasonal guidelines, accepting fall clothes in August and September, winter clothes from October through January, spring clothes in March and April, and summer clothes from May through July.

Once Is Not Enuf will accept women's and junior's clothes in sizes 2 through 26, as well as small decorative household items and accessories that they can sell for $10 or more. Their terms for acceptability are identical to those of Designer Re Runs: Clothes must be in style, no more than 1 to 2 years old, and delivered freshly washed and pressed or dry cleaned, wrinkle-free, on hangers, with seams, pockets, and zippers in good repair. They'll also consider some vintage items. Like Brendan Strasser of the Saucony Book Shop, the owner of Once Is Not Enuf sets sale prices for consignment articles based on her 30 years' experience in the business.

Their terms are also a lot like Kay Chrin's of Designer Re Runs: Articles are stocked for 8 weeks, with the items' prices reduced by 20 percent and then another 25 percent at intervals over the 8-week period if they don't sell. (I mentioned that the price reductions seemed hard to come up with, since they were in percentages rather than whole dollars, and the owner noted that there's a computer program that calculates the amounts precisely so they don't have to do all those calculations by hand!) Clients get 50 percent of the sale price, via a mailed check (if you don't want any unsold items) or at store pickup (if you come in to get your other items or it's less than $25). Like Designer Re Runs, Once Is Not Enuf expects you to keep track of your 8-week consignment period and pick up your unsold items within 2 weeks after the end of the period. Otherwise, they'll be donated to a charity.

Vintage and Funk

Closer to my house, Clares Closet in Kutztown, Pennsylvania, sells men's, women's, and vintage clothes on consignment. In addition to their inviting store, which also features locally made accessories and crafts like handbags, soaps, and wooden utensils, Clares has a thriving eBay store and takes items on consignment for it, too. (See Chapter 19, beginning on page 372, for more on the eBay side of things.) One of Clares's co-owners, Janet Brito, sets the prices for consignment items, again based on many years in the business. If your items have designer labels, the prices tend to be higher.

The attitude at Clares is a little more relaxed than at the other clothing consignment stores I patronize, in keeping with their "Fashion and Funk" theme and Kutztown's small-town charm. They technically accept items on consignment for 90 days, but will actually keep them longer, especially if they have confidence that it's something that will sell. "Sometimes a piece just seems to sit there, then one day someone comes in, takes one look, and boom!" Barb, one of Clares's veteran sales clerks, told me. Like the others, they accept seasonal clothes only because of space limitations, unless the item is seasonless (like jeans) or vintage, in which case they'll accept it at any time of year. You can call or drop by to make an appointment to consign.

Clients get 40 percent of the sale price at Clares, but unlike Designer Re Runs and Once Is Not Enuf, sale prices are fixed, not tied to the length of time the item is on sale, so the owner will get just as much if the item sells in 90 days as if it sells the first day it's brought in. If, after the 90 (or so) days, the item doesn't sell, the owner can come and retrieve it, or Clares will donate it to the local Hope Rescue Mission and give the (former) owner a receipt for tax purposes.

Because Clares Closet goes beyond the everyday clothes it carries to specialize in vintage and funky clothes and accessories as well, they sell a lot of clothing for private costume parties and, of course, for Halloween. And local theater groups, as well as the Kutztown University theater department, also check in regularly to see if Clares has gotten in anything they can use in an upcoming production.

The Young and the Restless

Because Kutztown is a college town, the Attic, a secondhand clothing store on the main street, specializes in clothes, vintage apparel and accessories, shoes, collectibles, and jewelry that students can relate to. The mother-daughter co-owners, Linda and Anne Kuronyi, specifically target 15- to 30-year-olds with an arty, vintage layout and a delightful assortment of clothes and vintage accessories, many from the sixties and seventies (buttons, anyone?). Like Clares, they also sell clothes for costumes.

You don't need an appointment to bring things in to the Attic. But unlike the other clothing stores, it's not a consignment shop—it pays cash or gives store credit on the spot for everything it takes (30 percent of their sale price in cash or 55 percent in store credit). "Because we pay cash, we're really picky about what we take," the college-age clerk told me when I stopped in. "Everything has to be in excellent condition." Being picky and buying less means that the Attic will buy clothing for any season at all times and will simply hold merchandise for the appropriate season. If they don't take your clothes and other items, they'll be glad to donate them to local charities. They summarize their business practices and philosophy on a postcard—no mean feat!—and have a great Web site, www.atticclothes.com, that tells you a lot more.

Furniture, Housewares, and All That

Clothes? Check. Books, music, and movies? Check. Household stuff? Still looking for a home. Well, seek and ye shall find. There may not be as many consignment shops for housewares as there are for clothes, but trust me, they are out there. Here are a few of the types you might encounter. As with everything else, try a store that specializes in your type of stuff if you want to get it sold.

Kid Stuff

Maybe my area has a lot of kids, but just driving around running errands takes me past four infants' and children's clothing, toy, and furnishings secondhand and consignment shops, all within half an hour of my house: Bears Repeating in

Consignments for a Cause

You can sell anything you want, from furniture, china, and crystal to jewelry, Christmas ornaments, quilts, and chess sets, at the Elephant's Trunk in Emmaus, Pennsylvania. But the Elephant's Trunk isn't just a consignment shop—it's a consignment shop for a cause. It's operated by volunteers for the benefit of Planned Parenthood of Northeast Pennsylvania. Since 1985, the Elephant's Trunk has raised more than $400,000 in support of Planned Parenthood's services.

And it's not alone. Pat Robertson, the owner of Antiques Etc., a shop in Maxatawny, Pennsylvania, mentioned that in her area, Nova Thrift Shop, which takes both consignments and donations, benefits battered women. Imagine the thrill of consigning your clutter to benefit your favorite cause! Call the causes you support and see if they have a consignment shop in your area. Like other consignment shops, benefit shops take a percentage of the sale.

the **Pros Know**

"Consignment stores are the perfect place to take unwanted clothing," says Janet Brito, co-owner of Clares Closet in Kutztown, Pennsylvania. If you're considering consignment, take her great advice to make your experience pleasant and profitable.

"Don't automatically pitch outdated clothing or clothes that have been stashed in the attic or basement," says Janet. "There is a huge resale market for retro clothing from the sixties through the nineties. Of course, the clothing has to have flair and not be stained, torn, and so on. Stores like ours will even come to your place and help you sort through it, especially if Mom or Dad passed and the job seems overwhelming to you."

Here's more of Janet's practical advice. "Find a way to monitor your current closet," she says. "One hint that we learned was to hang all hangers one way at the beginning of the season, and then if you wear an item, turn the hanger around. At the end of the season, you can see what you didn't wear and need to part with." What a great idea!

"Sort this unworn clothing into two piles, a donation pile and a consignment pile," Janet says. "Anything that is worn out, stained, mended, from discount stores such as Wal-Mart, pulled, pilled, or just not like new, put in the donation pile. Make a count of the donated items, along with their value (clothing items are worth a few dollars each), and take them to your favorite charity store. Make sure you get a receipt, because you can claim this donation on your taxes. Even if the charity store decides an item's not worth reselling, you can still take a deduction."

The items you have left are the ones Janet and her peers can help you get rid of. "The good-quality, brand-name, like-new items that are clean, wrinkle-free, pet-hair free, and smoke-free will be accepted at almost any reputable consignment store," Janet says. "You can earn a fair amount with these items for your mad money!"

Trexlertown, Rock-a-Bye Baby in Allentown, Once Upon a Time in Emmaus, and Back Again for Kids in Kutztown, Pennsylvania. And I'm sure that's just the tip of the iceberg!

At Back Again for Kids, housed in a huge, imposing old white farmhouse, they have room for a lot of stuff—and they get it. They're so busy that you need to book an appointment about a month ahead to bring in your stuff. They're not a consignment shop—they'll buy your things outright for 40 percent of what they'll price them at or give you 60 percent in store credit.

Like other stores, they accept only seasonal clothes—spring and summer starting in March, fall starting in July, winter clothes in October. But they'll accept "seasonless" clothes (like jeans) all year. They don't accept clothes for infants under 12 months but will take boys' clothes for up to ages 14 to 16. They'll also accept girls' clothes into the teens but are much more discriminating about them because "girls are so picky." And they take kids' stuff as well as their clothes—strollers, portable playards, playhouses, toys—"anything that's not beat up or scratched." These are typical arrangements; the shops take most anything that's in decent shape. Now, that *is* good news!

One caveat, though. My friend Anne advised me that kids' toys and furnishings are tested regularly for safety, and recalls are sometimes issued. It would be considerate and responsible to check into whether there have been any safety recalls on car seats, baby toys, or other items you plan to donate or sell, and refrain from giving any items that have been recalled.

Household Stuff

The cheerful volunteers at the Elephant's Trunk in Emmaus, Pennsylvania (see "Consignments for a Cause" on page 367), greet you as you come in the door. Unlike other consignment shops, the Elephant's Trunk is laid out more like an antiques shop, with plenty of room to walk around and items placed artistically on shelves instead of heaped in an intriguing jumble as if waiting to be discovered. As a result, it lacks the lovable "treasure-hunt" feeling of so many consignment and secondhand shops.

But there are indeed treasures waiting to be discovered! After seeing Christmas ornaments heaped like jewels in clear glass vases and hurricanes in a copy of *Martha Stewart Living*, I thought, "What a fabulous idea for a mantel display!" Then I priced the vases and hurricanes (ouch!). And *then* I headed to the Elephant's Trunk, where for $6 to $8 each I managed to acquire an impressive huge glass vase, a snifter, and a hurricane—and created my best-ever Christmas display. Just this week, I saw a set of marvelous dishes that I'd have loved to own (as if I had room for a second casual set). I'm planning to tell my friend Delilah, who enjoys using just that type of dishware for her outdoor entertaining and has entire cabinets for her china and glassware.

The Elephant's Trunk provides the ultimate brochure on exactly what they'll accept for consignment ("pictures, china, pottery, glassware, collectibles, dinnerware, silver, linens, fine jewelry, costume jewelry, objets d'art, lamps, furniture, antique quilts, kitchenware . . .") and what they won't ("novels, Avon products, clothing, records, used electrical appliances, draperies, computers, luggage . . ."). And they spell out their terms so there's no possibility of misunderstanding.

They have specific hours 4 days a week when you can make an appointment to bring in consignments, and you're limited to 20 items per week. You sign a "consignor agreement" and pay a yearly fee of $10. Items are consigned for a period of 6 weeks and are reduced 20 percent at the end of 4 weeks if they haven't sold. If you want them back after the 6 weeks are up, you can call to have them packed for pickup; otherwise, you can leave them as a donation and receive a receipt for tax purposes. (Items valued at less than $8 are ineligible for consignment but may be left as a donation.)

Clients receive 50 percent of the final selling price for all items, via check mailed the 10th day of the following month; they can also take the remaining 50 percent as a tax write-off. This shop is very specific about the importance of having items clean, polished (in the case of silver and the like), and in working order, with working batteries in items that use them, such as watches and clocks. They also accept holiday items for limited periods of time (for example, Christmas items from October 1 through December 15), and special rules apply to them: They're automatically reduced 50 percent the day after the holiday, and if they haven't sold, they're packed for pickup 2 weeks later.

Back in Kutztown, the 2nd Hand on the Saucony is a more traditional consignment shop, with stuff of all stripes and types loaded up on shelves and spilling onto the floor as far as the eye can see. You feel like you could find absolutely *anything* in there, and you probably could—including the owner's and friends' babies and kids running around or gurgling from the secure circle of their mothers' arms.

They'll take pretty much anything you have, as long as it's not beat up and (where applicable) still works, and you don't have to make an appointment to bring stuff in. There's no limit on the number of items you can bring, and they don't care about seasonality, either. They take housewares, linens, furniture, antiques, books, games, toys, clothing—you name it, it's in there. And their merchandise moves so fast that you don't see the same objects from week to week. (A good Main Street location certainly helps.)

ONWARD!

Now you should know whether consignment or secondhand stores are for you (and, of course, your stuff!). Let me remind you that they are addictive, so try to bear the "it is better to give than to receive" philosophy in mind when you step through those magic doors to sell your stuff.

Now it's time to tackle the big guy—eBay! If you're ready, turn the page and see what the mother of all online auctions has to offer you.

eBay and Other Online Auction Sites

This chapter provides a tour of the ins and outs of eBay. You'll learn how to do your homework without getting sucked in (after all, you bought the stuff once—you don't want to go online and find yourself bidding for more!), how to get the most from an eBay store, how to sell directly on eBay and set up an eBay store of your own, how to use other online sales venues, and the pros and cons of the various online sales options.

ALL ABOUT eBAY

Yes, you really *can* find just about anything (legal) on eBay, with a few exceptions like live animals and, say, your dream date. Recent "top buyer searches" included the Nintendo Wii, Xbox 360, PlayStation 3, iPod, and . . . Britney Spears's hair. (Further investigation revealed that sellers were offering Britney paraphernalia with and without hair, not her actual hair.) I myself have bought a Mark Knopfler guitar pick, a new Le Creuset Dutch oven in Lemongrass, a vintage Gunne Saxe dress, and a one-of-a-kind hand-carved tropical chess set (that I love but my boyfriend, Rob, hates because the two sides are almost the same shade of wood).

Pet Alert!

There are a few things you *can't* sell on eBay, and live animals are one of them. (Shame on you for even thinking of it!) So are animal parts and taxidermy specimens. Other eBay no-nos include guns and other weapons, drugs (including prescription drugs), and human body parts (someone once notoriously offered one of his kidneys on eBay). You can find a complete listing on the eBay Web site (www.ebay.com). Love your pets, love your eBay experience, but don't mix 'em up.

And I've noticed Rob checking the listings for his favorite Markland HO-scale model trains.

All of which is to say that, if you have something to sell, it's probable that at least a few of the more than 200 million worldwide eBayers will want to buy it. The question is, what will they pay for it, and is it worth the trouble? Because yes, it *is* a lot of trouble to sell something on eBay. QuikDrop, one of the many eBay drop-off store franchises, put it concisely in one of the understatements of all time when they said, "Buying on eBay is relatively easy. Selling is more complicated."

Not that it can't be done. I have friends who sell the occasional object on eBay, and well over a million people make their living selling stuff on eBay. But making a living selling lots of stuff for modest returns and making a killing on a single item are two very different propositions, and the latter is a rarity on eBay. (After all, most of us go on eBay looking for bargains, not planning to pay top dollar.)

So please, don't start your eBay sales career thinking you'll sell Great Aunt Rosa's original Ziegfeld Follies program for a million dollars and gain financial freedom. Instead, think of eBay as a great and relatively painless way to get rid of clutter that you can't give to family or friends, and make a profit in the bargain. Then, if something does end up in a bidding war and makes you a lot more than you expected, it will be a thrilling surprise. And if it doesn't, you'll still be bringing money in and kicking clutter out.

What eBay isn't, in my opinion, is a place to try to sell things that you know are actually valuable—fine jewelry, museum-worthy art, rare antiques, or a classic Rolls-Royce, for example. If you're certain what you have is valuable, or you have a suspicion that it is, have it appraised and sell it through an antiques dealer or another appropriate venue. (See Chapter 22—Antiques in Your Attic, starting on page 429, for more on this.)

Look at eBay as a great place to sell off your collectibles, household items, clothing, and other stuff that you might otherwise sell at a yard sale or see at a flea market. The eBay experts estimate that most people have about $2,000 worth of eBay-worthy items (we might be less tactful and call it clutter, or even dustables) lying around their homes. That $2,000 isn't going to make or break you, but it can sure help with the heating bills, car payments, or taxes. (And speaking of taxes, if you make a profit on eBay, you'll need to report it to our good friend Uncle Sam.)

TAKING IT TO THE PROS

To me, the most sensible way to offload your clutter on eBay is to take it to a store that specializes in selling stuff on eBay. They do the work, and you get the check. Maybe it's not as big a check as you'd have gotten if you sold the stuff yourself, but you don't have to do any of the work—and that includes listing the item on eBay, dealing with the buyers, and packing it up and hauling it off for shipping—or learn the ins and outs of eBay selling. If your goal is to get rid of your stuff and any money you make is a bonus, this is a really painless way to go. If, on the other hand, you're counting on making a killing, you may be very distressed to find yourself taking home a comparatively small piece of the pie. (But if that's the case, ask yourself if kicking the clutter is really a priority.)

I've found several types of eBay third-party sellers, and their approaches are all different. If you choose to go this route, scope out your area and see who's doing eBay selling. Check out a few places and see what you think. Then choose the one that works for you.

The "Little Guys"

One option is to go to a local shop that specializes in selling on eBay or sells some of their merchandise in a "bricks-and-mortar" store and some on eBay. It's not

the Pros Know

If you're thinking about turning to eBay to unload your clutter, first turn to the authority on eBay, *eBay for Dummies,* by Marsha Collier (Wiley Publishing, Inc., 5th edition, 2007, $21.99). Marsha, who's been selling on eBay since 1996, is the author of five other *Dummies* books about eBay that have collectively sold more than a million copies. In *eBay for Dummies,* she shares an insider's secrets—plus, of course, all the basics—of online selling on eBay. (And buying, too—but let's not even go there.) You can't go wrong following her advice! Just make sure you buy the latest edition of the book—it looks like they're updating it almost yearly to keep pace with eBay's evolution. Marsha's advice is so comprehensive that it's hard to pick out some pointers to show just how good it is. But I'll give you three favorites that aren't as intuitively obvious as they might seem.

The first is about the importance of timing. It's tempting to put stuff up on eBay as soon as you've decided to get rid of it—and getting rid of stuff ASAP once you've made that painful decision is usually good advice. But as with consignment shops that only accept clothing in season, seasonality can make a big difference in how much you get for an item sold on eBay if that item has a specific season. Sell your dirt bikes in spring and your snowmobiles in fall, not the other way 'round. Ditto for that Tasha Tudor-illustrated copy of *The Night before Christmas* or that fabulous pool float that feels like you're drifting on clouds. And of course, sell coats in winter and sundresses in summer!

The second tip is about getting your feet wet. Marsha suggests—quite rightly—that you shouldn't try to sell on eBay if you've never bought anything on eBay. But you're trying to de-clutter, not add clutter, right? Never fear. She suggests starting by buying *recipes*—which can be had for under a dollar and take up only the space of a sheet of paper. What an idea! But she's right on target; buying a few recipes will get you familiar with the eBay buyer process without costing you a bundle or flooding your house with stuff.

Another great tip is about spelling. Normally, correct spelling is a good thing, but on eBay, it can be a bad thing, if much of the buying population routinely misspells a word. Marsha points out that when buyers search for an object, eBay brings up the items that are spelled exactly the way they've searched for them. That means that if you spell something correctly when most people misspell it, you'll be passed over. (She uses "Caribbean" and "Carribean" as examples. Do you know which is correct?) The solution is to list it both ways, so both bad and good spellers can find it. Great idea!

For thousands of other great tips, get your own copy, or do as I did and have your local library order it for you. You'll be glad you did!

SANITY SAVERS

If you're selling something on eBay or entrusting your stuff to an eBay drop-off store (see page 382) or Trading Assistant (see page 378) to sell it for you, one word matters more than just about anything else: feedback. A seller's eBay feedback rating shows the entire community of buyers, at a glance, how trustworthy he or she is. It's the place on eBay where buyers can rate their transaction experiences as good, bad, or neutral, and leave feedback comments that can encourage buyers to purchase items from that seller or shun them like the plague.

If you want your items to sell on eBay, you want the seller you choose to have an excellent feedback rating (at least 98 percent positive)—and that's true if you sell it yourself, too. When I interviewed Patrick McWilliams about his eBay store, Kutztown OLDIES (see "Beyond Bikes"), his father appeared in the door to tell me that Patrick has a 100 percent positive feedback rating. Clares Closet's eBay store, Clares Closet/Fashion and Funk (see "The Pros Know" on page 368) also has a 100 percent positive feedback rating. Now, that's ideal!

People get good feedback by listing items exactly; maintaining good contact with the bidders and ultimate buyer, including answering questions promptly; making sure all terms are clear; mailing the item out well packaged and quickly—as soon as payment has been received or has cleared; and giving good, prompt feedback to the buyer. (Feedback is a two-way street—sellers can also see a buyer's feedback rating, review the comments he or she received, and decide whether or not to sell to him or her as a result.)

Mind you, a seller can have a 100 percent positive feedback rating but only have a handful of sales, so if you're entrusting your former clutter to someone else to sell on eBay, look for someone who's racked up a lot of sales and *still* has a great rating. Sales are counted as "points" on eBay and are listed in parentheses after the seller's eBay name (user ID). (It's actually more complicated, since—for one thing—sellers only get a point the first time they sell to each buyer, so their actual sales could be much higher than the number of points. But you can be sure the seller has sold *at least* that many items.) Clares, for example, has more than 2,400 points and is an eBay Power Seller. Marsha Collier, the author of *eBay for Dummies,* has more than 5,000 points and a 100 percent positive feedback rating. So start out right and save your sanity by choosing sellers you can trust!

difficult to find one that's selling stuff like yours, even in a small community like mine. I was driving to a friend's house for dinner last month and passed a used-car dealership I'd often seen before. But this time it looked different: They had put up a big sign that said, "Let us sell your used cars on eBay!" At my favorite antiques store (you'll read more about it in Chapter 22), Moyer's Stamps and Collectibles, co-owners Bruce and Karen Moyer sell all sorts of antiques in their shop, but Bruce also sells especially choice stamps and coins on eBay.

Let's take a closer look at another "eBay store within a store."

Beyond Bikes

Patrick McWilliams set up his eBay store, Kutztown OLDIES, in the back of his father's store, Kutztown Bike Shop, in (surprise, surprise) Kutztown, Pennsylvania. Patrick had sold stuff for himself and his siblings and friends on eBay since he got out of high school. After 8 years of that, he had the eBay bug big-time and decided to sell full-time for anyone who needed his services. Initially, he sold—what else?—bikes, but then he expanded into all sorts of goods.

Patrick printed up an informative card that spells out his terms for prospective buyers: Items should have an average sale price of $50. You pre-pay $10 for him to list the item on eBay. This fee includes professional photography, description, and basic research. He also monitors bidding for you. He'll normally list items for 7 days (the standard eBay auction listing), but other time listings are available. If the item is sold, the $10 is credited to you. Patrick's commission is 30 percent up to $1,000 and 20 percent over $1,000. The buyer pays shipping and handling; you pay the eBay and PayPal fees. (Huh? See "Tools of the Trade" on page 384.) Patrick handles packaging and shipping.

When I spoke to Patrick recently, he had some great insights to share about selling on eBay and when you should consider other options. His first piece of advice was to think about what the item can actually get at auction. Patrick stresses that it's not worth it to sell anything that will bring under $40 or $50 on eBay (the usual cutoff for eBay stores), but that, in reality, stuff either sells for way less or way more than that.

I asked Patrick what sells best—and what doesn't sell at all. In the "doesn't sell" category, he said that you don't get much for mass-produced stuff. Don't try to sell stuff like old records on eBay; it's not worth it. (Kutztown's flea market has a specialty shop that sells records, and it would make more sense to sell to the owner.) In Patrick's view, because of shipping costs and hassles, it's not worth trying to sell heavy stuff on eBay, either; he thinks it's better to use Craigslist (see Chapter 20—Clutter in the Classifieds, beginning on page 394, for more on this) or have a yard sale. So what *does* sell? Stuff that's no longer made, from rims for seventies bikes that probably cost $5 back then but can now sell for $250, to BMX bikes from the eighties that can bring in thousands on eBay.

Once you start looking for stuff on eBay, one thing you'll notice right away is that different listings for the same item can, in some cases, have one or two photos and a one-sentence description, while others have tons of photos and a wealth of text, describing in loving detail the glories of the product, its history, and any outstanding features. Ever since I started using eBay, I've wondered if a great description helps the item sell for more or if people couldn't care less and just go for the lowest price. In Patrick's experience, a good description with a history that's intriguing or compelling does help sales. Finally, for those of you providing your own photos, Patrick offers a tip: Upload your own digital photos through ImageShack (www.imageshack.us), an image-hosting service.

Trading Assistants

A different kind of "little guy" who can sell your stuff for you is the eBay Trading Assistant, someone local who already has a lot of experience selling on eBay and who is willing to act as a middleman to sell your items for a fee. You can find Trading Assistants in your area by going on the eBay site (www.ebay.com). All Trading Assistants listed have experience selling on eBay and are in good standing in the eBay community, with a feedback score of at least 100 and at least 97 percent positive feedback. Some Trading Assistants will sell all sorts of things on eBay, while others specialize in one or a few types of items, so make sure the one or ones you contact will handle the kind of stuff you're selling. You can contact Trading Assistants via the information in their Trading Assistant profile. Discuss fees and terms with them and make sure you're comfortable with the arrangement. (You can also ask for references from past clients.)

the *Pros* Know

Janet Brito and her sister, Barb O'Brien, are co-owners of Clares Closet, in Kutztown, Pennsylvania. (You may remember Clares from Chapter 18—Secondhand Shops.) Clares specializes in "Fashion and Funk" for men and women, including great vintage clothes and accessories, and sells both through a bricks-and-mortar store and on eBay. I've found great things at Clares over the years, from tie-dyed cushions and Hawaiian leis for a Jimmy Buffet–themed "Margaritaville" party my boyfriend, Rob, and I wanted to host, to the broomstick skirts I love to wear in summer. And whenever my friend Susan is visiting from Washington, DC, she insists on stopping at Clares to look for black skirts and jeans. I think you'll find Janet's answers to my eBay questions as helpful as I did!

Q: What are the advantages of selling through a professional service or eBay store like yours versus trying to sell on eBay yourself?

A: No matter what people say, it's hard work to sell on eBay. Plus, if you don't know what you're doing or don't look professional, you may not get as many folks looking at your items and you may not get as much as you could if you went to an eBay service. There are lots of tricks to the trade, lots of ways to list things to get attention, and lots of pitfalls if you don't know what you're doing. However, if you have just a few items or things that don't have too much value, it likely doesn't matter if you list them yourself.

Q: Are there things to look for—or look out for—when choosing an eBay store or service to sell your stuff through?

A: I think you need to look for someone who has experience and someone you feel you can trust. My sister, Barb, loves to get signed contracts. I love to work on a handshake. Either way, we need to have people trust us. I also think that you have to realize the actual value of what you have. There are lots of hyped-up stories about people selling things for a fortune on eBay. That's the exception and not the norm.

Q: How do you want people to approach you about an eBay consignment—make an appointment to bring stuff in, send an e-mail, or ask you to come over and see the stuff?

A: We're open to almost any way of folks initially contacting us. Since we have a retail store, many people do stop in. But when it gets down to evaluating their items, an appointment seems to work best.

(continued)

Q: What do you think makes a good eBay item—rarity, condition, interesting history— and what makes an unsuitable one?

A: Rarity and demand are the number one moneymakers. But if you have something rare and no one wants it, then you're out of luck. On the other hand, if you have a more common item but it's in great demand, then you will likely sell your item at a price that you're happy with. And of course, condition greatly affects the price your item will fetch. The tough variables are timing and luck. You can put up an item one week and no one will look at it, no one will bid on it, and you end up with no sale. However, you can turn around and relist the exact same item for the same price just a week later and it will get so much activity you cannot believe it. But remember, the market is really fickle, and the market is sometimes flooded with identical items that you may think are rare and valuable.

Q: Are there ever times you suggest that people consign the stuff in your shop instead of selling it on eBay, or vice versa?

A: If we feel it will not do well online, then we simply state that. However, there are lots of times that we tell folks that an item will do better in our bricks-and-mortar store than online. Hands-on impulse buying will generally fetch a higher price for a more common type of item. But there is a trade-off: Online, you have 200 million potential customers. Not so in a retail store. So online selling of a more common item may sell the item faster but fetch a lower price. In the retail store, an item may have to be displayed for months but will eventually sell for more. It's a tricky formula, and we try to do the best we can for our clients. We try to do a combination of keeping an item online as well as in our bricks-and-mortar store.

Q: What are your terms for selling on eBay for someone? How do you determine a baseline bid? How long do you keep things up for them? What happens if they don't sell?

A: We have gone through various types of terms and have landed on what we think is the most fair. We normally receive 50 percent of the selling price if and when something sells. If it sells for more than $200 or $300, we will

Like other eBay selling services, Trading Assistants will list the item on eBay, answer bidders' questions, ship or deliver the item to the buyer, collect payment, and send you a check once they've deducted all fees. Some will come to your house take a lower percentage. This business is very labor intensive and our time is valuable, so in order to stay in business, we have to cover our costs. Plus eBay and PayPal take a large chunk of the profit. Some places charge a nonrefundable fee for listing an item, which helps cover the eBay fees if an item does not sell. We do not, since we are trying to select items that will sell. But if an item doesn't sell, then the client is welcome to have it back.

Q: **Have you encountered false expectations from people who bring in stuff to sell on eBay ("I read in a book on ceramics that this was worth $500," or the like), and if so, what's your advice for potential eBayers on keeping their expectations realistic?**

A: Yes, there is a lot of hype about what you can make on eBay! Our advice is fairly simple. Be honest with the clients. It goes back to Economics 101: Supply and Demand. Pair this with a bit of luck, a good-looking listing, and a smart listing strategy, and you will get the most that you can at that moment in time. We never promise anything, but we will honor a minimum price if that is what the person wants, so that if it does not get bid on for that minimum, it does not sell. If a potential client has an unrealistic expectation, then we encourage them to keep the item for another time or reseller.

Q: **Do you have any general or specific tips or wisdom to share with people who are thinking of going the eBay route, either on their own or through an eBay store or service like yours?**

A: Be prepared for lots of work and lots of questions. If you are trying to sell your child's outgrown clothes, or your Longaberger collection, or a set of used tires, and you only want to make a few bucks, you will be fine on eBay. If you want a time-consuming hobby, then you can likely do eBay yourself. However, don't let all the hype about eBay fool you. It's a business—and a big business. There are lots of pitfalls, and with a few simple mistakes, you can end up making nothing or less than nothing. Most of our clients either have a truly collectible, valuable item or simply want the items out of their house and are grateful for whatever they get.

Check out Clares yourself by going to their eBay store: clares_closet, or their Web site: www.shopatclares.com.

to pick up the item initially. If an item doesn't sell, the Trading Assistant will return it to you; some also offer the option of donating it to charity for you.

Be aware that Trading Assistants are in no way a part of eBay; eBay simply provides the listing of Trading Assistants as a service to potential eBay sellers. Make sure you're comfortable with that before you choose to go the Trading Assistant route over an eBay drop-off store. (I'd go with the store, can you tell? But that's just me.)

The Big Guys: Drop-Off Stores

Because eBay is such a phenomenon, eBay drop-off stores that sell people's stuff for them on eBay are one of the fastest-growing franchises in the country. The biggest franchise is iSold It ("Turn old memories into new money with iSold It. It's easy."), followed by QuikDrop ("We sell your stuff on eBay!"). You can probably find several of each in your area. The franchises open in strip malls, so they're in standardized "box spaces" and they have a standard appearance. (iSold It sends its franchisees the entire inside of their stores via truck shipment in what they call a "store in a box.") Owners and employees are also professionally trained by the parent company. What this means is that you know what you'll be getting from any one of the stores—the only surprise is how the merchandise will sell on eBay.

I know a lot more about eBay drop-off stores today than I did last summer, when my friend Delilah and I ventured into one, hoping to make big bucks with our extra stuff. I'd noticed a sign for an eBay drop-off store while driving through Quakertown, Pennsylvania, and gotten all excited. I knew I didn't want to sell

$$\left[\text{ Tools of the Trade } \right]$$

Most eBay drop-off stores won't take items that would bring less than $30 (in the case of iSold It) to $50 (for QuikDrop). Instead of hauling a bunch of stuff to the store and being turned away, do your research first the way the store employees do it—through eBay itself. Go online to www.ebay.com and search for your item or something like it. You can use eBay's "Advanced Search" feature to look under "Completed Auctions" and see what like objects have recently sold for. Whether the news is good or bad, you're a winner: Either you may make some money at the drop-off store with your item, or you'll be saved the trouble of taking it.

stuff on eBay myself, but I enjoyed buying things on eBay and had watched the progress of many an auction with fascination, trying to figure out why one item sold for a bundle while the identical item didn't even sell. Here was a painless opportunity to get my feet wet from the seller's side, get rid of some surplus stuff, and make a little money.

Unfortunately, "a little money" turned out to be the defining part of the experience. Delilah, my co-conspirator in all things thrift store and flea market, was all for trying the drop-off store experience. We packed up a little stuff each—since it was just a trial—and headed over to the Quakertown drop-off store. The store experience itself has all the charm of waiting in line for your driver's license photo. But the employees certainly knew their business and knew how to do their research.

After checking us in and taking our data (including photocopies of our driver's licenses, which they stashed in a large notebook of other customers' similar pages), they turned their attention to our stuff. Delilah had brought some Dansk china and blue glassware, while I had a vintage movie poster and a couple of pieces of handmade pueblo pottery. After asking us a few questions about the items, the employees were able to scope out the sales of similar items on eBay. They then rejected my vintage poster, since another one on eBay failed to sell. But they accepted the rest of the items and filled out forms for each item (more on that in a bit), making sure to note down any potential flaws—they were very conscientious about wanting to represent the items exactly as they were. They also went over the terms, which were complex enough to leave both of us reeling. It was all very efficient and very impersonal. We returned to the car feeling shaken and dubious, but hoping for the best.

Things started looking up when we each got an e-mail with links to our items' auction pages so we could follow the auctions ourselves and track how our items were faring. The auction pages looked extremely professional, with great photos of the items. I can't vouch for Delilah, but I'll confess to checking the progress of mine several times a day for the 7 days the auction lasted. They did sell, but not for very much money. But the real sticker shock came when my check eventually arrived—for $7! (I think Delilah got about $38.) After all the fees and charges were taken out, there wasn't a lot left over. Neither of us even began to get back what we'd paid for our stuff, and we both felt that we could have done better elsewhere.

(continued on page 386)

Tools of the Trade

When you're talking about eBay, eBay drop-off stores may be the ultimate "tools of the trade." With 900 franchises and plans to expand to 3,000 in the United States—and more around the world—iSold It is the leading franchise, followed by QuikDrop. The iSold It Web site (www.i-soldit.com) gives a concise overview of how the drop-off process works that is true to my own experience:

"Our experienced staff can conduct some quick online research to help estimate [your object's] value. During the check-in process, our store staff will work with you to capture any key copy points you'd like to make in your eBay listing. Once you've checked in, we place the item in our inventory and hand you a receipt. Then we get to work photographing and listing your item on eBay. Once we've listed your item on eBay, we'll send you an e-mail with a link to the auction, so you can watch all the action as it occurs. Once the transaction is complete, we send you a check. Or, if you prefer, we can send the proceeds to your favorite charity."

iSold It will sell items with an expected value of $30 or more, that weigh less than 150 pounds, and that measure less than 130 inches in length and girth combined. They typically list auctions for 7 days but can shorten that to as little as 1 day for time-sensitive items like concert tickets or tickets to sports events. If an item doesn't sell, they'll send you an e-mail and you can either pick it up within 10 days of the end of the auction or they'll donate it to charity. Sellers can set an opening bid of $9.99 or higher, but they're warned that that can limit bidding activity. Sellers can expect their checks within 30 to 45 days after they drop off an item at the store.

QuikDrop's services are similar. They'll sell items with an expected value of $50 or more, typically list them for 7 days, and give you 15 days to pick up anything that doesn't sell (then they'll donate it to charity). On their Web site (www.quikdrop. com), they note that they provide a gallery photo for all listings. This means that prospective buyers can see the photo when they do an item or category search rather than seeing an annoying camera symbol letting them know that if they click on the entry there will be photos. (Worse still is when there's no symbol, which means there's no photo of the item—bad idea.) QuikDrop also uses bold titles in their listings, which they say gives the items more exposure. Like the other services, Quik Drop tracks each auction, answers questions from prospective buyers, processes payment, packages the item, and ships it to the winner when the auction closes.

Now for the downside: transactions fees. Just how much are they, and why do you have to pay them? Well, get ready to whip out your calculators (though both iSold It and QuikDrop have charts with examples of selling prices and the fees associated with them on their Web sites, so check them out for more details).

First, the why: Well, obviously the store owners have to pay off the $65,000 to $100,000 startup costs for their franchises, not to mention the ongoing operating costs. But, as they rightly point out, they're also doing all the work for you, from researching, photographing, and listing your stuff on eBay to conducting all the transactions, getting your money from the winner, packing and shipping the item, and sending you a check. Plus, they're paying eBay (and often PayPal) listing and payment processing fees. And they're guaranteeing those all-important high positive feedback ratings that will get potential buyers to choose their items over similar objects from sellers with lower ratings. In return for all these services, you're turning over a hefty percentage of your profits.

Both eBay and the drop-off stores base their commissions on a sliding scale. For eBay, the initial listing and gallery photo fee is 75 cents, followed by a commission of 5.25 percent of the first $25, 2.75 percent of the next $975, and 1.5 percent of any amount over $1,000. The typical iSold It commission is 35 percent of the first $500 and 20 percent of the remaining amount over $500, with a minimum commission of $5 per item. For QuikDrop, it's typically 42 percent of the first $200, 34 percent of the next $300, and 25 percent of the remaining amount over $500. Then there are the payment processing fees: iSold It charges $1.05 plus 2.55 percent of the total transaction value (sales price, shipping and handling, and sales tax). QuikDrop charges 2.9 percent for payment and processing fees, plus sales tax.

So how does all this break down? If your item sells for $100 on eBay, you'll get a check for $57 (57 percent of the final selling price) from iSold It; if it sells for $1,000, you'll get $642 (64 percent of the selling price). If you sell an item for $100 through QuikDrop, after eBay's commission of $8.86 and QuikDrop's of $42, you'll get a check for $49.14; if it sells for $1,000, after eBay's commission of $64.36 and Quik Drop's of $311, you'll get $624.64. Again, see their Web sites for more examples.

There are plenty of other eBay drop-off stores to choose from, all of which are run along similar lines. For example, AuctionDrop stores operate out of United Parcel Service (UPS) stores. They'll take items worth over $75 on eBay, as long as they weigh less than 25 pounds. AuctionDrop typically starts bids at $1 and lists for 7 days, but you can pay them a fee of $19.99 that gets you "premium service" and lets you set an opening bid that's higher than $1. (AuctionDrop will credit the $19.99 toward its commission fee if the item sells.) AuctionDrop's commission is 38 percent on the first $200, 30 percent on the next $300, and 20 percent on the remainder over $500. Check them out online at www.auctiondrop.com. For other drop-off store franchises, look online for www.theonlineoutpost.com.

That's not the end of this story, however, or I wouldn't be recommending drop-off stores to you. If I'd had the sense to do some online research or had been more focused on de-cluttering and less on making some money, my attitude about the whole experience—which was fast, painless, and professional—would have been quite different. For one thing, I'd have found out that almost nobody gets the street or book value of an item, much less as much as they paid for it. And I'd have found out about all the fees, so I could have prepared myself for the sticker shock.

As I now see it, the correct attitude is: At these stores, people take your unwanted stuff away and replace it with money! In the words of my ex-father-in-law, "It beats a jab with a sharp stick." All of which is to say, I wouldn't recommend eBay drop-off stores as a way to build your retirement savings or pay off your credit cards—though of course some lucky customers do strike it rich with a big auction price. Don't count on it, though. Instead, bring in your yard-sale stuff, sit back, and enjoy the spare change when those checks come in.

What to Sell

What sells best at a drop-off store? At iSold It—assuming your items are clean and in good condition—the list is long. Their Web site lists antiques and collectibles, appliances and small furniture, cameras and video recorders, designer apparel and accessories, electronics and phones, event tickets, housewares, musical instruments, sports equipment, and vehicle parts. Musical instruments, electronics, and vintage or antique items also move fast at QuikDrop. And both stores will sell your vehicles, too.

What if you're trying to unload something big? They can handle big stuff at iSold It, too, but they'll ask you to leave it at home, take 10 or more photos of the object, fill out an Item Questionnaire, and bring the photos and questionnaire to an iSold It store instead of the object itself (you can find guidelines and the questionnaire on their site, or see "Tools of the Trade" on page 384 for details). Once an item sells, they'll arrange for the winning bidder to pick up the piece at your house or arrange for a freight service to transport it. Some stores also offer a "house calls" service where, for a fee, a store employee will come to your house to photograph your stuff and fill out the questionnaire for you. Check with the other drop-off stores for their policies on large items.

According to iSold It, popular large items on eBay (besides vehicles) include game-room items like jukeboxes, pool tables, and arcade games; pianos and other musical instruments and equipment; luxury name-brand furniture (like Eames) and high-end appliances (like Viking); big screen and plasma TVs; motorized equipment (such as golf carts, wheelchairs, and Rascal scooters); architectural elements and artwork (such as woodwork, flooring, and oil paintings); and large antiques and collectibles. (Again, if your antiques, collectibles, and artwork are really valuable, please read Chapter 22—Antiques in Your Attic, beginning on page 429, before consigning them to eBay.)

GOING IT ALONE

If you decide to take the plunge and sell your own stuff on eBay—you just wouldn't listen to me, would you?—for heaven's sake, do your homework. Get your hands on a copy of *eBay for Dummies* (see "The Pros Know" on page 375) and read it. Check out the eBay site to see if they're holding an eBay University anywhere near you. It's a daylong seminar that, for a mere $59, will show you the ropes of selling on eBay. You can also take the course online for free, so do it! (eBay University also offers an advanced course online for $19.95, or at the local sessions for $59.)

Spend a lot of time on eBay, exploring the "Seller" portion of their site and monitoring auctions. Look at the various listings and see how the sellers have set up their pages. Check out sellers' feedback and see what you can expect. Go to Marsha Collier's Web site, www.coolebaytools.com, which is directed at eBay sellers, and sign up for her free newsletter. Make sure your photography and computer skills are up to snuff.

This is *work*, you all. If you're a seller, you'll be responsible for taking the photos; writing the description; setting the terms; listing the item on eBay; monitoring the auction; answering bidders' questions; determining shipping, eBay, and PayPal fees, as well as sales tax; collecting and processing payment; packing and shipping the item; and tracking and reporting profits to Uncle Sam. About 165 pages in *eBay for Dummies* are devoted to getting you up to speed as a seller—and that's the most basic of the *For Dummies* eBay sellers' books! That doesn't mean it can't be fun, but it does mean that you should learn the ropes before you start, and then start very small.

Before you put a single item up for sale on eBay, you need to register on the site as an eBay seller, with a credit card on file with eBay. Go to the "Seller" area of their site (www.ebay.com) and follow their directions to register. Then fill out your "Sell Your Item" page and you're ready to list your first item and go for it!

What to Show and Say

Take it from the pros when it comes to creating your own listing. You can't do better than what the eBay drop-off stores request from you in the way of photos and descriptions—except, of course, in terms of adding more color to your descriptions and histories, plus a really great title.

In terms of photos, you should take a bunch and choose the best to use in the listing. (eBay allows up to eight, but you have to pay an additional fee for every photo after the first one, which is free.) Make sure the photos are in focus and well lit. Photograph the object from all sides, and take close-up photos of all features, both good (manufacturers' names, design details) and bad (scratches, dents, discolorations, stains). If you don't have a digital camera, have your 35mm photos developed onto a CD-ROM (most photo processing stores can do this).

As for what to say, you should start by choosing a category or categories in which to list your items. Start with the general (antiques) and add what you need to help potential buyers find your item (collectibles, dolls, Shirley Temple dolls).

After the category, you need a title—the thing buyers see (along with the gallery photo) when the list of items they've requested comes up onscreen. It should be descriptive and catchy, so people both know what you're offering and are pulled in. You have only 55 characters (meaning both individual letters and spaces between words), so they all have to count. "Rare Signature MARK KNOPFLER Martin Acoustic Guitar" or "Cool Vintage Spiro Agnew Collectible Tee-Shirt '70s Chic" both tell buyers what you have on offer. For an extra fee, you can add a subtitle to say a few more things about your object, if you need to.

Next, provide a detailed description, including the item's color(s), name, make and model, dimensions (height, length, and width), weight, accessories, age, and anything else you can think of to enhance the item's appeal to a buyer (as long as it's accurate). "Original 1976 Diane von Furstenberg silk wrap dress, size 8, white with blue and gold paisley design, mint condition, vintage designer couture collectible" tells potential buyers a lot more than "White wrap dress with blue and gold design, size 8," don't you think? Whatever it is, describe it lovingly.

Note any flaws in your item and show a close-up photo of the flaw in your listing to make sure buyers know exactly what they're getting and can happily report that the item was as described. (Protect your feedback rating!) Better to note that your rare vintage Lys acoustic guitar has a small scratch by the soundhole than risk endless grief when the buyer gets it in the mail.

Moving beyond drop-off store basics, it's time for the cream, the stuff that hooks an already-interested buyer in your particular item, as opposed to just anybody's. In the case of the dress, you could give some background on Diane von Furstenberg: talk about her rags-to-riches story, colorful life, and appointment as head of the Council of Fashion Designers of America in 2006, making her arguably the most powerful woman in fashion. You could talk about the stellar success of the wrap dress design—one of Ms. von Furstenberg's is on display in the Metropolitan Museum of Art—and its current revival. You could position your particular dress in its history—did it come out the first year Ms. von Furstenberg created the style? (The first year was actually 1973, so no luck on that one.) And you could add some personal history, such as how and why you got it. ("I wore it on my honeymoon in Paris," or "Mom bought it and wore it to see her first play in New York.")

In the case of the Lys guitar, you could give a history of its creator, Robert Godin, who began with the Lys line in Canada in the sixties and went on to found Godin Guitars, with six different highly successful lines. You could discuss the rarity of Lys guitars today, their collectibility, their great sound. Give the history of your guitar. Give a few examples of famous musicians who play Godin guitars today.

Whatever your item is, see what other people are saying about it on eBay by searching for it in other auctions. If what they're saying is both compelling and accurate and refers to the brand as a whole, not just their individual item, consider adding it to your description (in your own words, of course). Check out companies, designers, and well-known objects on Wikipedia (www.wikipedia.com). Search for them at www.google.com to see what you can find for your listing. Go to the companies' or designers' own Web sites. The more you know, the better your listing can be.

However: You *don't* want to drone on and on about your object, numbing the prospective buyer, and you don't want to give a bunch of meaningless verbiage. Make sure what you say is interesting and informative, and that it would appeal to you as a buyer.

Other Essentials

What else matters when you list something on eBay? Auction terms, auction time, shipping (and handling), and methods of payment. As far as auction terms, you can set a low opening bid, a higher opening bid, a reserve, and/or a "Buy It Now" price. Low opening bids—as in a dollar or less—tend to attract bargain-hunting buyers. But what if somebody actually *buys* President Lincoln's mother's sister's bird's-eye maple dresser for $1? Horrors! But it ain't necessarily so.

Obviously, you can set the starting bid at the lowest price you'd be willing to accept, but eBay insiders have found that that discourages bidders. So they often get around the low-low opening bid by setting a reserve price for the item—which is usually also the lowest price they'd be willing to accept. Potential buyers will be attracted by the low opening bid, but will see that there's an undisclosed reserve price, and will also see whether or not the reserve has been met. (If it hasn't been met by the end of the auction, you don't have to sell the item.) Items with reserves are intimidating to bargain hunters—who knows how much the seller is expecting?—so given a choice between an item with a reserve and a similar one that broadcasts "NR" or "no reserve" in its title, they'll gravitate toward the one without a reserve. You can try to counteract that by putting "low reserve" in your title, or telling bidders right in the description what the reserve is and why you've set it. That way, they'll know if your object is within their financial reach.

There's also the optional "Buy It Now" feature. It's another way to offer bidders the option of buying something they really want at a price you're willing to accept (always higher than the opening bid, but, depending on the bid, not necessarily much higher). This is a gamble on your part—if a buyer takes you up on it, you might make less than you would from an auction. But if bidding doesn't get as high as the "Buy It Now" price, you'd have been better off if someone had taken you up on it. In any case, if anyone places a bid, your "Buy It Now" option disappears (unless you've set a reserve, in which case it will disappear once a bidder meets the reserve price), and then anything goes.

Auction time is a factor because eBay, which is based in San Jose, California, runs its auctions on Pacific Standard Time. And since most bidders monitor auctions closely as they near their end, you don't want them to end at some ungodly hour when many of your would-be buyers are asleep. (eBay's peak hours of operation are 5:00 p.m. to 9:00 p.m., and that's probably true of 5:00 p.m. to 9:00 p.m. in your time zone, too, whatever time it is on the West Coast.) eBay ends its auctions 7 days from the exact same time that they started, so you'll know when they'll end an auction based on when you begin it.

You choose when to start your auction, so make sure it will end at a reasonable time for people in your part of the country. Why? Because given a choice of several of the same item in different locations, people are more likely to bid on objects closer to them, since—all else being equal—the shipping will be lower. (Marsha Collier has a free eBay time calculator to help you with this; look for it on her Web site, www.coolebaytools.com.) And speaking of timing, sellers' wisdom says to run auctions over holidays if you can, since people are at home and online then. Marsha advises that you run the auction so it ends the Tuesday after the holiday Monday.

Because you've measured and weighed your object carefully, you can calculate and list shipping charges so the buyer knows what to expect. (You can also put an automatic shipping calculator in the listing so a would-be buyer can calculate the cost for him- or herself.) This matters, since the winner will pay for shipping. If you don't list shipping costs, lots of buyers will pass over your listing in favor of someone else who has a similar item and does list shipping. Specify where you're willing to ship—the continental 48 states, all 50 states, the United States and Canada, internationally?

The US Postal Service has partnered with eBay to provide a wide array of shipping services online, including one-price shipping anywhere in the United States if the item will fit in a Priority Mail flat rate box, plus free carrier pickup. Go to http://pages.ebay.com/usps/home.html to check out all the options.

If you'll allow the winning bidder to pick up the object in person, as opposed to paying shipping, it might attract even more bidders. (But that means meeting people someplace or letting them come to your house, so you'll need to decide if you're comfortable with that.) In addition to the shipping charges, note whether you require insurance for the package and how much, if anything, you'll charge for "handling" (acquiring packing materials, packing up the item, and hauling it off to be shipped). I'd say make this number as small as possible, or waive it altogether and include those costs in your opening bid or reserve.

Then there's that little matter of payment. Let your hopeful buyers know what forms of payment you're willing to accept—and the more forms, the better. Options include eBay's own online payment service, PayPal (www.paypal.com), which allows money to be transferred from one bank to another electronically, like magic, and also handles credit card transactions so you don't have to deal with them. PayPal does assess fees to sellers, but not to buyers, and its convenience to both makes it a popular option. Lots of sellers also accept personal checks, cashier's checks, and money orders, for folks like me who'd rather put the check in the mail. Be very clear about your terms: how soon after the end of the auction you expect payment; that you won't mail out an item until a personal check clears (usually within 7 to 10 business days); and if you'll charge the buyer sales tax if he or she lives in your state and, of course, if your state has sales tax. (Needless to say, if you sell to an in-state buyer in a sales-tax state and you don't charge the sales tax to the buyer, you'll have to pay it, but offering to do so is another possible sales tactic.)

Once you've collected the money—and kept the documentation for those potentially pesky IRS auditors—you'll need to remit the fees you owe to eBay and PayPal (if you use it). Remember all those fees I talked about in the drop-off store section?

Well, you'll need to calculate the 20 cents to $80 listing cost and 2 to 8 percent of the final price that you owe eBay, plus any additional fees from PayPal.

What happens if your high bidder defaults on the payment? Luckily, eBay lets you contact the second-highest bidder with an exclusive "Second Chance" feature that offers them the opportunity to buy the item at their highest bid. And if they decline, and you want to, you can continue to offer the "Second Chance" to other bidders until you get a buyer.

ONWARD!

Obviously, this is just the tip of the eBay iceberg. But I hope it's been enough to give you a good idea of your options and to decide what you'd like to do as far as selling your stuff on eBay or another online auction site. Now it's time to move on to a more old-fashioned and local (but nonetheless effective) technique, the good old classifieds and their online descendant, Craigslist. Grab a paper—or turn on your computer—and let's go!

Chapter 20

Clutter in the Classifieds

Extra, extra! Local woman makes a tidy profit off her former clutter while creating space she never knew she had! In this chapter, you'll learn your online and in-print options, from newspapers to Craigslist, as well as how to write an ad that will sell your stuff, tailor ads to the sales venue, evaluate buyers and their methods of payment, and make the exchange after you've made the sale.

THE CLASSIFIEDS: READ ALL ABOUT IT!

Despite the advent of Internet sales venues, many people still sell their stuff through classified ads in their local papers or in special "bargain" papers like my own area's *Merchandiser* and *Penny Pincher,* both of which are ads- and classifieds-only publications. With classifieds, you're limiting your market not just locally, but to readers of the paper or publication where you place the ad. However, if you live in an area with cheap (or even free) ad rates or you're advertising a more expensive item, it makes sense to advertise in one of these papers because it requires almost no effort on your part, it attracts the people most likely to come to your home to haul off the stuff while paying you for the privilege, and an item that sells for a lot of money will more than cover the cost of a cheap ad.

What to Say

As in any other sales venue, your classified ad is competing with pages of other ads for the attention of busy, distracted readers. Your goal is to make your ad jump out at a reader who might want your stuff. How can you tell what will catch somebody's eye? Look at your local paper's classifieds and see which ads catch yours, and why. If one of them makes you want to actually *buy* something, then you know you're on to something. Study it closely and see why it's so intriguing.

The hook for your ad may be the title or capitalized first few words, but the core of your ad is the description you write of the item or items you're offering for sale, so make it as vivid and inviting as possible. Look at various ads for the same thing—say, golden retrievers or exercise equipment or bedroom sets or Harleys—and see which ones paint the best and most inviting picture. That's your goal, too. For example, "beautiful warm cherry" sounds a lot better than "cherry finish," doesn't it?

A great ad I saw recently for a dining-room table read like this: "DINING TABLE beautiful AICO brand, w/8 chairs, exquisite detail, inlaid bird's-eye maple, heavy, high-quality estate piece, 1 yr old, flawless, must see! Can e-mail photos." Just above it was an ad that said "DINING ROOM TABLE with chairs." You choose!

Remember, when you place a classified ad, you're paying by the word or line, and classified columns are just 28 spaces per line, so you want to say the most possible in the fewest words. How can you do that? Start by writing down *everything* you want to say about the item you're selling. Once you've gotten it all down, take a good look at what you've written and see what you can get rid of (because it's not going to increase sales), what you can combine (when you've said basically the same thing in different ways), and what you need to keep. The *Express-Times* puts this best in their tip on editing your ad: "Remove nonessential information and insert more benefits for prospective buyers."

Note the abbreviations in the sample ad above. Abbreviations cut down on lines—a good thing, as long as they're easy to understand and there aren't so many of them that a buyer feels like he or she is reading HTML. (Some papers, like the Nashville *Tennessean*, recommend against using abbreviations because not everyone knows what they mean.)

Tools of the Trade

Wondering how to make your classified ad stand out in a sea of ink? Here's a checklist of ways to get buyers' attention.

✳ Put the first few words in bold type to get your readers' attention.

✳ Make sure the words you put in bold type are attention-getting. You can say something startling ("BETTER-THAN-NEW JOHN DEERE RIDING MOWER is guaranteed problem-free."), or something unexpected ("JOHN DEERE MOWER. FREE up your time. Switch to a riding mower."). "HUGE SALE!" and "BIG SALE!" are also attention-getters if you're selling a number of items. Others to think about: "GREAT DEAL!" "HERE IT IS!" "LIMITED EDITION!" "NEVER USED!" (if that's true) "REAL BARGAIN!" "CHECK IT OUT!"

✳ Don't forget to say what the item is as part of the bold listing, so it will be listed with its competition and people scanning the ads for, say, a piano, will see it with the other pianos.

✳ Follow the heading with a benefit. Why does a buyer need your stuff? ("Stop sweating behind a push mower." "Save 75 percent over a new mower.")

✳ What's unique about your item? How is it better than or different from similar items that will have ads running alongside yours?

✳ If you have room, such as in a Craiglist ad where you can write as much as you want for free (see page 398 for more on Craigslist), add a statistic to reinforce the value of what you're selling. ("This model John Deere riding mower was rated #1 for its year by *Consumer Reports*." "I just checked the cost of metal pillar candle molds like the ones I'm offering, and you can buy my three bins of candlemaking supplies—*including* 10 metal pillar molds—for less than it would cost to buy five new molds!" "This Braun coffee maker got top user ratings by Amazon reviewers.")

✳ Give your description oomph by adding attention-getting words (if they're true): "excellent condition," "limited edition," "new in box," "still in plastic," "first edition," "never used," "original," "designer," "vintage," "antique," "high quality," "mint condition," "exquisite," "valuable," "precious," or "adorable." You get the idea. And you can mix and match them as you describe the item.

✳ Add a call to action at the end of the ad. ("Like-new condition, won't last. Call today." "Don't wait at this price. Respond now.")

If you look at a paragraph or page of text and want to keep it all, put it aside for a day and look again when you're more detached, or give it to your spouse or a friend and ask them to read it and "edit" it for you. Make every word count. Above all, make every word accurate. Make sure you're not (even accidentally) misleading potential buyers.

Now you're almost done. After the description, you still need to list the price you're asking for the item. Follow that with your contact data (phone number or numbers and/or e-mail address) so buyers can reach you. The *Express-Times* notes, "Many sales are lost because the advertiser was just too difficult to reach." Add that "call today" closure if you want to. That's it!

How to Do It

Check your local paper's classified ad guidelines to see their directions and charges. When I looked up how to place a classified ad at my local paper's Web site (www.mcall.com), it couldn't have been easier. It uses a software service called Advertise123.com by AdStar that walks you painlessly through the process. Once you tell them that you're a private-party advertiser (as opposed to a business), it takes you through its "Ad Placement System," which helps you place the ad in the right category, compose the ad, and schedule it, and even provides tips to help your ad stand out! I also checked the Web site of my hometown paper, the Nashville *Tennessean* (www.tennessean.com), and found that they used AdBaseE software to create a very easy-to-use system that also walks you through the process. (They also provide ad-writing tips, and so did the paper my boyfriend, Rob, used to work for, the *Express-Times;* check out their Web sites at www.pennlive.com and www.nj.com.)

So what does it cost? For my paper, the *Morning Call,* the rates are by the line rather than by the word. For a weekend (Saturday and Sunday) ad in both the paper and on its Web site, the rate is $39.44 for four lines and $7.11 for each additional line. For 5 days (Monday through Friday), it's $68.44 for four lines and $14.36 for each additional line. For 7 days, the rate is $91.58 for four lines and $20.14 for each additional line. Every ad gets a full 7 days on the paper's Web site, and weeklong ads also get placed in the paper's extra weekend edition, *The Chronicle*, and on the *Chronicle* Web site for 7 days.

In Nashville, the *Tennessean*'s rates are a lot friendlier, and they vary by type of item. In fact, if you're selling stuff for less than $50, you can place a five-line ad in Saturday's *Tennessean* and on its Web site (www.tennessean.com) and upload up to 10 photos online for FREE (as they'd say in the classifieds). Additional lines cost just $1 each. For stuff over $50 and under $250, the rate is five lines for $19.50, additional lines for $1 each. Again, you can upload up to 10 photos, and you can also list multiple items, as long as the total price is under $250. You'll also get your ad in their weekend special, the *Rage*. Stuff over $250 is $26 for five lines and $3 for each additional line. If you're selling a cheap car ($1,000 or less), you can place an ad in the *Tennessean*, the *Rage*, and online on www.cars.com for just $10 for five lines and 50 cents for each additional line; for more expensive cars, the rate is $40.25 for five lines and $2 for each additional line. All ads run for 7 days.

As you can see, a classified ad may not compare to the cost of a "real" ad, but, depending on where you live, it may not be cheap, either. That's why most classifieds are for higher-priced items like pianos, home gyms, mattresses, large equipment and power tools, large furniture, good jewelry, and collectibles, rather than yard-sale stuff. (That bird's-eye maple dining table and chairs I mentioned earlier were offered for a firm $3,000, for example.) It's also why, if you do see less expensive items, they're often grouped together in a single ad. Before you place a classified ad (unless, of course, it's free), make sure you'll get enough for your item to make it worth the cost.

CRAIGSLIST: THE "OTHER" CLASSIFIEDS

Craigslist, which started out in 1995 in San Francisco as a sideline hobby for a guy named—guess what?—Craig, has become the eBay of classified ads. You can find it in more than 450 cities worldwide, and more than 10 million people use it a *lot*—it gets over 5 billion page views per month, making it the eighth-ranked Web site in the United States. It's also the leading classified ad service, with over 10 million new ads posted each month.

Obviously, if you post a classified ad on Craigslist, you'll have a lot of competition. But you'll also have a lot of potential buyers. It's free to list an ad on Craigslist, and listings are posted for 45 days. You have nothing to lose by trying—except your clutter!

Checking Out Craigslist

To see how it worked, I went to the Craigslist home site (www.craigslist.org), then clicked on "Pennsylvania" to see what was available in my area. (You could click on individual states, large US cities, or countries.) A page appeared asking me to choose the city or area nearest me, so I selected "Lehigh Valley." This opened up the Allentown listings. So far, so easy.

A pageful of categories appeared on the screen, so I clicked on "collectibles" and found listings by day, with today's date at the top. I could choose from a Bethlehem Steel jacket, candlemaking supplies, a collection of 45 rpm records, a circa-1900 clawfoot bathtub, a Longaberger pie plate, a Hotwheels service center or garage, an antique men's shaving mirror, the "entire Hess truck collection," a photo of Dorney Park (a local amusement park) taken in 1902, and a 10-gallon aquarium with light lid, all listed (with other stuff that I'll spare you) the first 3 days of this week. Prices ranged from "make offer" (for the Dorney Park photo) to $950 (for the Hess trucks), though most were in the under-$50 range.

The one that jumped out at me had the heading "Want to sell snake skins—$10!" (I am *not* making this up.) Sure enough, when I clicked on it, it turned out that some guy was offering his pet snakes' shed skins to interested Craigslisters. He included a short and heartfelt sales pitch, noted that he "has a very pretty corn snake at the moment who sheds perfectly," and added the clincher: "Beautiful collectibles if you are interested." If you happened to collect Hess trucks instead of snake skins, the Hess ad offered nothing but the years of the trucks and number per year—not much for your $950, to my way of thinking, but I guess it told fellow enthusiasts all they needed to know. The person who put the Longaberger plate up for sale knew more about advertising—her headline read, "Longaberger Pie Plate Brand New in Box—$20."

Then there were the owners of the candlemaking supplies. When I clicked on their listing, it took me to a couple of pages of copy, very chatty and personal, but also quite informative, about how they were moving and were trying to sell three Tupperware bins full of candlemaking supplies that had been used and needed some cleaning and were currently in their basement. (To quote their ad, "Note: Items have been used and are a bit messy. If you don't want to dig through and get your hands dirty, this isn't the deal for you.") They carefully listed the stuff—an extensive list—with descriptions of each item, quantity and other specs, condition, and so forth. And they added some strong hooks to interest potential buyers: "I have a great deal for you! It's a candlemaking 'grab-bag' of sorts. Most likely, there's even more stuff than I've listed, but I can say that there's a lot of stuff." After itemizing the stuff included in the deal and adding that anything that they'd forgotten to list in the Tupperware bins was also part of the sale, they added some compelling statistics (what even a fraction of the stuff sold for when new), pointing out that just a couple of items would make it worth the trip to get the supplies. And they remembered to thank potential buyers for looking.

By contrast, the owner of the fish tank's ad simply read "10-gallon fish tank with light lid $7 may e-mail or call me thanks." And the guy who offered the collection of 45 rpm records mentioned at the end of the ad that he'd throw in his 45 record player as part of the deal! ("I will include 45 record player which has been sitting here also. I am not sure what kind of shape the player is in." Hmmm, after reading *that,* I'd bet I could guess what kind of shape it was in!)

So the ads are really all over the place, from barest of bare bones to fullest of full disclosure. Read some in your area, then go for the style that you find most appealing. It's free and you've got all the room in the world, so you can say what you want. But follow the basic rules for writing a classified ad (see page 396): Tell the readers what they need to know about the item—description, dimensions, date of manufacture, color(s), condition. You can add distinctiveness and appeal to your ad with some history or anecdotes, but remember not to bore your buyers or waste their time. They're trying to shop, not read, after all! I myself liked the snake guy—talk about an eye-catching ad!—and the candle people, though their ad could have been a couple of paragraphs shorter without losing anything.

Placing Your Ad

By now you've nailed your style and it's time to place your ad. You access the Craigslist site (www.craigslist.org) and find the list nearest you, then click on the link to it. Next, click on the "create posting" link. You'll be sent to a page that asks you to choose a posting category. (Like me, you'll probably choose the "for sale/wanted" category, since you're trying to sell your stuff.) Click that link and you'll be sent to a page that asks you to choose a category (once again, I chose "collectibles"). Now, you're sent to the actual listing page, where you fill out all the data about your object—title, description, price, and location. You can also attach and edit photos.

Craigslist will assign you a numerical e-mail address so responders can't see your actual e-mail address but can still contact you by e-mail, and of course you can list a phone number as well. (Don't forget to check the little box at the bottom that tells potential spammers and the like that no, it's not okay for people to contact you about other products or services.) When you've finished filling everything out, click "continue" and you're on your way!

Does Craigslist work? Absolutely. When my friend Susan's colleague Lisa switched jobs and moved across country, she persuaded the former owners of her new house to sell her their futon so she'd have a place to sleep until her furniture arrived. But futons are notoriously uncomfortable, and this one was no exception, so once her bed arrived, Lisa posted the futon on Craigslist. "A few days later, someone e-mailed me about it," she says, "and that resulted in a nice young couple coming by my house with a pickup truck, handing me $200, and driving off with the futon. Voilà! I love Craigslist."

Does Craigslist always produce results? No. My father's girlfriend, Alice, tried to sell a "designer" custom-made fence and lighting system for her tennis court on Craigslist, to no avail. It also might not be available—at least not yet, but keep checking—in your area. But if it is available, it's free, it's easy, and it's worth a try! Free is good, and it's also good ad-writing practice. If you're in no hurry to sell, you might list something on Craigslist first, then move on to a (paid) newspaper classified ad if you don't get a buyer through Craigslist. If the newspaper ad is also free or you have to get the item out *now,* list it in both.

SEALING THE DEAL

No matter which method successfully sells your stuff, be sure to use common sense when screening buyers, and stay within your comfort zone when handing over your item. Bear in mind that, if you're selling something, people will probably want to come over to your house to look it over before agreeing to pay for it. Unless you have a houseful of Rottweilers, it makes sense to have one or more other people around when prospective buyers come over. You might ask the neighbors to do a few yard chores or otherwise make their presence known when you let them know a buyer is expected. Don't let buyers come over at hours that strike you as unreasonably late.

Then there's the matter of payment. Ask prospective buyers how they plan to pay, and choose the one whose terms suit you best. Cold, hard cash is always appealing for less-expensive items. (If somebody can't withdraw $40 from their checking account and hand it to you, I don't know about you, but I'd be a little leery of accepting their personal check.) If they want to pay by check for a more expensive item like a piano or piece of furniture, remember that even eBay lets their sellers wait until the check clears to ship an item. You should make it clear that you'll do the same. If you'll accept a money order or cashier's check, let buyers know that. As with every part of a transaction, the clearer you can be about your terms and expectations, the easier and more pleasant it will be for everyone involved.

Speaking of shipping, make sure you and the buyer agree on how large items will be transported. Will they come to your house with a truck or U-Haul and cart it off? Will they arrange for third-party transport? Are you prepared to haul it to their house?

For small items, you can let the buyer come and get them, take them to the buyer, ship them to the buyer (make sure it's clear who's paying the shipping and what those costs will be), or meet at a convenient midpoint. My friend Delilah once bought some (live) ducks from a seller about 100 miles away, and I went with her to pick them up. Rather than have us try to find their farm, the couple met us at a McDonald's just off the highway at the exit nearest them, bearing a box of quacking ducks in the back of their truck. I can tell you, the ride back was like traveling with the Marx Brothers!

ONWARD!

What about that old-fashioned fair-weather weekend event, the yard (aka tag) sale, and its foul-weather twin, the garage sale? We'll take a stroll around the yard (sale) in the next chapter. And we'll also look at some fun ways to get rid of stuff you don't want to or don't think you can sell. So start your engines and look for those yard-sale signs. . . .

Chapter 21

Yard Sales, Swaps, and Giveaways

Call 'em yard sales, garage sales, tag sales, or rummage sales, what's really for sale is your clutter. Here's how to set one up, how to display and price your stuff, whether to organize a block party or go it alone, how to make the sale, when to hold your sale, and, most importantly, what *not* to do. You'll also get a primer on the good old-fashioned art of bartering—who to approach, how to approach them, what's a fair swap, and what to expect. Plus: Great ways to persuade total strangers to come pick up your junk, take it away, and love it!

OUT IN THE YARD (OR IN THE GARAGE)

My friend Tom's idea of heaven is an endless weekend of yard and garage sales. Every weekend, he cruises around his neighborhood and scans the classifieds looking for promising sales. Does he need anything? No. Is he looking for anything particular? No. But to Tom, it's an entertaining way to spend free time (with an emphasis on "free"—it costs nothing to attend yard sales, after all), a treasure hunt that might yield a really great bargain or a one-of-a-kind jackpot—or just some useful stuff at a reasonable price.

Tom's not alone in his passion for yard sales. Despite the popularity of eBay and other online venues like Craigslist, more than 60 million people go to yard sales in the United States each year. One of them could be yours!

Three Kinds of Yard Sales

In my area, there are three kinds of yard sales. First are the ones that people have because they're moving, or because it's spring and they're trying to unload some stuff as part of spring-cleaning, or because they just ended up with a whole bunch of stuff when their parents moved to a retirement home or died. Those are the "once-in-a-while" sales, the kind where you see the little handmade signs by the road as you're driving around.

Next, there are what I'd call the "professional yard salers." These people have the long folding tables, the plastic covers, the folding chairs, sometimes even tents—the whole shebang. And every weekend from early spring through fall, those tables are set up and covered with stuff. These people tend to have homes on busier roads, and they don't bother with signs—people know where to find them or see them as they drive by. They're sort of halfway between a yard sale and a flea market. Clearly, they get stuff from other sources—maybe from "once-in-a-while" yard sales—and resell it at their sales.

Finally, there are the neighborhood yard sales, where two or more families pool their resources and hold a big sale, again hoping to clear out their collective clutter. These are "once-in-a-while" sales on a bigger scale and are held in the flattest yard or the one with the most on-street parking or the one that's easiest to see from the main road (or, in bad weather, at the house with the biggest garage). If you mention the multi-family angle in your advertising ("Block Sale!" "Neighborhood Yard Sale!" "Monster Multi-Family Garage Sale!"), you'll almost certainly attract more people, since there's the promise of more to check out.

GETTING YOUR YARD SALE NOTICED

By now, you probably know that there are four keys to really successful sales: good merchandise, good advertising, good pricing, and good selling (customer) technique. It's true of every sales venue, from classified ads to eBay, and it's certainly

the **Pros Know**

Did you know that there are professionals who can hold your yard sale for you? Like auctioneers and eBay drop-off stores, they'll take a commission on sales (usually 20 to 30 percent). But in return, they'll handle all the advertising, pricing, display, and actual sales of items, and they'll even deal with the customers. These people are pros at selling housewares and collectibles. They know what prices they can get, and some of them have client lists, so they can contact buyers if you have stuff of interest to them.

Of course, professionals won't think it's worth their while to spend a day or a weekend in your yard if what you have to sell is worth pocket change. But if you have some good stuff (furniture, silver, crystal, china, better collectibles, electronics) and you really don't want to do all that work yourself, or you don't feel confident about pricing or selling, contact area professionals and find someone to do it for you. Look for them in your local classifieds under "Yard Sales," "Garage Sales," or "Merchandise."

true of yard and garage sales. (There's a fifth key, too. It's called "luck" and typically involves the weather and location.) Making *your* yard sale the must-see sale of the weekend is your goal, and to do that, it has to stand out from the competition.

> [There are four keys to successful sales: good merchandise, good advertising, good pricing, and good selling technique.]

Here are some ways to get your sale some attention:

❑ Post notices on bulletin boards at local libraries, markets, and other community bulletin boards. Print them out on a full-size 8½ x 11-inch sheet (copier-paper size). Use big, bold type that's easy to read and add plenty of color. (Just make sure the type itself is dark enough to read easily.) Add digital photos of some of your more appealing items with a brief description under each photo. If you want, add balloon icons, borders, or stickers to remind people to look for the balloons on your mailbox.

- Put classified ads in local papers; they'll typically also put them up on their Web sites' classified sections. (See "Placing Your Ad" on page 409.)

- Post a notice on the garage sale section of your area's Craigslist Web site (www.craigslist.org) and other community Web sites.

- Use words and phrases that help your ad stand out: "1-Day-Only AMAZING Garage Sale!" "Mother of All Yard Sales!" "AWESOME Garage Sale!" "Grandma's OVERFLOWING Attic Sale!" "Basement BLOWOUT Sale!"

- In the item descriptions, list the biggest and most interesting items first.

- If your sale has items that are surefire crowd magnets, like vintage clothes, baby clothes and equipment, kids' clothing and toys, costume jewelry, dolls, and tools, feature them prominently in your ad. Then make sure you draw attention to them at the sale itself by grouping them together and putting up a large display sign (like a lavender sign that says "Vintage Clothing!" in flowery Victorian lettering, with a hand icon pointing down at the table).

- Good signage makes good sales. Hang big signs over your tables telling what's on them in bold, easy-to-read letters that can be seen across the yard.

- People love food, so if you have the manpower to deal with a small refreshment table set somewhat apart from the rest of the sale, take a tip from church sales and offer (or sell) treats like mini chocolate-chip cookies and doughnut holes and small paper cups of water, lemonade, or iced tea at your sale. Don't sell anything gooey, and set big trash cans near the table so people can gulp their treats and dump the cups and plates before heading back to the sale tables. Of course, put up a big "Refreshments" sign over the table. If you don't want to charge for them, consider setting a glass jar with some coins in it on the table to encourage people to toss in a quarter or two for their treats. Don't forget to mention the refreshments in your ad! If you do offer them, be aware that you may get some spills and crumbs on your stuff. But it will definitely set your yard sale apart!

- Have a bargain or grab-bag table (or combine both at one table, with signs over the table for bargains and grab bags). Sell your bargains for $1 and under and your grab bags for 50 cents, and note that prominently on the signs. If you set out boxes of costume jewelry or other little items on this table, have signs on each box listing the per-item price ("Anything in this box is $1!") and also, if you want, a multiple-item price ("Any three for $2!"). This kind of pricing also lets you move stuff over to the bargain table toward the end of the sale if you see it isn't selling.

❑ Don't put out anything you aren't prepared to sell, with the exception of the display tables, folding chairs for sellers, cash box, bins for tags, and boom box (and hide that under a table beside a seller). Don't be surprised if people want to buy them, too. If you put bright tablecloths, sheets, or other textiles under your stuff to "set it off," someone will inevitably want to buy the textile and end up feeling disgruntled when you won't sell it (or you'll end up disgruntled if you decide to oblige and have to pull off all the stuff on top of it, then put it all back). Worse, the pattern in the textile will distract people from the stuff that *is* for sale and make it harder to see it, too. So use plain white sheets or leave the tables clean and bare.

❑ Give your sale an inviting "block party" feel by adding some music—salsa, Jimmy Buffet, something upbeat and inoffensive. Don't crank up the volume—you want to hear buyers easily, you want couples to be able to confer with each other, and you don't want to disturb the neighbors! But don't make it so soft that it doesn't contribute to a happy atmosphere.

❑ When people arrive, act like you're glad to see them. Don't sit there sulking (or hiding) behind your table. Smile, come up and greet people, thank them for coming, ask if there's anything special they're looking for. (If they say they're looking for something you don't have, do not just say "I don't have that." Instead, say something along the lines of, "If we have one of

the **Pros Know**

Want to learn more about holding a yard sale? The undisputed yard-sale queen in America is Cathy Pedigo, author of *How to Have Big Money Garage Sales* (Winning Edge, 2002, $10.95) and coauthor with Sonia Weiss of *The Pocket Idiot's Guide to Garage and Yard Sales* (Alpha, 2003, $9.95). Check out her Web site (www.win-edge.com/GarageSale.shtml), where you can order her book—which she promises will more than triple your garage or yard sale income—or get a downloadable version for $8.95 (or both for $12.95).

those, it would be on that table/in that bin over there," or "I don't think we have one, but you might be interested in. . . ." Once they start looking at something else, you have a good chance of making a sale.)

Placing Your Ad

My boyfriend, Rob, was for years an editor at the *Express-Times*, which serves both the Easton, Pennsylvania, area and parts of New Jersey. I decided to look there for good yard sale ads. I noticed immediately that the *Express-Times* categorizes sales as "Estate & Tag Sales," "Garage/Yard Sales," and "Yard Sales," a rather mystifying set of distinctions, since the ads seem to be identical. Each ad gave the town, street address and directions, date(s) of the sale, and time of the sale (8:00 a.m.–2:00 p.m., 9:00 a.m.–?).

After listing the basics, some ads managed to be both concise and enthusiastic ("Yard/Moving Sale! Housewares, antiques, furniture, tools, gardening items, camping equipment, 1,000 items and more!"). Some were quite specific ("Leather pull-out sofa, mahogany 4-poster bed, iron & glass table/chairs, cherry desk/ chair, baker's rack, piecrust table, Waterford, Lenox, grandfather clock, housewares"). Some listed quite a bit more. Others threw in catch phrases like "Everything must go!" "Rock-bottom prices!" "Plus much more," "Parents moving," and "Too much to list."

In the Nashville paper, the *Tennessean*, the garage- and yard-sale ads were even more exuberant. The paper provided eye-catching headings if you wanted to list your sale as a moving sale, kids sale, or estate sale. A quick scan of the ads themselves showed me hooks aplenty, including "New & used items!" "Tons of new stuff!" "LOTS of stuff!!" "Rain or shine!!" "Super Estate Sale!" "All must go today!!" "Fabulous Finds!!!" "Something for everyone!" and my favorite, "Y'all Come!"

Churches and bigger sales added the lure of food to their yard sales ("Bake sale with hot foods," "Cake and refreshments will be sold"), which I thought was a great idea. And one of them threw in a cool bargain element ("Bag day will be Saturday") to add even more appeal.

Note that, unlike classified ads for individual items, the goal of a yard-sale ad is to cover as much ground as possible—to entice buyers with popular categories of items (like vintage clothing) and with the breadth of the offerings (1,000 items) rather than descriptions of individual items. Note, too, that they start with the big-ticket stuff (antiques, leather pull-out sofa), then move on to the small potatoes.

What Does It Cost?

Like placing a classified ad for one or more individual items, the cost of placing an ad for a yard or garage (or tag) sale varies with the paper. In the *Tennessean,* it costs $31 to place five lines for a garage sale listing and $2 for each extra line. The paper also offers a free garage sale kit if you advertise and lets you advertise the leftovers from your sale for just $5. The *Express-Times* boxes their garage sale ads, so you're paying for a 2-inch-deep box rather than individual lines. They charge $46.50 to run your ad for 4 days (Thursday through Sunday), or $43.50 to run it for your choice of any 3 of the 4 days. In either case, your ad will also be featured online at www.nj.com and www.pennlive.com for 30 days, included in the cost, and you'll get a free kit from them, as well.

In my local Pennsylvania *Merchandiser,* an all-ads community paper with two special editions and a Web site, you can run a garage/yard sale ad for $4.20 for up to 20 words and 10 cents for each additional word per issue per week. Ads can run up to 12 weeks in one or both editions and will automatically be featured on their Web site. They'll run a "super ad" in all-bold type for $6.05 per ad, per week, per publication.

So check the Web sites of your local papers for pricing (or call the classifieds departments of the papers and speak to a sales rep). And remember, it's smart to advertise in *all* your local papers, as long as it won't cost you so much it will eat away your yard-sale profits. (If that's the case, see which one or ones have the most garage/yard sale ads and go with it or them.)

How Does It Work?

All the newspapers I checked have forms on their Web sites, making it as easy to create an ad for a garage or yard sale as it is for a classified ad. You just fill in the blanks! Some, like the *Express-Times,* have a different form for a garage sale than for a single- (or multiple-) item classified, while others, like the *Merchandiser,* use the same form for both kinds of ad. See Chapter 20—Clutter in the Classifieds, beginning on page 394, for more tips on ad writing.

COUNTDOWN TO THE SALE

Okay, you've checked it all out and decided to try a yard or garage sale for yourself. Congratulations! Here's what you should do as you plan your yard sale.

1. **Get permission.** Check with your township or city hall to see if there are regulations governing yard sales or if you need a permit to hold a yard sale in your area. If so, make sure all the paperwork's in order before you place your ad. While you're at it, if you live in a state that charges sales tax, check to see if you'll need to collect it at your sale. (In most states, that's not necessary if you hold four or fewer yard sales a year, but be sure to check— better safe than sorry!)

2. **Collect your stuff.** Gather everything you want to sell, bearing in mind that seasonality might count—in spring, people will be more likely to be looking for lawn mowers than snow blowers. You could divide up the stuff into spring/summer, fall/winter, and "anytime" piles, and hold two yard sales, one in spring and one in early fall, assuming you have someplace to store the off-season stuff in the meantime. Put the "anytime" stuff out with both sales. Don't be too hasty to assume something's too junky or broken to sell. As yard-sale whiz Jackie (see page 422) reminds us, one man's trash really is another man's treasure. "People will buy *anything*," Jackie says, "even empty hat boxes." You can always donate it, put it out for the trash, or have it hauled off afterwards if it doesn't sell.

3. **Talk to the neighbors.** See if any of your neighbors are interested in participating in the yard sale with you. Bigger yard sales draw more buyers, and you can split the costs of advertising; the setup work; cost of hiring a professional (if you all decide to go that route); and actual work of monitoring tables, talking to customers, taking money, making change, bagging or boxing up purchases, and other tasks. If several families agree to participate, choose the largest, most visible yard (with the best on-street parking) for the sale, or, if there's lots of stuff and the houses are adjacent to each other, you can have stuff on display in every yard to create the

impression of a *really* big sale. If your neighbors (or your relatives, for that matter) do go in on a joint sale with you, make sure all the arrangements are spelled out, including what will be done with the stuff that doesn't sell by the end of the sale. Even if your neighbors aren't interested in participating, they may offer you some of their clutter to add to your sale— or they may come over and buy some of yours!

4. **Call in the pros.** If you're planning to hire a professional, now is the time to find one and have him or her come over and evaluate your stuff (and your neighbors', if you're having a group sale). If you do bring a pro on board, this is pretty much your last step—they'll usually take it from here, even down to cleaning and polishing your stuff. (See "The Pros Know" on page 406 for more on hiring a yard-sale pro.)

5. **Clean up your stuff.** You'll be less stressed if your stuff is clean and ready to sell before you set your sale date. Make it look as good as it can. Sort clothes by type (tee-shirts, jeans, skirts) and size; separate men's, women's, boys', and girls'. Sort junk, like a collection of rusty small tools; odd batches of screws, nails, and hooks; sewing odds and ends; and other little things into grab bags or boxes. Put marbles, buttons, and other potentially decorative junk into glass canning jars. If you're trying to get rid of extra sewing or quilting fabric, tie several complementary pieces together with ribbon, like they do in quilting shops, and sell them as a bunch.

6. **Watch the weather.** Try to hold your yard sale on a nice day. You can monitor weather in your area up to 10 days in advance on sites like Weather. com (www.weather.com) and Weather Underground (www.wunderground. com), or check the local paper for a 5-day forecast. NOAA weather radio also gives extended forecasts. No forecasting system is perfect, but it's better to wait if bad (especially severe) weather is predicted, and hold your sale another weekend. Decide if you can hold the sale in your garage (or a neighbor's) if the weather turns bad despite your efforts, and if not, set (and advertise) a rain date.

7. **Finalize the timing.** Jackie, Nashville's yard-sale queen (see page 422), recommends holding a yard sale when there's a big flea market in town, since people will come from all over for the flea market, and many of them scour the area for yard sales while they're visiting. In their excellent book

Scaling Down, authors Judi Culbertson and Marj Decker suggest holding your yard sale between July and September if you live in an area that attracts tourists. There's also the question of how many days the sale should last. Jackie suggests holding a 2-day sale on Friday and Saturday, unless you have only a small amount of stuff, in which case it should be a 1-day sale on Saturday. Judi and Marj recommend always holding a 1-day sale (they also recommend Saturday), regardless of the size; they don't think second days are worth it. Other experts, like Michael and Pam Williams (see "Price your stuff," on page 414), claim that 3-day sales from Friday through Sunday are the most successful. (Yard-sale veterans refer to the "usual after-church crowd.") You decide, or try it two or all three ways (if you hold several sales) and see which works better for you. Marj and Judi advise against holding a yard sale over a major holiday weekend, since people will be having family gatherings and are less likely to head out to a sale. Time of day also matters. People won't buy what they can't see, so unless you have exceptional outdoor lighting or are holding your sale in a well-lit garage, make sure the sale ends before dark.

8. **Write your ad.** See "Getting Your Yard Sale Noticed" on page 405 for more on this. You can also check out Chapter 20—Clutter in the Classifieds, beginning on page 394, for ad-writing tips from the pros, and check your local papers' Web sites' classifieds sections, since they often provide ad-writing tips. Make sure your ad says what you're selling, when you're selling it (days and times), what your address is and how to get there, and includes a rain date if you decide to have one.

9. **Place your ad.** Put your ad in all the local and area papers, including special marketing papers like (in my part of Pennsylvania) the *Merchandiser* and the *Penny Pincher.* If you have special-events papers (the Nashville version is called the *Scene*), advertise in those, too. Post your sale on Craigslist and other community Web sites. (See "Placing Your Ad" on page 409 and Chapter 20—Clutter in the Classifieds, beginning on page 394, for more on placing ads in the paper and on Craigslist.) Tack up notices on community bulletin boards at local libraries and markets. When you place an ad in your local paper's classified section, if you have an option as to how long it runs, I'd opt for starting it the day before the sale and running

it each day of the sale; Jackie, who certainly knows her business, suggests running it the days of the sale. Some papers simply run the ads for a week. Whatever the case may be, find out by calling the classified department several weeks before your sale. The last thing you want is to place your ad too late for it to make the paper in time!

10. **Price your stuff.** Decide on a price for each item or box or bag of items. Do your research! Check out pricing at local yard sales and see what other people are asking. Go to local flea markets, where the sellers are pros, and see not only what they're selling their stuff for (assume you'll get less), but how they tag or otherwise show the prices of their stuff. In their book *Garage Sale Magic!*, authors Michael and Pam Williams suggest pricing items at 25 percent of retail cost, but discounting clothes and outdated electronic items much more. Books and magazines are other items that won't sell unless they're deeply discounted. But it's still possible to make a profit, even if you have a whole table of 25-cent stuff. In fact, most of the big-money garage salers who made hundreds and even thousands of dollars and bragged about it on yard-sale diva Cathy Pedigo's Web site said upfront that they had only two or three $25–$50 items, and most of what they sold was priced at 25 cents to $15. Judi Culbertson and Marj Decker recommend pricing everything in 25-cent increments, so you don't need to keep dimes, nickels, and pennies on hand for change. Make sure you tag every item with a price (in large, easy-to-read, waterproof ink, please) and attach the tags where buyers can see them. No staples, please! I don't like having to pry a stapled price tag off a piece of clothing and risk pulling threads (or worse), and I'm sure you don't, either. If you're having a multi-family sale, take a tip from the pros and give each family its own color of tags so you can tell who's made what at the end of the sale. Getting all the prices figured out, written out, and attached in advance will really cut down on stress on sale days!

11. **Get your setup assembled.** Don't wait 'til the last minute to gather all the tables, rolling clothes racks, bins, chairs for you and your family to sit in, signage, cash box or money belt, and other necessary supplies, or your yard sale will be a disorganized mess. You'll be most successful if your stuff is neatly displayed and you have plenty of room between tables and displays. Make sure you have enough table and bin space to display every small item

and enough floor or yard space to set up clothes racks, large stuff, and tables (and your chairs), and still leave plenty of walking room between tables or objects. (Again, you can learn a lot by checking out other people's yard sales and flea market setups—both what to do and what *not* to do.) Practice setting out the stuff. If your sale is in the garage (What? You have room for it in the garage!), it will be easy to do a practice setup and make any needed adjustments to make the layout work. If it's in the yard and driveway, set up a table in the house and practice displaying the stuff on it. (Needless to say, folding tables and chairs work best for yard sales, even if you have to beg everyone you know to lend you some for the weekend.) Eyeball the tables and large stuff and your yard space until you're sure you have enough room for everything *and* for, at times, 30 or more browsing buyers. Make sure you have tarps or big plastic sheets (and a secure way of anchoring them!) to put over everything if it's a yard sale and you plan to set up the night before or keep everything set up over 2 or 3 days.

12. **Buy some balloons.** You'll need some big, bold, colorful balloons on your mailbox to help buyers find you on the big weekend.

13. **Decide where to put your signs.** You'll need to know this before you actually make the signs, since where you'll put them will determine the driving directions you write on each sign as well as how many signs you'll need. You'll want to put them at all major intersections near your home, at both ends of your road, and along the road (these will just require the address and arrows, not directions). Put a big, bold sign in the yard itself ("Here It Is!!!"), and make sure it can be seen from the road.

14. **Make your signs.** You want your signs to stand out, but it's even more important that they be easy to read. I love color, but have you ever seen signs posted along the road on paper that was such a dark pink, red, or whatever that you couldn't read what was on them? Remember that people will see these signs while they're driving past at 25 to 55 miles an hour, so you need to make them as easy to see as possible. A pale shade of a bright color (like pink, yellow, or orange) might work if the ink is really bold and black. Try it and see! Make sure the sign is big enough to actually read, which is probably going to be a lot bigger than you think. Use paper or cardboard that's stiff enough that the signs will not fold, bend over, or wrap around a telephone

pole in the wind and thus be unreadable. Practice writing your signs until the lettering is huge, dark, and easy to see (or create it on your computer using the same criteria). Waterproof ink, please! Don't forget stakes, staples, tape, and anything else you'll need to actually put up your signs. Once you think you've got it down, put up one of your signs, then drive by and see if you can read it. If you can't, fine-tune it until you've nailed it.

What should you put on your sign? Start with a headline. Why say "Yard Sale" or "Garage Sale" when you can say "Mother of All Garage Sales!" or "Basement Blowout Sale!" Tell folks when it is (days and times), where it is (address and simple directions), and the rain date (if there is one). Don't forget directional arrows, which can be a different color (like red) to add an eye-catching touch. (Remember that the directions and the way the arrow points will be different for the different streets where you put the signs—don't write the same thing on every sign.) Add a drawing of balloons or some colorful, big balloon stickers to remind people to look for the balloons at your house, or, when it's time to put up the signs, attach actual balloons to the signs themselves. Judi Culberston and Marj Decker recommend that you also make signs to post downtown if you live in an area that gets lots of tourists.

15. **Clean up the yard.** Or the (gasp) garage, if you're holding the sale inside. It's very important to make a good impression on prospective buyers—you want them to have confidence in you and your stuff. A neat, tidy yard (or garage); an attractive front door; and well-organized, attractively displayed merchandise (hey, it's no longer "stuff"—it's for sale!) can work wonders in boosting both stops and sales. For tips on how to neaten up, see Chapter 16—Sprucing Up the Yard and Garden, beginning on page 330, and Chapter 15—Cleaning Out the Garage, beginning on page 311.

16. **Put out your signs.** Put up your signs the morning before your sale begins (Thursday morning if the sale starts Friday), so people can plan their weekend accordingly. I've seen signs go up in my area even earlier.

17. **Get small change.** Stock up on cash and change so you'll be ready for your customers. They'll probably arrive with $20 bills from the ATM, so you'll want to have plenty of tens, fives, and ones on hand, as well as loads of quarters. Because people like to bargain, I think it makes sense to have small change on hand, too—if somebody offers you 20 cents for that 25-

cent paperback, are you really going to turn them down? Once you have the money, practice using the money belt or cash box so you (and anyone else who's using it) will be comfortable.

18. **Get refreshments and supplies.** If you're selling (or offering) refreshments like doughnuts, cookies, bake-sale items, lemonade, iced tea, or water, get your supplies together. Do you need napkins, paper plates, little paper cups? How about plastic wrap (if you're selling the stuff)? Do you have a couple of trash cans for the cups and food wrappers? If not, can you borrow some? Do you have enough bags and newspaper to bag or wrap up all your stuff? If not, now's the time to bug friends and neighbors to fork over their extras. (You can offer them a doughnut and some lemonade in exchange!)

19. **Set it up.** If it's a garage sale or a big yard sale, unless you want to be out there at 3:00 a.m. stumbling around in the dark, set everything up the afternoon before the sale. That way, there's still time to borrow an extra table, rearrange the display, or run off for some additional supplies if you realize things are missing. Put up your signage and make sure it's secure so folks can actually read it. Double-check to make sure several people can walk abreast between tables and displays. Set out bigger stuff to double-check the display, but take rolling clothes racks, furniture, and other portable items back inside for the night and bring them back out on the mornings of sale days. Obviously, keep your cash box in the house! Put out the balloons on your mailbox, keeping some in reserve in case of vandals. Look everything over and make sure you're pleased with the way it all looks.

Yard-sale veterans recommend putting some of the bigger, higher-priced items in the front of the display to attract more buyers. Go out to the road and make sure that what you see looks inviting, abundant, well organized, and intriguing. And make sure you can see your sign. To make things even more inviting, you can set pots of colorful flowers at the base of your sign and on the cashier's table—but if you do, be prepared to sell them!

20. **Keep your focus.** People go to yard sales for fun. Do what you can to make it a fun experience for them *and* for you. Remind yourself and all involved that your goal is to get rid of stuff, not to haggle and try to make a huge profit. Yard-sale diva Cathy Pedigo recommends having music playing. Laugh, chat, be cheerful, have a good time!

21. **Go for it!** It's finally the big weekend. Make sure you're up and out early. Set out refreshments (if you're having them), get everybody in position, and make sure everyone knows what they're supposed to be doing. Set out the big stuff and remove the tarps or plastic from the tables. Make sure all signage is still in position. Finally, lock the doors to the house and you're ready to roll. Good luck!

Troubleshooting

There are a few precautions you can take to prevent the most common mishaps from striking your yard sale. I'm going to assume that you've already checked with your township or city hall, gotten any necessary permits, and followed any regulations. I'll also assume you've been clear with your neighbors about everyone's roles and responsibilities, and if you've hired a yard-sale professional, you're clear on what they're offering (and taking in return). And I'm going to assume you have a Plan B for bad weather. Here are some other things to watch for and what to do to keep them from happening (or at least, getting out of hand).

❏ **Haggling.** People love a bargain, and they love trying to get a lower price. And for a lot of people, that's what yard sales are all about. Expect to hear variations on, "Is this your best price?" "Can you do better on this?" and "I'll give you X for this." Judi Culbertson and Marj Decker suggest that you price slightly higher so you can come down and help people feel like they're getting a bargain. (Emphasis here on "slightly"—several yard-sale pros note that if someone thinks one item is overpriced, they're likely to conclude that everything is and leave without buying anything.) If their offer is too low, you could always offer to throw in something—a second paperback, another toy. But remember that your object is to offload the stuff! No matter what—even if someone tries to bring down a price by saying awful things about the item they want to buy—remain pleasant, cheerful, and courteous. You owe it to yourself. And other buyers are listening!

❏ **Stealing.** The best ways to keep someone from making off with stuff is to have it all well organized and displayed, with plenty of room between tables, and to have enough people manning the sale that anyone who arrives and lingers will be asked very pleasantly, "May I help you find something?" It's a lot easier to take stuff when the stuff is all piled and jumbled in a chaotic mess or there's one lonely person trying to deal with a line of paying customers.

❏ **Unwanted visitors.** Speaking of thieves, while you're out in the yard, it's possible that an uninvited guest is in your house. And besides simply snooping or trying to buy your everyday china, someone could be casing the house or stealing something. It's one thing for a light-fingered passerby to make off with a piece of costume jewelry and quite another for a thief to remove your spouse's Rolex or your diamond earrings. I don't know about you, but I'd make sure all doors to the house were locked and all downstairs windows closed and locked. (If one of your family or the sales group needs to get inside, you can give them the key.) Of course, if you have professionals handling the sale, you can be inside keeping an eye on things—but I'd still lock the doors.

❏ **Early birds.** Veteran yard salers start early because, like the early bird, they want that worm. That means that, if you advertise a sale starting at 8:00 a.m., you might look out your windows bleary-eyed at 6:00 a.m. and find people pulling up to the curb and pawing through your stuff. There are two ways to deal with this—advertise the sale as starting at 9:00 and get out there at 7:00, or do as a number of folks did in the Nashville *Tennessean* and say "NO EARLY BIRDS!" in your ad. (I'd opt for the first approach to avoid turning away customers, but if you're not an early bird

(continued on page 422)

the Pros Know

I was lucky enough to be writing this chapter while visiting my father and his girlfriend, Alice, down in Nashville. When I mentioned it to them, Alice pointed out that a friend of theirs, Jackie, was the yard-sale queen of Nashville. So of course I got on the phone with Jackie and asked her to tell me all about it. Read on for an insider's view of all things yard sale!

When Jackie started holding yard sales, she did it all herself, and she still recommends that approach if you have just a small amount of stuff or none of it is worth very much. But if you have a lot of stuff, or you're going in with some neighbors, or you have some valuable pieces—"if you're unloading your house, not just your basement," as she put it—do as Jackie did and hire a professional to handle your yard sale. (Jackie found hers through word of mouth; see "The Pros Know" on page 406 for other options.) She points out that professionals are interested in the bigger and better stuff, like dining room sets, and are very selective about taking on yard sales.

But if you have the goods, a professional is fabulous: For 25 percent of the take (in Jackie's case), Ron, the professional she works with, comes over with a team of two to three assistants. They evaluate the stuff and ticket every item. If several families are holding a joint sale, they'll use different-colored tickets for each family so it's easy to tell who's made what at the end of the day. Ron creates a great ad and places it in the local paper and anywhere else he thinks will help draw a crowd. They set out signs on critical corners.

On sale days, one of the assistants acts as cashier while the others monitor the crowd, guard the house (unobtrusively, of course), collect the money, wrap or bag items for buyers, and are generally helpful. Throughout the process, they keep meticulous records. At the end of the sale, Ron looks over what didn't sell, then takes any pieces he thinks he can sell at his flea-market stand and gives Jackie the money when each item does sell. What about the items he doesn't want to take? "He gets somebody to come out with a truck and haul it all away, and then they send me a check," Jackie says. No fuss, no muss!

Does it pay off? "My biggest sale made $4,000 over one weekend," Jackie said. Wow. That's more than most of us could hope to get from even a big yard sale—usually anything over $1,000 is considered fantastic, and if it's a small sale, you should be happy to make a few hundred. Whatever you make is good. "After all," as Jackie says, "it's found money, from stuff that's just lying around."

At the end of it all, even somebody as successful at yard saleing as Jackie isn't really in it for the money. "I do it for the challenge of it," she says.

Yard Sale Specifics

I asked Jackie to share some insights with all of us, and she generously agreed. Here are some tips you can use to make your yard/garage/tag sale a winner:

✳ **When to have the sale.** Jackie says you should hold your yard sale on a Friday and Saturday, unless it's really small, in which case do a 1-day sale and hold it Saturday. She always aims to hold sales when there's a big flea market or antiques event in town. "People come from all over to attend these events," she says. "They bring the paper along and go from yard sale to yard sale as well as the flea market."

✳ **When to expect the crowds.** Jackie says the most people will come early, especially on the first day. "If you advertise that the sale starts at 8:00, they'll be lined up in your driveway at 6:00," she warns. (This is another case where those yard-sale professionals can come in handy.) She says activity will continue to be heavy through the morning and early afternoon, then start tapering off around 3:00 p.m.

✳ **When to advertise.** Advertise on the days you hold your sale, Jackie advises. If you're planning a 2-day sale starting on Friday, place your ad to come out on Friday and run again on Saturday.

✳ **Where to put up signs.** Jackie says to put up signs at the principal intersections in your area, as well as at the turn-offs to your road, and, of course, in front of your house. Announce that it's a yard, garage, or tag sale (depending on what it's called in your area); give days, times, and the address; and add an arrow pointing in the direction of the sale.

✳ **What to expect.** Surprises, according to Jackie. "Stuff that means the least to you is the stuff that sells first," she says. She also warns that you need a thick skin when you're selling off things you care about. "You may have loved that painting, and you'll be shocked by the unkind comments you hear about it."

✳ **Who to expect.** "The dealers come first," Jackie says. They'll snap up the things they think they can sell, then resell them at their flea-market stands. Once they've picked over your stuff, the yard-sale enthusiasts (like my friend Tom) are likely to show up. These are the people who love yard sales enough to get up early on a weekend and turn out for them when they could be sleeping or lounging around in their pajamas drinking coffee. Finally, the general public drops by.

(continued)

✳ **What sells.** Tools, costume jewelry, vintage clothing, dolls, books, baby clothes and equipment, kids' stuff, kitchenware, glassware, and linens all do well. "If you've moved to a condo and no longer garden, get rid of those tools," Jackie advises. She says people are always looking for dolls and baby stuff. People love costume jewelry, and lots of people make stuff out of it, including other jewelry. Vintage clothing is so popular that "it's like the running of the bulls" when Jackie advertises it in one of her yard sales. Grandparents who've long since gotten rid of all the kid stuff in their homes often shop yard sales for games, toys, and equipment like trikes and bikes once the grandkids start visiting. I was surprised to hear that books did well, but Jackie says as long as you don't want much for them (you might have to sell three or four paperbacks for a dollar), both paperbacks and hardcovers sell well. And, as Jackie points out, urging us all to cull our collections regularly, "How many books can your bookshelves hold?" Other strong sellers—both surprises to me—were artificial flowers and bric-a-brac.

✳ **What doesn't sell.** Outdated technology, for the most part. "I could not give away a typewriter, no matter how good or expensive it was," Jackie laments. On the other hand, old camera equipment is often bought by collectors, and people sometimes buy old Mixmasters and other kitchen equipment as decorations if they want to create a vintage or period look in their

yourself, you might want to go for the other. But don't be surprised to see a few vultures circling even if you do put the warning in your ad.)

❑ **Parking.** On-street parking is good; blocking your driveway (and potentially crashing into other cars while pulling in and out) is bad. Keep it from happening by setting up display tables, clothes racks, or on-sale equipment or furniture in the driveway, far enough toward the street that no one can pull into the drive.

❑ **Accounting.** As people pay for each item, remove the tag and put it in a small plastic storage bin. (If you accept a different price than the one on the tag, cross out the original price and write the new one on the tag before you toss it in the bin.) This is another reason not to staple on tags—you need them for your records, so they should be easy to remove. If several families are involved, have a separate small bin for each color of tag, so kitchens. Yard sales are also one venue where designer clothes do not bring a premium. "My daughter tried to sell some expensive designer clothes at a yard sale, and they brought only $4 to $5 apiece," Jackie says.

❋ **What to do first.** Make sure you look carefully at everything you're setting out. Jackie points to the time she'd put out a box of costume jewelry and a conscientious customer brought her a heavy gold man's bracelet that had a broken catch and had been tossed into the box years before and been long forgotten. She wasn't as lucky the time she mistakenly put her new weed eater into the yard sale instead of the broken one and sold it for $2. When she realized her mistake, Jackie contacted the buyer, but he refused to give it back. And then there was the time she was selling a golf bag. The prospective buyer looked in a pouch and discovered a pair of her husband's underwear! (He bought the golf bag anyway.)

❋ **What to watch out for.** If you let buyers into your home, it's every man for himself. When her mother died, Jackie held an estate sale at her mother's home. Her yard-sale professional, Ron, and his team had roped off most of the house, but had let people into the den and the kitchen. Though nothing inside the house was supposed to be for sale, Jackie watched one couple buy the kitchen cabinets right off the wall and haul them away (she was planning to renovate the kitchen anyway) and another woman slip under the barricade and return demanding to buy the living-room curtains, rods and all.

that, at day's or sale's end, it's super-easy for each family to add up their sales and take their share of the profits.

FINDING STUFF A HOME

Not everyone has what it takes to hold a yard or garage sale. Maybe you don't want zillions of people coming to your home. Maybe you don't think your stuff is good enough to sell. Maybe, like me, you live on a death-defying road that curves right before your house and has absolutely no curb between the lawn and the road. (Drat! But I haven't given up hope. Rob and I are scheming to hold a group yard sale with our friends from our Friday Night Supper Club. Now we just have to let them know.) Or maybe you just don't want to be bothered. But you'd still like to unload some stuff.

Never fear! There are some really fun things you can do to get rid of stuff you don't want—and maybe get stuff you need, in the bargain.

The Freecycle Network

A great resource is the Freecycle Network (www.freecycle.org). Like Craigslist, the Freecycle Network started as a small idea in 2003—a way to keep stuff out of Tucson landfills—and grew into a network of almost 4,000 local groups. That's because the idea is so easy and great. You sign up with your local Freecycle group, and you can view all the free stuff they're offering online, or post your own stuff. There are just three restrictions—that anything offered be free, legal, and appropriate for all ages. Their motto is, "Think globally, recycle locally."

This is a great way to get rid of stuff you might otherwise have to contact someone to have it hauled off. My friends Jeff and Nitya, who purchased a home in rural Pennsylvania, wanted to get rid of a falling-down garden fence. So they put it on Freecycle. To their amazement, a Yuppie guy contacted them about it, then arrived to haul it off, explaining that his wife was redecorating one of their bathrooms and wanted to use the decrepit fence to give the bathroom walls a rustic look!

Meanwhile, in Washington, DC, my friend Susan's condo tenant broke up with her boyfriend, who decamped with some of her stuff but left his bed behind. Sure enough, she listed it with Freecycle and someone carried it away (for free!). No more bad memories for her!

Susan herself signed up for Freecycle and was able to find people to come pick up a bag of books she'd been carting around in her car for months (meaning to donate them to the library but never managing to do it) and some cans of Science Diet salmon cat food, a flavor her boyfriend's cat had refused to eat. Within 2 hours of posting them, she had offers for both. (You get to choose who to give your stuff to from the respondents; she chose first-come, first-served.) She sent directions, put the stuff out on the porch, went out to run errands, and by the time she got back, poof! They were gone!

Susan was just amazed to see what her local group was listing (and asking for). Among the listings were a bag of plastic coat hangers someone had rescued from the trash, a working television, size 6 shoes, a set of flash cards for calculus, a food processor, and a whiteboard. On the "want" side, someone was looking for empty pillboxes for an art project. As she says, "All of a sudden, de-cluttering began to feel more like a stroll through a flea market." (But don't get any ideas—remember, you're trying to offload stuff, not haul it off to your home!)

It's super-easy to navigate the Freecycle Network site and to find your local group and sign up. You do need moderator approval, though, and to get it you have to explain why you want to join the group. My local group had 485 members when I signed up!

Just for Books

Want to get rid of some books and have fun at the same time? Check out Book-Crossing (www.bookcrossing.com). It's based on "Where's George?" (www.wheresgeorge.com), a tracking system for dollar bills that lets people who find specially stamped bills log onto a Web site and note where that particular bill has turned up. Started by a software and Web site developer and his wife in 2001, the nonprofit BookCrossing now has more than 500,000 members internationally.

To "read and release" books, you register on the BookCrossing Web site. Then they send you book labels that you put in the book you want to pass along. You leave it somewhere, and when the next person picks it up, they go to the Web site and log where they found it—and what they thought of it. Then they pass it on.

My friend Susan was very excited to discover BookCrossing and couldn't wait to try it. She signed up, got the bookplates, and left her first book in a café in Greenbelt, Maryland. Then she began obsessively checking to see if anyone had picked it up. Unfortunately, it was a physical anthropology text on hominids, so she had a longer wait than most, but sure enough, one day she received an e-mail from BookCrossing with a post from the next person who'd picked it up and her review of it. (She enjoyed it and was looking forward to the sequel.)

Good Old Barter

Don't forget that primordial trade technique, swapping. You can always offer goods for services or goods for goods. My little farmette of six heirloom chickens lays more eggs than Rob and I can eat, so I often take a six-pack (a half-egg carton) or two of delicious, organic eggs to the weekly gathering of my Friday Night Supper Club. In return, I'll get homegrown produce, fresh herbs, baked goods, jams and jellies, or whatever anyone has on hand. It's an informal arrangement that works well for all of us.

My friend Carolyn swaps pet-sitting duties for eggs from our friend Nitya's small-farm enterprise. My friend Delilah will exchange her unwanted kitchenware and collectibles for items she does want or store credit at local antiques stores and flea markets. (I'm sure this wouldn't work everywhere, but I've never heard of a vendor turning her down, and I've been present at some of these exchanges.) Delilah and I swap extra plants, and there's a whole group of us who exchange extra seeds each spring. My neighbor had a tree removed in exchange for giving the arborists the wood.

If you know of someone who wants some of your stuff and you'd like something of theirs (or some kind of service, like lawn mowing), give it a try and see what you can do. It's fun, it's a great feeling to know you're giving someone something they want, and it's wonderful to get stuff and services you actually want in exchange for your clutter.

Barter at Work

If your co-workers are up for it, arrange to unload your stuff at an office swap. Have people bring a limited number of items (say, a maximum of five) and set them out on a table in the employee break room or somewhere else out of sight of clients and bigwigs. Either let people take what they want, have everyone gather at a set time and take turns, or draw numbers and choose based on the order in which their numbers came up—1 goes first, 2 goes second, and so on. (Bear in mind that you are trying to kick your clutter and don't have to take *anything* unless you actually need it!) If everyone enjoys the experience, you could have "swap day" once a month.

Make sure your colleagues agree about what to do with the stuff once the swap is over. Will everyone take home their stuff if it wasn't chosen? Will it be left on the table for a certain (predetermined) amount of time with a "Free" sign in case someone comes by and wants something? At the corporation where I worked, there was a small snack kitchen on my floor, and it was understood that any employee who had something to give away would leave it on the table in that room, and anyone who wanted something could take it. I'll confess that I found a few good books there, and left a few, too!

If your neighborhood is close-knit, there's no reason why you couldn't hold neighborhood swaps, too. Every year, I give my neighbor extra plants from my water garden (mine's small, so the plants are always spreading too much, and his is bigger and can hold them) in exchange for snow shoveling in winter. If you'd like to involve several neighbors or even the whole block, you should set it up like a yard sale. ("My Trash, Your Treasure! Neighborhood FREE Yard Sale!") Have everyone bring stuff to the most convenient yard and put it on display tables.

Make sure everybody knows when the swap will happen (day and time) and what to expect in terms of bringing and taking stuff. They should bring their own bags and boxes to haul stuff off in and should return at the end of the day to take back any of their stuff that wasn't claimed. Providing cupcakes, doughnuts, cookies, or other snacks would be a nice touch. Just don't be surprised if strange cars start pulling up when they see stuff on tables!

Barter Online

If you find you enjoy bartering or you want something your friends and family can't give you, you can go online. Craigslist (www.craigslist.org) lists a barter category in its classifieds. In the Allentown area, I saw ads from a guy seeking to exchange painting or drywall work for a dirt bike, boat, motorcycle, car, or truck in any condition; someone wanting to exchange computer work for tattoo work; someone offering to do tattoos in exchange for a digital camera; a Harley mechanic who would trade work on your bike for tools or electronics; someone who wanted to trade his dirt bike for an old manual truck; someone offering to give flying lessons in exchange for Web and graphics work; and someone who would paint your home for a piano, to name just a few.

There's also a service called Trashbank (www.trashbank.com) where you register, list your item (with description and photo) in the appropriate category—antiques, jewelry and watches, toys, sports, books, collectibles, computers, music, movies, and so forth—and then can offer to swap it for another item or service or sell it. It's free to register, post your item, and request trades (there are no fees or charges). As they succinctly put it, "Barter, Swap, Trade, Buy, or Sell Online Absolutely Free!"

Other Unloading Options

Still trying to find free homes for your stuff? Craigslist (www.craigslist.org) lets you post stuff that's free on its Web site. (See Chapter 20—Clutter in the Classifieds, beginning on page 394, for more on Craigslist.) Or you could do what tons of people in my area do—set the stuff out on the curb (when dry weather's predicted, please). I've seen more sofas and mattresses on area curbs than I could ever imagine. Some put "Free" signs on their stuff; others assume people will figure it out for themselves. Either way, I'm always amazed at how soon that stuff disappears!

Of course, you could call your local sanitation service and arrange for pickup, especially if you're really trying to dispose of trashy stuff. Or contact a local franchise of a junk-removal service like 1-800-GOT-JUNK (www.1800gotjunk.com), TrashBusters Garbage and Trash Removal Service (www.trashbusters.com), or Junk It! Garbage Removal Service (in Canada; www.junkit.ca). There are plenty of local services that will come clear out your basement, attic, garage, or shed; check the classifieds under "Services." (One in my area has the great slogan, "If you call, I'll haul.")

And don't forget all those donation options we discussed in Chapter 17—Donations and Write-Offs, beginning on page 351. Where there's a will to kick the clutter, there's a way!

ONWARD!

Yard sales, eBay, classifieds, and giveaways are great when you have less-valuable clutter to kick. But what if you have Uncle Edmond's original Arts and Crafts bookcases, or Grandma Stella's Tiffany lamp, or a platinum-and-diamond cocktail ring that's come down in your family, and you don't want them? It's time to turn to the next chapter and head for your very own antiques roadshow. So let's hit the road!

Chapter 22

Antiques in Your Attic

If your clutter is actually valuable (to someone, anyway)—for example, you've inherited Great Aunt Sophie's cherished Sèvres collection, or a Cubist painting, and you don't like it—the best way to sell it may be through an antiques store or specialist. But how do you find the right one, and how much can you expect to get? Should you contact a museum or head to the local flea market? This chapter tells you how to match your stuff to the appropriate dealers, how to get their attention, what to expect, pitfalls to avoid, and more.

WHAT TO EXPECT AT AN ANTIQUES STORE

Like my parents, I've always been an avid antiques hound. I love going to antiques stores and flea markets, and also to museums and historic houses that are open to the public. But, though I've bought many antiques over the years, I've never tried to sell them. So when I wanted to get the scoop for this chapter, I went to the pros.

One of my favorite antiques stores is Moyer's Antiques and Collectibles in the picturesque village of Monterey, Pennsylvania. I decided to begin my investigations there, with owners Bruce and Karen Moyer. Karen and Bruce buy lots of their stuff from people like you and me who just drive up and bring things in from their cars or who call for an appointment to show their heirlooms.

Karen told me right away that people often have unrealistic expectations because of what I call *"Antiques Roadshow* Syndrome." They see an episode where someone's blackened flowerpot turns out to be an original Paul Revere sterling silver punchbowl worth a bazillion dollars. (Remember the story in Chapter 18—Secondhand Shops, about the guy who went into a thrift store with a few dollars and came out with a copy of the Declaration of Independence worth $250,000?) So they think, "Gee, I have some old stuff. It must be worth a bazillion dollars, too!" Or they collect a particular type of vintage ceramic or coin. They buy a book called a price guide that gives the value of every known style of that kind of ceramic or coin. Then they bring a piece in to a dealer and are dismayed when the dealer offers less than "book value."

It's a hard lesson for all of us, especially if, like me, you are an enthusiastic collector and have spent time and money acquiring pieces that you can't sell for close to what you paid for them, much less at a little profit. But the takeaway lesson is this: For the antiques dealer, the bottom line is not what the piece is "worth." It's what they can get for it. And of course, they need to make a profit on the sale, so what they'll offer you is still less.

Karen has some advice to help you avoid disappointment when you bring your stuff to a shop: Do some research first. Go on eBay and look for similar items. (Remember how to do that? Go to www.ebay.com, then type in the name or keyword of the item you want to find in the title search field. Select the "Completed Items Only" check box. Click "Search," and it will show you what the item actually brought at recent auctions.) You can also check out local antiques stores; if you can find someone selling the same object, you'll see what they're asking for it. (Remember, you'll probably be offered less.) Once you're better prepared, you'll be less likely to be disappointed.

Mind you, if you happen to have the exact same object that was just featured on *Antiques Roadshow* and appraised for a gadzillion dollars, then maybe you've found that pot of gold. Good luck!

Antiques Store Checklist

This checklist should help you get the most from your antiques store experience. Look it over, and do your homework before you bring your stuff to the store.

1. **Keep a clutter-kicking mind-set.** Remember why you're getting rid of this stuff—to get rid of it. If someone offers you $25 for a piece you thought was worth $250, or $250 for a piece you hoped might bring $2,500—and you've done your homework and know you can't get a better offer elsewhere—it's still money you didn't have before, and it's one less piece of stuff taking up space in your home.

2. **Be realistic.** Remember that what an item will bring on the market isn't usually as much as it's worth—and often, it's not even close. Find out what items like yours are selling for in your area and on eBay or other online auction sites (see page 392 for a list of Web sites). Then bear in mind that the dealer has to get a percentage, so you'll actually get less than the sale price.

3. **But be aware of what you have.** If you have something that you feel or know is really valuable, for mercy's sake, get it appraised. (See pages 435–36 for more on this.) You do *not* want to be the person who dropped off that copy of the Declaration of Independence at the thrift store! And you probably don't want to sell it through a local shop, either, unless that shop specializes in what you're selling or is very high-end. Which brings us to . . .

4. **Pick the right shop.** If a shop specializes in vintage comic books and sports cards, you are not likely to have much luck selling them your jardiniere or Bakelite jewelry. Even if they took it, it's not likely that they'd pay more than a pittance. But if you took your jardiniere to a shop that specialized in garden antiques or your Bakelite to a shop that specialized in vintage jewelry and accessories *and* had a good selection of Bakelite, you'd be more likely to make a good sale. Of course, if the store already had 5 or 10 identical pieces, they might not want yours, too—at least not right now. In that case, you could ask them to recommend another store that might want your item, or ask them to call you if they sold the ones in the shop and needed more. You could also simply check back every few months to look over their inventory. A shop that sells a variety of antiques and collectibles, like Moyer's Antiques and Collectibles, is also a good choice. A generalist might not offer as much as a specialist, but they'd be likely to take the piece if they thought they could sell it.

5. **Comparison shop.** It's perfectly fine to say, "Thanks, let me think about it," if you don't like the price you're offered for a piece. Then you can take

it to a few more shops and see if you can get a better deal. What's *not* fine is to argue with a store owner about the price they offer. You may know everything about the piece, but they know their market. Take it or leave it, but mind your manners.

6. **Don't forget antiques malls and flea markets.** I live in an antiques-rich area, and there are huge antiques malls in several communities near me with both general and specialty shops. There are also lots of established weekend flea markets with regular vendors. When you're scouting around for a good fit for your stuff, don't overlook them—you might find the perfect match. Flea markets are usually a better choice for less-valuable collectibles (Disney figures, Hallmark ornaments, Matchbox cars) and old rather than antique furniture—stuff that might be too good for a yard sale but not good enough for an antiques store. But you never know!

UP FOR AUCTION

At Antiques Etc. just down the road from me in Maxatawny, Pennsylvania, owner Pat Robertson has a different take on how you should sell your antiques. "Sell them through an auction," she told me. That's where she buys the vast majority of the antiques she features at Antiques Etc. and in her two other antiques stores.

Pat says it's easy to find auctions online through sites like AuctionZip and Auction Guide. (See "Tools of the Trade" for more on them.) Once you've found them, she reminds you to do your research! Choose an auction that sells what you have. For example, if you lived in my part of Pennsylvania and had art to sell, Pat says, you should take it to Alderfer's Auction Company in Hatfield, Pennsylvania, which is known for its art auctions.

Like seasonal goods at consignment shops, auctions have their seasons. Pat says that winter's a bad time to try to sell something at auction, but anytime from spring through fall is good.

Speaking of consignment shops, Pat's a big believer in taking things there. (See Chapter 18—Secondhand Shops, beginning on page 357, for more on them.) Her advice is, once again, to match your stuff with the shop. For example, if you have nicer things, you should try a more high-end store. Pat recommended Select Consignments in Quakertown, Pennsylvania, as an example; it's now on my agenda

[Tools of the Trade]

If you're trying to find an auctioneer near you or to decide on one that's a good fit for your antiques, AuctionZip (www.auctionzip.com) is a wonderful tool. It's an online live auction locator. (A "live" auction is one that's held in person rather than online at a site like eBay.) At AuctionZip, you can search by state (when I searched for Pennsylvania, it not only took me to the Pennsylvania section, but also featured "This Week's Top 10 Most-Viewed PA Auctioneers" and "Top Five Most-Viewed PA Auctions"), by auctioneers, and by category (click on "Antiques Auctions," for example). If you click on an auctioneer's name, it brings up their listing, which features all their contact data, a link to their Web page, and an overview of current auctions. There's even a feature that lets you check out all the auctioneers within a given distance of your zip code. How convenient!

Want to learn more about auctions—what they are, what types of goods are sold, how they work, and so on? Go to Auction Guide (www.auctionguide.com), and you can find out the difference between a Dutch auction and a Yankee auction (no, it's not their location!), how to place a bid (wait, you're trying to get rid of clutter), and how a reserve works, for example. Just go to "Tips 'n Hints" on their home page and then click on "Traditional Auctions" (as opposed to "Online Auctions," which has tips for you eBayers out there). Auction Guide also lists auctioneers, both nationally and internationally, and categories of items for sale, from livestock and wine to seized goods and surplus. And of course, you'll find antiques, too.

---

for an upcoming visit with my thrift-shop coconspirator, Delilah. Or put your stuff where you feel it can do the most good. Pat gives her things to the Nova Thrift Shop, which benefits battered women and accepts both item donations and consignments.

Auctioning Off Your Stuff

If you've ever been to an auction but aren't a devotee, you know how intimidating they can be—the auctioneer pattering away at a mile a minute, items flying across the stage, people bidding all around you. (Or are they? And what is that auctioneer saying, anyway?) Luckily, if you're selling something, you don't need to know the ins and outs of bidding. But if you're curious, attend a few live auctions, or check

the **Pros Know**

The Web site www.guidetoauctions.com has links to a lot of auctions and auction sites. Go to their home page, then search "Related Topics" for "Antiques Auctions," click, and check out the links. (They even provide a history of live auctions from ancient Babylon to the present!) They also feature two valuable tips for people who are thinking about selling their antiques at auction. The first is to sell your antiques when they're hot, since items that are in demand will get more and higher bids. For example, it would have been a good time to sell a Louis XVI chair after the movie *Marie Antoinette* came out, or a vintage Indian motorcycle after the movie *The World's Fastest Indian* revived interest in the brand. Their other great tip is to resist the urge to monkey with, modernize, or "improve" your antiques. An antique in original condition can be worth hundreds or even hundreds of thousands of dollars more than one that's been refinished or painted. Both these tips hold true if you're trying to sell your antiques to a store, too.

out the run-through on the Auction Guide site (www.auctionguide.com). (See "Tools of the Trade" on page 433 for more about this.) In fact, once you've turned your stuff over to an auctioneer, you should follow the pros' advice and *stay home* while it's being auctioned—otherwise, you might find yourself bidding on it and paying for it twice!

Instead, find an auctioneer or auction house that meets your criteria, either online, via the Yellow Pages, by a referral from an antiques dealer or museum, or in your local paper. (My own local paper, the Allentown *Morning Call,* recently featured a prominent ad from Tom Hall Auctions, Inc., under the headline "Something to sell? Auction is the answer!" with the announcement, "Sell your fine antiques and heirlooms to the highest bidder in our Internationally Advertised Auction." If this weren't inducement enough, besides providing contact data, they note "28 Years' Experience—Over 10,000 Satisfied Customers.")

Auction houses typically work like this: You contact them, and they call you and try to make sure the sort of things you have are things they want to (and can) sell. If so, they'll come to your house and decide what they want. Then they'll arrange for pickup and schedule your stuff in one of their auctions (probably several months out). They'll send you a list of the items, with their estimates of what they expect each piece to bring. (Note that these are *estimates* based on their experience. Don't get your hopes up too high.) Finally, auction day arrives and the items (hopefully) sell. Within 30 days of the auction, you'll receive a listing of what each item sold for and a check for your part after the auction house deducts its commission (usually 30 percent) and any transport fees. As with anything else, ask about fees up front so you'll be prepared for the auction house bite.

GETTING AN APPRAISAL

When I moved to Pennsylvania and rented my first apartment, my parents gave me a framed Toulouse-Lautrec that my mother thought "might be something." The small artwork of a couple enjoying a country drive in their carriage had come from a shop in Nashville, and my parents considered it quite a find.

Not long after my move, I saw that the Allentown Art Museum was having an antiques appraisal event, where for a small fee you could have professional appraisers from one of the big houses—Sotheby's or Christie's, I can no longer remember which—look at your treasures and tell you if they were trash or the real thing.

Clutching my Toulouse-Lautrec, I joined the long line of other hopefuls with their vases, lamps, furniture, jewelry, art, and other heirlooms. My hopes began to dim as I saw the bored looks on the appraisers' faces and the demoralized expressions of the disappointed appraisees.

Finally, it was my turn. As I placed the Toulouse-Lautrec on the table, the appraiser suddenly became animated. My heart pounded as he excitedly called his colleagues over for a look. They turned the frame over, conferring quietly. Then the others returned to their stations and the original appraiser turned back to me.

"Is this the frame your parents bought this in?" he asked. I replied that it was.

"Then I'm afraid it's just a print and has very little value."

Visions of financial security drained from my sight as I crawled away. I still have—and still enjoy—my Toulouse-Lautrec. But, like most of my lottery tickets, it wasn't a winner.

Nonetheless, if you have art or antiques that you think (or know) are truly valuable, and you want to sell them, you need to get them appraised. (There are lots of ways to do that; see "The Pros Know" on page 436 for some of the best.) Read on to find out how to take *your* antiques on the road.

As it happens, my father's girlfriend, Alice, was a renowned art-gallery owner in Nashville for many years, so when I wanted to know about getting something appraised, I turned to her. I wasn't disappointed with her advice! Her tips can help you as well, whether you have art or antiques that you need to have appraised.

Alice said the first thing she'd suggest would be to take the work back to the gallery where you bought it and have it appraised there. (They might buy it back or even suggest potential buyers.) She said that you could also call Sotheby's or Christie's, the two auction giants, and find out what similar works had sold for recently. (This service is free.) If it's a very valuable item, Alice recommended that you consign it to Sotheby's or Christie's for sale.

Other options? Alice suggested that you look online or in the Yellow Pages for an appraiser who is registered with a reputable national or regional professional association like the American Society of Appraisers, Appraisers Association of America, or New England Appraisers Association. You could also call a local museum and ask them to recommend appraisers to you. (Tell them what you have so they can make an accurate referral.) Or do as I did and take your heirloom to a museum appraisal event. (Call your museum to see if and when they have them.)

Your Own Antiques Roadshow

Antiques Roadshow, PBS's Emmy-nominated antiques appraisal show, is beloved by all of us who hope Grandma's cream pitcher is worth thousands—or even hundreds of thousands—of dollars. But the long-running program inspires both love *and* hate in antiques dealers. Love, because it's done so much to raise public awareness about antiques, and that's great for business. Hate, because the show's "jackpot" approach has created *"Antiques Roadshow* Syndrome," where everyone selling something old to a dealer thinks it's surely worth its weight in gold—at least. If you've ever enjoyed watching an episode or are an *Antiques Roadshow* addict, you know what I mean.

But whether you watch the show, want to be on the show, or couldn't care less about the show, if you have antiques to sell, *Antiques Roadshow* is your friend. That's because of their wonderful companion Web site, Antiques Roadshow

Online (www.pbs.org/roadshow). It has, of course, features about the show, tips from the show, and a great list of terms used in the antiques world and to describe antiques, called "Antiques Speak."

If you'd like to attend one of the six yearly appraisal events hosted by *Antiques Roadshow* and held in cities across the country, you can apply online or via post-card and hope that yours is one of the applications randomly selected for a free ticket. If you get one, you're entitled to show up at the event with two objects that will be appraised by one of the 70 to 80 appraisers who attend each event. The appraisals are also free. Go to their site's FAQ (frequently asked questions) for application and event details.

But the real beauty of the site, in my opinion, is its list of appraisers and auction houses that are affiliated with the show. You can go to their appraisers index and look up appraisers alphabetically or by specialty. (For example, if you collect pueblo pottery, as I do, you'd search the listing of appraisers under American Indian/Ethnographia. You'd get a listing of appraisers who work in this specialty. I was astounded to find one in Franklin, Tennessee, just down the road from my family home!) There's a profile for each appraiser and contact data, so you can contact them directly. There's also a section on auction houses affiliated with the show (including all the big guys, like Sotheby's, Christie's, and Skinner's), with summaries of their history, what they sell, appraisal practices, and contact data. (Where contact data isn't provided, you can access them easily through a Google search.)

Going on the *Antiques Roadshow* Web site is like gaining access to your own personal cache of appraisers and auction houses. So if you haven't already done so, make friends with *Antiques Roadshow* today!

ONWARD!

You've almost done it. You've cleared out the clutter from every part of your house and yard—even the car—and you've hauled it off, donated it, sold it, swapped it, or given it away. There's just one thing left: Keeping it from coming back. And that's the subject of the next section, Controlling Clutter Creep. Before your clutter has a chance to sneak back, turn the page and read about how you can finally kick your clutter out forever!

PART FIVE

Controlling Clutter Creep

Chapter 23

Kicking the Clutter Habit

Okay, you've gotten it out. But like with losing weight, where getting the excess poundage off is just half the battle, getting rid of the clutter is only half the solution. Now, you have to keep it out—or, just like the diet gurus are always telling you, you'll gain it all back and then some! But by now we've given you some great techniques for de-cluttering every part of your house and yard, so you're prepared to clear the clutter as soon as you see it creeping back. And in this chapter, you'll find a smorgasbord of effective ways to catch yourself (and others) before the old habits—and new clutter—start taking hold.

IT'S BA-A-A-ACK!!!

Has this happened to you? You go on a cleaning frenzy and empty the house of all the clutter and junk. Whew! What a triumph! As you survey your domain, you can't see a single piece of clutter taking up space. You think, "Well! Thank heavens *that's* over!" and go back to your usual occupations. One day—maybe 6 months from that triumphant moment—you look up and see . . . clutter. Wait a minute—how did that happen? You don't even remember bringing all that stuff back in.

Like weight, clutter has a sneaky habit of creeping back up on you the second you think you've got it licked. You think you might need your "fat" clothes again sometime, so you stuff them in the back of the closet. That three-for-one sale at the local shopping club was too good to resist. Your sister-in-law had a few pieces of furniture she didn't need but was convinced you'd love. You upgraded your coffee maker but kept the old one, "just in case." Your husband promised to replace the deck railing, but somehow all the materials ended up in the garage. Before you know it, your home starts to look junky and crowded all over again. And you'd worked so hard to clean it out!

Don't panic. Here are some ways to recognize when clutter's creeping in through the back door and kick it out *before* it becomes an issue.

> # [The easiest way to keep clutter out is not to bring it in.]

Use It or Lose It

"Try to find a place or use for everything," advises my friend Chris. "If you don't have an immediate use for it, don't buy it or get rid of it." If only it was that easy! But try to keep Chris's advice in mind when you're thinking about whether or not to buy something, and use it to cull objects you already have whenever you can.

Avoid Temptation

Just as you'd avoid the pizza or ice-cream parlor if you were trying to lose weight, if you can't resist buying when you go into stores, find other ways to shop.

"I try to avoid looking at catalogs or going to the mall so I don't buy things I don't need or have space for," says my friend Jennifer.

Jennifer has another excellent tactic for buying what she needs without being tempted to buy anything else. "I buy things online whenever possible, especially if the store offers free shipping," she says. "That way, I save gas and time, and I avoid seeing—and buying—extra things I don't need or have space for."

Know Your Limits

Your space limits, that is. When stuff starts overflowing its allotted space, it creates both visual and actual clutter.

"I allocate space in my home for categories of things—such as a bookcase for my books and a cabinet for my glassware," my friend Jennifer says. "Once I exceed that space, if I bring another item home, I have to get rid of one."

And don't forget the advice of Diane, one of my colleagues at the Kutztown Curves (you met her in Chapter 1): Her rule is, if one item comes in, *two* have to go out. If you can manage that, you'll not only keep clutter from coming into your home, you'll reduce the amount of stuff you have over time.

Take Five (or One)

Keep your clutter in check by constantly culling your stuff. If you can find a few items to put in a donation bag for your local thrift store each day, you'll be amazed at how soon things get back under control. I do this with my dressers, closets, and cabinets, taking it a little at a time. When my bag is full, I drop it off at Goodwill or the Salvation Army and start a new bag. Easy does it!

Toss the Little Stuff

Be ruthless with worthless junk-drawer clutter like twist-ties, rubber bands, bottle caps, and paper clips. If you must, keep just enough to fill a sandwich-size zipper-lock bag and toss the rest. You'll have plenty for any household needs, you'll be able to get them when you need them, and they won't take over the drawer. Get rid of restaurant packets that come with take-out orders. Cull coupons regularly, and clip only the ones you'll use—don't clip coupons for every item that looks like it might be worth trying someday.

Find Better Things to Do

Shopping is entertaining—certainly for me, probably for you. But when shopping results in buying, clutter will be coming in the door with you every time you return from a shopping trip. Escape this trap by planning outings that don't produce clutter: Go for a walk, go to the movies, go to a concert. Research and plan vacations (even if you never take them, it's fun to think about your dream vacation locations and put together the perfect weekend, cruise, spa trip, or the like). Check out the books, magazines, CDs, and DVDs or video tapes at your local library. Get a subscription to Netflix. If you simply *must* shop, indulge your shopping habit by going to the most upscale stores you can imagine—jewelry, antiques, fashion, furnishings—where you *know* you won't be tempted to buy anything but can enjoy looking at the best.

Trade Up

Remember the concept of trading up from Chapter 1? It's another take on "one in, two out" that's especially helpful for Collectors like me. Take a handful—or armful, or carful—of less-good stuff from your collection and sell it, then use the money you make to buy just one very good (or at least, much better) thing. You could get rid of a box of so-so jewelry and get the piece you've had your eye on all season, or exchange your starter woodworking equipment for the router you've been drooling over. Take a box of books to the used-book store and use the store credit to buy one or two really nice books. In the case of art and collectibles, sometimes the store or gallery where you bought the pieces will take them back (don't expect to get what you paid for them, though). Then you can apply whatever money you make to the price of the piece you want to buy.

Take Small Steps

Any time you think clutter is starting to get a foothold again, turn back to Chapter 4—Five Simple Steps to Kick Your Clutter, beginning on page 54. Review the steps and see if you should be using one or more of them more often. The sooner you act, the faster you'll bring the clutter under control and get your house back to where you want it.

Take a Picture

Give yourself a clutter-fighting chance by taking photos of each room or area of your house and yard after you've gotten the clutter out of it. If clutter starts creeping back, take out the pictures and see how great everything looked. You'll be inspired to get the space cleared out again.

Review Your Visualizations

Another good way to bring clutter creep to a screeching halt is to look at the "After" visualizations you wrote down in Parts Two and Three of this book. If the family room is starting to look shabby or the front yard is getting away from you, reread that visualization and once again picture your dream space. It will motivate you to kick the clutter back where it belongs. Review the tips in the relevant chapter to remind yourself of all the ways you can show clutter the door.

Try Some Tools

The right tools can make all the difference in any task, and clutter-control is no different. If you haven't tried any of the tools I recommend in Chapter 3—Tooling Up (beginning on page 35), go back and look them over. Pick one thing—even if it's a single storage container or a showerhead bottle holder—and treat yourself. It really makes a difference! Or go to an organizing store in your area or online, and see how many ideas you get just from looking around. It's inspiring!

Enjoy Yourself

As I hope you've found out by now, lots of the ways you can use to get rid of clutter are actually fun! Whether you have been bitten by the eBay bug, feel like you've finally mastered the art of yard-saleing, have made a little cash on consignment, or just enjoy hauling bags and boxes to the thrift store, remember the fun part when you see clutter start to creep back. Figure out what you're going to do with each type of clutter—have another yard sale next month, put it on Craigslist or Freecycle, take it to the eBay store. Choose the option you'll enjoy most, and go for it!

Don't Give Up

You've worked hard to get the clutter out. But if there are things still lying around that you can't figure out how to get rid of, don't despair. Even if you have to call

Dear Claire,

My kids are clutter hogs—or maybe they're just hogs. I worked all month to get our family room shoveled out, and by the next weekend, the kids had totally trashed it. I didn't even get to enjoy it! I know it's not really as bad as it was, but it will be soon if something doesn't happen. What can I do?

Hog-Wild in New Haven

Dear Hog-Wild,

How do you get your kids to do their homework, chores, and other social obligations? Choose the incentives (or punishments) that have worked in other situations and apply them here. Tell them that they're free to trash the family room as much as they please as long as they're in there, but that everything must be taken to their rooms or put in its place when they leave the room. And, dear, before you start meting out punishments, make sure that when you took out the clutter, you remembered to put in lots of storage solutions. If you forgot this vital part of the de-cluttering process, do it now, and then explain to the family what you expect from them. Show them where to stow their stuff, *then* lay down the law.

Good luck,
Claire

in a hauling company and pay them to cart stuff off, it beats continuing to live with it.

As Pat Robertson of Antiques Etc. (see page 432) put it, "If you want to get rid of your stuff, there's a way."

ONWARD!

Just two things left to read and you've done it! The first is Chapter 24—The Top 10 Clutter Traps, starting on the next page. It's an at-a-glance guide to the most common ways clutter can creep back into your home. Last—but far from least, for most people—is Photo Finish, beginning on page 450. As you might guess, it's a guide to all the ways you can (finally) bring your photo clutter under control.

The Top 10 Clutter Traps

I'll leave you with a checklist of the most common ways clutter can creep back into your house . . . and your life. You might want to photocopy them and post them on the fridge as a reminder. But then again, you might decide that's just more clutter!

1. **Buying in bulk.** Yes, buying 24 rolls of toilet paper instead of four might save you money. But if you don't have room to store the 24 rolls, you're creating clutter. And an attractive, uncluttered home is worth more than the few cents (or even dollars) you'll save by buying in bulk!

2. **Getting free stuff.** "Buy one, get one free!" "Free matching purse with this raincoat!" Free stuff sells stuff, as canny marketers know. But unless you actually *need* the free stuff, it's just clutter. Turn it down or donate it.

3. **Keeping unwanted gifts.** Aunt Jane gave you that urn as a wedding present. Your parents generously bestowed that sofa on you when you left home. Whatever it is, you never liked it, but you're afraid you'll hurt someone's feelings if you get rid of it. But who's getting hurt because you're keeping it? You and your family, that's who. Unload it. (See Chapter 1 for ways to do it discreetly.)

4. **Keeping stuff you don't like because you paid for it.** I know you spent good money on that orange-eucalyptus herbal tea or the dress that was just like the one that looked so wonderful on Angelina Jolie. But you can't stand the tea, and when you put on the dress, your bratty teen asked if you'd

decided to go to a costume party dressed as a hippo. Know what? If you don't like something now, you're not going to decide you love it months (or years) from now. And meanwhile, it's taking up space. Take the tea to the office and set it out with a "free" sticker. Sell the dress through a consignment shop and make back some of your money. Mistakes happen, and they do cost money. But don't compound your original mistake by letting it turn into clutter.

5. **Keeping stuff too long.** I'm as guilty of this as anyone. I wear shoes I love until the heels have practically worn off and have been known to wear my favorite tees until they're so threadbare holes actually appear in them. But deep down, I know—and you know it, too—that keeping clothes, appliances, food, you name it, past its prime is doing you no favors. The hairdryer that takes three times as long to dry your hair as it did when it was new is wasting three times as much of your life every single morning (and probably wasting electricity, too). Worn-out clothes, however beloved, are *not* becoming. Treat yourself (and your wardrobe) with some respect, and replace worn items before strangers start offering handouts!

6. **Letting paper pile up.** Don't have time for the paper? Magazines, catalogs, and bills spilling off the coffee table, kitchen counters, and dining table? Paper is one of the worst clutter traps because every family member has his or her own, and nobody likes to get rid of it. ("Don't throw out my magazine!" "I haven't read that section yet." "I might want to try that recipe.") Getting tough on paper pileups will save you a lot of clutter headaches in the long run. Set strict deadlines about how long different kinds of paper can stay in the house before they're recycled, and stick to them. Consider reading the paper online if it looks like nobody's reading the print version. If someone wants to hang onto their guitar or cooking magazines, they should be shelved neatly in magazine files. No room on the shelves? Either they or something else up there's gotta go.

7. **Keeping your kids' stuff.** The kids are in college . . . they've got their first apartments . . . they're married and haven't lived at home for 15 years. But somehow, their stuff is *still* living there, because however long they've been gone, there's always some reason why they can't take it. Call a halt. Tell them they have 3 weeks (or 3 months) to get over to your place and take

what they want—or it's going to Goodwill. Nurturing them was one thing; nurturing their clutter wasn't part of the deal. Tell them your home isn't a self-storage unit, and they're welcome to rent one if they need to.

8. **Getting the whole set.** Collector, know thyself! Why have just one or two (or ten, or . . .) shells, marbles, Barbies, Sting albums, Ansel Adams prints, or first editions when you know there are more—so many more—waiting somewhere out there just for you? When you can't see or store your stuff, it's stopped being a collection and become clutter. Cull it, and start enjoying your treasures again. Sell off the ones you like less and invest in one you've always wanted. It may feel like a big sacrifice at the time (and I know whereof I speak here), but it really won't kill you not to buy every single one, or even the next one. Think of what else you could do with your money, like paint the house or replace those ancient shoes. This goes for getting more china, crystal, and silverware than you need. In the days when families were large and family gatherings were even larger, 16-piece place settings were the norm. But if your family is small and your dinner parties are modest, don't buy 12 glasses when you need 6 . . . or 2. Save your money and your space.

9. **Keeping "extras."** You bought a new coffeemaker to replace the one that went on the fritz, but the old one ended up in the basement, "just in case." The old lawn mower's still in the garage. You have all three electric can openers you got at your bridal shower. Pick the best and toss, recycle, sell, or donate the rest. The space you save will be your own.

10. **Keeping stuff for "someday."** The sewing machine you got a great deal on when you decided to make your own clothes (but never did). The black walnut boards you were going to make into a table. The older we get, the more stuff like this we have. No, we didn't end up taking up painting, or the trumpet, or model-building after all. But we might, someday, so we hang on to all our supplies, even if we can't remember where, or even what, they are. Well, here's a little secret: If "someday" really *does* come, you can buy the stuff again. Meanwhile, stop letting it clutter up your home. Sell it, donate it, give it to someone else who's actually doing the craft, art, or work. Perhaps in return they'll give you a finished project that you can display and enjoy!

Photo Finish

Because so many people have a lifetime of photos, negatives, and envelopes stuffed all over the house, I decided to break this section out as a special appendix to make it easy to find. Read on for ways to corral, catalog, and curb your photo clutter!

Let's start with the printed photos, negatives, and associated clutter. (We'll get to the digital versions in a minute.) Follow these steps to make them manageable.

1. **Collect your photos.** You probably have them stashed everywhere—in drawers, boxes, maybe even (gasp!) albums. You can tackle the entire assortment at one time, which will make it easier to figure out what you actually have and, thus, what you'll want to keep. Or, if that's just too much to deal with, you can take on a single box, drawer, album, or envelope at a time and work through the mountain of photos bit by bit.

2. **Toss what you can't see.** This step should be easy, but I know too many people who can't seem to part with any photo, however abysmal. *Please* don't let yourself get stuck here. Unless it's the only known photo of Great-Great-Uncle Leo or it's a pioneer photo or rare shot of your Civil War ancestor in uniform, if it's too dark or out of focus, toss it.

3. **Vanquish the vampires.** Red eyes, grimaces, half-headed monsters (this one's my specialty, alas). If someone doesn't look good in a photo, for whatever reason, unless it's a vintage shot and you can't take another photo

of that person, throw that photo out. Think about how you'd feel if it were a photo of you, and be kind!

4. **Ditch duplicates.** If you've inherited (or are yourself guilty of taking) 1,000 identical or nearly identical shots of the Eiffel Tower, London Bridge, or your dog Milton, give it a rest. (Father, cover your ears, please.) Pick the best shots for your own collection. If you have duplicates of the best shots, set them aside for your kids, friends, traveling companions, or relations—*if and only if* you know they'd be interested. (And don't forget that you can pick up the phone and ask them!) Put those in envelopes marked with each recipient's name. Then toss the rest.

5. **Don't save strangers' photos.** No idea who's staring back at you from that old photo? Don't make yourself a hostage to ancient clutter. If you think it's an ancestor or relative, send or take it to the family historian or an older relative for an ID. You might discover that it's your mom's college roommate! Can't remember the name of your BFF from sixth grade? Say good-bye. Same for your granddad's colleagues from the mill. If you get an ID and the photo is of someone who matters to you, label it and save it. If you've ID'd Great-Uncle Al and couldn't care less, send it to his kids or grandkids. But if nobody has a clue who it is and you don't really care, throw it out. (If it's a nice old photo, you might be able to sell it to an antiques store.)

6. **Ditto for strange places.** If you don't have a clue what that scenic photo's showing, it might be of some obscure place your grandparents visited during the Depression. Unless it means something to you or someone you love, throw it out. (Or again, if it has that vintage look, take it to an antiques store.)

7. **Label everything.** Once you've pared everything down, if the people, place, occasion, and date aren't already on the back of the photo, write them on or write the data on a label and attach it. You don't ever want to go through this again—or put your kids through it, either! If you don't know the date, give an approximation with a question mark.

8. **Store them together.** Stash the photos you've decided to hang on to in photo albums by family member, place, theme (such as Christmas or pets), or time frame. (Or choose your own organizing theme. I have an album of photos documenting the construction and contents of my greenhouse.)

Paste a label on the spine of each photo album so you can see what's in it at a glance, and keep them all together on a shelf for easy retrieval.

Besides those basic principles, here are some additional tips for photo storage:

Know where they are. If you're like me, family photos are one of the top things you'd try to save in case of a fire, along with your pets, purse, and best jewelry. Make sure you know the exact locations of the albums and framed photos that matter to you most. Keep those precious albums closest to the door. Drill yourself and your family to see how fast you can grab the must-keep photos off walls and shelves and take them outside to safety.

Use acid-free paper. Photos are fragile and react quickly and sometimes dramatically to their environment. If you're storing them in photo boxes or scrapbooks (available from crafts or scrapbooking stores and Web sites), make sure you choose acid-free paper to protect them. The same sources sell acid-free labels to use as IDs on the backs of photos.

Keep them out of the basement. That goes for the attic, too. Store photos in a dry, climate-controlled room—one you'd be comfortable in yourself.

Repair the damage. If you find a precious family photo that's nicked, cracked, splotched, or otherwise damaged (I told you to keep them out of the basement!), you can have it professionally restored thanks to the wonders of modern technology—call a photo shop near you. Or, if you're up for it, you can do it yourself with a program like Adobe Photoshop LE and a scanner.

Peel 'em off. Apparently, stick-on photo albums were all the rage in the seventies—and, as you might expect, the sticky stuff did no one's photos any favors. If you happen to have any of these albums lying around, extract your photos and put them in today's archival-quality sleeves.

Show them off. Look through your stash for photos that are especially evocative. If you find some good ones, have them enlarged and frame them for display. In their living room, my friends Gary and Carolyn have a marvelous black-and-white photo of their daughter Michelle holding a goose. My boyfriend, Rob, framed some wonderful shots of his road trips to Utah, Wyoming, Colorado, and the Four Corners area of New Mexico, and he displays them in his office at the college where he teaches. Why have photos if you don't look at them?

Box 'em up. If you decide to store photos in an archivally sensitive acid-free photo box, add tabbed dividers to sort photos by topic (pets, vacations, Grandma's house, birthdays, Christmas, whatever). You can find them at stores like West Elm (www.westelm.com) and, for larger prints, Exposures (www.exposuresonline.com).

Make some memories. Photos and scrapbooking just seem to go together. As you create a scrapbook around a given theme, whether it's Christmas or that never-to-be-forgotten trip on Route 66, add some photos to bring your multi-media treatment to life. It's a great way to preserve your photos as well as your memories!

Keep up. Whenever you get printed photos—from the pharmacy or from your printer—immediately write who, what, where, and when on the back of each photo you choose to keep. Don't put off this vital step! If you cared enough to take the photo, you care enough to document it. And please, toss the bad shots as you go through.

Try compact options. Catalogs like Solutions (www.solutions.com) offer ways to store lots of photos in small spaces. They allow you to display 100 photos, 4 by 6 inches each, in a single wooden frame that lets you flip through the photos to display your favorites; or organize 400 of your 4- by 6-inch photos in six-compartment photo storage boxes. You can group them by theme or person, whatever works for you.

Nix the negatives. I know this is heresy to lots of people, but in these days of photo scanning, when anyone can reproduce their photos ad infinitum and any pharmacy or photo shop can duplicate a photo from the original photo, negatives seem pointless to me. Unless you're a professional photographer, they're just anachronistic photo clutter. I recommend tossing your negatives—you (and your photo library) can live without them.

Or keep them close. If you can't bear to toss your negatives, I suggest storing them in envelopes attached to the inside back of the album where the photos contained in them are displayed. That way, they're at hand if someone asks for a copy while thumbing through the album, and you always know where they are.

Get some ammo. My friend Susan says her cousin Chuck has discovered a great way to store negatives. "Chuck bought a bunch of army surplus ammo boxes for storing negatives and other family treasures," she says. "The ammo boxes, he says, are designed to keep things from getting damp."

Buy a bin. For a more professional option, you can buy a special negative-storing box designed to store more than 2,000 negatives (35mm format). It's a steal from www.mvconservation.com.

Keep them safe. Some organizing experts, like Linda Koopersmith, the Beverly Hills Organizer, recommend storing your negatives in your safe deposit box. That way, if your actual photographs are lost in a fire, flood, or other disaster, you'll still have the negatives. If you choose this option, you might want to consider getting a light-resistant, protective storage case made especially for negatives. You can get an inexpensive one that holds 2,000 negatives from www.mvconservation.com.

Label your negatives. Write the date and content of your negatives on each envelope so you can identify the contents at a glance.

Pass them on. Do you have framed photos of your son's ninth-grade soccer team, your daughter's riding trophy, the twins' wrestling medals? Yow. Pass them on to the child concerned; it's his or her history. Ask yourself, do I *really* want this?

Digital Dilemmas

Just because digital cameras don't (necessarily!) leave a paper trail, that doesn't mean you can just ignore digital photo clutter. Here's some advice to help you reduce and organize the digital photo flow.

Ditch digital duds. They may not be piling up around the house like printed photos and negatives do, but those digital dupes and "oops" are still filling up your memory card. My boyfriend, Rob, loves his digital camera, and he tends to go overboard whenever he's taking photos of pets, family, or scenery from one of his famous road trips to the Southwest. To make sure he always has plenty of space for new shots, he's diligent about deleting duplicates, fuzzy shots, and anything he doesn't absolutely love as soon as he finishes a shoot.

Shop for software. Software programs like Adobe's Photoshop Album (www.adobe.com), Paint Shop Photo Album (www.corel.com), Google Picasa (www.picasa.com), Apple iPhoto (www.apple.com), and Photo Mechanic (www.camerabits.com) let you sort and store digital photos by subject, event, or date. Picasa is free, and the others have free trial versions that let you test them before you buy.

Use your e-mail. E-mail systems like Yahoo! have free online photo storage sections ("My Photos," in the case of Yahoo!) that let you archive and e-mail favorite photos.

Download onto CDs. Not only does downloading digital images to CDs (or DVDs) free up your photo card, it also gives you great archives and gifts. (Just make sure you edit all those digital photos rather than mindlessly dumping them all onto CDs!) Many image-editing software packages feature a contact-sheet option that lets you create customized CD case covers with choice images from the shoot that's on the CD.

Label your CDs. For what strikes me as a rather hefty initial investment, you can buy a CD/DVD title printer that will print a professional-looking title on your photo CDs. You can buy a compact printer with five type fonts, 14 languages, and 650 symbols from catalogs like Hammacher Schlemmer (www.hammacher.com) for $129.95.

Store your CDs. Stash those photo CDs in soft plastic CD photo sleeves from the Container Store (www.containerstore.com). The inexpensive CD storage pages keep four photo CDs safely stowed on each side.

Box 'em up. If you have a lot of photo CDs or DVDs, check out Atlantic Inc.'s super-affordable CD File Box, which holds up to 80 CDs or DVDs in protective hanging file folders in a blue fabric cube. Get it from www.atlantic-inc.com.

Frame your digital photos. Wood meets electronics in a digital photo frame from Solutions (www.solutions.com). The 6- by 3¼-inch framed view accepts your digital camera's memory card and shows your photos like a slideshow or one at a time.

Put them on a chain. Catalogs like Solutions (www.solutions.com) offer key chains with viewing capacity for up to 56 digital photos on a 1.4-inch screen. Software for both Macs and PCs lets you edit photos on your computer, then download them to the key chain.

INDEX

Underscored page references indicate boxed text.